Studying Horror Cinema

Studying Horror Cinema

Bryan Turnock

auteur

First published in 2019 by
Auteur
24 Hartwell Crescent, Leighton Buzzard LU7 1NP
www.auteur.co.uk

Copyright © Auteur Publishing 2019. All Rights Reserved
Designed and set by Kim Lankshear
Printed and bound in the UK

Cover images: *Rosemary's Baby* (c) William Castle Productions / Paramount Pictures; *The Old Dark House* (c) Universal Pictures; *Let the Right One In* (c) EFTI / Sandrew Metronome / Filmpool Nord / Sveriges Television (SVT) / WAG / Canal+ / Fido Film AB / Ljudligan / The Chimney Pot; *It* (c) New Line Cinema / RatPac-Dune Entertainment

British Library Cataloguing-in-Publication Data
A catalogue record for this book is available from the British Library

ISBN: paperback 978-1-911325-88-8

ISBN: cloth 978-1-911325-89-5

ISBN: ebook 978-1-911325-90-1

Contents

My thanks go to John Atkinson at Auteur for his advice and encouragement throughout the life of this project, and to Dr. Emma Robertson of La Trobe University, without whose assistance and support this book would not have been possible.

For Matilda Grace.

Introduction

The horror genre richly deserves its abject status among critics and audiences… It seems to me incontrovertible that the horror genre in the American cinema has been primarily exploitative, artless, frequently without taste or restraint or sense, and generally unworthy of serious attention. (Solomon 1976:112)

Although the above quote was written over forty years ago, there would be more than a few film critics nowadays who still agree with the sentiment. Since its inception, horror has been one of the most universally derided and dismissed of film genres. Yet at the same time it has consistently been one of the most enduring and commercially popular. While there have been periods where it seemed to have reached a dead end, it has always managed to re-invent itself and rise again; like the monsters that it so often depicts, the horror film has proven time and again that it cannot be killed.

At the time of writing, horror cinema is experiencing something of a renaissance, enjoying box office success and even critical acclaim. With hundreds of films produced around the world each year, horror exists across an incredibly diverse range of sub-genres. While Robin Wood's oft-quoted 'basic formula' for the horror film, 'normality is threatened by the Monster' (Wood 1979:175), still holds true, the genre itself has never been less predictable. Gone (for now) are the days when audiences sat down to watch what had been described to them as a 'horror film' knowing exactly what to expect in terms of narrative and film style. The modern horror film is the result of over a hundred years of development, and the aim of this book is to identify and explore the various technological, cultural and social forces that have worked to shape the genre into what it is today. Thirteen case study films have been selected to represent some of the key developments in horror cinema. Some herald the beginnings of a new trend, others illustrate a wider shift in horror sensibilities, whilst some mark the pinnacle of a particular stage in the horror genre's evolution. To illustrate some of the broader ideas discussed, each chapter will also provide recommendations of other films worthy of viewing alongside the case study.

Film Genre

Before we go any further, it's worth taking a step back for a moment to understand exactly what we mean when we talk about 'film genre'. The concept is essentially a product of the classic Hollywood studio system, which existed from around the early 1920s to the mid-1950s. With a dizzying array of films being launched into the marketplace each year, the major Hollywood studios saw the ability to categorise their output as a powerful marketing tool. In labeling their latest release a 'gangster picture', or a 'Western', the studios were entering into an understanding with their audience as to what they should expect from a particular film. Hence, the major genres were created and evolved through the contributions of film-makers, publicists, audiences, exhibitors and critics. Studios took note of which components of a film proved popular or effective, and through their re-use these became generic 'codes and conventions'.[1]

These components can be found not only within the actual film, but also in advertising materials such as trailers and posters, and often in the film's title itself. Advertising frequently references previous well-known films to attract audiences; more than a few horror films have been billed as 'the scariest since *Psycho*!' or, depending on the confidence of the publicist, 'even scarier than *Psycho*!' In theory, even if they knew nothing else about a new release than its genre, a filmgoer who had previously enjoyed a film of the same type would be more likely to want to see it. Once a genre was sufficiently established with a mass audience, the studios could be confident in producing a program of similar films in the knowledge that a ready market existed. Certainly, a studio that continually produced films unlike anything previously seen would have a hard time in marketing and attracting audiences for each of them. Even today, films that do not belong to an easily identifiable category can face difficulties in being successfully financed, produced and marketed.

The Hollywood system during the studio era was an industrial operation heavily geared towards genre film production. Having invested in sets, costumes and props for a particular film, studios were able to re-use them in similar productions, helping to reduce budgets and production times. At the same time creative personnel including producers, directors and writers who were suited to a particular type of film were kept under contract by the major studios. All of this meant that the larger studios tended to concentrate their efforts on a single genre or a small number of closely related ones, differentiating their product from those of other studios and fostering an audience 'brand loyalty'. So, for example, Warner Bros. tended to specialise in crime and gangster films, MGM in lavish musicals, Universal Pictures in Gothic horror films, and so on.

Influential films in any particular genre are those that introduce new elements which go on to become conventions, or that use existing conventions in a new way which is subsequently taken as the norm. Such films become known as 'genre-defining', and by their nature can only be recognised as such in hindsight, once the elements they introduce have been accepted by audiences and film-makers as convention. This process can occur over a prolonged period or can happen extremely quickly, but it is through these changes that a genre evolves. By the end of the 1950s, Hollywood had established and significantly developed the vast majority of film genres that exist today. However, for any genre to survive it must be able to innovate and adapt its conventions, to both attract new audiences and give their existing audiences some degree of variation. There would be few viewers willing to pay to watch exactly the same film over and over again, and therein lies a fundamental problem for film-makers: genre audiences expect to see familiar elements, but with enough variation to appear fresh and original.

Through tying their most popular actors and actresses to exclusive contracts, studios were able to utilise the 'star system' to further market their films. So, anyone going to see a film starring Gary Cooper would assume that they were seeing a Western, just as James Cagney would imply a gangster film, Doris Day a musical, and so on. These contracted artists could also be loaned out to other studios producing one-off films in that star's 'usual' genre. In this way, popular actors and actresses found themselves associated with a particular type of film to such an extent that they became a 'genre icon', where their very image or presence in a film was regarded as a generic convention. One of the benefits of having a recognisable genre star was to allow the makers to add more variation to other aspects of the film, for example plot or style, and so introduce the element of novelty that genre audiences demand. Similarly, plot holes or character attributes could be implicitly filled in by the audience through their memory of roles the star had previously taken or through perceived biographical knowledge of the star themselves.[2] Examples of genre icons in the horror film would be Boris Karloff and Bela Lugosi in the 1930s and 40s, and Christopher Lee, Peter Cushing and Vincent Price in the 1950s, 60s and 70s. Genre iconography and the star system will be discussed further in our chapters on *The Old Dark House* (James Whale, 1932) and *Psycho* (Alfred Hitchcock, 1960) respectively.

Studying Film Genre

While practical film schools have been around for a century or more, the subject of film studies as we know it today was virtually non-existent up until the mid-1950s. Prior to this, publications relating to film were restricted to fan magazines (usually produced by the studios to promote their latest stars) or high-level genre overviews. Film was seen purely as entertainment rather than any kind of art, and treated as such. With the demise of the Hollywood studio system, however, there was a change in critical attitudes. During the second half of the 1950s and through the 60s a group of writers attached to the French periodical *Cahiers du cinema* established what they termed *politique des auteurs* (known as *auteur* theory or auteurism). This highly influential approach rejected the dominant view of cinema (particularly Hollywood cinema) as nothing more than mass-produced popular entertainment, and sought to highlight the artistry of individual directors.

The aim of the *Cahiers* critics was to promote the idea that, regardless of Hollywood's commercial function and production-line approach, it was possible for talented directors to create genuine works of art. Despite the constraints imposed by working within the confines of a set genre or studio system, these directors had been able to establish a distinctive 'world view' throughout their body of films. By projecting this personal view, through consistencies in theme and stylistic technique, directors such as Alfred Hitchcock, Orson Welles and Howard Hawks were considered to be the sole authors (the '*auteurs*') of their work. Such an approach therefore concentrates on the elements brought to each film by the director, at the expense of any kind of traditional generic examination. In effect, the films by a particular director are classed as a genre in and of themselves, with their own codes and conventions. We will discuss the idea of the *auteur* more fully in Chapter 10, when we look at the films of Canadian director David Cronenberg and how his own particular world view influenced the wider horror genre.

By the late 1960s, the emergence of film studies as a valid academic discipline led to new directions in film theory. Auteurism came to be seen as unnecessarily restrictive, and too simplistic in its attitudes towards how and why films were made; in particular, the emergence of the 'blockbuster' in the mid-1970s reiterated the importance of the commercial aspects of film production over the artistic. As well as the arrival of Marxist, psychoanalytic and feminist approaches to film theory, there was a return to the study of genre. Early work in 'genre theory' consisted of purely textual analysis to discover and trace recognisable codes and conventions, to define boundaries and understand which features of a film assign it to a particular genre. More recently genre theory has grown to encompass an examination of the influence of elements external to the films themselves, for example to understand why a particular genre (or sub-genre) should be more popular at one time than another.

While there will be textual analysis of the films featured in this book, it is important that we recognise the relationships between those films and the outside world. Our case studies highlight the effects on the genre of external factors including economic, cultural and societal changes (in particular censorship, which has been a major driver behind the genre's evolution), the rise of independent film-making, technological innovations such as special effects, and so on. Of course, we must remember that this is not a one-way street; films can themselves be an influence, and the horror genre's interaction with popular culture is something that we discuss at length in our later chapters.

Horror as Genre

Now that we have an idea of how and why the concept of film genre came about, we will briefly discuss the history of the one which is of immediate interest to us: horror. What we see in the genre today is the result of over a hundred years of evolution. As with other genres, over time horror developed codes and conventions that became typically associated with what we would now term a traditional horror film. Generic conventions include settings (for example an isolated old mansion or a dark castle), plot elements (a thunderstorm, or a climactic chase sequence), and characters (a mad scientist, or a masked killer). Thematic conventions are those that are concerned with the overall story, and tend to be more fluid and cyclical than other conventions. For example, many horror films in the 1940s and 50s would feature scientific experiments gone wrong, whereas 'slasher' films of the 1980s were based around stories of revenge for past misdeeds. Generic codes, found in the stylistic aspects of the film (cinematography, lighting, *mise-en-scène*, editing, and sound), can also affect the narrative, by way of so-called generic motivation. For example, horror films have generally used low-key lighting and shadows to evoke an air of mystery and fear. How many such films have you seen which are set at night, or in an otherwise dark location, and have had an event occur which means that the protagonist is left with only a candle, lantern or flashlight to help them find their way? Here the stylistic concerns of the genre have imposed themselves onto the causality of the film's text.

Particularly since the arrival of the 'modern' horror film in the early 1960s, the genre has displayed a degree of freedom from many of its more traditional conventions. Nowadays, especially in comparison to other distinct genres such as the Western or the gangster film, a horror film is not necessarily identified as such by its setting or characters. Rather than being categorised through discrete elements from which it is built, a horror film can be identified from the effect that the film as a whole is intended to have on the viewer. The horror film's *raison d'etre* is to scare its audience, literally to horrify them. Arguably, any film that sets out with the objective of provoking fearful emotions can be described as a horror film, regardless of plot, characters, setting, or anything else. And, just as the success of a comedy film rests on its ability to make its audience laugh, so the horror film may be judged on its ability to frighten. As we shall see through examination of the case studies in this book, and as discussed in our final chapter, there are any number of ways to provoke such emotions, from dread through the slightest suggestion of the supernatural, to outright repulsion through a bombardment of blood and guts.

In comparison to more straightforward genres, then, horror cinema is particularly adaptable in terms of narrative. A horror film can be set anywhere, and at any time, and it may contain any number of characters, of any age and background. The commercial aspect of this flexibility at least partly explains the initial success of the genre. For the big Hollywood studios, horror films could re-use sets and costumes from their more usual genre output, so were less of a commitment in terms of investment. For the smaller studios they represented a type of film that could be produced cheaply and quickly using whatever sets and costumes they had to hand. Certainly, it has been unusual for major studios to invest large amounts in the genre, with very few big budget productions. Nowadays horror is favoured by independent film-makers and smaller studios, and has proven extremely effective at achieving commercial, and occasionally critical, success on limited budgets. We discuss this at length in our final chapter.

For all its adaptability, the plot of the horror film almost without exception has a straightforward linear structure, and obeys the classical Hollywood narrative of cause-effect. As we discuss in Chapter 7, the use of 'artistic' expression in the horror film is arguably counter-productive. Drawing attention to the fact that what we are seeing is a film and not reality, in which the film-making process is highlighted, is not what is required.[3] For this reason it is unusual to find any 'art' films in the genre. Even directors who have a reputation for more experimental films have tended to be conservative in their approaches to tackling horror. Examples of this would be Werner Herzog with *Nosferatu The Vampyre* (1979), Nicolas Roeg with *Don't Look Now* (1973), and Roman Polanski with *Rosemary's Baby* (1968).

Like the majority of narrative cinema (and indeed literature), most horror films fit the traditional three-act structure of 'order-disorder-order'. Into an orderly world comes a disruptive element or threat (in horror this would be the 'monster'), which must be neutralised or assimilated to restore the world back to its balanced state. The conventional horror film tends to follow this structure quite rigidly, with the threat itself being the main differentiating factor. For each film we need to ask: what is the nature of the monster and what does it represent? Is it 500 feet tall, breathing fire? Is it made up from parts of dead bodies, with a damaged, criminal brain? Is it Death itself, dispatching those who have cheated it in ever more ingenious ways? Is it a tribe of cannibals? Is it a possessed car? A house? A doll? Outside of the narrative the monster can often be seen as a metaphor for a larger threat, a universal fear that touches the society and culture within which it was produced. Horror cinema enables the cathartic expression of such fears.

In his seminal book examining horror in all its (art) forms, *The Philosophy of Horror*, Noël Carroll describes the narrative structures he views as characteristic of the genre. These are primarily the 'overreacher plot' and the 'complex discovery plot', from which can be derived a number of simpler plots. Works based around the 'overreacher plot' are concerned with the negative consequences of the pursuit of knowledge or power through the (mis)use of science and/or magic by a misguided protagonist. The disequilibrium of the narrative is caused directly or indirectly by the character's actions in this pursuit, which must then be reversed, by either the protagonist or the larger community, for equilibrium to be regained. Such a plot-line can be found in a number of the films discussed in this book, such as *Der Golem* (Paul Wegener, Carl Boese, 1920) and *The Fly* (David Cronenberg, 1986).

The 'complex discovery plot' consists of four narrative stages: onset (the audience is made aware of the monster), discovery (one or more of the central characters discovers that the monster is the cause of immediate threat), confirmation (the wider community is convinced of the monster's existence) and confrontation (humanity confronts the monster and may or may not be victorious). In the construction of narratives derived from this plot, each of the four stages may be repeated, extended, or dropped altogether. A relatively straightforward example of a complex discovery plot in our case studies would be *Night of the Living Dead* (George A. Romero, 1968). *Psycho*, by contrast, delays the onset stage until late in the film, dispenses with the discovery stage, and merges confrontation and confirmation in its climax. Hitchcock's methods of manipulating audience expectation, of which this is one of many, are discussed more fully in that chapter.

With particularly broad film genres (or 'umbrella' genres) such as horror, the use of 'conventional subsets' in a group of films results in further classification of films by way of 'sub-genres'. If we look at some of the films discussed in this book, we can find haunted house films, zombie films, demonic possession films, vampire films, and so on. Such sub-division makes it easier for the potential audience member to understand and decide if it is something they would want to see: not every fan of haunted house films would be interested in watching a film about flesh-eating zombies. As with the umbrella genres, sub-genres are defined after the fact. So, for example, once films such as *Friday the 13th* (Sean S Cunningham, 1980), *My Bloody Valentine* (George Mihalka, 1981) and *The Burning* (Tony Maylam, 1981) had established the conventions of what it was to be a 'slasher', earlier films which were not necessarily part of the current cycle, such as *Black Christmas* (Bob Clark, 1974), and even Hitchcock's original *Psycho*, began to be included retrospectively in the 'slasher' sub-genre.

Once established, sub-genres can include entries decades apart, and will continue to evolve. A 'cycle', on the other hand, will generally (but not always) exist for a relatively short period of time, and will use a rigid subset of generic conventions. Between 1931 and 1956 Universal released dozens of films in what is commonly termed the 'Universal monster cycle'. We look at these in more detail in our chapter on the studio's 1932 film *The Old Dark House*. These early releases from Universal introduced numerous generic icons that have endured throughout horror cinema and popular culture (including familiar representations of Count Dracula, Frankenstein's monster, the wolf man and the mummy), as well as countless codes and conventions. To take a more recent example, while 'slasher' is regarded as a sub-genre, the original set of 'slasher' films from 1978 to 1983 are considered a cycle due to the extremely limited set of codes and conventions that they employed. The particular codes and conventions associated with this cycle and the larger sub-genre are discussed more fully in our chapter on Mario Bava's *Bay of Blood* (1971).

Parodies, films that deliberately push generic conventions into cliché, generally appear towards the end of particular cycles, when audiences have become sufficiently aware of the key elements to be able to easily recognise them, even outside of their usual context.[4] For the Universal monster cycle, this happened with the *Abbott and Costello Meet...* films of 1948 to 1955, beginning with Charles Barton's *Abbott and Costello Meet Frankenstein*. The British comedy *Carry on Screaming* (Gerald Thomas, 1966) was a parody of both the Universal cycle and Hammer's Gothic horror films of the 1950s and 60s. More recently the *Scary Movie* films (from 2000 onwards) began life as a parody of the 'postmodern slasher' cycle initiated by *Scream* (Wes Craven, 1996), but have since developed to encompass horror, science-fiction and fantasy films in general.

One method of introducing audiences to new elements is through the use of so-called 'genre-hybrids'. These are films that straddle two or more distinct genres by including enough conventions from each that they could be said to belong to any one of them. Examples of these include the Western-musical 'singing cowboy' films of the 1940s, and the horror-comedy-musical *The Rocky Horror Picture Show* (Jim Sharman, 1975). Obviously this approach should be treated with caution, as the combining of two inappropriate genres can have potentially disastrous results. When their traditional brand of Gothic horror was on the wane, Hammer Films teamed up with Shaw Brothers of Hong Kong to produce *The Legend of the 7 Golden Vampires* (Don Houghton, 1973). Mixing their long-running Dracula series with elements of the then-popular martial arts cinema, they came up with what was promoted as 'the first kung-fu horror spectacular'. Unfortunately for the companies involved, the audience for kung-fu films at the time was too far removed from that for typical Hammer fare, and the film was a commercial failure.

While horror/science-fiction has been a particularly popular and successful hybrid, the boundary between the two genres has traditionally been fuzzy. *Lifeforce* (Tobe Hooper, 1985) concerns the invasion of Earth by a race of 'space vampires' who suck the life from humans. Whilst the presence of vampire-like creatures (not to mention the director of *The Texas Chain Saw Massacre* [1974]) indicates that it could be a horror film, it will usually be found listed under science-fiction. On the other hand, *Night of the Living Dead*, which features a plague of re-animated corpses who return from the grave to devour humans, will always be classed as a horror film and not science-fiction, despite the fact that the narrative implies the source of the plague is a returning space probe.

Of course, genre was developed as a marketing tool, and it's important to understand the commercial influences of the industry on films' classification. Many of what are termed science-fiction films from the 1950s are typical 'monster movies' that if made in the 1930s or 40s (or 60s or 70s) would have been recognised as belonging to the horror genre. The fact that public interest in modern technology meant that the films performed better at the box office by being labelled and marketed as 'science-fiction' does not necessarily reflect their content. The Lon Chaney Jr. vehicle *Man Made Monster* (George Waggner, 1941), a conventional Universal horror picture, was re-released in the 1950s as a science-fiction film under the title *The Atomic Monster*. Looking back at these films today, they could legitimately be described as horror, science-fiction or a hybrid of both. 1950s science-fiction cinema will be discussed further in our chapter on David Cronenberg's remake of *The Fly*.

Audiences' knowledge and understanding of genre are also used in marketing. At the height of their success in the 1960s Hammer Films had become so associated with horror that everything they released was considered a horror film, even though some (for example *Stranglers of Bombay* [Terence Fisher, 1960] or *The Terror of the Tongs* [Anthony Bushell, 1961]) were more period action films than anything else. When their psychological thriller *Straight on Till Morning* (Peter Collinson, 1972) was described in its trailers and publicity materials as 'A love story … from Hammer', the audience's recognition of the type of films associated with the studio made it clear that this was not going to be a love story in the traditional sense. There is also the possibility that a film is deliberately marketed as belonging to a genre to which it does not. *The Walking Dead* (Michael Curtiz, 1936) may be a horror/gangster hybrid, but Warner's publicity materials misleadingly highlighted a 'Karloff-as-monster' angle that is at odds with the actual content of the film. Such an approach was extremely prevalent in the 1960s and early 70s, when exploitation distributors would frequently retitle films to appeal to whatever market was popular at the time. We discuss this practice, and the exploitation film in general, in our chapter on *Night of the Living Dead*.

The Origins of Horror

Whilst it is undoubtedly true that horror cinema has regularly drawn inspiration from older written works, as well as myth, legend and folklore from around the world, the literary origins of what we now call the horror genre are generally traced back to early-to-mid eighteenth-century Britain and the works of the so-called 'graveyard poets'. Seen as a reaction to the Age of Enlightenment,[5] the works of writers such as Thomas Parnell and Edward Young regularly featured 'graves and churchyards … night, ruins, death and ghosts, everything, indeed, that was excluded by rational culture' (Botting 1996: 32). Viewers of horror cinema will certainly recognise these iconic elements, and during the latter half of the century such ingredients were to be found also in a huge number of popular Gothic tales, beginning with Horace Walpole's 1764 novel *Castle of Otranto*, through Ann Radcliffe's *The Mysteries of Udolpho* (1794) and Matthew Lewis's *The Monk* (1797), and culminating in the epic *Melmoth the Wanderer* (Charles Robert Maturin, 1820).

Such fiction continued the earlier anti-rationalist stance, describing the journey from familiar everyday settings into a darker, more primitive and often supernatural world. Heavy on atmosphere and light on plot, they abandoned the restraint of the conventional literature of the period to indulge in excess. Favoured narratives involved the trials of a young, virginal female protagonist who found herself pursued through the labyrinthine ruins of a castle or abbey by a nefarious villain. That these antagonists were usually foreign (more often than not continental European) highlights the idea of 'otherness' that informs the horror film's treatment of 'the monster'. Thematically, Gothic literature revolves around the transgression of boundaries (light/dark, good/evil, life/death, reality/dream, young/old, and so on) and the concept of 'the uncanny', something at once familiar yet alien, typified by the *doppelgänger* or double.

In line with similar developments throughout Europe, particularly in Germany and France, the early nineteenth century saw a Romantic emphasis in the English Gothic novel. The movement away from stock caricatures of good and evil towards a more ambivalent study of alienated character resulted in the appearance of more recognisable horror stories, at least to modern audiences. Conceived on a single night in 1816 following the group reading of German ghost stories, both Mary Shelley's *Frankenstein, or The Modern Prometheus* (1818, revised and re-issued in 1831) and Dr John Polidori's *The Vampyre* (1819) proved extremely popular, and were common stage dramatisations from the 1820s onwards. Whilst *Frankenstein* can be credited with introducing the image of the true 'monster' (as opposed to the villain or ghost) into Gothic literature, Polidori's work represents England's first serious vampire tale. Meanwhile, in America, Edgar Allan Poe's two-volume collection of short stories *Tales of the Grotesque and Arabesque* (1840), followed by classics such as *The Masque of the Red Death* (1842), *The Tell-Tale Heart* (1843) and *The Raven* (1845), introduced elements of madness and psychological horror.

The psychological aspect became more prevalent towards the end of the nineteenth century when, fuelled by a popular interest in spiritualism, ghost stories moved out of the realm of the Gothic castle and into more everyday settings. Popular early works in this style include *The Signalman* (1866) by Charles Dickens, and Joseph Sheridan Le Fanu's *In a Glass Darkly* (1872), a collection of previously published short stories that includes the vampire tale 'Carmilla'. Other notable authors of the psychological ghost story include Henry James (*The Turn of the Screw*, 1898) and M. R. James, who produced several collections, beginning with *Ghost Stories of an Antiquary* in 1904. However the two most important publications during this period, as far as the evolution of the modern horror genre is concerned, were Robert Louis Stevenson's novella *The Strange Case of Dr Jekyll and Mr Hyde* (1887) and Bram Stoker's *Dracula* (1897). Influenced by Le Fanu's short story and his own knowledge of Transylvanian history, Stoker's novel combined elements of Romanticism (including the concept of the aristocratic vampire from Polidori's earlier work) with more traditional Gothic horror and European folklore. Both of these met with instant success, and along with Shelley's *Frankenstein* would provide the burgeoning film industry with inspiration for a number of early productions in the 1910s and 20s.

Thomas Sipos uses these three works – *Dracula*, *Frankenstein* and *Dr Jekyll* – to exemplify what he describes as horror cinema's 'three subgenres': 'the supernatural, the monsters of nature and science (horror/sci-fi), and the human psyche's dark side (horror psycho)' (Sipos 2010: 10). Together, they contain many of the themes that define the genre as a whole and which will be explored through the individual case studies in this book: in particular, the dangers of science/forbidden knowledge, bodily transformation, the undead, threats of modernity, split personality, the *doppelgänger* and the 'exotic other', and the linking of sex and death. The release in 1931 of official film versions of these three cornerstone works of Gothic horror fiction, and the commercial success that accompanied them, confirmed a desire in cinema audiences for tales of fantasy and the macabre. Whilst nowadays there can be little doubt that Universal's *Dracula* (Tod Browning, 1931) should be classed as a horror film, at the time of its release it was marketed as a romantic drama, opening on Valentine's Day and billed as 'the strangest love story ever told'. It was only following the later release of *Frankenstein* (James Whale, 1931), and the British censor's response in creating the H (for 'horrific') classification, that the term 'horror film' came into common usage.

Studying Horror Cinema

While the narrative structures and themes of the genre may have remained largely unchanged since the Gothic literature of the 1700s, the way in which these have been represented to audiences has undergone great changes in the past hundred or so years. From the trick photography of Georges Méliès at the turn of the twentieth century, through the arrival of sound, colour film, special make-up effects and computer-generated imagery (CGI), advancements in the technology of cinema itself have been a major driving force behind genre production. Each of these will be discussed in relation to the individual case studies, but from its inception the cinematic art form in general has been viewed as particularly suited to tales of the fantastic, where the ghostly images projected (and viewed) in the dark manifested the stuff of dreams – or nightmares.

The chronological arrangement of our case studies, beginning in 1920 with *Der Golem* and ending in 2017 with *It*, allows us to trace the evolution of the genre against the backdrop of a tumultuous century. Two world wars, the Cold War, rapid scientific and technological change, economic boom and bust, growing fears for the environment and the future of the planet – we cannot understand horror cinema without making reference to the real world events that have characterised the era. The Universal horror films of the 1930s have frequently been read as allegories of the Depression, with Frankenstein's monster representing the downtrodden proletariat and Dracula symbolising the threat of European immigration. Similarly, the sci-fi/horror hybrids of the 1950s may represent fears of science out of control and of Cold War paranoia. Graphically violent American films of the late 1960s and early 70s (*Night of the Living Dead*, *The Last House on the Left* [Wes

Craven, 1972] and *The Texas Chain Saw Massacre*, amongst others) have been seen as reactions against the Vietnam War, and reflections of the country's general atmosphere of unrest at the time. More recent British films such as *Mum and Dad* (Steven Sheil, 2008) and *Eden Lake* (James Watkins, 2008) can be read as responses to popular concerns of a 'broken society', while left-leaning commentators have been keen to align the genre's current return to popularity with the rise of Donald Trump. Our approach to studying horror cinema therefore illuminates broader social, political and cultural histories.

Horror films are a product of their time, then, and films that were once considered upsetting may today be more likely to raise a giggle or a yawn than a shiver. At a more individual, subjective level, what terrifies one person may have no effect on another. Yet there are elements in the earliest horror films that are still apparent in the genre today, and we intend in this study to examine how and why such elements have evolved during the past hundred years. What do these films say about the audiences and the film-makers of the time? Can we find anything in them to understand why modern-day audiences still flock to see the latest genre releases? Until relatively recently it was difficult to find more than a cursory mention of horror cinema in any academic film study. As a genre, it has existed almost on a par with pornography in terms of the denigration it has received from scholars. The films have been accused of pandering to the basest needs of a questionable audience, with genre classics often dismissed as unworthy of serious discussion.[6] Even those involved in the production of genre films have tended to distance themselves from the connotations of the word 'horror'. Interviewed in 1974 about the films he made for Hammer, Christopher Lee said that he would 'prefer to call them fantasy pictures, or morality plays, or fairy stories'. Thankfully these attitudes have changed in recent years and horror cinema is now acknowledged as deserving of critical attention. Indeed, the genre has been the subject of highly complex, if not always sympathetic, theoretical analysis. In this volume we hope to provide an accessible overview, one that simultaneously gives horror the critical attention it deserves and unashamedly celebrates its capacity to (pleasurably) terrify audiences since the dawn of cinema.

Bibliography

Brosnan, John (1976) *The Horror People*. New York: St. Martin's Press.

Carroll, Noël (1990) *The Philosophy of horror, or Paradoxes of the Heart*. London: Routledge.

Jancovich, Mark (1996) *Rational Fears: American Horror in the 1950s*. Manchester: Manchester University Press.

Sipos, Thomas M. (2010) *Horror Film Aesthetics: Creating the Visual Language of Fear.* Jefferson: McFarland & Co. Ltd.

Skal, David J. (1994) *The Monster Show: A Cultural History of Horror.* London: Plexus.

Solomon, Stanley J. (1976) *Beyond Formula: American Film Genres.* New York: Harcourt Brace Jovanovich, Inc.

Wood, Robin (1979) 'An Introduction to the American Horror Film' in Grant, Barry Keith (ed.) (1984) *Planks of Reason: Essays on the Horror Film.* London: the Scarecrow Press, Inc.

Worland, Rick (2008) *The Horror Film: An Introduction.* Oxford: Blackwell.

Endnotes

1. Common stylistic approaches to lighting, editing, cinematography and *mise-en-scéne* are referred to as a genre's 'codes', whereas common narrative elements such as setting, character types and plot developments are 'conventions'.

2. To foster audience recognition, studios' publicity departments often promoted supposedly candid images of an actor or actress that further tied them to their screen roles or reinforced desirable traits.

3. An obvious exception to this is the 'found footage' film, introduced in *Cannibal Holocaust* (Ruggero Deodato, 1979) and popularised by *The Blair Witch Project* (Daniel Myrick and Eduardo Sanchez, 1999).

4. Note that this is not always the case. Mel Brooks' *Young Frankenstein* (1974) appeared well after the end of the classic Universal monster series it parodies, and at least part of the failure of *Student Bodies* (Mickey Rose, 1981) can be attributed to the fact that it appeared relatively early in the slasher cycle.

5. Also known as the Age of Reason, the Age of Enlightenment is generally considered to span the latter half of the seventeenth and the majority of the eighteenth century. Driven by a philosophical movement that strove to explain the place of man in terms of rational and scientific law, its cultural influence can be found primarily in the literature and Neo-classical architecture of the period.

6 There are exceptions. Alfred Hitchcock's *Psycho* is one of the most written-about films in the history of cinema. However, it is often discussed in terms of a thriller, or 'suspense' film, or as part of Hitchcock's *auteur*-ial output.

Chapter 1

Early European Horror

Der Golem: Wie er in Die Welt Kam
(The Golem: How He Came into the World)

Paul Wegener and Carl Boese, Germany 1920

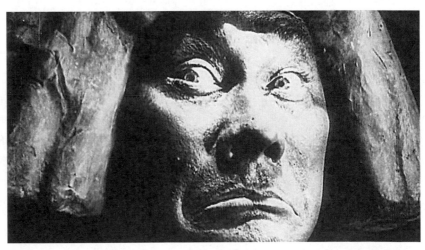

Recommended viewing

Der Student von Prag (Paul Wegener and Stellan Rye, 1913)

Das Kabinett des Dr Caligari (Robert Weine, 1919)

Nosferatu (F W Murnau, 1922)

Das Wachsfigurenkabinett (Paul Leni, 1924)

M (Fritz Lang, 1931)

Introduction

In his influential article on the American horror film, Robin Wood offers what he calls a 'basic formula' for all works of the horror genre: 'normality is threatened by the Monster' (1979: 175). He goes on to suggest that whilst the genre's definition of 'normality' remains relatively fixed, the form of the monster (and perhaps more crucially the relationship between it and normality) continually evolves and develops in response to societal and cultural change. Although ostensibly an external menace, the monster often represents the physical manifestation of some repressed aspect of self or society, of subconscious anxieties hidden just beneath the surface. As we will see throughout the course of this book, examination of the identity of the monster, the nature of the threat it carries, and the method of its subsequent rationalisation (through destruction or assimilation), provides insightful information about the society and culture from which horror films emerge. In response to the question of what constitutes a monster, Noël Carroll suggests that as well as posing a deadly threat it must also be 'impure', and puts forward four 'symbolic structures of impurity': fusion, fission, magnification/massification and metonymy (1990: 42-52). Essentially, each of these represents an unnatural transgression of some commonly accepted boundary, usually, but not necessarily, physical. Fusion involves the simultaneous occupation of two or more normally exclusive categories, such as living/dead, human/animal, human/vegetable, and so on (for example zombies, vampires). Fission involves the occupation of two or more categories, at different times (werewolves, Dr Jekyll and Mr Hyde) or in different spaces (the *doppelgänger*). Magnification/massification takes an existing source of potential horror and either magnifies it (giant spiders) or masses it (swarms of cockroaches). Finally, metonymy involves the representation of something inwardly monstrous, though appearing normal, through association with a recognisable source of horror (Norman Bates' association with the stuffed corpse of his mother).

Although we have stated that the monster is a prerequisite of all works of horror, the term 'monster movie' is often taken to represent a recognisable sub-genre, and carries with it specific audience expectations in terms of plot and characterisation. In this chapter we look at an early example of such a film, wherein a society is threatened by the intrusion of an inhuman, physical force intent on death and destruction. As well as identifying elements that would go on to become 'monster movie' convention, we also examine the film's style and themes as they relate to the wider horror genre.

Background

From the first flickerings of Lumiere's Cinématographe in the mid-1890s, the new art form brought to life images of the fantastic, the marvellous and the macabre. Studies within any branch of fantasy cinema invariably begin with the work of French conjurer and film-maker Georges Méliès, and this book is no exception. Although his influence is also felt in the science-fiction and fantasy genres we know today, Méliès took particular delight in presenting images of horror and the supernatural. In 1896 alone he introduced audiences at his Paris magic shows to the sight of a woman metamorphosing into a skeleton (and back again) in *The Vanishing Lady*, an attack by giant insect in *A Terrible Night*, and even Satan himself, calling forth ghosts and skeletons from a bubbling cauldron in *The House of the Devil*. Over the next decade-and-a-half, he wrote, directed and appeared in hundreds of such so-called 'trick films', often containing what we would now consider to be iconic horror film images of cobwebbed castles, coffins, skeletons and swooping bats. Ever more elaborate and ambitious, Méliès' productions culminated in his epic *The Conquest of the Pole* (1912), in which he presented the spectacle of a giant (pipe-smoking and man-eating) snow creature being discovered and destroyed by a group of Arctic explorers. Whatever the subject, the attraction of Méliès' films was always the optical effects, including many which would subsequently become standard in fantasy cinema, such as stop-motion photography, double exposure, split-screen, and the manipulation of film speed through under- and over-cranking. Although his film-making career would end with him in poverty, the cinematic illusions created by the 'Wizard of Montreuil' were embraced by audiences and copied by film-makers the world over.

Georges Méliès is justly remembered as a pioneer in fantasy cinema, creating unique, popular and sought-after films at a time when the movie-making business was essentially a free-for-all. Even as Méliès' film career ended there was not yet a Hollywood, and America was just one amongst a number of countries producing popular films for consumption worldwide. In Europe it was France, Italy and Scandinavia who led the way, with not insubstantial output from countries such as Russia, Britain and Spain. With hundreds of film-makers competing across the world, cinema quickly evolved from short, unsophisticated material to a longer, more structured and narrative-based form, essentially moving from a vaudevillian entertainment to one more akin to theatre. Such a transition was ultimately dependent on the ready availability of source material, and in an effort to raise the artistic and cultural values of the cinema film-makers increasingly turned to existing written works. It has been estimated that by 1910 over half of all films being produced were adaptations of novels or plays, and the continuing popularity of

Gothic and Romantic literature meant that by 1913, for example, Robert Louis Stevenson's *The Strange Case of Dr Jekyll and Mr Hyde* had become one of the most adapted stories in cinema's short history.

Stevenson's theme of split personality and dual existence, although a staple of the Gothic novel since its inception, had been especially prominent in Romantic literature from the late eighteenth century onwards in the form of the *doppelgänger*. According to myth, to see or meet one's own *doppelgänger*, or double, is a sign of impending danger or even death. In 1913, Edgar Allan Poe's *doppelgänger* tale 'William Wilson' (1839) was, along with Goethe's 'Faust' and the fantasy tales of E. T. A. Hoffmann, the inspiration for arguably the first classic of German cinema: Paul Wegener and Stellan Rye's *Der Student von Prag* (*The Student of Prague*). A well-respected stage actor at Max Reinhardt's prestigious 'Deutches Theater', Paul Wegener was fascinated with the new possibilities offered by the technology of film, much as Georges Méliès had been almost twenty years earlier.[1] But whereas the Frenchman had been satisfied to simply amuse audiences with the novelty of his filmed illusions (an approach which ultimately led to his demise as a film-maker), Wegener wanted to use the medium of cinema to bring to life familiar tales of the horrific and the macabre. Believing that films' content should be dictated by the unique effects which the new art form offered, he regarded the medium's natural subject as the fantastic, the mythical, the supernatural, anything in fact which challenged the accepted laws of reality. As an actor, he saw film as a means to break through the limitations of theatre and, excited by the idea of performing opposite his own self, Wegener proposed a film based around the concept of the *doppelgänger*. With *Der Student von Prag*, rather than using the camera to simply present tricks for their own sake, the effects produced would be an integral part of the narrative. Germany's most innovative cinematographer at the time, Guido Seeber, developed Méliès' split-screen and double-exposure techniques to bring Wegener's ideas to life in the tale of a young man who unwittingly sells his soul to the Devil. *Der Student von Prag* was extremely successful in Germany, gaining a reputation as the first of a new breed of 'high art' film, and prompted a number of productions based around similar themes.

It was during the filming of *Der Student von Prag* that Wegener first heard the legend of the golem, a clay man sculpted and given life by the medieval Rabbi Judah Loew Ben Bezalel to protect the Jews of the Prague ghetto from persecution.[2] The story fascinated Wegener, and inspired him to co-direct and star in a trio of films of which only the third has survived intact; indeed, there has been some debate as to whether the second in the series, the light-hearted *Der Golem und die Tanzerin* (*The Golem and the Dancer*, 1917), ever existed as a completed film. In transferring the golem's story to the screen, Wegener and his scriptwriters embellished the basic legend with their own mythological details. According to Wegener's films, the golem is given life by having a piece of paper inscribed with a secret word placed inside a pendant (a 'shem') decorated with a pentagram on the golem's chest; remove the pendant and the golem returns to inanimate stone. (In most versions of the legend writings from the Torah are written on the Golem's forehead, or placed inside its mouth or skull.) The first of the films, *Der Golem* (*The Golem*, 1914), co-directed by Henrik Galeen, is set in contemporary Prague. The lifeless clay giant (played by Wegener) is discovered in the ruins of an old synagogue by a group of workmen and passed on to Troedler, a knowledgeable antiquarian played by Galeen. Troedler locates an ancient book of necromantic rituals and succeeds in bringing the golem back to life. The creature initially obeys its new master, using its great strength to help him with physical tasks. However, when it falls in love with and is rejected by the antiquarian's daughter, Jessica, the golem goes on a violent rampage through Prague. Finally tracking Jessica and her lover to a party, it pursues the pair to the top of a tower where, after a brief struggle, Jessica removes the shem and the golem topples to its destruction on the cobbled streets below.

From this brief description of the events in the first film you may already recognise some of the narrative features that have since become conventions in so-called 'monster movies'. However, it must be said that the cinematic influence of this first entry in the series was severely limited. When initially released, at the beginning of the First World War, there was little appetite for the nation's films outside of Germany itself. Indeed, during the war years (and for some time after) many countries banned the import of German films altogether. Before we move on to the case study for this chapter - the third of Wegener's golem films, from 1920 - it is important to understand the changes that took place not only in German cinema but also in the film industry as a whole during the intervening years.

Prior to the start of the First World War the German film industry had been relatively modest, with American and European imports providing much of the material shown at the country's cinemas. This situation began to change in 1914 when the outbreak of war limited the supply of film imports, and accelerated in early 1916 when the German government placed an embargo on all foreign films excepting those from Sweden and Denmark. Cinema-going had become an incredibly popular pastime for a German public eager to escape the horrors of war, and with the supply of foreign films curtailed there was an immediate explosion in local production. The number of independent German film companies quickly multiplied, and soon the German government began to take an active role in the shaping of a national film industry, beginning with the formation of Ufa (Universum Film

Aktiengesellschaft) in 1917. Initially a consolidation of some of the country's larger studios, Ufa would continue to absorb smaller production companies over the next few years. In a move that mirrored the major Hollywood studios, which were by now beginning to dominate the American film industry (and to which Ufa was Germany's direct response), the company introduced what was termed 'vertical integration'. Under this structure, a studio could have complete control over the distribution and exhibition of its films by either building or buying up cinemas or merging with existing exhibition chains. But whereas the Hollywood studios' actions were motivated by profit and market share, the German government's interest in controlling the industry was at least partly political, regarding film as a powerful tool for the dissemination of propaganda both during and after a war which was growing increasingly unpopular at home.

From the start of Germany's import ban in 1916 until the early 1920s, the country's film industry was largely isolated from events that were taking place elsewhere in the world. During this time, with much of the rest of Europe having ceased film production for the duration of the war, America rose to a position of almost complete market domination. While the narrative and stylistic forms practiced by the Hollywood studios were quickly becoming accepted as the de-facto standard elsewhere, German film-makers continued to experiment with innovative and unique styles and production methods. At the end of the First World War the German film industry was in a very strong position financially: the country's dire economic situation meant that German films were extremely cheap to buy for overseas exhibitors, and with hundreds of independent production companies in operation there was an abundance of material. As a result, German cinema at this time exerted much more of an influence on the rest of the world, especially Europe, than vice versa. Even after the embargo on foreign film was lifted at the end of 1920, the prohibitive costs of importing films from America and elsewhere in Europe meant that local film production continued apace, with exports far outstripping imports for a number of years and for a time making Germany the largest film producer outside of Hollywood.

Following the war, and in an effort to differentiate their films from those produced or influenced by the Hollywood studios, German film-makers sought a unique style which they could claim as their own, and which could be combined with German subject matter to project a distinctive image of their country. It was also hoped that the introduction of an artistic aspect in their product would help to rehabilitate German cinema in the eyes of the rest of the world. The result was German Expressionism, a style often thought of as the dominant form in German film of the post-war period, although only around thirty or forty such films were actually produced. The Expressionist movement itself had begun in the early years of the twentieth century, initially through the work of a group of Dresden-based avant-garde artists known as 'Die Brucke' (The Bridge), which existed between 1905 and 1913. As a response to what they saw as the superficial objectivity of French Impressionism, Expressionist artists sought to avoid naturalistic depictions of external reality and instead project the artists' subjective vision. Their images, often representative of inner turmoil or disturbed psychological states, contain extreme abstract stylisation along with vibrant contrasting colours, sharp angles and geometric patterns.

These themes and styles had also been taken up in theatre and literature, so whilst their migration to film was not entirely unexpected, the introduction of such an 'artistic' influence was also part of a concerted effort to reach more sophisticated, middle-class audiences.[3] From its beginnings as a fairground novelty, cinema had been seen very much as cheap mass entertainment for the lower classes, a view that was certainly not restricted to Germany. For the country's film producers, not to mention Ufa and the German government, anything that served to attract wider audiences to German film was to be welcomed. Thematically, films of the movement tend to share a pre-occupation with tales of threat and oppression, angst, or depression. Their narratives often feature fantastical characters such as *doppelgängers*, alchemists and supernatural beings; all direct confrontations to established rational norms. Aesthetically, the films utilise canted camera angles (known as 'Dutch', or more accurately '*deutsche*', angles), distorted perspectives and unnatural architecture, and tend to use high-contrast ('chiaroscuro') lighting resulting in deep, well-defined shadows.

Unsurprisingly, given the style's natural ability to project a haunting, otherworldly atmosphere, the best known German Expressionist films of the post-war period are in what we would now call the horror and fantasy genres, primarily *Das Kabinett des Dr Caligari* (*The Cabinet of Dr Caligari*, Robert Wiene, 1919), *Nosferatu* (F.W. Murnau, 1922) and *Metropolis* (Fritz Lang, 1927). Of these, *Caligari* is commonly regarded as the first, and certainly the purest, of all German Expressionist films, with its disturbed psychological themes, subjective camerawork, anti-naturalist acting style, exaggerated make-up and distinctive set design. Expressionist film-making is suited to the use of indoor sets where every condition can be precisely controlled, and for *Caligari* this went as far as physically painting the exaggerated shadows directly onto its backdrops. The worldwide success of *Caligari* (including a screening in Paris which led to France re-opening its borders to German cinema) influenced the appearance of the films that followed, although none would incorporate such an extreme style. That films of fear and horror were popular at this time in Germany is perhaps not surprising, with its population recovering from a lost war, and the country suffering mass unemployment, financial meltdown and social unrest. However, both before and during the war, films featuring elements of the fantastic and the supernatural had already proved popular in Germany, and the introduction of the Expressionist style merely added another level to what was already evolving into a commercially successful genre.[4]

The case study for this chapter was released by Ufa one year after *Caligari*, and is a film that undoubtedly qualifies as cinema's first ever horror prequel (or what would nowadays be termed an 'origin story'). For *Der Golem: Wie er in Die Welt Kam*, Paul Wegener returned to the original legend as told to him in Prague, while incorporating the mythology he had created for the first golem film in 1914 and adding a few melodramatic flourishes. Stylistically, the differences between the 1914 and 1920 productions are worth noting. Viewing what little footage remains of the first, a modern-day audience will be struck by the realistic style in which it is shot, with bright outdoor locations and contemporary surroundings. It is certainly a long way from the closed sets and shadow-filled architectures created for the 1920 production. Although Wegener later claimed that he did not deliberately set out to make an Expressionist film with his golem prequel, it is difficult to believe that he would not be attracted by a style so suited to the anti-realist themes he favoured. Although *Golem* is undoubtedly more subtle than *Caligari*, whether by accident or design the Expressionist influence is apparent throughout the film, in both its visual style and narrative themes.

Textual Analysis

In sixteenth-century Prague, the Rabbi Low foretells from the stars that a great disaster is to befall his people and constructs the golem, a giant clay man of enormous strength, to protect them. With the planets in precise alignment, the demon Astaroth is summoned to provide the life-giving word, and the golem is awakened. The creature is used as Low's servant, obeying his every command, and when it saves the emperor and his court from the wrath of the gods the decree expelling the Jews from the ghetto is rescinded. However, a realignment of the planets causes the golem to turn against its creator and Low removes the life-giving amulet, vowing to destroy his creation. Before he can do so, Low's assistant Famulus, overcome with jealousy after finding the Rabbi's daughter Miriam with one of the emperor's knights, resurrects the golem. The creature grows increasingly violent, killing the knight, kidnapping Miriam, setting fire to the Rabbi's laboratory and causing mayhem throughout the community. Wandering outside the walls of the ghetto, it encounters a group of young girls, one of whom innocently removes the amulet from its chest. Returned to inanimate clay once more, the Jews rejoice as they carry the golem back into the ghetto.

The plot of Wegener's film is often compared to that of Shelley's novel *Frankenstein*, but, whilst there are undoubted similarities, they diverge significantly in one important aspect. Although both works can be said to follow what Noël Carroll calls the 'overreacher plot', as described in our introduction, the motives behind Victor Frankenstein and Rabbi Low's actions are very different. As we shall discuss more fully in our chapter on *The Curse of Frankenstein*, Shelley's protagonist was driven by a thirst for knowledge and a desire for power over life and death, typically selfish traits of the 'overreacher'. Rabbi Low, on the other hand, creates the golem for the benefit of the community, in a desperate attempt to protect his people from the actions of the emperor. He does so reluctantly and fearfully, describing the life-giving word extracted from the demon Astaroth as 'terrible', and prays to Jehovah for the strength to survive the invocation. It is the rabbi's assistant Famulus who, having taken advantage of the golem's strength in his everyday chores, sees the creature as a source of power to be unleashed against his love rival. Once the golem is revived the film enters more familiar 'monster movie' territory, and what would later become recognisable generic conventions appear thick and fast.

Before taking a more in-depth look at the film's plot, and in particular those climactic scenes, we will embark on a brief overview of the film as a whole. Most discussions of German Expressionism's influence on the horror genre tend to concentrate on stylistic traits such as the distinctive lighting and camerawork, and the break from traditionalist modes of visualisation and representation. Whilst this is certainly an important area, we must not neglect the thematic concerns of films such as *Der Golem*, *Caligari* and *Nosferatu*, which bind them both to the Expressionist movement and to the horror genre as it would later develop. Although politically the Expressionists sought to promote individualism and freedom, their films tend to take place in a world whose characters are trapped in situations outside of their control, and where hierarchies of power work to frustrate any attempt to break free. The movement's pre-occupation with unpredictability, irrationality, chaos and instability found voice in tales of fatalism, alienation, ambiguity and loss of personal control or identity. Such themes are found in much Gothic and Romantic literature of the eighteenth and nineteenth centuries, and have continued to evolve throughout the history of horror cinema.[5]

For its US release, Wegener's original 1914 golem film was retitled *The Monster of Fate*, and it is man's powerlessness against fate, in effect his lack of free will, which is the overriding theme of the prequel. In this film, the planets control the actions of every character, including the golem itself, and their significance is highlighted from the opening shot of the film. It is through his reading of a star-filled sky that Low learns of the impending danger to his people, and when the decree banishing them from the ghetto is revealed it is in a clenched fist superimposed over the same starry backdrop. The movement of the planets dictates the timing of the golem's birth, and their realignment precipitates its violent change in behaviour, shattering the illusion of control that the rabbi has over his creation. Even the emperor, ostensibly sitting at the top of the film's power hierarchy, is acknowledged as having previously used Low's astrological skills for predicting the future, and his order that they leave by the next new moon again betrays a reliance on astrology and the influence of the cosmos. (His attitude serves also to highlight another general concern of the Expressionists, that of the irrationality of social authority and the misuse of power: the emperor chooses to banish the Jews for their practising of the 'black arts', yet later summons Low to the castle to entertain the court with his magic.) The notion of the heavens predicting bad luck remains a common device in the horror film, serving to create a sense of dread and hinting at possible supernatural occurrences. Although it has little bearing on the narrative's later events, the reading of ominous horoscopes, accompanied by stylised shots of solar flares, in the opening scenes of Tobe Hooper's *The Texas Chain Saw Massacre* helps to set up an atmosphere of foreboding which endures throughout the whole film.

Working on *Der Golem*, Wegener was fortunate to have alongside him two highly-skilled craftsmen in Karl Freund and Hans Poelzig. With Guido Seeber lost to illness for most of the filming, Wegener turned to cinematographer Freund, who had previously worked on F. W. Murnau's now-lost version of *Dr Jekyll and Mr Hyde*, *Der Januskopf* (*The Head of Janus*, 1920) and would go on to shoot both *Nosferatu* and *Metropolis*. Acclaimed architect Poelzig designed the life-sized reproduction of the Jews' medieval ghetto, and oversaw its construction in Ufa's Berlin studios. Working closely with both men to design the film's distinctive look, Wegener rejected *Caligari*'s sharply-defined angles of stark black and white, instead relying on the effects of subtle light and shadow and distorted, organic looking sets to emphasise the fantastic aspect of the story. The opening shot presents a highly stylised silhouette of the Prague ghetto against a night sky, with curved buildings that look as if they have grown and developed as part of the natural landscape. When we cut to a shot of the rabbi and his telescope, the tower on which he stands resembles a claw reaching up to the sky. The design of the rabbi's home looks as if it has been carved or shaped from natural surroundings; the staircase that winds down from the tower in particular has the appearance of a conch shell or inner ear, and the branch-like hinges on the door of the Rabbi's workshop look as if they have grown of their own accord. The buildings in the ghetto feature cavernous interiors full of dark spaces and are sparsely furnished, whilst outside towering roofs lean precariously across crooked, labyrinthine streets. The impression given is one of instability and, contrasting with the perfectly symmetrical architecture and bright and lively *mise-en-scène* of the emperor's court, clearly marks the ghetto as otherworldly and fantastical, protected from the outside world by an oversized, triangular gate.

Geometric shapes, a common feature of Expressionist art, occur frequently in the visuals of the film. Unsurprisingly, given the dominant theme described above, the symbol of the star (in various forms, including the Star of David and the pentagram) is a recurring motif, from the opening shot through to the closing image. Similarly circles (here representing the never-ending 'circle of fate') fea-

Figure 1.1

ture heavily, beginning with the subjectively masked view from Low's telescope in the film's opening and ending with the circle of girls playing outside the ghetto's gate. The Jews' clothing features a circular motif on the chest, and their triangular pointed hats are matched by the doors and windows of the ghetto's buildings, as well as in the iconic pose of the golem as it holds the broken beams of the banqueting hall above its head (see Fig 1.1). Smoke and fire are recurring motifs, beginning with that curling from the bubbling test tubes and out onto the roof (acting to tie the 'good science' of chemistry with the 'bad science' of astrology), through to the climactic conflagration in the ghetto. The set-piece of the film brings all of these motifs together, as Low summons the demon Astaroth from within a circle of flame whilst clutching a pentagram, and the life-giving word is revealed in smoking letters – an Expressionist visualisation of sound that had also been used in *Caligari*.

Whereas with *Caligari* Weine had mainly utilised the Expressionists' theatrical approach (concentrating on set design, acting style and make-up), Wegener makes more use of cinematic techniques, such as shot masking, camera effects and point-of-view (POV). Although it is now a common feature of the horror film, usually used to infer the presence of some unseen danger, the POV shot is by definition a subjective, and hence expressionistic, device.[6] Classical Hollywood cinema, which provides the viewer with an omnipresent 'third person' view from which to appreciate narrative events, had little use for such a restrictive viewpoint. The exception would be where a particular character has the optimum view, or when it is necessary to point out that a character has seen something not immediately apparent. In such a case the point-of-view shot would be preceded and/or followed by an objective reaction shot of that character (for example a character is seen to look at their watch, followed by a shot revealing that character's view of the watch).

In *Der Golem* the subjective shot of the emperor's court as seen by the golem does not convey any privileged information; we are simply presented with a subjective view of the scene. The use of masking, cutting off the top and bottom portions of the shot, indicates to the audience that what we are seeing is subjective, as well as suggesting a distancing of the golem from the real world. In terms of the narrative, it reveals that the golem is aware of what is going on; rather than being a soulless automaton there is a flickering of self-awareness, a foreshadowing of its impending release from the rabbi's control.

There is little doubt that *Der Golem* can be classed as what we now term a 'monster movie', a categorisation reflected in the American title of Wegener's original version. The golem itself is impure; as an inanimate object made mobile it is neither living nor dead, and its uncanny human appearance betrays its true origins. It is alien to the everyday world as depicted in the film, sending women and children fleeing even when performing such benign tasks as collecting the rabbi's shopping. However, if this was all there was to the creature, the film could not be described as a 'monster movie', or even a horror film. Rather, it would be a mild fantasy, wherein a statue is brought to life by magic to perform good deeds, and its plot would be very slight indeed. As it is, *Der Golem* structurally matches what is universally acknowledged to represent a 'classical narrative', consisting of a three-part sequence: equilibrium (characters are introduced within an ordered existence); disequilibrium (a problem threatens or actively disrupts that order); equilibrium (the problem is overcome and order restored). This simple structure is utilised in the majority of films of whatever genre, and most (though not all) of the films featured in this book. Essentially the first hour or so can be classed as the initial equilibrium section of the plot, and the moment that the golem turns evil sparks disequilibrium. The transformation of the golem from harmless creature to threatening monster confirms *Der Golem* as a horror film under Robin Wood's 'basic formula', and its sudden display of violence elicits shock and fear in an audience that has already witnessed its superhuman strength. The audience's confusion at the golem's sudden change in behaviour is quickly removed by yet more mythology from the rabbi's ancient book, although the relief following the removal of the shem is short-lived. Dramatic irony, where the audience now knows more than the characters on screen, works to generate tension as we watch Famulus resurrect the creature. Although at first it appears to obey his instructions, we know it has developed a violent life of its own. In future films of this type, the ensuing mayhem would take up much more of the narrative, and the restoration of equilibrium would be more involved than the chance encounter that finally returns the golem to clay.

Der Golem's opening title asserts that what we are about to see is 'based on events in an old chronicle'. A popular ploy in Gothic novels was to claim that the work was based on 'found' documents (Stoker's *Dracula* consists entirely of diary entries, journals and letters by and between the book's protagonists, and both *Frankenstein* and *The Strange Case of Dr Jekyll and Mr Hyde* rely heavily on such devices), and this is something that has continued through to the horror film. In a genre which depends on the audience's ability to suspend disbelief, the writer or film-maker will welcome any approach that lends their work authenticity; a horror story will be scarier, and hence more effective, if its audience thinks that what they are reading or watching actually happened in real life. Nowadays, given the increase in home movie-making and the proliferation of amateur video, the same effect can be generated by claiming that the film is made up of actual 'found footage'. Whilst the Italian *Cannibal Holocaust* remains the first and arguably most effective of this type of horror film, more recently the device has been popular in films purporting to document supernatural events, for example *The Blair Witch Project*, *Paranormal Activity* (Oren Peli, 2007) and *The Last Exorcism* (Daniel Stamm, 2010). Obviously the technique is suited to some subjects more than others; whilst many viewers are willing to believe in the supernatural and will be open to such material, suggesting that footage showing a giant reptile terrorising a major city was genuine may stretch audience credulity, the success of *Cloverfield* (Matt Reeves, 2008) notwithstanding.

Similarly, the use of an ancient book or manuscript to validate the mythology being used is a popular device in the horror film, an attempt by the film-makers to add an air of authenticity. In *Der Golem*, Rabbi Low consults a tome entitled 'Necromancie: The Art of Bringing Dead Beings to Life', which reveals the origin of the golem and the importance of the 'shem', all in fact created by Wegener and his co-writers. Similar life-giving artefacts in horror fiction are the 'Scroll of Thoth', introduced in Karl Freund's *The Mummy* (1932) and used in several sequels and remakes, and the 'Necronomicon', or 'Book of the Dead', which appears in H. P. Lovecraft's 1924 short story 'The Hound' and several of his later works. The 'Necronomicon' in particular has proven popular with horror film-makers, and has featured (barely disguised) in Sam Raimi's *Evil Dead* series (1982 onwards), Lucio Fulci's *The Beyond* (1981) and *Jason Goes to Hell: The Final Friday* (Adam Marcus, 1992), amongst others.

We have already mentioned the narrative connection between *Der Golem* and Shelley's *Frankenstein*, and in terms of cinematic influence Wegener's film is often discussed in relation to James Whale's 1931 version of the novel. Both films feature a mute, lumbering man-made monster which turns against its creator, a common trope in literature going back to Milton's *Paradise Lost*, and a recurrent feature of the horror film. As with Boris Karloff in Whale's film, Wegener manages to portray the golem as both sympathetic and terrifying. The horror evoked when the creature turns evil is heightened by the close up of its face, the eyes staring out of the screen as its previously blank expression turns into a bestial snarl. Contrast this with its bemused smile when it is offered a flower in the emperor's court or when it gently lifts up the little girl at the film's close. These latter two sequences undoubtedly informed the infamous incident in Whale's film where the monster encounters a young girl by a lakeside and joins her in throwing flowers into the water, before picking her up and throwing her to her death. The subsequent scenes showing an angry, torch-carrying mob hunting the monster down would become something of a cliché, particularly in Universal's horror films of the 1930s and 40s, and again its genesis can be seen in the climax of Wegener's film.

The establishing shot of Famulus, poring over bubbling test tubes while the rabbi studies the stars, suggests a fusion of science and magic that is ultimately unexplored. In later films of the genre such a combination would inevitably spell disaster, and the figure of the scientist-alchemist, common in Gothic literature, would be popularised in Hollywood's 'mad scientist' sub-genre of the late 1930s and 40s. Interestingly, Wegener's only American film, MGM's *The Magician* (Rex Ingram, 1926), in which he stars as a Frankenstein/Caligari hybrid, contains many of the elements described here, as well as introducing another stock genre character in the form of the protagonist's disfigured assistant. Fritz, the crippled assistant of Whale's *Frankenstein*, also mirrors Famulus inasmuch as they can be held responsible for the failure of their respective master's experiment. Just as Famulus foolishly resurrects the golem, so Fritz's clumsiness leads to him stealing an abnormal brain rather than a healthy one.

Stylistically, the influence of Wegener's film, and in particular the visualisation of the golem itself, can be felt throughout the horror genre. One of the most celebrated shots in Murnau's *Nosferatu* (paid *homage* in *Bram Stoker's Dracula* [Francis Ford Coppola, 1992], amongst others) is when the vampire Count Orlok rises from his coffin in the hold of the Demeter, stiff and unnatural, as if defying gravity. Although it remains an eerie sequence, Wegener had used the exact same technique to equal effect two years earlier, during the golem's resurrection by Famulus. When Rabbi Low first brings the creature to life, its eyes open and appear to glow, staring out of the darkness. Again, it is a disconcerting effect, and one re-used with varying degrees of effectiveness in films as diverse as Tod Browning's *Dracula* and the Italian *Demons* (Lamberto Bava, 1985). The image of the monster's hands crashing through a locked door, seen when the golem eventually gains entry to Miriam's room in pursuit of Florian, is a frequently-used shock effect, and can be seen in a number of films, including *Night of the Living Dead* and *The Evil Dead*.

Whilst its influence can be seen in all of these films, in terms of plot structure,

Wegener's film is actually much closer to what is still considered the ultimate 'monster movie', *King Kong* (Merian C. Cooper and Ernest B. Shoedsack, 1933). Here, the giant gorilla transported to New York and displayed as an attraction not unlike the golem in the emperor's court, escapes, runs amok and kidnaps the heroine. Like the golem, Kong is fatally attracted to things of beauty, a failing that would affect many a

Figure 1.2

movie monster. The final line of the film, delivered after Kong falls to his death from the Empire State Building and asserting that, 'it was beauty killed the beast', could equally be applied to the ending of *Der Golem*, where the creature's rampage is brought to an end by the innocent young girl. However, as is typical in the 'overreacher' plot, the result of the experiment poses a particular danger to those closest to the protagonist, and the main target of the golem's attention is the rabbi's daughter Miriam. The image of the monster carrying (or in this case dragging) off the heroine is a recurring one in the horror genre, and the golem's attempted ravishing of the swooning Miriam and her subsequent kidnap in flowing white nightdress is pure Gothic (see Fig 1.2).

Discussion of the character of Miriam raises another important point, which again differentiates the film from classical Hollywood product. She is not the pure and virginal heroine common in the horror movies that followed, and that would evolve into the 'Final Girl' of the slasher films discussed in Chapter 9. In contrast to the demure and giggling women of the emperor's court, Miriam seems positively lustful, brazenly throwing herself at Florian against her father's wishes and allowing him into her bed as soon as the rabbi is away. Such ambiguity again reveals an Expressionist influence, where psychologically complex and unpredictable characters add to the air of confusion and instability, and is present in each of the film's main characters. The rabbi, whilst regarded as an authority figure representing the 'heart and voice' of the Jewish community, displays a cruel side in forcing Miriam to her knees when he sees her attraction to Florian, and ultimately seems more interested in basking in the praise for his achievements than in destroying his potentially deadly creation. Florian, ostensibly the hero riding into the ghetto on his white horse and protecting Miriam against the advancing golem while Famulus cowers in a corner, is also a schemer, using his money and power to gain access to the rabbi's daughter. His violent demise, leaving the way clear for the blackmailing

Figure 1.3

Famulus to go unpunished and get together with Miriam, would almost certainly not have happened in contemporary mainstream Hollywood, with its unambiguous sense of right and wrong. Similarly, one would expect a Hollywood film of the period to end with unqualified repentance from the protagonist, the destruction of the creature and a vow never to repeat the experiment. Instead the body of the golem is carried back to the ghetto, perhaps to be stored for future use; the fact that the rabbi's underground workshop is strewn with diagrams and clay body parts hints at previous creations. Wegener's ultimate message may be that, in the circle of fate, man is destined to repeat the same mistakes over and over (see Fig 1.3).

Reception and Aftermath

As evidenced by the film's enormous sets, the spectacular set-piece of the invocation, and the huge numbers of extras used in the climactic ghetto scenes, *Der Golem* was viewed as a major production by Ufa. They could be confident that German audiences, at least, would have already been familiar with the concept of the golem through Wegener's earlier film version and the popular 1915 novel *Der Golem* by Gustav Meyrink. There had also been a number of successful theatre productions based on the legend, including one by Max Reinhardt in 1908. On its release, Wegener's film was hailed as a landmark of German cinema, and is still regarded as the definitive screen version of the golem legend. Despite being set in the sixteenth century, its modernist themes, warning of the dangers of meddling with things best left alone, resonated with a German population recovering from devastating defeat in the first 'modern' war. It has also been suggested that the golem character serves as a metaphor for Germany itself, alienated and ostracised following the First World War.

1922 saw the release of *Nosferatu*, perhaps the best-known German horror film of the period, from a script by Henrik Galeen based on Bram Stoker's *Dracula*. Although its full impact was weakened by a protracted legal battle with Stoker's widow over copyright, Murnau's film eventually made it to American screens in 1929 and together with *Der Golem* was to have a profound influence on Hollywood's horror genre as it would develop in the following decade. More generally, in the years immediately following the release of *Der Golem* film production in Germany continued to expand, to such an extent that Hollywood studios feared for their dominant position. However, as the decade progressed there occurred a number of events which adversely affected the German industry, the first of these being an ironic side-effect of its new-found international popularity. American audiences saw the films emerging from Germany and elsewhere in Europe as more artistic than the entertainments being produced locally, and the success of quality films such as *Caligari* and *Der Golem* quickly created an appetite in both American and European audiences for German cinema. However, this appetite was in part met by the release of older, inferior works produced during the war years. Lacking the artistic qualities and interest of the post-war films, audiences' initial enthusiasm was quickly dampened by this surfeit of lower-quality releases and the reputation which Germany had achieved through the introduction of Expressionism quickly declined.

At the same time, stabilisation of the German economy in the mid-1920s meant that the country lost the export advantage it had enjoyed since the end of the war. This led also to an increase in foreign capital flowing into the country, including investment by Hollywood studios quick to set up their own local production and distribution businesses. German film companies saw budgets increase and profits decline, and responded by turning away from production and towards the exhibition of primarily foreign films. Despite government efforts to protect the German industry through the introduction of a quota system, those studios that continued production found themselves struggling against the tide of American imports. A number of German studios who were struggling financially and eager to have their product distributed in the US market reluctantly entered into deals with the Hollywood majors. These included Ufa who, after a string of big-budget failures and in the midst of funding the phenomenally expensive and commercially disastrous *Metropolis*, signed a deal with Paramount and MGM in 1925.[7] The 'Parufamet agreement' gave the American studios the use of Ufa studios and cinemas, as well as access to technicians and actors, in return for a loan of some four million dollars. In a remarkably short space of time, Hollywood had not only defeated its most powerful competitor but also gained a huge level of control over what little of the domestic industry remained.

Of course Germany was not alone in its struggles against the dominance of Hollywood. Although its film industry had come out of the war in an extremely strong position, other European countries such as France and Italy, successful prior to the outbreak of war, had subsequently cut back production and lost much of their industry. The creation of Film Europe in 1924 represented an effort by European film industries, including that of the Soviet Union, to form a co-operative force to compete against America. Under the scheme, countries across Europe would work together in the distribution and exhibition of each other's films in preference to those of the US. Whilst the project did enjoy some degree of success, one major effect was a dilution of the distinct styles of film-making across the continent. As the aim was to foster and supply a huge pan-European market to rival that of the US, films produced under the scheme needed to be in a style accessible to audiences in a number of different countries. By the end of the 1920s Germany's Expressionist cinema as a formal movement had all but disappeared,[8] while Soviet montage cinema (typified by Sergei Eisenstein's *Battleship Potemkin* [1925]) and French Impressionism (for example *J'Accuse* [Abel Gance, 1919]), both of which had flourished in the post-war years, similarly declined. Although the initial aim of the Film Europe co-operative had been to resist the domination of Hollywood studios and the standard 'classical Hollywood' style, the films being produced in Europe were looking more like their American counterparts than ever before.

With the onset of the worldwide depression in the late 1920s, many countries withdrew from international co-operation in favour of more protectionist policies. However, the final nail in the coffin of Film Europe came from the introduction of cinema's first major technological advancement: sound. Prior to the arrival of subtitles and dubbing, the language barrier made it extremely difficult for sound films produced in one European territory to be successfully distributed in another, and many of the smaller countries did not have enough of a market to support their own film industry.[9] Germany was hit particularly hard by both the effects of the Depression and the imposition of foreign trade barriers, and the agreements signed with the Hollywood studios soon became worthless. Following the rise to power of Adolf Hitler in 1933, the imposition of strict censorship and the increasing state control over the arts curbed the production of macabre films. The last great German horror film of the period, *M* (Fritz Lang, 1931), starring Peter Lorre as a serial child-killer, was banned in its home country in 1934.

During the 1930s and 40s Paul Wegener remained in Germany, continuing to work both as a director and actor in the theatre and in film. In actual fact a pacifist, he has gained a reputation as a Nazi sympathiser due to his involvement in a number of propaganda films, beginning with a role in the infamous *Hans Westmar* (Franz Wenzler, 1933). In the light of this, *Der Golem* has in recent years attracted accusations of anti-Semitism, particularly in relation to the association of the Jews with black magic. Certainly, there are some dubious aspects to the film, amongst them the juxtaposition of the elders' prayers to Jehovah with a shot of a black cat, a traditional symbol of witchcraft and subsequent horror film convention; the seemingly interchangeable use of the pentagram and the Star of David; the dark and dishevelled appearance of the Jewish elders, frequently lit from below to make them appear even more sinister; and the final juxtaposition of the golem with the innocence of Aryan youth. On the other hand, the legend of the golem does state that Rabbi Low brought it to life through magic, and we have already noted Low's apparent reluctance to perform the invocation. It is also clear that the audience is meant to identify with the plight of the ghetto's inhabitants, both before and during the creature's rampage. As discussed in the introduction, the power of any horror film lies in its ability to generate audience empathy for the characters under threat, and from the opening sequence the film it is obvious that these are the rabbi, his daughter and assistant.

Whatever his intentions, by remaining in a country where the state held such a grip on the arts Wegener's professional position was undoubtedly compromised, and this was a situation few of his compatriots desired. One lasting effect of the US-German agreements had been to open the door for European film-makers and actors, who were finding desirable work increasingly hard to come by in Germany, to relocate to Hollywood. As we will see in the following chapters, the migration of talented directors and technicians such as Paul Leni, Karl Freund, Fritz Lang, Michael Curtiz and Curt and Robert Siodmak throughout the 1920s and 30s brought not only Expressionist themes and film-making techniques of lighting, camerawork and *mise-en-scène*, but also the European myths, legends and folklore that would find a place in many of the films produced during Hollywood's 'golden age of horror'.

Bibliography

Carrol, Noël (1990) *The Philosophy of Horror*. London: Routledge.

Eisner, Lotte (1969) *The Haunted Screen*. Berkeley: University of California Press.

Hoffgen, Maggie (2009) *Studying German Cinema*. Leighton Buzzard: Auteur.

Kracuaer, Siegfried (1969) *From Caligari to Hitler: A Psychological History of the German Film*. New Jersey: Princeton University Press.

Prawer, S. S. (1980) *Caligari's Children: Film as Tale of Terror*. Oxford University Press.

Tybjerg, Casper, 'Shadow-Souls and Strange Adventures: Horror and the Supernatural in European Silent Film'. In Prince, Stephen (ed.) (2004) *The Horror Film*. London: Rutgers University Press.

Wood, Robin (1979) 'An Introduction to the American Horror Film' in Grant, Barry Keith (ed.) (1984) *Planks of Reason: Essays on the Horror Film*. London: Scarecrow Press, Inc.

Endnotes

1. Méliès had himself produced a number of films based around portions of the Faust story, including *The Damnation of Faust* (1903), *Faust and Marguerite* (1904) and *The Merry Frolics of Satan* (1906).

2. The word 'golem' derives from Hebrew, meaning 'thing without shape', and numerous writings about such creations were recorded centuries before the emergence of the Prague legend.

3. It is worth noting that by the end of the 1910s the popularity of Expressionism in painting and literature was already waning. Also, Expressionist influences could already be seen in a number of German films produced prior to this, most noticeably in the six-part serial *Humunculus* (Otto Rippert, 1916). Based on conventional Gothic themes, and borrowing heavily from Mary Shelley's novel *Frankenstein*, the now-lost *Humunculus* is often cited as a direct influence on both the 1920 version of *Der Golem* and Murnau's *Nosferatu*.

4. Germany has a long-held reputation for embracing the darker aspects of human existence, exemplified by the enormous success of *schauer-roman* ('shudder novel') literature of the late eighteenth and early nineteenth century. An offshoot of the more traditional Gothic novel, this uniquely German variant increased the horror, sex and violence to often excessive levels. It has been suggested that the horror film flourished there during and after the First World War 'because it was felt to be peculiarly German, thanks to the widespread contemporary acceptance of the idea that the German national character was particularly attuned to "twilight" and the supernatural' (Tybjerg, 2004: 31).

5. It is also worth remembering that these films emerged soon after Germany's defeat in a brutal and deeply unpopular war, where millions of men had been sent to their deaths in often futile battles by their authoritarian masters, and as such reflect the resentment of much of the German population towards 'the powers that be'.

6. The POV shot is nowadays considered a characteristic feature of the horror film in general, and of the slasher sub-genre in particular. As such, it will be discussed in more detail in our chapter on *Bay of Blood*.

7. Ufa continued to lose money, and its American interests were bought out in 1927, after which the company was increasingly used as a mouthpiece for the National Socialist Party.

8. It should be said that Film Europe cannot be solely blamed for this. As the social and economic situation in Germany stabilised there was also a conscious move away from the fantasy themes of Expressionism towards the social realism of the so-called 'New Objectivity' movement, typified by the films of G. W. Pabst. The National Socialist Party under Adolf Hitler later banned the production of overtly Expressionist films in Germany, along with most other art that could be considered modernist or 'avant-garde'.

9. During the early years of sound, a number of the Hollywood studios invested in foreign-language productions of their bigger productions. One of the best known of these is Universal's Spanish-language version of *Dracula* (George Medford, 1931), filmed at night on the same sets as the Tod Browning version, to which it is widely regarded as superior.

Chapter 2

American Gothic

The Old Dark House
James Whale, US 1932

Recommended viewing
The Phantom of the Opera (Rupert Julian, 1925)
Dracula (Tod Browning, 1931)
Frankenstein (James Whale, 1931)
The Mummy (Karl Freund, 1932)
The Black Cat (Edgar G. Ulmer, 1935)
The Bride of Frankenstein (James Whale, 1935)

Introduction

The essential element of any horror film, as discussed in the previous chapter, is 'the monster'; without the threat that the monster presents, there would be little suspense or fear. In this chapter we look at another convention of the genre – the 'Terrible Place', identified by Carol Clover as somewhere ('most often a house or tunnel') which at first appears to be a safe haven but which in fact acts to trap the victim with the monster (1992: 30-31). As mentioned in our introduction, chases through labyrinthine tunnels were a staple of Gothic literature, where the Terrible Place commonly took the form of a ruined abbey or castle. Often representing a physical embodiment of the psyche of its current or previous inhabitants, the location is a timeless place where evils of the past return to haunt the present. This is exemplified most famously in Edgar Allen Poe's 1839 short story, 'The Fall of the House of Usher', in which the doomed Roderick Usher is compelled by the ancestral madness contained within the walls of the family house to bury alive his twin sister, only for her to return and wreak deadly revenge. Poe's descriptions of the house, as it influences the thoughts and actions of both Roderick and the story's first-person narrator, evoke an enveloping atmosphere of dread, the story culminating in the physical destruction of the building during a ferocious storm.

The case study for this chapter is a production by a Hollywood studio whose name was to become synonymous with the horror genre. 1931 saw cinematic adaptations of *Dracula*, *Frankenstein* and *Dr Jekyll and Mr Hyde*, and the commercial success of each of these revealed a previously unrecognised audience appetite for such dark tales. Horror was rapidly established as a standard Hollywood genre, and the early 1930s saw investment in horror films by all of the major studios, but none more so than the company behind both *Dracula* and *Frankenstein*: Universal Pictures. At one time the biggest production company in Hollywood, by 1930 Universal had found itself in severe financial trouble yet it embarked on a programme of films that represented the birth of the cinematic horror genre as we know it today. In this chapter we look at the origins of Universal's original horror cycle, and how the Hollywood 'star system' ensured that it continued. We also take a look at the issue of film censorship and its effect on the evolution of the genre for the first, but certainly not last, time.

Background

Carl Laemmle, a German émigré born in 1867, began his career in the film industry in 1905 operating nickelodeons in Chicago. Within two years he added a distribution business, and then in 1909 formed the Independent Motion Pictures

Company, through which he began producing his own films. Mergers with several other production outfits resulted in the formation of Universal Film Manufacturing Company, and by 1915 he had complete control over one of Hollywood's first major film studios and ownership of the 230-acre Universal City production facility. A shrewd businessman, Laemmle advocated the standardisation of film product, re-using successful storylines and character types but with just enough variation to keep audiences interested. This streamlining of operations, effectively creating a production line of similar films, was eventually taken up by all of the major studios in Hollywood, resulting in what we now call the 'studio system'. It was an effective strategy, and Universal quickly became the biggest production company in Hollywood, in terms of both size and output.

Universal's fortunes changed rapidly following the end of the First World War, however. During the war years rival studios had begun acquiring or merging with cinema chains, while distributors and exhibitors were increasingly expanding into production. This 'vertical integration' of production, distribution and exhibition meant the larger studios were able to ensure that their own films were shown at the most prestigious (and expensive) 'first-run' cinemas, with releases from smaller studios restricted to less profitable 'second-run' outlets. Cinemas that remained independent were often tied to deals with the studios in which they paid to exhibit a package of films (usually consisting of one major release together with a number of less attractive films) without prior viewing, practices known as 'block booking' and 'blind bidding'. Successful releases by the major studios could remain on first-run screens for weeks or even months before moving to the smaller cinemas, and the profits they returned were quickly ploughed back into bigger and more extravagant productions. At Universal, Laemmle had remained cautious, refusing to integrate and determined to keep production costs low, and by the beginning of the 1920s the studio found itself overtaken by the so-called 'Big Three' companies: Paramount, Loew's (which later became MGM), and Associated First National (which would later be taken over by Warner Bros.). Highlighting the importance of vertical integration at this time, both Loew's and First National began life as cinema chains before expanding into production, whilst Paramount resulted from the merger of production company Famous Players and distributor Paramount Pictures. Alongside Universal in the second-tier 'Little Five' group were Fox (who would later merge with 20th Century), Producers' Distributing Corporation, Film Booking Office, and Warner Bros.; beneath these were a collection of smaller companies including Columbia and United Artists.

In 1923 Universal produced an adaptation of Victor Hugo's novel *Notre Dame de Paris*, under the title *The Hunchback of Notre Dame* (dir. Wallace Worsley). The film's ambitious young producer, Irving Thalberg, frustrated with what he saw as the restrictive caution of Laemmle, deliberately pushed it over budget in an effort to compete with the prestige films of the Big Three. The fact that the film emerged as Universal's biggest profit-maker of the year did little to change Laemmle's stance on budget levels and integration, or to keep Thalberg in his job. Although more of a historical melodrama than what we would now call a horror film, *Hunchback* began Universal's association with what has been described as 'a cinema of the grotesque' (Brosnan 1976: 2) as well as creating the medium's first horror star in Lon Chaney. The actor had already gained a reputation in Hollywood for putting himself through painful procedures in order to play physically crippled characters in films such as *The Miracle Man* (George Loane Tucker, 1919) and *A Blind Bargain* (Wallace Worsley, 1923), as well as designing his own make-up for a variety of unusual characters including a monstrously decrepit Fagin in *Oliver Twist* (Frank Lloyd, 1922). For his role as Quasimodo in *Hunchback*, Chaney devised an elaborate costume, including a 30kg hump which forced him to be bent double for much of the three-month shoot and heavy facial make-up which prevented him from closing his mouth or seeing through one eye. For designs such as this, Chaney became known as 'the man of a thousand faces' (a moniker used as the title of a 1957 film based on his life, starring James Cagney), and a popular saying at the time was 'don't step on it, it may be Lon Chaney!'

The success of *Hunchback* led Universal to cast Chaney in the title role of *The Phantom of the Opera* (Rupert Julian, 1925), an adaptation of Gaston Leroux's 1908 novel. Much darker in tone than the earlier film, *Phantom* represents a significant step towards the type of product for which Universal would later become known. The story features a classic Gothic narrative, with the virginal heroine pursued through and imprisoned within the labyrinthine sewers of Paris by Erik, the hideously disfigured villain. Chaney's make-up for *Phantom* was even more horrific than that for Quasimodo, and the unmasking scene in which the camera cuts to a close-up of Erik's skull-like face is one of silent cinema's most horrific moments, and horror cinema's first truly iconic image. *Phantom* represented another major box-office success for Universal Pictures, who were by now beginning to carve a niche as producers of macabre films.

It is important to note that *Hunchback* and *Phantom*, as well as similar productions from other studios, were very much grounded in reality. True, they featured evil or grotesque characters, and contained horrific and frightening moments, but they lacked any of the supernatural elements of *Der Golem* or *Nosferatu*. In fact, the success of these German films presented something of a quandary for the Hollywood studios, who believed that cinema audiences wanted realism, not fantasy.[1] This view was reinforced by the commercial failure of the Douglas Fairbanks Jr. epic *The Thief of Baghdad* (Raoul Walsh, 1924), at the time the most expensive film ever made. Stylistically, Walsh's film was heavily influenced by the work of German director Fritz Lang, and served to highlight the differences between Hollywood film-makers and their German counterparts. The aesthetic side of what we now refer to as the 'classical Hollywood' cinema, the form that by the 1920s had become recognised as the standard for fiction film-making, was built on ideas of objective realism. The classical Hollywood style was designed to convey a film's narrative to the viewer in as clear and unambiguous a way as possible, primarily through the use of standardised continuity editing techniques. These stylistic devices, pioneered chiefly by director D. W. Griffith, of shot/reverse shot, cross-cutting, eyeline matching, and so on, work to give the viewer as much information as possible in a naturalistic way: that is, without drawing attention to the fact that such techniques are actually being used. This was in stark contrast to the aesthetics of the German Expressionists, who deliberately highlighted the filmic process through the use of non-naturalistic lighting, obviously painted sets, flamboyant acting, canted camera angles and suchlike.

Nevertheless, Carl Laemmle took a great interest in the development of the German Expressionist movement, and worked harder than most studio bosses in bringing his home country's talent to Hollywood.[2] Universal enjoyed a major presence in the European market, and Laemmle saw the recruitment of their technicians and actors as an important part of the company's continued success in the region. He also viewed the Expressionist style, if not the content, as a potential distinguishing feature of Universal's product in the highly competitive American market. One of the first German directors to be given a contract with the studio was Paul Leni (previously a set designer at Deutches Theatre, working alongside Paul Wegener), whose macabre *Das Wachsfigurenkabinett* had particularly impressed Laemmle. Leni's Hollywood debut was *The Cat and the Canary* (1927), an adaptation of a 1922 stage play by John Willard. In it, a young woman is forced to spend the night at mysterious Clifton Castle with a collection of strange relatives, following the reading of a will to which she is the sole beneficiary. However, the will's executor is murdered, and the heiress finds herself terrorised throughout the night by what may or may not be an escaped lunatic going by the name of The Cat. As well as the traditional Gothic elements of castles, cobwebs and thunderstorms, the film features Expressionistic shadows, canted angles, distorted architectures and a constant atmosphere of dread.

The Cat and the Canary exemplifies a format that had proved popular on Broadway since the early 1900s. A fusion of Gothic horror and detective story, these productions involved a murder and its subsequent investigation, played out in a remote or secluded location while a ubiquitous thunderstorm crashed outside. The setting would be an old country manor, castle, asylum or similar isolated building, complete with secret panels and hidden passageways and holding a disparate collection of inhabitants. Although the story often suggested that supernatural events were taking place, that the location was haunted or inhabited by some type of strange creature, when the time came for the murderer to be unmasked this was invariably shown not to be the case. Throughout, the gruesome proceedings would be lightened by the inclusion of doses of humour and comic characters. The format became a popular one for cinema, beginning with D. W. Griffiths' *One Exciting Night* (1922), which featured a famously extravagant thunderstorm climax. Multiple adaptations of plays such as *The Bat* and *The Thirteenth Chair* followed, and *The Cat and the Canary* itself was filmed again by Universal in 1930 (as *The Cat Creeps* [Rupert Julian]) and by Paramount in 1939. Paul Leni's final film for Universal, completed shortly before his death from blood poisoning at the age of 44, was another such adaptation, *The Last Warning* (1929).[3]

The arrival of 'the talkies', beginning with *The Jazz Singer* (Alan Crosland, 1927) from Warner Bros., heralded a major upheaval in film production and exhibition in America. Almost overnight, audiences deserted silent films, preferring instead to pay more to watch sound films regardless of their comparative quality. Interest in the new technology also worked to reverse the trend of declining audience figures, at least until the arrival of the Great Depression. The resulting increase in box-office returns enabled studios to invest heavily in ensuring that the switchover to sound happened quickly and smoothly. Many smaller, independent theatres that could not afford the conversion were forced to close or sell up, further increasing the dominance of the integrated majors. One important side effect of the rapid switch to sound was that studio bosses suddenly found themselves in urgent need of dialogue-heavy screenplays. Thus, although stage adaptations had always been popular, the first years of sound saw a massive migration of material and talent (particularly actors, directors and scriptwriters) to Hollywood from Broadway, London and elsewhere.

By 1929, Universal was in the hands of Carl Laemmle Jr., the studio having been gifted to him as a twenty-first birthday present. Laemmle Jr. was more ambitious and less cautious than his father, and had big plans for the company. From now on, he declared, Universal would produce big-budget, prestige pictures based on well-known source material and using big-name talent loaned from the larger studios. To help fund this new strategy, he sold the few second-run theatres that the company owned and invested the proceeds straight into film production. Despite some major box-office hits, including *All Quiet on the Western Front* (Lewis Milestone, 1930) and a number of lavish musicals, Universal found itself struggling in the aftermath of the stock market crash. Reluctantly, Laemmle Jr. was forced to admit defeat and revert back to what Universal knew best: the production of low-budget, formulaic films. There was, however, one title that had been picked up during the studio's brief big-budget phase that particularly appealed to the new studio boss's love of the macabre. Encouraged by the success of a Broadway production of Bram Stoker's *Dracula*, Laemmle Jr. bought the film rights and hired Hamilton Deane and John L. Balderston, the writers of the stage adaptation, to provide a film script. Although much of their submitted script was subsequently rewritten, Balderston would go on to be instrumental in the writing of many of the studio's most successful horror films in the period that followed. Originally planned as one of Universal's prestige productions, the film had been held up due to potential problems with censorship, something that had previously deterred other studios, including Paramount, from tackling the novel. By 1930, however, the censors were not wielding anywhere near as much power as they had previously enjoyed.

Through the 1910s and early 20s Hollywood had seen a succession of scandals, most notoriously the 1921 death of starlet Virginia Rappe, which ended the career of one of the industry's top comedy actors, Roscoe 'Fatty' Arbuckle. As well as off-screen controversies, the films themselves were increasingly coming under attack for their graphic depictions of violence, crime and nudity. Concerned by the growing influence that Hollywood was having over the public, particularly impressionable children, a number of states set up local censorship bodies throughout the 1910s. Beginning with the Pennsylvania State Board of Censors in 1911, these bodies had the power to unilaterally ban or restrict the showing of films deemed unsuitable. When New York State, at the time the biggest market for Hollywood film, set up its own censorship board in 1921 the studios jointly decided that self-regulation would be preferable to increasing governmental interference. Thus, the Motion Picture Producers and Distributors of America (MPPDA) organisation was established in 1922, with former Republican politician Will H. Hays as president.

Although the local censorship bodies that already existed would remain in place, the passing of a film by the MPPDA ensured that it would be looked upon in a more favourable light. In addition, the formation of an internal organisation reduced the possibility of a powerful federal censorship body being created, something which could have had serious consequences for the studios. The MPPDA also acted as main point of contact for complainants and lobby groups, as well as being a middleman between the studios and the unions; in effect, the 'Hays Office' became the public face of Hollywood. Certainly, the creation of the MPPDA stemmed the tide of local censorship bodies, and in Hays the industry believed they had a figure whose sympathies lay with the commercial interests of the studios. Nevertheless, over the next few years, Hays worked hard to clean up Hollywood both on- and off-screen, including the effective blacklisting of over a hundred actors and actresses whom he felt to be a bad influence. He also compiled a list of elements that he felt unsuitable for film, including the depiction of violence and nudity, and the promotion of drunkenness, gambling and criminality. This 'Hays Formula' was expanded in 1927 to include an additional 25 subjects which should be treated carefully to avoid censorship problems, including drug-taking, rape, and animal and child cruelty, in what became known as the list of 'Don'ts and Be Carefuls'.

The fundamental problem with the self-regulatory system, however, was that submission to the MPPDA was entirely voluntary. The smaller studios, with their lower budgets, were prepared to take risks and often would not submit scripts or completed films for Hays' authorisation. Although money was lost from cinemas unwilling to play unauthorised films, this could be more than made up from inquisitive audiences at smaller and less reputable venues. While the bigger studios had originally been prepared to live with this, the stock market crash and the onset of the Great Depression led to more selective audiences who forewent the more expensive first-run theatres in favour of second-run and independent cinemas. Now that the majors were competing directly with the smaller studios, the number of films being released by them which did not adhere to the Formula began to grow, and the number submitted for approval by the board fell dramatically. By the end of the decade the board was receiving ever-dwindling numbers of story and film submissions, and the Formula in all of its forms was abandoned in 1930.

At Universal, Laemmle Jr. saw *Dracula* as the ideal vehicle to mark the return of their original horror star, Lon Chaney, to the studio. Following the success of *Phantom*, Chaney had signed a contract with MGM, where he appeared in popular films such as Tod Browning's *The Unholy Three* (1925), *The Unknown* (1927) and *London After Midnight* (1927). Browning had forged a successful partnership with Chaney in the production of macabre films, and as such was Universal's first choice to direct him in their version of *Dracula*. While the move to talking pictures had signalled the end of many silent stars' careers, Chaney had unequivocally demonstrated his versatility in the new medium: in a sound remake of *The Unholy Three* (Jack Conway, 1930) the actor performed using no less than five different voices, providing a signed affidavit that he was responsible for all of them. However, tragedy struck and Universal's plans for *Dracula* were sent into disarray when Chaney succumbed to throat cancer and died suddenly in late 1930. As his replacement, Browning brought in a little-known Hungarian actor he had used in an adaptation of *The*

Thirteenth Chair (1929), and who had previously starred as the count on Broadway, Bela Lugosi.

Watching Browning's *Dracula* today it can come across as slow, even boring, and it is difficult to imagine any audience being particularly frightened by it. In part this can be blamed on the origins of the script; mindful of the copyright problems that had dogged *Nosferatu*, Laemmle Jr. had bought the rights to the stage version rather than the novel, which dramatically scaled down the story and confined the action almost exclusively to a couple of interior locations. Aesthetically, the film was also hampered by the limitations of the new sound technology. Early microphones had a very short range, and actors were forced to speak straight at them, slowly and distinctly, in order to be heard clearly. This led to less expressivity and movement and more stilted dialogue. In addition, the heavy equipment used to house and move cameras around the set created a lot of background noise, so camera movement was kept to an absolute minimum. As a result the cinematography by *Der Golem*'s Karl Freund[4] is very restrained, although one early atmospheric shot, in which the camera glides silently through Dracula's fog-shrouded cellar, gives some indication of what could have been. It is difficult to believe that six years earlier Freund had been responsible for the cinematography of *The Last Laugh* (F. W. Murnau, 1925), a remarkable production in which the camera is in almost constant motion, making the film at once more dynamic and interesting and a far cry from the staginess of *Dracula*.

Nevertheless, *Dracula* was a commercial success for Universal, emerging as their biggest earner in 1931 and demonstrating that there was an audience for fantastical films. Indeed, whereas earlier productions had used their climax to explain away any seemingly supernatural elements, *Dracula* took the opposite approach; at the end of the film Edward van Sloan (who played Professor Van Helsing) emerges from behind a curtain to deliver a speech directly to the audience, warning them that, when it comes to vampires, 'there are such things!' Although critical reviews of Browning's film were mixed, Lugosi received almost universal praise for his performance as the count and the studio began to view him as a long-term replacement for Chaney. Plans were quickly made for him to star as the monster in a film version of Mary Shelley's *Frankenstein*, again based on a pared-down theatrical adaptation and to be scripted by John Balderston. By now Browning was back at MGM and the project was assigned to French director Robert Florey, who planned to employ a more overtly Expressionist style. Aided by Freund, he began studying German classics such as *Der Golem* and *Metropolis* in preparation. The production stalled, though, when Laemmle Jr. deemed initial test footage, shot on the *Dracula* sets and featuring Lugosi in golem-like make-up, unsatisfactory. At the same time, as part of a lucrative contract with the studio English theatre director James

Whale was offered his pick of Universal's current projects. He chose *Frankenstein*, suggesting fellow Englishman Colin Clive for the title role alongside Lugosi's monster. Lugosi eventually turned down the role, however, reportedly unhappy with the character's lack of dialogue and the heavy make-up required. As Whale's search for a replacement began, Florey and Lugosi were assigned to *Murders in the Rue Morgue* (1932), a loose adaptation of Edgar Allen Poe's novel, featuring a murderous gorilla under the control of the deranged Dr Mirakle (Lugosi). Again photographed by Freund, the film is thematically and stylistically very similar to Robert Weine's *Caligari*, and arguably the most Expressionistic of all the Universal horror series.

According to Hollywood myth, James Whale became intrigued by the face of a bit-part actor he spotted while having lunch in the Universal canteen. As Whale began sketching the man's features on a tablecloth a now-familiar image of the Frankenstein monster began to take shape. The actor was Boris Karloff, an Englishman born William Henry Pratt, who had already appeared in some eighty films without note and was delighted to accept the role turned down by Lugosi. The make-up designed by Jack Pierce to cover the actor's features would provide an icon for the genre that has endured like no other. The flat-topped skull, the heavy eyelids beneath a high, scarred forehead, the bolts in the neck, and the huge asphalt-spreader's boots combined to create a monster that would haunt the dreams of cinemagoers for decades. Just as any impersonation of Dracula will involve Lugosi's heavy Hungarian accent and drawn-out speech patterns, so Frankenstein's monster brings forth Karloff's lumbering walk, arms outstretched. From the opening scene in the cemetery, where mourners sob beneath a troubled sky, church bells toll and the 'mad scientist' and his hunchbacked assistant lurk behind slanted gravestones, through to the climax of angry villagers and exploding laboratories, *Frankenstein* introduced numerous generic conventions that would appear again and again in subsequent productions. The climactic 'angry mob' sequence, in which the film's monster is chased to its death by villagers carrying flaming torches, had originally been adapted from Wegener's *Der Golem* for *Phantom of the Opera*, when preview audiences demanded that Chaney's character suffer a more damning end than being found slumped dead over his organ keyboard. From *Frankenstein* onwards, however, it became a ubiquitous part of the Universal monster formula.

As what we now term a horror film, *Frankenstein* succeeds on just about every level, and is in a different league to *Dracula*. Unlike Browning's film, it attracted almost universally favourable notices from reviewers who realised they were witnessing the birth of something new and exciting. Whereas *Dracula* had been marketed as a fusion of Gothic mystery and romantic thriller, there can be no doubt that *Frankenstein* was devised with the sole purpose of terrifying its audience; indeed, some prints were released with a green tint, billed by Universal publicists as 'the colour of fear'. The enormous box-office returns of Whale's film sparked the first Hollywood horror cycle into life, and within twelve months such films were in production at all of the major studios.

There have been a number of explanations mooted for why the horror genre would become popular with both film-makers and audiences at this time. Technologically, the arrival of sound enabled the use of aural effects that enhance the genre experience (creaking doors, thunderstorms, screaming, and so on), while improvements in film stock allowed the integration of German Expressionist lighting (already associated with darker subject matter) with the more conventional Hollywood cinematic style. More practically, in the economic downturn of the Great Depression the use of heavy shadow and fog-shrouded locations typical of the horror film cut down on expensive set design. At the same time, audiences became more responsive to escapist entertainments, with make-believe horrors a welcome distraction from the miserable situation many found themselves in. It has also been suggested that the monsters of the Universal films acted as identification figures for an increasingly disaffected society. Certainly, Karloff's performance as the tortured and ostracised creature in *Frankenstein* is responsible for much of the film's popularity, stealing every scene from Colin Clive's less-than-sympathetic creator. And this highlights one important aspect of these films in comparison with those that had gone before. Whereas previously, romantic leads such as Rudolph Valentino, swashbuckling heroes such as Douglas Fairbanks Jr., and loveable comedians such as Charlie Chaplin or Harold Lloyd were the stars, Universal's top attractions were Lon Chaney, Bela Lugosi, Boris Karloff and, later, Lon Chaney Jr. The effect of this, of course, was that once these actors became recognised as horror stars they rarely managed to find roles in other genres. The fact that audience loyalty and interest appeared to lie with the 'villain' rather than the more conventional hero marked a distinct shift, and is an aspect of the horror genre that endures today.

Following the unprecedented critical and commercial success of *Frankenstein* Lugosi found himself unceremoniously toppled as Universal's prime horror property, and Boris Karloff was quickly signed to a lucrative contract. The studio's publicity department implied that the actor was the true successor to Chaney (incredibly going as far as crediting him with the design and application of the Frankenstein monster's make-up), and he became involved in discussions concerning remakes of both *The Hunchback of Notre Dame* and *The Phantom of the Opera*.[5] As it was, his next major film for Universal reunited him with director James Whale on a new production, albeit based on a 1927 novel by English writer J. B. Priestley: *The Old Dark House*.

Textual Analysis

Three American tourists, Philip and Margaret Waverton and their friend Roger
Penderel, are forced by a storm to seek shelter overnight in a large house in the
Welsh mountains, populated by the eccentric Horace Femm, his God-fearing sister
Rebecca and their mute servant, Morgan. The Femms reluctantly allow them to stay,
but Horace seems particularly nervous of what may happen during the night. While
Helen is dressing for dinner, Rebecca scares her with her threatening behaviour, and
reveals that her father, the evil Sir Roderick, is upstairs. As the group begin dinner
another pair of stranded travellers arrives, successful businessman William Porterhouse and his companion Gladys DuCane. Roger and Gladys, obviously attracted to
each other, venture to the Wavertons' car for some whisky and decide to shelter in the
stable. Back at the house the electricity goes off and Philip is sent upstairs to retrieve
a lamp. Left alone, Margaret is attacked by a drunkenly violent Morgan but manages
to run to Philip, who knocks him out. Upstairs, Margaret and Philip are told by the
bedridden Roderick Femm that his other son, the psychopathic Saul, is locked in a
room at the top of the house. Horace then warns them that Morgan has recovered
and released Saul, who will undoubtedly burn down the house and kill them all. With
William and Philip dragging Morgan to the kitchen, Gladys and Margaret hide in a
cupboard while Roger confronts Saul. In the ensuing fight, the two men fall through
a balustrade from the landing to the floor below, killing Saul, whose body is mourn-
fully carried back upstairs by Morgan. The following morning, the rain has stopped
and the floods subsided. Margaret and Philip set off for help, leaving a still-dazed
Roger with Gladys and William. Roger proposes to Gladys, who accepts.

The Old Dark House is an interesting case study, inasmuch as it takes extra-textual
elements of the burgeoning horror genre and transposes them onto the more established *Cat and the Canary*-style narrative. Unlike *Dracula* and *Frankenstein*, *House*
does not contain any supernatural occurrences, ghosts or conventional monsters,
yet it was very much devised as the latest in Universal's horror series, its publicity
highlighting the return of *Frankenstein* director James Whale and the presence of
Boris Karloff. The studio's efforts in attempting to build Karloff as a horror star
are apparent from the film's opening title card:

> PRODUCER'S NOTE: *Karloff, the mad butler in this production, is the same Karloff who
> created the part of the mechanical monster in "Frankenstein". We explain this to settle all disputes in
> advance, even though such disputes are a tribute to his great versatility.*

With his character in this film not too dissimilar to that of Frankenstein's monster,
presumably Karloff's 'great versatility' here relates more to his appearance than
his acting skills (publicity for the film again suggested, falsely, that the actor had
been responsible for his own make-up), while in describing his role as that of 'the
mad butler' the note prepares the audience for another villainous turn (Fig 2.1).

Figure 2.1

Even before it has started, then, the film is acting to typecast Karloff. By the time the publicity for his next Universal horror film, Karl Freund's *The Mummy*, appeared he was being marketed as 'Karloff the Uncanny', thus cementing his association with the genre. It is also worth noting that the opening of *House* refers to Karloff by surname only, as did the posters for the film when it was released. Whilst such billing had occurred previously, most notably with (Greta) Garbo, to apply it to an actor with only one previous starring role was unprecedented. We will take a closer look at Karloff's role following a brief overview of the film's themes and style.

At the time of *House*'s release it was still unusual for non-diegetic music to feature prominently in talking films, and was generally restricted to the opening and closing credits or to set the mood for an important scene.[6] The early Universal horror films are often noted for their use of excerpts from Tchaikovsky's *Swan Lake* as the accompaniment to their opening credits; in fact, only four productions used this: *Dracula*, *Murders in the Rue Morgue*, *The Mummy*, and the lesser-known *Secret of the Blue Room* (Kurt Neumann, 1933). On the face of it, the choice of ballet music to open a horror film is an unusual one, but the haunting melody and rising passion of Tchaikovsky's piece, as well as its European flavour, works well for each of these films. *House* departs from this in using an original composition from Bernhard Kaun, who had also supplied music for *Frankenstein*, as its opening theme. Kaun's music sets the scene for the film, suggesting mystery, thrills and spooky goings-on, and is accompanied by crashes of thunder and a howling wind. Over a shot of storm-wracked trees the film's title swoops down in a blurred, ghostly form, suggesting supernatural themes. Prior to the release of *Dracula* and *Frankenstein*, audiences attending a film such as this would have expected a rational story, or at least a story with a plausible explanation. However, following those fantastic tales, who could know what to expect from Universal Pictures, James Whale and Karloff?

As it turns out, there is nothing supernatural about the events in *House*, nor any real pretence that there is. The film relies on the characteristics of the house itself and the unpredictable nature of its human inhabitants to generate suspense and fear. Like the travellers who arrive at the Femms', the audience are taken out of their normal everyday surroundings and put on a rollercoaster ride, which ends only when the sun rises. Although the film retains the Welsh setting from *Benighted*, the J.B. Priestley novel on which it's based, to be fair it could have been set anywhere. One of the more striking traits of the Universal horror films of the 1930s and 40s was that although they often feature American protagonists (or protagonists with American accents), they are invariably set overseas, and generally in Europe. That *House* follows this pattern differentiates it from, say, *The Cat and the Canary*, which made much of the fact that its own old dark house was situated on the banks of New York's Hudson River. Whilst Universal's use of European settings reflects the origins of many of the novels or legends that formed the basis of the films, as well as the background of many of the film-makers involved, it has also been suggested that this choice for the source of horror played on American fears and prejudices of the period. During the Great Depression there were widely-held beliefs that the country's economic woes stemmed from events in Europe, particularly a wave of bank closures which had spread across the region. Concerns were also raised about the influx of European immigrants seen by many to be flooding the country and taking American jobs. Whatever the veracity of these theories, the message given by the Universal films is that yes, in the words of Van Helsing, there may well be such things, but they certainly aren't American. When Universal horror did finally arrive on American shores, specifically the Louisiana swamps of *Son of Dracula* (Robert Siodmak, 1944), it was made obvious that the monster's origins lay overseas.

With this in mind, it is clear that the three American travellers introduced in the opening of *House* are to be the audience's identification figures. The sarcastic, bickering Wavertons and annoyingly cheerful Penderel get the film off to a snappy start; their quick-fire exchanges obviously benefit from the director's previous theatre experience, and wouldn't be out of place in a screwball comedy (a popular Hollywood genre beginning in the mid-1930s). Indeed, the opening sequence of the film provides the first glimpse of a comedic bent that would be a strong feature of Whale's two subsequent horror films for Universal, *The Invisible Man* (1933) and *Bride of Frankenstein*. Accompanying the travellers on their journey, the viewer is quickly made aware that they are moving into the realm of the unknown. Their map is unreadable and Penderel doubts that their location would be on it anyway, later describing the journey as 'travelling along roads that aren't there', but he assures Margaret that if they just keep driving they'll arrive 'somewhere, sometime'.

Penderel's choice of words here is interesting. Not only does the house they arrive at exist in its own separate space, literally in the middle of nowhere, it appears to be suspended in time, held back by ghosts of the past. Horace Femm's dry comment that they make their own electricity, 'and we aren't very good at it', is a demonstration of the family's inability to move forward, although Rebecca's later comment that she'll 'have none of this electricity' reveals reluctance on her part to do so. When Margaret returns from changing her clothes in Rebecca's room, the fact that she has lost all sense of time suggests a temporal distortion that is matched by the increasingly warped reflections in the room's numerous mirrors. It is here, where Rebecca's 'godless' sister Rachel once lay screaming to be killed, that the evils of past events reach out to the present most powerfully. Within the space of the house itself, then, there are various realms and boundaries, not least the grand staircase connecting the relative safety of the ground floor and the increasingly treacherous upper levels. Like a Gothic descent in reverse, the further the travellers venture towards the top of the house, the more dangerous their predicament seems to become. The contrast between the warmth and light of the downstairs and the shadowy, cobweb-filled upper levels is frequently highlighted in Whale's choice of shots, most noticeably in a long shot when the newly-arrived travellers first gather around the blazing fire: the balustrade runs across the pitch-black landing like a castle battlement in the night, effectively splitting the screen in two. It is a boundary that will be physically broken at the film's climax, when Saul and Penderel crash through it during their fight to the death.

The framing of that early sequence, from an angled position far behind the gathered travellers, is the first of numerous shots (most notably from the staircase during the supper scene) that suggest the presence of an unseen character, watching from the shadows. This 'first person perspective' has since become an enormously popular technique for generating suspense in the horror genre. When a similar shot is presented later, looking out from behind the flames of the blazing fire (see Fig 2.2), we can only assume that the unseen character is the house itself. It has a tangible presence, as responsible for the feelings of fear and danger as any of its weird and eccentric inhabitants; early in the film Philip tells Penderel that the house 'gives him the creeps,' while Margaret later shivers with fear as she describes it as 'an aw-

Figure 2.2

ful house.' In perhaps the most disturbing scene of the whole film (and indeed all of Whale's films for Universal), following the physical and verbal threats against Margaret in Rebecca's room there is a sequence of psychological horror that we must presume is purely subjective. In it, the image of Rebecca is reflected in the room's ever more distorted mirrors, repeating the descriptions of her family's misdemeanours, followed by brief shots that seem to suggest that Morgan is watching from the shadows, all the while accompanied by the sound of the crashing storm. Despite the potential threats of both Rebecca (who will later make a more dangerous move for Margaret's throat in the same location) and Morgan, the real source of Margaret's fear is the location – the house itself, and that room in particular.

The use of stormy weather to set up trouble ahead is a common convention (think how many scary stories begin 'it was a dark and stormy night'), and a popular tactic of Gothic literature was to use adverse weather conditions to symbolise the mental or physical state of its human characters. In *House*, the storm itself plays an active role in forcing the travellers to take refuge in the house and keeping them there, as well as aiding the house in generating fear, through windows that suddenly fly open, creaking doors and an eerily whistling chimney. These effects, together with the howling wind and crashing thunder, show how film-makers were quick to use new technology to generate atmosphere, using diegetic sound rather than music. The ability of sound and image to bring to life a seemingly inanimate object is demonstrated in the very first shot of the house, its imposing structure shot from a low angle and accompanied by a deafening crack of thunder. At the same time, it is worth noting that Whale also acknowledges the film's silent heritage; when Rebecca first leads Margaret down the long corridor to her room, the curtains billow in like ghosts in the darkness, blown by the wind in an exact recreation of the opening tracking shot of Paul Leni's *Cat and the Canary*. Whilst not a 'haunted house' movie, *House*'s representation of the building almost as a living entity influenced a number of supernatural productions that followed, such as *The Uninvited* (Lewis Allen, 1944), *The Haunting* (Robert Wise, 1963) and particularly *The Legend of Hell House* (John Hough, 1973).

In terms of the film's plot, it is the interaction between its set of disparate human characters, presented as a source of both amusement and fear, which provides much of the interest in what is quite a slim story. In Sir William Porterhouse, a brash and boisterous 'new money Northerner' and Gladys duCane, his down-to-earth chorus girl companion, some of the original novel's observations on the British class system remain, yet they do little to enhance the plot. Despite the director's own background, *House* fails to dispel the American perception of Britons as strange and eccentric, and of course none are stranger than those portrayed by Boris Karloff. The relief experienced by the travellers when the door to the house is first opened is short-lived when Morgan's disfigured face, lit from below to make him even more menacing, appears. Throughout the film he is seen slipping silently into and out of the shadows, and at other times, like the house itself, his appearance on screen is accompanied by a crash of thunder. From the opening title card

Morgan is singled out as a source of potential danger, and is repeatedly referred to by Horace as 'uncivilised' and 'savage', a description in keeping with his unkempt hair and beard. His lumbering movements and inhuman utterances remind audiences of the actor's role in *Frankenstein*, with the monster's pathos in evidence at the film's climax, when he mourns over the lifeless body of Saul.

The first appearance of Karloff, slowly and menacingly emerging from behind the door, is similar to his introduction in both *Frankenstein* and *The Mummy*; however, a more noticeable repetition from the earlier film occurs later, in a series of distinctive 'jump cuts' during Morgan's attack on Margaret. By repeatedly cutting to a tighter shot of Karloff's face without changing the camera's position or angle, Whale chose to ignore one of the established continuity rules of classical Hollywood film-making (the so-called 'thirty-degree rule', although Whale is well-known for abandoning other continuity rules). Coupled with the lack of sound, the effect here is to disorientate viewers, making them catch their breath, repeatedly bringing the source of horror closer and forcing them to watch. Obviously a personal favourite, Whale repeated the technique again in both *The Invisible Man* and *The Bride of Frankenstein*, while thirty years later Alfred Hitchcock used identical camera and sound work to horrific effect in *The Birds* (1963), when closing in on the face of an eyeless corpse. The repetition of shots and scenes, as well as the casting of Karloff in similar roles (at Universal and other studios) worked to quickly associate the actor with a certain type of film. Such was his iconic status the description of a film as a 'Karloff picture' would give prospective viewers enough of an idea of what they could expect. This was the studio 'star system' in action. For the actor himself it meant a career of monster and mad scientist roles,[7] the association reaching a dubious height in *Abbott and Costello Meet the Killer, Boris Karloff* (Charles Barton, 1949). Whilst it is common to display a star's name 'above the title' in publicity materials, to have Karloff's name within the actual title itself demonstrates how much of a draw the actor remained, almost two decades after his most famous role.

Ernest Thesiger, who plays Horace Femm, was another English stage actor who had moved to Hollywood, and was a personal friend of director Whale. Although more often remembered for his role as the demented Dr Praetorius in *The Bride of Frankenstein*, his prissy performance is one of the highlights of *House*. Thesiger's flamboyant acting technique and angled posturing is not unlike the German Expressionist style, and his introduction, as he descends the staircase to meet the travellers, is suitably theatrical. The strong lighting from below accentuates his cheekbones and nostrils giving him an appearance reminiscent of Chaney in *Phantom*; indeed, throughout the film his face appears subjected to harsher lighting than the rest of the cast, with his gaunt features and haunted, sunken eyes making him look like a living corpse. As he greets the travellers from the second stair, Horace's head is level with a demonic gargoyle that sits at the bottom of the banister, like a shadow of his own profile. Behind the gargoyle, the shadow of smoke rising from the fire completes a somewhat Hellish scene. However, any sense of threat is quickly dispersed in the next shot, when Penderel introduces himself while leaning confidently on the banister. The camera angle and perspective emphasise Horace's slight figure, and the way in which he plays nervously with his hands shows that he is probably more apprehensive than his unexpected guests.

Figure 2.3

The characters of Horace and his sister are more complex than they may at first appear. It is obvious that Horace doesn't feel safe in the house, and we later learn that he is there only because he is on the run from the police. The antagonism between Horace and his sister Rebecca is initially amusing,[8] such as when he unceremoniously tosses a bunch of flowers onto the fire after noting that she was 'in the process of arranging' them, or the delight he takes in her disapproval over handing out gin to the travellers. However, Rebecca's responses ultimately reveal a sadistic and controlling character, mocking a genuinely scared Horace for his fear of death. Driven by puritanical beliefs, she takes the storm as a sign of God's anger and constantly chastises others for what she sees as sinful behaviour and attitudes. She is particularly fanatical about sexual activity, repeatedly shouting that the travellers 'can't have beds', and accuses Margaret of 'revelling in the joys of fleshly love' after telling her of the orgies that once went on in the house (see Fig 2.3). It must be said that some of the language and insinuations in this particular scene are quite strong, and it's doubtful whether they would have been allowed under the Hays Code or the Production Code that replaced it in the mid-1930s.

For all the eccentricities of Horace and Rebecca and the physical threat of Morgan, the most dangerous character in the house is not revealed until late in the film. Throughout, the Femms hint that something lurks in the upper levels of the building, but it is their father Roderick who finally reveals that his psychopathic son Saul is locked in an attic room. No sooner do Margaret and Philip (and the audience) learn this than Horace tells them that he is now on the loose, courtesy of a drunken Morgan. So begins the film's most sustained period of suspense; we know that there's a homicidal maniac in the house, determined to burn the building to the ground, and Whale draws out the tension almost to breaking point. The first shot of Saul is ominous, a disembodied hand inching down the banister, projecting a deep, distorted shadow on the wall behind it. There then follows a series of quick cross-cuts: the terrified travellers looking up from the foot of the stairs; Morgan staggering down towards them; Rebecca pleading with him to return Saul to his room; Morgan lunging for Margaret and being dragged away by the men (note the disorienting breaking of the 180-degree rule as Morgan is taken down the corridor to the kitchen); Penderel bundling the women into a cupboard and returning to the staircase. Saul's hand reappears on the banister and we hear a maniacal laugh, tension reaching its peak as the audience braces itself for the horror that is to be revealed.

The fact that Saul turns out to be an apparently weak and nervous little man throws the audience, and Penderel, momentarily off guard. That his appearance coincides with another crash of thunder is a hint that he is not as harmless as he seems, and suspense is reignited through dramatic irony, when we see his benign face turn into an evil snarl while Penderel's back is turned. The ensuing stand-off and fight is effective if a little drawn-out and melodramatic. Undoubtedly audience sympathies are with Penderel, having followed him throughout the film and witnessed his blossoming romance with Gladys, so whilst his survival following the final struggle that kills Saul allows the audience to breathe a sigh of relief, it is hardly unexpected.[9] Using the ending of Priestley's original novel, where Penderel dies, would have been unthinkable even for Universal; whatever happens during the course of the film, classical Hollywood cinema thrived on giving audiences a happy ending. Thus, with the arrival of the morning light, not only has the evil Saul been defeated but Penderel finds true love when Gladys accepts his offer of marriage.

Reception and Aftermath

Critically, *The Old Dark House* was received even more favourably than *Frankenstein*, and is generally regarded as a better-made film. Having delivered Universal their biggest hit, the director was allowed a degree of artistic freedom with *House*, injecting a sense of humour lacking in the earlier film while avoiding the out-and-out comedy elements associated with other 'old dark house' adaptations of the period. As with *Dracula*, *Frankenstein* and the rest of Universal's horror series, the film embraces the lighting and *mise-en-scène* of the German Expressionists, while for the most part retaining the more conventional Hollywood style of performance, framing and continuity. A hugely successful formula for the studio, these films ensured that horror would go on to become a popular and enduring cinematic genre. In the first half of the decade all of the Hollywood studios attempted to replicate Universal's output, with varying degrees of success. Boris Karloff found himself in constant demand; when not working for Universal he was loaned out to the majors for films such as MGM's *The Mask of Fu Manchu* (Charles Brabin, 1932) and *The Walking Dead* from Warner Bros. as well as lower budget productions, including *The Ghoul* (T. Hayes Hunter, 1933), the first British film to receive the 'H' classification (see below). Smaller Hollywood studios also cashed in on the genre's popularity, with the casting of Karloff or Lugosi used to entice audiences. Lugosi in particular found himself involved in some extremely poor productions, a situation that would continue until his death in 1956.

In 1935 Karloff and Whale were re-united for *The Bride of Frankenstein*. With its publicity making heavy use of iconic images of Karloff's monster, the film was a phenomenal commercial and critical success, and is today considered by many as the finest of Universal's horror cycle. Nevertheless, at the time of its release the future of the horror genre was looking increasingly uncertain. When Frederic March won the Best Actor Academy Award for Paramount's prestigious *Dr Jekyll and Mr Hyde* (Rouben Mamoulian, 1931), the horror film achieved a level of recognition that it would rarely reach again. In hiring director Tod Browning, MGM hoped to outdo Universal in the horror stakes, giving his macabre outlook free rein on the 1932 film *Freaks*. Now regarded as something of a masterpiece, *Freaks* was at the time the subject of a massive backlash, with the director's use of real-life circus performers proving too shocking for audiences. Disowned by the studio, the film effectively ended Browning's career and resulted in calls for stricter rules on film content, calls that were eventually met with the adoption of the Production Code in 1934. Although once again self-regulatory, the Production Code, administered by the Production Code Authority, was more effective than the earlier Hays Code, remaining in force until 1968. We will discuss the Production Code more fully in our chapters on *Night of the Living Dead* and *Rosemary's Baby*.

Concern about the newly-emerging horror genre was certainly not confined to the US. Representing at the time the biggest single overseas market for Hollywood product, British film censors struggled with the sudden influx of horrific films. Nineteen thirty-two alone saw the banning of both *Freaks* and *The Island of Lost Souls* (dir. Erle C. Kenton), and the heavy censoring of films from major studios including Universal's *Murders in the Rue Morgue*, Warners' *Doctor X* (dir. Michael Curtiz), RKO's *The Most Dangerous Game* (dirs. Irving Pichel & Ernest B. Shoedsack) and Paramount's *Dr Jekyll and Mr Hyde*. Intense lobbying from children's charities such as the NSPCC led to the BBFC introducing the 'H' (for horror) classification in May 1933. Whereas previously films had been passed as either 'U' (particularly suitable for children) or 'A' (suitable for all), it was advised that children not be allowed to view those classified 'H'. Whatever the BBFC's intention, the introduction of the new category did little to stem the flow of horrific films, instead ensuring that productions which would previously have been banned could now be released (Carl Dreyer's *Vampyr* [1932], for instance, was deliberately held back until the new classification was in place).

It was the graphic cruelty of Universal's Karloff-Lugosi vehicle *The Raven* (Lew Landers, 1935) which eventually led to the BBFC declaring war on the horror genre, publicly warning film-makers that future entries in the genre would be subject to more rigorous censorship. Political pressure from both the BBFC and the PCA coincided with American audiences' waning interest in the genre, as smaller studios cashed in with a surfeit of poor quality, low-budget releases. By this time Laemmle Jr. had relinquished control of Universal to an investment bank, and the new owners were keen to concentrate on producing cheap, family-friendly fare. Following the release of *Dracula's Daughter* (Lambert Hillyer, 1936) the studio suspended horror film production, a decision also taken by the rest of the Hollywood majors. Responding to this development, the BBFC announced the abandonment of the 'H' classification in 1936. However, following pressure from government, local councils and cinema achains, and in an effort to re-standardise national film classification, they introduced the 'H' certificate in 1937. Unlike the previous *classification*, which had been merely advisory, the 'H' *certificate* explicitly excluded children under 16 from attending 'unsuitable' films, and remained in use until the 1950s (see Petley 2017: 138).

The years 1937 and 1938 saw no investment at all in the genre by the majors, the PCA actively dissuading studios from even contemplating such films. Struggling financially, the new-look Universal Pictures found their biggest successes in Deanna Durbin musicals and comedies based around the characters Ma and Pa Kettle. Five years after the birth of the Hollywood horror film it appeared that the genre was already dead and buried, the victim of market forces and political pressures. The films had shown that there was an audience for horrific material, but was there enough of an audience to make it an established Hollywood genre? The answer came from a theatre-owner in Los Angeles, his business close to bankruptcy, who in a final act of desperation booked two out-of-favour pictures to play as a double-bill in August 1938. The pairing of Universal's *Dracula* and *Frankenstein* proved to be a sensation, generating queues around the block and prompting the studio to arrange a nationwide re-release. With box-office returns surpassing those from 1931, followed by an equally successful re-release of *The Old Dark House* in 1939, the decision was made to resurrect the monsters that had made the studio famous.

The first production to emerge from this was the impressive, highly Expressionistic *Son of Frankenstein* (Rowland V Lee, 1939), the last of the series to feature Boris Karloff as the monster and another critical and commercial success. So the Universal monster cycle resumed, but under the direction of the studio's new owners: from this point onwards, the quality and budgets of their genre output quickly headed downwards. The franchise approach that had worked with their musicals and family comedies was brought to bear, with a series of films featuring the mummy, Dracula and the Frankenstein monster, culminating in the *Abbott and Costello Meet…* comedies. Where once they had terrified film audiences, Universal's monsters were rapidly becoming figures of fun, and the horror film was in danger of quickly dying an embarrassing death. A fresh approach was needed, and with the majors reluctant to return to the genre, the opportunity arose for another down-at-heel studio to step out of the shadows and take over Universal's mantle as the home of true cinematic horror.

Bibliography

Brosnan, John (1976) *The Horror People*. New York: St. Martin's Press.

Curtis, Barry (2008) *Dark Places: The Haunted House in Film*. London: Reaktion Books.

Doherty, Thomas (1999) *Pre-Code Hollywood: Sex, Immorality, and Insurrection in American Cinema 1930-1934*. New York: Columbia University Press.

Nollen, Scott Allen (1991) *Boris Karloff: A Critical Account of his Screen, Stage, Radio, Television and Recording Work*. Jefferson: McFarland & Co.

Petley, Julian, 'Horror and the Censors'. In Benshoff, Harry M. (ed.) (2017) *A Companion to the Horror Film*. pp. 130-148. Chichester: John Wiley & Sons.

Schatz, Thomas (1988) *The Genius of the System: Hollywood Filmmaking in the Studio Era*. New York: Pantheon.

Sevastakis, M. (1993) *Songs of Love and Death: The Classical American Horror Film of the 1930s*. Westport: Greenwood Press.

Spadoni, Robert (2007) *Uncanny Bodies: The Coming of Sound Film and the Origins of the Horror Genre*. Berkeley, CA: University of California Press.

Endnotes

1. This rationale may go some way to explaining the popularity of what we would now call 'cheat endings' in a number of American pseudo-horror films of the 1920s, for example MGM's *London After Midnight* (Tod Browning, 1927), in which Lon Chaney removes his vampire disguise at the film's climax to reveal that he is in fact a mere mortal detective.

2. Immediately prior to the signing of the Parufamet agreement (see Chapter 1) Laemmle had been in talks to loan Ufa the funds that they eventually received from Paramount and MGM, in return for mutual distribution and boardroom voting rights.

3. *The Last Warning* re-used many of the theatre sets that had been built for *Phantom*. Leni's second film had been a lavish adaptation of Victor Hugo's *The Man Who Laughs* (1928), a Gothic historical epic very much in the style of *Hunchback* and *Phantom*. Heavy on Expressionism, the film starred *Caligari*'s Conrad Veidt as a Chaney-like grotesque, with make-up by Jack Pierce.

4. Freund had migrated to Hollywood to try and market a technique he had created for colour film and was quickly put under contract at Universal, originally with a view to directing an American remake of Wegener's *Der Golem*.

5. Neither of these remakes, when they were eventually produced in 1939 (by RKO) and 1943 respectively, would feature Karloff.

6. It was only after the success of *King Kong*, the first film to have a full score specially composed for it, that there was a conscious move away from stock music clips to original full soundtracks. We will discuss more fully the importance of music to the horror film in later chapters.

7. Unlike many subsequent actors who found themselves typecast in the horror genre, Karloff often expressed his gratitude to the genre for providing him with such a long and successful career. It is also worth noting that in later films, once his 'monstrous' reputation had been cemented, he was occasionally cast against type, as a red herring to draw attention away from the real villain.

8. It is interesting to note the similarities in the characters and interaction between Horace and his sister and those of the Wavertons, especially the exchanges during the film's opening scene.

9. Gladys's cries of 'He's alive! He's alive, I tell you!' in this sequence are yet another reference to Whale's *Frankenstein*.

Chapter 3

In the Realm of the Fantastic

Cat People
Jacques Tourneur US, 1942

Recommended viewing:
The Wolf Man (George Waggner, 1941)
I Walked with a Zombie (Jacques Tourneur, 1943)
The Curse of the Cat People (Robert Wise, 1944)
The Body Snatcher (Robert Wise, 1945)
The Haunting (Robert Wise, 1963)

Introduction

According to philosopher Tzvetan Todorov, 'the realm of the fantastic' is entered when, '[i]n a world which is indeed our world, the one we know, a world without devils, sylphides, or vampires, there occurs an event which cannot be explained by the laws of this same familiar world' (1975:25). He goes on to suggest that such a state exists only as long as there is indecision over whether the event is indeed a supernatural occurrence or a product of the imagination; once this is determined, we leave the realm of the fantastic for that of either the 'marvellous' or the 'uncanny'. Although Todorov's studies of narrative are primarily concerned with literature, we can extend his theories to our discussion of the cinematic horror genre. For a film to be 'fantastic' in this sense we can say that the viewer must be held in this state of hesitation, when both rational and supernatural explanations for what they are witnessing carry equal weight.

The case study for this chapter is the first in a series of 'fantastic' horror films produced by Val Lewton for RKO Pictures in the 1940s. Famous for their use of suggestion and ambiguity, they are widely regarded as classics of the genre. Like Universal Studios before it, RKO used the horror film to transform itself into a major Hollywood force, injecting new life into a genre that had by then become staid and predictable. Their success came at a time of mounting problems for the majors, and when independent studios and film-makers began to play an increasingly important role in the industry. With the genre all but abandoned by the big studios, the independents would have a powerful influence on the future of the horror film as it evolved over the following decades.

Background

The late 1930s and early 40s saw a series of setbacks for the major Hollywood studios. As the result of a 1938 anti-trust suit the Big Five were forced to abide by 'the Paramount Decree', a ruling that significantly reduced the power they had over theatres, outlawing the practice of blind bidding and placing strict limits on the number of films that could be block-booked. A direct result of this was a gradual reduction in the number of low-budget movies produced by the big studios, now unable to guarantee sales by packaging them with higher-profile films. This in turn led to an *increase* in output from independent studios specialising in 'B' movies. The concept of the double-bill, where a major release (the 'A' movie) was paired with a lower-budget ('B') movie had emerged in the early 1930s as a method of attracting audiences back to cinemas during the Great Depression. It was a highly successful strategy, and remained in place for many years after. Outfits such as

Monogram, Republic and PRC produced short, cheap pictures that were sold as the bottom half of double-bills. Excluded from the decree, these so-called 'Poverty Row' studios were able to continue the practice of block-booking their films to subsequent-run theatres. With cinema attendances rising steadily between 1938 and 1946, the independents were ideally placed to take advantage of the changes being introduced.

Market forces also shaped the type of films that the smaller independents produced, as, with the onset of the Second World War, Hollywood studios found their foreign markets shrinking. With the UK outlawing the exhibition of horror films for the duration of the war, deeming them bad for morale, the genre was practically abandoned by the majors. The few notable exceptions were films which returned to the literary origins of earlier successes, and which played up the melodramatic aspects of the stories at the expense of the horrific. MGM's big-budget version of *Dr Jekyll and Mr Hyde* (Victor Fleming, 1941), starring Spencer Tracy and Ingrid Bergman, was a critical and commercial success nominated for three Academy Awards, while Universal's lavish Technicolor *Phantom of the Opera* (George Waggner, 1943) went one better in being nominated for four and winning two (for art direction and cinematography). Whilst it is debatable whether either of these qualifies as a true horror film, it would be another thirty years before Hollywood again saw the genre as worthy of big-budget productions (or Academy Awards).

Enter the independent studios, who discovered a lucrative market in catering to the thrill-seeking audiences now ignored by the majors. They knew that there was enough of a dedicated audience for the genre, fostered chiefly by Universal, that practically any film could turn a profit provided costs were kept under control. Their horror films tended to centre on deranged scientists or other monstrous humans, often featuring either Boris Karloff or Bela Lugosi, who was by now experiencing difficulty in attracting quality roles. Columbia Pictures in particular, who like Universal were largely unaffected by the anti-trust action against the majors, released a series of 'mad scientist' films starring Karloff, with titles such as *The Man They Could Not Hang* (Nick Grinde, 1939) and *The Man With Nine Lives* (Nick Grinde, 1940), all playing on, and adding to, the actor's iconic status. With the best film-makers moved to other genres, horror films of the 1940s are generally regarded as poor in comparison to those of the previous decade. To keep costs low, the majority were set in the present day, and demonstrated a pre-occupation with science and modernity reflected in the naturalistic style they employed: gone were the Gothic sets and elaborate schemes of light and shadow, and in their place were badly lit, sparsely furnished laboratories.

The migration of behind-the-camera talent from the horror genre coincided with important technical advances in the industry. The development of faster film stock towards the end of the 1930s meant that film-makers were able to operate with lower light levels (an important consideration for studios keen to reduce costs), as well as allowing greater contrast and a wider variety of shades between light and dark. The first important film to take advantage of this new stock, *Citizen Kane* (Orson Welles, 1941), took Expressionist use of light and shadow and combined it with deep focus photography (where objects in the foreground, mid- and background planes are shown with equal clarity) to increase the air of oppression and tension. Although a commercial failure at the time, *Kane* is now regarded by many as one of the best films ever made, and its influence on the aesthetic of film in general, particularly during the 1940s and 50s, should not be underestimated. However, of more relevance to our discussion is another non-horror film from the same year, which proved to have a much more immediate impact. The camerawork of Arthur Edeson, cinematographer on both *Frankenstein* and *The Old Dark House*, is arguably the most impressive aspect of the highly-successful Warner Bros. detective film *The Maltese Falcon* (John Huston, 1941). With its atmospheric use of light and shadow, skewed camera angles, ambiguous characterisation and constant air of tension, *Falcon* transferred the Expressionist aesthetic from the horror genre to a new type of film, one commonly regarded as reflecting America's wartime fears and paranoia: *film noir*.

Nowadays primarily associated with American detective and gangster films of the 1940s, *noir*'s origins can be traced to the so-called 'poetic realist' films produced in France throughout the 1930s. Poetic realism merged socio-realistic elements of the emerging documentary film movement with the aesthetics of French Impressionism to produce artistically stylised yet gritty films, usually concerned with the lives of the socially disadvantaged or criminal underclass and set in rain-swept city streets. In projecting a downbeat vision of a country between wars, film-makers consciously rejected the conventions and aesthetics of classical Hollywood. Poetic realism represents a theme and style rather than any particular narrative structure, and as such the fatalistic subject matter, low-key lighting and often dream-like cinematography of films such as *L'Atalante* (Jean Renoir, 1934) and *La Bete Humaine* (Jean Vigo, 1938) can be seen as a continuation of the original German Expressionist movement. The widespread adoption of poetic realism as *film noir* represents perhaps the first major movement in Hollywood based around a style rather than a genre, and the application of this aesthetic was seen by the studios as a way to add something fresh to already existing genres. By its nature, films utilising such lighting and cinematography projected an air of menace and claustrophobia, so, whilst there were some comedies and romance films made in the *noir* style, it was generally regarded as more suited to thrillers, particularly the detective and gangster genres.

As such, the term *film noir* became associated with a number of conventions present in these types of films, including first-person narration, flashbacks, doomed protagonists and *femmes fatales*. Typical narratives feature themes of entrapment and oppression, where the (almost always) male protagonist is drawn into and affected by a series of events outside of his control. He will find himself faced with obstacles that are psychological or pathological, rather than physical; relationships, which in a conventional melodrama would have been made difficult by external influences, are instead complicated by the personalities of the characters themselves. Conventional heroes often have a dark side, and the films' endings are rarely altogether happy. Such themes and stylistics continue to inform more recent films, including much of the work of David Lynch and so-called 'neo-noirs' such as *Blade Runner* (Ridley Scott, 1982) and *The Dark Knight* (Christopher Nolan, 2008), while the more direct influence of poetic realism can be seen in the Italian Neo-realist films of the 1940s and the French New Wave. The importance of both of these movements to the horror genre will be discussed in subsequent chapters.

Two early *noir* films are worth mentioning briefly here due to their relevance to the horror genre. *Black Friday* (Arthur Lubin, 1940) was a Universal film co-written by Curt Siodmak and starring Boris Karloff (as a surgeon) and Bela Lugosi (briefly, as a gangster). On the face of it a typical Karloff mad scientist movie (involving the transplanting of a professor's brain into the body of a gangster), it is set in a contemporary crime milieu more suited to the later *noir* thrillers. The film's cinematographer, Elwood Bredell would later work on a number of *noir* including the classic *The Killers* (Robert Siodmak, 1946), as well as Universal monster sequels such as *The Mummy's Hand* (Christy Cabanne, 1940) and *The Ghost of Frankenstein* (Erle C. Kenton, 1942). It is interesting to note that the camerawork in Bredell's *noir* demonstrate much more of an Expressionist influence than do his monster movies, something which owes much to the imagination and competence of their respective directors.

The second film of note pre-dates *Black Friday*, and is often cited as the first true Hollywood *noir*. *Stranger on the Third Floor* (Boris Ingster, 1939) features Peter Lorre, who had starred opposite *Frankenstein*'s Colin Clive in Karl Freund's final horror film as a director, *Mad Love* (1935) and would later feature in *The Maltese Falcon*. Although it contains none of the scientific or supernatural aspects of *Black Friday*, at the time of its release *Stranger* was marketed by RKO as a horror film, and features Lorre as a psychotic killer, not unlike his role in Fritz Lang's classic German drama *M*. *Stranger* is concerned with a reporter who is haunted by the fear that his testimony has led to an innocent man (played by Elisha Cook, Jr.) being condemned for a murder he did not commit. His mental anguish is relayed through the use of narration (a common feature of *noir*), and a seven-minute, surrealistic dream sequence in which he finds himself on trial and condemned for murder. The cinematographer of *Stranger*, Nicholas Musuraca, would later photograph the case study for this chapter, *Cat People*.

In addition to cultural influences, Hollywood film-making in the early 1940s was subject to economic and structural developments within the industry. One important concept relevant to this chapter is that of the 'producer-unit', a mode of production that had grown in popularity within the studios since the early 1930s. During the early years of production, in the 1910s and 20s, one central manager had usually been responsible for supervising a studio's entire output, for example Carl Leammle (and subsequently his son) at Universal. Beneath these general managers would operate a finance manager, production manager, security manager, and so on, each responsible for a particular aspect of the studio's operation as it affected each and every production. Whilst such an operational structure may have suited a general manufacturing company, by the early 1930s the studios were concerned that this rigid hierarchy was responsible for perceived audience dissatisfaction with stereotyped product. This was hardly surprising given a single general manager controlled every single picture the studio released, even down to the final cut, and could not be an expert in all types of film. Pioneered by Columbia Pictures in 1931, and subsequently followed by most of the other studios, management was restructured into units, each of which would be responsible for individual films, rather than overseeing the studio's whole output. Unit producers would concentrate on all aspects of a handful of films, usually belonging to a particular specialised genre or style, seeing them through from conception to release. Such an approach, it was supposed, would increase quality and variety in product. Perhaps more importantly, in the midst of the Great Depression, it would reduce costs through efficiency and the elimination of waste, and allow producers to keep a closer eye on any budget overruns.

One by-product of this re-organisation was that a number of important producers, perhaps resentful of their loss of control, left the majors to set up their own independent studios. These were a far cry from the poverty row independents, however, and by the end of the 1930s independent producers were wielding a great deal of power in Hollywood. None was more powerful than David O. Selznick, who had left MGM in 1935 to form Selznick International Pictures, where he produced such high-profile successes as *Gone with the Wind* (Victor Fleming, 1939). Selznick's phenomenal success was in stark contrast to one of his previous employers, who by the early 1940s was in dire straits and struggling to stay afloat. Despite commercial success with films such as *King Kong* and *The Hunchback of Notre Dame* (William Dieterle, 1939), RKO Pictures had been in consistently poor financial shape throughout the 1930s and into the 40s, relying on series films based around popular characters such as The Saint and a string of Fred Astaire-Ginger Rogers musicals to survive. By 1942 the studio was suffering the additional financial burden of *Citizen Kane*, and in desperate need of a winning formula.

Mindful of the continuing (relative) success experienced by Universal's monster movies, as well as the more opportunist genre productions of the smaller independent studios, RKO's new studio head Charles Koerner drew up plans for a production unit which would specialise in short (under 75 minutes) and cheap (under $150,000) horror films. Despite the low budgets afforded them, these were to be quality productions to compete with the best of Universal's genre output, rather than those being made by Monogram, PRC and the rest. Charged with running the unit was Val Lewton, a Russian-born screenwriter and producer who had built an impressive reputation at MGM, initially as editorial assistant and story editor for Selznick. In his new role at RKO Lewton was to be given a movie title (market-tested by the studio to ensure an audience as far as possible)[1] and complete freedom (within the stated budgetary and length restrictions) to deliver a finished film. Whilst the films themselves were put together by a number of talented individuals who went on to be highly successful in their own right, such was the influence of the producer in every aspect of the film-making process that they are regarded first and foremost as 'Val Lewton films'.

'Cat People', the first title given to Lewton by RKO, was undoubtedly inspired by the success Universal had seen with *The Wolf Man* (George Waggner, 1941). By the early 1940s Universal was in the midst of its second wave of monster movies which had begun with *Son of Frankenstein*. Not content with reviving previous successes, the new owners at Universal wanted their own monster, and *The Wolf Man*, which launched Lon Chaney Jr.'s career as a genre actor, continued the tradition of the rest of the studio's horror series. Ostensibly set in contemporary Wales, although re-using familiar central European village sets and costumes from earlier monster movies, Chaney stars as Larry Talbot, an American who is infected by the bite of a werewolf (Bela Lugosi) while visiting his father's estate. Like Wegener with his *Golem* films, Universal's scriptwriters took existing legends and embellished them with their own mythology, as well as featuring a number of narrative conventions established in earlier genre films. Screenwriter Curt Siodmak, a Jewish migrant who had left Germany for Hollywood in 1937, expanded on existing European legend by asserting that werewolves can only be killed by silver, and that they can identify their next victim by the sign of the pentagram. The script also introduced the now-famous rhyme, adapted and reused in a number of subsequent productions:

Even a man who is pure in heart
And says his prayers at night,

May become a wolf when the wolf bane blooms
And the autumn moon is bright.

If the RKO bosses had expected a re-tread of *The Wolf Man* when they came up with their inaugural title, then they were to be disappointed. Lewton hated the way that Universal were increasingly bringing their monsters out of the shadows, making them less frightening and threatening to turn them into figures of fun. Lewton wanted to use his films' low budgets to his advantage, relying on shadow and suggestion to generate horror, rather than make-up or special effects. By filling much of the frame with shadow, the films were able to hide the lack of expensive set dressing while at the same time evoking a claustrophobic and threatening atmosphere. Lewton's view that audiences are more scared by what they can't see than what they can meant that supernatural and psychological threats took the place of monsters and mad scientists. The result was a series of films that brought critical acclaim to a genre that was in serious danger of becoming a laughing stock.

Textual Analysis

In contemporary New York, maritime draughtsman Oliver Reed strikes up a conversation with a Serbian fashion artist, Irena Dubrovnik, at Central Park Zoo. Invited back to her apartment, Oliver is intrigued by Irena's fascination with cats and her story of the legendary 'cat women', devil-worshipping shape-shifters who were banished from her village long ago. Obviously attracted to her, Oliver arranges to meet her again the next day, when they express their love for each other. They marry soon after, but Irena feels unable to consummate the relationship and agrees to see a psychoanalyst, Dr Judd. Under hypnosis, Irena tells Judd of the cat women and that she fears that she herself will turn into a cat and kill her husband if she is aroused. Returning home, she is embarrassed to discover that Oliver has told his workmate Alice about their problems. Irena grows jealous of Alice and stalks her as she walks home. Later that night several sheep are found mutilated in the park. Oliver and Irena's relationship deteriorates, and after a confrontation with Irena while taking a swim Alice finds that her robe has been shredded by what appears to be large claws. Concerned by Irena's increasingly strange behaviour, Alice and Oliver approach Judd for advice. He suggests they have her committed and they arrange a meeting but Irena does not show up. Instead Alice and Oliver go to the office where they find themselves menaced by a big cat. Judd engineers a secret meeting with Irena, during which he forces himself upon her. Irena turns into a cat and mauls him to death, but not before being stabbed by the broken sword of his cane. Back in human form Irena returns to the zoo. Unlocking the panther's cage, she allows it to knock her to the ground, pushing the sword through her body and killing her.

Cat People opens with credits played over an art-deco painting of a panther, followed by a title card containing a quote taken from 'The Anatomy of Atavism' by the film's psychologist, Dr Louis Judd:

> *Even as fog continues to lie in the valleys, so does ancient sin cling to the low places, the depressions in the world consciousness.*

Behind the title card, the painting has been replaced by a sculpture of King John of Serbia running a cat through with his sword, the first of several occasions in which Judd is linked with the mythical figure of King John.

In the original script, the quote was to have been attributed to Sigmund Freud, and it is obvious from the theories he expounds that Judd is heavily influenced by Freud's work. During the 1940s psychoanalysis in general and Freud in particular had a significant influence on many films produced in Hollywood, primarily in the horror and thriller genres, which began to place more emphasis on the psychological aspects of their protagonists. During the 1930s many eminent European psychiatrists had migrated to the west coast of America, where it had become fashionable in Hollywood circles to 'enter analysis', and this popularity was matched by a rise in interest in psychoanalysis across the country. Freudian theories of dream interpretation and analysis were widely known, and the 1940s saw a marked increase in the number and relevance of dream sequences in film, one of the most well known being that produced by Salvador Dali for Alfred Hitchcock's *Spellbound* (1945). Such sequences introduced into otherwise classical Hollywood films an Expressionistic aspect, where the subconsciously repressed fears and memories of the protagonist could be presented visually. The dream sequence which appears in *Cat People*, featuring animated cats and Dr Judd dressed as King John, is typically surreal. We will discuss surrealism in relation to horror cinema further in our chapter on *Wes Craven's New Nightmare*.

The role of the psychologist in solving a crime or assisting an investigation also became more prominent in Hollywood thrillers from the 1940s, and this is one of a number of areas where *Cat People* goes against convention. In more mainstream productions, such as *Spellbound*, psychoanalysis is used to successfully explain or solve some mystery. By contrast, *Cat People* makes the point that, when dealing with the supernatural at least, psychoanalysis does not have all the answers. A stock character in the horror genre is the 'knowledgeable expert' typified by Dracula's mortal enemy Van Helsing, who has a unique insight into whatever threat is present, no matter how fantastic or unbelievable it may be. It is usually this professional's role in the film to convince the rest of the characters of the seriousness of their predicament. *Cat People* reverses this by having the other characters (Alice and Oliver) needing to convince the expert of the reality of the situation. In doing so, the film foreshadows later genre entries, beginning with the science-fiction films of the 1950s and fuelled by growing disillusionment with, and distrust of, authority figures in general during the 1960s and beyond. This shift will be discussed further in our chapter on *Night of the Living Dead*.

Figure 3.1

Whilst it would have been convenient for Judd to be an expert on cat legends and to know of the existence of cat people, taking the opposite approach actually strengthens two of the film's key areas: its realism and its ambiguity. Had Dr Judd been introduced and asserted that there are indeed such things as women who turn into cats when aroused, not only would it stretch the audience's credulity, but the ambiguity that had been built up so far would have been lost. In fact, due to its climactic scenes *Cat People* ends up being perhaps the least ambiguous of all Lewton's horror films, although for much of its running time both rational and supernatural explanations appear equally valid. Constrained by his rationality, and by his stubborn belief that he can explain away Irena's beliefs as stemming from some forgotten childhood trauma, he scoffs when Alice suggests that Irena may actually be able to turn herself into a cat. Obviously attracted to Irena and determined to 'cure' her through physical contact, Judd is so unlikeable that the audience feels almost compelled to reject his assertion that Irena's problems are all in her mind and to believe the supernatural explanation. Indeed, it can be said that Judd is the closest thing to a real villain in the entire film, and in its less-than-favourable depiction of its expert (as a lecherous opportunist with dubious motives) *Cat People* demonstrates a *noir*-ish pre-occupation with psychologically flawed characters (see Fig 3.1).

One conventional mainstay of the *noir* is the *femme fatale* – a desirable and mysterious woman who leads the classical hero into dark and dangerous territory. Although *Cat People*'s Irena possesses some of the traits of the traditional *femme fatale* (a forwardness demonstrated early by inviting Oliver into her apartment, a mixture of vulnerability and danger, a powerful allure that inexplicably draws him to her) she differs from them in one important aspect. Unlike the characters played by Barbra Stanwyck in *Double Indemnity* (Billy Wilder, 1944) or Lana Turner in *The Postman Always Rings Twice* (Tay Garnett, 1946), she does not deliberately seek to entrap or seduce Oliver, although she does have a controlling power over their physical relationship. As the film progresses, it becomes obvious that Irena is the true victim of the story, although Lewton is happy to play to the audience's *noir* expectations to keep them off balance.

When Oliver comments that he 'never cease[s] to marvel at what lies behind a brownstone front', he is obviously referring to the contrast between Irena's strong-willed personality and innocent appearance. Of course, little does he know at this stage exactly what lies behind her seemingly harmless facade, but he is keen to find out. As he approaches her apartment door the shadows thrown by the window frame recall the opening image of the panther in the zoo. The impression we get is of Oliver is being drawn into a cage, while the music on the soundtrack takes an ominous turn. A common use of shadow in *noir* (seen in both *Citizen Kane* and *Stranger on the Third Floor*, amongst others), the bars in fact symbolise Irena's own feelings of entrapment and the inability to escape her ultimate fate. Furthering the move begun by Universal a decade earlier, the antagonist of the horror film is here depicted as more victim than monster. Despite being marked as 'other' through her foreign-ness, the audience can be forgiven for eventually siding with the tragic Irena given the generally unsympathetic nature and duplicity of the rest of the film's characters.

Although the script is credited wholly to Bodeen DeWitt, the original idea for the film goes back to a short story that Lewton wrote for 'Weird Tales' magazine in 1930. 'The Bagheeta' concerns a shape-shifting half-woman, half-leopard creature that preys on those tainted by sins of the flesh. Beautiful and seductive, the baghee-ta can only be slain by a virgin, one who is able to resist her sensuous charms. Many writings on *Cat People* tend to concentrate on its links with and similarities to *The Wolf Man*, though thematically it more closely resembles an earlier Universal horror film, *Dracula's Daughter*. In this direct sequel to Tod Browning's *Dracula*, a young woman arrives in England from Transylvania following the death of the count, hoping in vain to be freed from the curse of vampirism. Countess Zaleska generates audience sympathy yet is also distanced by her European origins (as well as the fact that she is most definitely a vampire, and probably lesbian). Like *Cat People*, *Daughter* also features a disbelieving psychologist, although it is the returning Van Helsing who takes on the conventional role of knowledgeable expert.

Despite such narrative similarities, Lewton consciously sought to distance his RKO productions from the horror films being produced at Universal. He wanted to present believable and empathetic characters that become unwittingly involved in strange and incredible situations. Thematically, the film is concerned with the intrusion of the 'other' into normal life; as in *Dracula* and its sequel, the arrival of an exotic foreigner impacts the everyday lives of the film's protagonists. However, rather than being set in the past, or in a generic European neverland, the danger is here brought home to modern-day America. From the opening scene, the film presents its narrative in as natural a way as possible, immersing the viewer in the familiar real-life surroundings of 1940s New York City. The Central Park Zoo set that features heavily throughout the film was familiar to viewers from, amongst other RKO productions, the popular Astaire-Rogers musical *Shall We Dance* (Mark Sandrich, 1937). Transplanting horror to the recognisable here and now, and suggesting that the events in the film could happen to an everyday person in the street, cannot help but increase its effectiveness.

One event that was impacting real life at the time of the film's release was World War II, and, whilst it is not specifically mentioned in the film, the situation is reflected in the characterisation of the two female leads. Irena is obviously a refugee from war-torn Central Europe; she tells Oliver that she has recently arrived from Serbia and has no friends. When we first meet Alice she is confidently taking charge in the draught studio; she exemplifies the modern and independent woman working in a 'man's world', a phenomenon brought about by wartime shortages in the male workforce. The fact that Irena is employed in the decidedly more feminine area of fashion design is just one of many narrative and stylistic oppositions set up between the two female characters. Most obvious, though, is that whilst Alice is a no-nonsense, straight-talking all-American (blonde) girl, Irena is a coy, mysterious (dark) outsider. It is a reflection of Oliver's disillusionment over his relationship with Irena and his new-found attraction to Alice when, in the coffee shop next door to his office, he opts for traditional American apple pie and coffee rather than Minnie's exotic 'Chicken Gumbo'.

Although *Cat People* is very much character- rather than plot-oriented, there are two narrative sequences for which it is particularly well known, and which have become classic genre set-pieces. The first occurs when Alice is walking home following her meeting with Oliver at the coffee shop. After an argument with Oliver during which he reveals that he has been discussing their relationship with Alice, Irena tries to contact him at the office. When Alice picks up her telephone call, Irena's suspicions appear to be confirmed. In fact, Oliver is sitting alone at the coffee shop and it is only by chance that Alice meets him there. During the conversation that follows we learn that Alice is prepared to play a waiting game when she tells Oliver to make up with Irena; she knows that the marriage will break down, given enough time. However, by now Irena has left the apartment in a jealous rage, and the shots of her stalking the dark city streets wouldn't have been out of place in any *noir* of the period, working to evoke the image of a dangerous *femme fatale*. As Irena watches from the shadows, the couple say their goodbyes with a platonic handshake and Alice heads off down a street-lit concourse towards Central Park.

Now the set-piece begins. The audience has been primed: we know that Irena is angry and jealous, that she has been following the couple, and that Alice is now walking alone down a dark street. Cut to a shot of Irena surrounded by trees, the light from a streetlamp behind her resembling a full moon hanging low in the sky. One half of her face is brightly lit, the other in shadow, an obvious and

Figure 3.2

common visual representation of split personality. She pauses briefly, wrapping her fur coat tighter before walking towards the camera, silently, until she is completely enveloped by shadow (see Fig 3.2). The impression we get is that, without any physical transformation, the cat persona has taken over Irena. Reaching the corner where Oliver and Alice have just said their goodbyes, she heads in the direction taken by Alice. The film cross-cuts between the two women walking along the path, each passing the same streetlights, as Irena gradually closes in. The following shots track the women's shoes, Irena's footsteps echoing off the concrete, highlighting the fact that she is walking faster than Alice. She is gaining on her stealthily, like a cat closing in on a mouse.

The camerawork and editing throughout the rest of this sequence actively work to build tension. Back to a full-length shot, and we see Alice walk out of frame right. But we do not cut to Irena as has been the pattern so far, and instead the camera holds momentarily on an empty wall. We then expect to see Irena enter frame left, having caught up, but she doesn't. We hear Irena's footsteps fade and then disappear. The viewer is momentarily disoriented, wondering where Irena is (or what she has become). Cut back to Alice and we follow her as she walks past another streetlight, and then into darkness. Alice is front-lit, but around her is nothing but darkness. Tension builds. Is Irena about to pounce from the darkness? When she reaches the next streetlight, Alice pauses and turns. Cut to a POV shot looking down the street behind her. It is deserted and silent. Worried, Alice speeds up, again walking into darkness, hurrying now and quickly looking back as she walks and then runs. With each cut back to Alice, the framing is tighter. By showing less of the area around her the sense of paranoia and claustrophobia is heightened; although Alice is walking through the open space of the concourse, visually she is trapped within an ever-shrinking frame. As it closes in around her, so too does the off-screen danger, leaving Alice vulnerable to attack from any direction.

Alice starts to run, clinging to the next streetlight and again looking back. Finally, as the tension becomes almost unbearable, there is a loud hiss and a screech as a bus pulls up right in front of her. Relieved, Alice begins to climbs on-board, but looks up to see the trees above swaying, as if something had jumped up the wall behind her and through the branches. The effect used at the climax of this sequence, where the audience's steadily-built tension is broken by a sudden audio and visual intrusion calculated to make them jump, has since become known as a 'Lewton bus'. Commonly referred to as a 'shock cut' (or 'startle effect'), they differ from the normal 'jump cut' in that they are calculated to shock the audience, either through what is seen (for example, a mutilated body suddenly falling from a tree) or through the information that is given (that a killer is in the room). They do not even have to include an actual cut, in that objects may suddenly appear in the frame, or lunge towards camera, or the camera may zoom in or focus on some hitherto unseen menace. They are usually accompanied by a loud aural effect, such as a non-diegetic orchestra stab or, as in this case, the sudden arrival of something noisy.

These types of sequences can be found in many subsequent horror films, and due to their effectiveness remain popular with film-makers today. Its use here, as a red herring, is also common, and is nowadays often used as part of a double-whammy to catch the viewer off-guard. First the red herring (for example, a pet cat jumping through the window), followed closely by the real shock (the discovery of a severed head in the fridge when getting the cat some milk). Whatever, the success of the shock cut depends on the ability of the film to build tension prior to the jump, and it is often preceded by a long take or sequence that causes the audience to hold their collective breath. In *Cat People* the camerawork, editing and sound combine to create an atmosphere of danger, without the need to show anything other than a lone woman walking down a dark street. It is an excellent example of Lewton's philosophy of less being more; just the suggestion that Alice is being followed by someone who may or may not have the power to turn into a panther is enough to generate tension.

The second famous set-piece also occurs during a bout of jealousy on the part of Irena, and whilst it doesn't crank the tension up quite as much as the bus episode, it makes the audience more fearful for Alice's immediate safety. Following a visit to the museum, where Alice and Oliver effectively abandon Irena, we cut to a taxi pulling up outside an apartment block. Alice climbs out of the taxi and enters the building. Another taxi pulls up and out climbs Irena (again in her fur coat), who pauses outside the main door. Inside, Alice is followed down to the swimming pool changing room by a black kitten, which runs off in fright when it senses Irena approaching. Spooked by a shadow at the top of the staircase, Alice dives into the swimming pool and nervously looks around. As before, light and shadow play an important part in the effectiveness of the sequence. In an otherwise dark room, the pool is lit from below, its rippling water casting ghostly shapes that shimmer and dance around the walls. The sound of dripping water fills the soundtrack as Alice treads water, slowly rotating. Again, the audience knows that Irena is prowling but this time, rather than her prey being out in the open, Alice is trapped within the confines of the pool. Suspense and tension rise. A large shadow momentarily blacks out one of the walls. Alice turns quickly but sees nothing. What *looks* like the shadow of a big cat looms briefly on the wall, followed by a scream, before Alice herself screams, the piercing sound echoing around the room. Panicking, she shouts out for help and Irena emerges from the shadows to switch on the lights, another example of a shock cut without a cut.

Irena's demeanour during the exchange that follows suggests that she is taking delight in tormenting Alice, and recalls an earlier sequence in which she toys with a canary in its cage until it dies of fright. In particular, Irena's smile when Alice moves to get out of the pool before backing off shows the pleasure she is getting from Alice's fear. With Irena leaving and the confrontation over, it seems that we can breathe easy again, but this proves not to be the case. When Alice is presented with her robe she discovers that it has been ripped to shreds by what appear to have been large claws. The audience is caught off-guard. Was the shadow on the walls around the pool that of Irena in the form of a panther, or merely a fear-induced distortion of the kitten seen from Alice's viewpoint? Obviously the shredded robe wasn't the work of the kitten, but was it caused by panther claws, or by a knife, or something else? Whatever the answer, the encounter is enough to convince Alice, and the audience, of the physical danger that Irena represents.

The ambiguity over Irena's supernatural powers is kept up until the film's final major sequence, when Dr Judd meets with her in the apartment. Judd's response to Alice's warnings not to be alone with Irena, asking if he should carry 'a gun…with a silver bullet', is an obvious reference to the phoney folklore of Universal's *The Wolf Man*.[2] The revelation that he has a sword in his cane, though not a silver one, recalls the statue of King John which foreshadows the tragic events of the film's climax. Resigned to her fate, Irena doesn't resist when Judd pulls her to him and kisses her. As he steps back, the camera focuses on Irena's face, smiling serenely. Slowly the image darkens, and her eyes begin to shine brighter before she drops out of frame (see Fig 3.3). This is the closest the film comes to a traditional 'transformation scene', the elaborate dissolve editing of *The Wolf Man* and its sequels replaced by imaginative use of light and shadow. In the struggle that follows we see Judd grappling with what is, unmistakeably, a panther, managing to stab it with his sword before he is mauled to death.

Figure 3.3

The shots showing an actual panther in this sequence were inserted at the behest of RKO, and against the producer's wishes. The need for a clear and unambiguous resolution, in which any hanging plot points are tidied up, questions answered and mysteries solved, is an underlying feature of classical Hollywood cinema. Although the endings may not necessarily be happy, studio bosses wanted audiences to go home feeling satisfied, not struggling with questions about what they had just been watching. In the original script, Oliver and Alice were to discover the body of a panther, skewered by Judd's sword in a recreation of Irena's drawing from the film's opening scene. As it is, the revelation of what form Irena has taken in death remains off-screen, though when Oliver tells Alice that 'she never lied to us' we know that Irena was indeed one of the cat people. We leave the realm of the fantastic for that of the marvellous.

Reception and Aftermath

Although today considered a classic of Hollywood cinema, RKO executives were initially unimpressed by what they saw of the film. After the first few days of production they threatened to fire director Tourneur, complaining that the film was too slow moving and not at all frightening. Given Lewton's determination to go against everything that the Universal films stood for, if they were expecting another *Wolf Man* then such a reaction is perhaps understandable. Although Lewton persuaded them to keep Tourneur as director, there was little faith on the part of the executives that the film would do anything to alleviate the studio's financial problems. The commercial performance of *Cat People* on its release, however, proved that there was a market for more intelligent genre films, and vindicated Lewton's belief that, when it comes to scaring an audience, less can be more.

Playing at first run theatres for over three months, the film took in excess of $4 million worldwide and played a large part in keeping RKO in business. Indeed, such was the success of the film that RKO were forced to hold back the release of the next two Lewton films while *Cat People* continued to draw audiences. Over the next three years, Lewton's unit produced ten further films, all but two of them in the horror genre and all featuring a similar atmospheric style. The first of these, *I Walked With a Zombie* (Jacques Tourneur, 1943), was co-written by Curt Siodmak and based loosely around Charlotte Bronte's novel *Jane Eyre*. The final three (all period films) featured Boris Karloff, brought to RKO by new studio head Jack Gross, who had previously been at Universal. Gross was keen to see a shift to Universal's style of genre film, a move that Lewton successfully, and thankfully, resisted. Nevertheless, the studio bosses still came up with the titles, and *Curse of the Cat People* reunited producer and scriptwriter along with the three main stars of the original. Despite publicity promising 'feline fingers that could rip young flesh to shreds!' the sequel's narrative is notable for having virtually nothing to do with that of the first film, with Irena appearing as a benign imaginary friend of Amy, the neglected young daughter of a now-married Oliver and Alice.

Although the success of the series didn't result in a rash of similar productions from other studios, Lewton's style influenced a number of films from directors who had been involved with him at RKO, including Tourneur's *Night of The Demon* (1957) and Robert Wise's *The Haunting* and *Audrey Rose* (1977). Lewton's low-key atmospherics and effective use of shadow and off-screen sound continues to influence supernatural films from *The Legend of Hell House* through to the recent *Paranormal Activity* and *Conjuring* franchises. *Cat People*'s narrative approach of bringing horror 'home' was one that would be embraced in the decades that followed, beginning with Alfred Hitchcock's *Psycho* and continuing through films such as *Rosemary's Baby* and *The Exorcist* (William Friedkin, 1973). These latter two films also share *Cat People*'s association of horror with female sexuality, another important concept in the genre discussed in more detail in later chapters.

RKO's commercial success failed to inspire the Hollywood majors to return to the genre that had been so popular a decade earlier. Whilst the poor quality of many of the films emerging from the smaller studios such as Monogram and PRC during the early 1940s undoubtedly played some part, the decline of interest in the traditional horror film is perhaps easy to explain. In an environment that saw the birth of the atomic bomb, a real-life terror capable of wiping out cities at a single stroke, creaking coffins in Transylvanian castles no longer seemed so scary. It was a fact acknowledged by Universal who, following the relative success of *Frankenstein Meets the Wolf Man* (Roy William Neill, 1943), added Dracula to the mix in *House of Frankenstein* (Erle C. Kenton, 1944) and *House of Dracula* (Erle C. Kenton, 1945), before ultimately descending into all-out parody in the *Abbott and Costello Meet...* films.

A preoccupation with technology, along with Cold War paranoia and an explosion of interest in UFO sightings, saw the mad scientist films of the late 1930s and early 40s evolve into the sci-fi/horror hybrids of the 50s. Films featuring society under attack from giant monsters (usually caused by radiation or some scientific experiment gone awry) began with *The Beast from 20,000 Fathoms* (Eugène Lourié,

1953, itself prompted by a hugely-successful re-release of RKO's *King Kong*) and continued through *Them!* ([Gordon Douglas, 1954] featuring giant ants), *Tarantula* ([Jack Arnold, 1955] a giant spider) and numerous others. We will discuss the development of this hybrid genre in more detail in our chapter on David Cronenberg's 1986 remake of the sci-fi/horror film *The Fly* (Kurt Neumann, 1958).

Across the wider industry, Hollywood emerged from the Second World War in an extremely strong position, with domestic audience numbers higher than ever, reaching a peak of up to 90 million attendances per week in 1946 (see Lev 2003: 7). However the American film business, and the Hollywood majors in particular, quickly encountered a succession of political, technological and societal changes that would precipitate the decline of the studio system and ultimately threaten the entire industry.

In the immediate aftermath of the war, foreign market income from countries such as Britain and Italy was hit by quota systems on American film imports, introduced in an attempt to get national industries back up and running. Closer to home, in 1947 Hollywood was rocked by an investigation into communist infiltration in the film industry, which resulted in a number of actors, screenwriters and directors being called to testify before the House Committee on Un-American Activities. So-called 'friendly' witnesses incriminated colleagues who they believed to have involvement with the Communist Party; 'unfriendly' witnesses refused to testify and were jailed and blacklisted. The following year, the finalisation of the 'Paramount Decree' legally enforced production companies to separate their exhibition businesses over the next five years, effectively dismantling the system of vertical integration and bringing an end to the studios' domination of the industry.

However, the final, and potentially most dangerous, problem confronting Hollywood was the arrival of television in the late 1940s. In the seven years to 1953 cinema audiences steadily decreased by 50 per cent, whilst the number of television sets in the US grew to over 20 million. In this same period, increasing numbers of American families were moving out of cities into the suburbs, restricting their access to cinemas and leading to the emergence of the drive-in. Situated out of town, the drive-in attracted young families and teenagers, often playing low-budget, independent and foreign films. The whole landscape of the American film industry was changing, and the initial response by the studios was to cut back production, tighten budgets, and dispense with staff. Relying on tried and tested formulae, they became more conservative in the types of films they released; in the wake of the HUAC hearings none of them wanted to be accused of producing un-American material.

Abandoned by Hollywood, the horror genre had faltered once again and was in desperate need of new blood. Step forward a modest British studio who saw opportunity in the changes sweeping the industry, and whose success in revitalising the traditional horror film would make it the genre's dominant force for over a decade. The next phase in the evolution of the horror film would be marked by a return to Gothic literature, and the re-appearance of some familiar characters.

Bibliography

Bansak, Edmund G. (2003) *Fearing the Dark: The Val Lewton Career*. Jefferson: McFarland & Co.

Clarens, Carlos (1969) *Horror Movies: An Illustrated Survey*. London: Secker & Warburg.

Lev, Peter (2003) *Transforming the Screen, 1950-1959*. Berkley: University of California Press.

Newman, Kim (1999) *Cat People*. London: BFI.

Prawer, S.S. (1980) *Caligari's Children: The Film as Tale of Terror*. Oxford University Press.

Rigby, Jonathan (2007) *American Gothic: Sixty Years of Horror Cinema*. London: Reynolds & Hearn Ltd.

Endnotes

1   The use of titles specifically designed to bring in audiences was a technique that would prove popular amongst exploitation film-makers and distributors, particularly during the 1950s and 60s, and will be discussed in more detail in our chapter on *Night of the Living Dead*.

2   Such self-reflexivity is a prominent feature of the so-called 'postmodern' horror films that proliferated in the late 1990s, and will be discussed at length in our chapter on *Wes Craven's New Nightmare*.

Chapter 4

English Gothic

The Curse of Frankenstein
Terence Fisher, UK 1957

Recommended viewing
Dracula (Terence Fisher, 1958)
The Mummy (Terence Fisher, 1959)
Frankenstein Must Be Destroyed! (Terence Fisher, 1969)
The Wicker Man (Robin Hardy, 1973)
The Company of Wolves (Neil Jordan, 1984)
Hellraiser (Clive Barker, 1987)

Introduction

Given the country's input in the success of the Hollywood horror films of the 1930s, in terms of source material as well as technicians and actors, horror film production in Britain was remarkably slow to emerge. This was due in no small part to the stringent censorship rules of the BBFC, who did their best to dissuade British studios from making such films. With the introduction of the 'X' certificate in the mid-1950s, the opportunity arose (for those brave enough) to foster a new generation of horror fans now effectively ignored by the Hollywood studios.

In this chapter we take a look at the British horror film industry. In particular we investigate how one studio took up the reins of the genre and went on to dominate it for almost two decades. Matched only by the golden age of Universal in the 1930s and 40s, Hammer Films produced some of the genre's most iconic images and characters through dozens of productions, while breaking box office records around the world. As our case study for this chapter we will look at the company's first foray into the genre, one which would lay the foundations for their success and set the template for the English Gothic horror film as it flourished into the 1960s and 70s.

Background

Following the introduction of the 'H' classification, and later certifcation (see Chapter 2), the British Board of Film Censors expressed a hope that producers and exhibitors would be deterred from dealing with such films (see Conrich 2002: 59). The local industry at least took heed, as very few such films were made in Britain during the 1930s and 40s. Nevertheless, the exhibition of 'H' films remained a source of constant concern for the country's moral guardians, and between 1942 and 1945 there was a ban on the import of horror films into Britain and on the issuance of 'H' certification for local product (see Pirie 1973: 22; Petley 2002). As such, noteworthy British genre films made prior to the 1950s are few and far between: Alfred Hitchcock's *The Lodger* (1927); T. Hayes Hunter's *The Ghoul*, starring Boris Karloff and displaying a German Expressionist influence through the work of cinematographer Gunther Krampf and former Ufa make-up artist Heinrich Heitfeld;[1] *The Man Who Changed His Mind* (Robert Stevenson, 1936), again starring Karloff in a forerunner of the 'mad doctor' series of films he would make at the turn of the decade for Columbia Pictures; and Ealing's influential portmanteau *Dead of Night* (Alberto Cavalcanti, Charles Crichton, Basil Dearden and Robert Hamer, 1945). Although other horror-themed films were made in Britain during this time, their standard in general is poor and they are rarely if ever seen today. In particular, the actor Tod Slaughter brought audiences murder and mayhem in a number of Vaudeville-tinged melodramas throughout the 1930s and 40s with titles such as *Sweeney Todd, The Demon Barber of Fleet Street* (George King, 1936) and *The Face at the Window* (George King, 1939).

By the early 1950s, the British film industry in general was in poor shape. Rank, the country's dominant studio since the late 1930s, teetered on the edge of bankruptcy. The company was still recovering from the hugely expensive box-office disaster *Caesar and Cleopatra* (Gabriel Pascal, 1945) and audiences were tiring of their brand of inoffensive, bland productions. Ealing Studios, whose gentle, if socially-conscious comedies had been extremely successful over the previous decade, was also in decline. British cinema audiences were changing, just as they were in the US, and studios were finding it difficult to attract the growing youth market. At the same time the Wheare Report (1950), a governmental review of British film censorship, recommended changes to what was viewed as a confusing and restrictive classification system. The U, A and H ratings were replaced by U (suitable for all), C (especially suitable for children), A (suitable for all but containing adult themes) and X (for adults only). The introduction of the X certificate (which strictly forbade anyone under 16 from viewing) allowed the responsible release of non-horror films for adult audiences that would previously have been banned or, as had been the case with the violent gangster film *No Orchids for Miss Blandish* (St. John Leigh Clowes, 1947), cause an outcry if released as suitable for all viewers.

The arrival of the X rating was a double-edged sword for exhibitors, however. Although the onus of discretion had been taken from them as to deciding who should be allowed to see what, this new 'adults only' classification brought with it certain undesirable connotations. From the late 1940s, films had been emerging from continental Europe that increasingly centred on sexual relationships, featuring mild nudity or sexually suggestive imagery. Now passed as suitable for adult viewing, such films played at independent 'art' cinemas and private cinema clubs, attracting what became known as the 'dirty mac brigade'. As such, the X certificate quickly became associated with foreign sex films and cheap exploitation pictures, and high-street cinemas were reluctant to show anything that could be perceived as disreputable. At this time two cinema chains, Rank and ABC, dominated film exhibition in Britain, and both were struggling with rapidly shrinking audience figures. Whilst Rank's 'family-friendly' approach meant that they initially refused to exhibit X-rated films out of principle, ABC were concerned about showing films from which much of their potential audience would be excluded by law. The knock-on effect was that British film-makers were unwilling to produce anything which would receive an X rating, and even mainstream foreign-language films were heavily cut by their distributors to ensure an A rating.

However there were some in the industry who viewed the new rating as an opportunity rather than a barrier. Witnessing the commercial success of the macabre French thriller *Les Diaboliques* (Henri-Georges Clouzot, 1954), the management of a small independent British studio saw a lucrative market for mainstream, but X-rated, entertainment.

Formerly a music hall comedian performing under the pseudonym of Will Hammer, businessman William Hinds founded Hammer Productions in 1934. One year later he joined with Enrique Carreras, a Spanish immigrant who ran a small chain of cinemas, to form the distribution company Exclusive Films. After producing only five films, including the Bela Lugosi vehicle *The Mystery of the Mary Celeste* (Denison Clift, 1936), a decline in fortunes forced Hammer Productions into bankruptcy. Nevertheless, Exclusive continued to operate as a distributor throughout the war years, and in 1946 produced a series of short documentaries. Building on the relative success of these, Hammer Films was resurrected to produce low-budget feature films. Following a series of forgettable crime dramas Hammer struck gold with an adaptation of a BBC radio serial, *Dick Barton – Special Agent* (Alfred J. Goulding, 1948). For the next six years the company was extremely prolific, churning out cheap but successful films based on radio serials featuring well-known characters such as PC49 and The Saint, as well as original crime dramas and short musicals. In 1955 Hammer released yet another adaptation, this time based on a hugely popular television science-fiction serial by Nigel Kneale broadcast by the BBC in 1953, originally entitled *The Quatermass Experiment*. Although viewed by Hammer as another low-budget project with built-in audience appeal, the film was to have an enormous impact on the fortunes of the company, shaping the path that it would follow for the next twenty years and a legacy that would last far longer.

The Quatermass Xperiment – as it was retitled, in a nod to the X certificate – tells the story of Victor Carroon, an astronaut whose rocket crash lands in the English countryside. As the authorities try to ascertain what happened to two missing crew members Carroon begins to mutate, escaping from hospital and embarking on a violent terror spree. His transformation complete, the octopus-like creature he has become takes refuge in Westminster Abbey and prepares to spawn. However, Professor Quatermass, responsible for the rocket project, tracks the creature down and orders its electrocution. Quality-wise, the film is a vast improvement on Hammer's previous output, thanks primarily to writer-director Val Guest and the acting of Richard Wordsworth as Carroon. Wordsworth's mute performance, reminiscent of Karloff's in *Frankenstein*, generates pathos and fear in equal measure as he undergoes his hideous transformation. Just as Hammer's adaptations of radio serials had given audiences something new (the ability to watch as well as listen), so their film version of *Quatermass* offered more horror and violence than would be allowed on the BBC at that time. As such, it was inevitable that it would receive an X rating, and Hammer were happy to emphasise the fact in its titling for its UK release (much to the dismay of the BBFC). Borrowing a tactic from *Les Diaboliques*, publicity materials made a point of playing up the film's more horrific aspects, and dared audiences to watch it alone. The tactic worked, and it was a huge box-office success in both the UK and America, where it was released as *The Creeping Unknown*.

With *The Quatermass Xperiment* becoming their most financially successful film to date, Hammer immediately shelved the historical and radio adaptation projects they had lined up, and scheduled more science-fiction films. *X-The Unknown* (Leslie Norman, 1956), from an original screenplay by Jimmy Sangster, was again titled to highlight the adults-only rating, while *Quatermass 2* (Val Guest, 1957) was based on Nigel Kneale's follow-up TV serial from two years earlier. The success of both of these enhanced Hammer's reputation for producing quality adult-oriented entertainment, but it was to be their next release that cemented it. In 1956, the manager of a small American company, Associated Artists Productions, had approached the studio with a script by Milton Subotsky and Max Rosenberg based on Mary Shelley's *Frankenstein*. The idea appealed to Hammer's appetite for projects with built-in audience recognition, and a deal was struck for AAP to provide 50 per cent of the film's funding. The remainder was to come jointly from Hammer and ABPC, owners of the ABC cinema chain, who were now more appreciative of the box-office potential of X-rated product.

The film, to be entitled *Frankenstein and the Monster*, was originally viewed as a low-budget black-and-white production, and Hammer began by making enquiries into the availability of Boris Karloff to star as the baron. At the time Karloff was out of favour in Hollywood, finding much of his work in theatre and television, but had appeared in a number of genre B-movies and was seen as a potentially inexpensive box-office draw. These enquiries no doubt attracted the attentions of Universal, who were quick to warn Hammer that any copyright infringements would be severely dealt with. Although Shelley's novel itself was in the public domain, Universal would not allow the use of any elements introduced in their own series of films; in particular, the monster must not resemble their creation in any way. On reviewing Subotsky and Rosenborg's treatment, Hammer bosses concluded that it contained too many references to the Universal series, especially the first two sequels. The script was rejected but the project remained alive, and writing duties were handed to Jimmy Sangster. The script that he submitted, now titled *The Curse of Frankenstein*, impressed the studio so much that they immediately sanctioned a budget increase and proudly announced that theirs would be the first Frankenstein film shot in colour.

Although tinting had been used in Hollywood film since the early 1920s, it is worth noting that even after three decades many in the industry still saw the use of colour as self-defeating (see Buscombe 1985). Rather than increasing realism, they said, colour actually highlighted the artificiality of film, with flesh tones in particular notoriously difficult to reproduce, and required expensive lighting. Until colour photography became suitably life-like, many film-makers were of the opinion that, far from enhancing the realistic film experience, colour gave the impression of a make-believe world. This view is exemplified by the 1939 film *The Wizard of Oz* (Victor Fleming), where the opening and closing sequences depicting Dorothy's everyday life in Kansas are in monochrome, while her fantasy adventures in Oz are shown in vivid colour. Well into the 1940s, full colour tended to be used almost exclusively in genres such as the musical or the historical spectacle, to produce 'larger than life' visuals. It was only with the introduction of cheaper and more practical competitors to Technicolor in the early 1950s that colour film really took off. Along with innovations such as CinemaScope, 3D and stereo sound, it was seen as a valuable tool in the battle against the threat of television.

In the beleaguered British industry, the added cost of colour stock meant that black-and-white film would remain popular well into the 1960s. Nevertheless, the success of *The Quatermass Xperiment* had convinced Hammer that there was a market for horrific films, and the visual possibilities presented by Sangster's script made it worth the extra investment. Given the task of bringing *Curse* to the screen was Terence Fisher, a prolific director of low-budget British crime dramas who had previously worked for Hammer on the science-fiction films *Four-Sided Triangle* (1953) and *Spaceways* (1953), amongst others. It is safe to say that Fisher did not subscribe to Val Lewton's view on the power of suggestion, commenting that 'it's popular and fashionable to say that the unseen is the most scaring; I don't believe this! I believe the seen is the most scaring thing I can think of...' (quoted in Frank 1977: 66-67). Fisher turned down the opportunity of watching the original Universal films, determined to create something new and exciting for modern audiences. Bearing in mind Universal's threats of legal action, he would also want to avoid subconsciously introducing elements of the earlier productions into his own film.

Whilst their previous X-rated films had utilised (relatively) well-known American actors as a draw for US audiences (Brian Donlevy as Quatermass, and Dean Jagger in *X-The Unknown*), for *Curse* Hammer were confident enough to use an all-British cast. The pairing of Peter Cushing and Christopher Lee in the lead roles was one that would be repeated many times over the following two decades, as they quickly became iconic figures both at Hammer and in the wider horror genre. At the time, however, their careers were on very different levels. Cushing was already familiar to

British television audiences through his award-winning work in a number of prestigious BBC television adaptations, including the roles of Darcy in *Pride and Prejudice* and Winston Smith in a Nigel Kneale-scripted version of George Orwell's *1984*. He had also starred alongside Laurence Olivier in his film of *Hamlet* (1948), and in Nigel Kneale's BBC play *The Creature*, itself later adapted into a film (*The Abominable Snowman* [Val Guest, 1957]) by Hammer. Conversely, Lee had struggled for his big break in acting, appearing in dozens of films of little note. He blamed his height for holding him back, a trait that effectively won him the role of Frankenstein's monster. Like Karloff before him, Lee was happy to be made unrecognisable under heavy make-up, on the basis that he wasn't getting anywhere looking the way he did without it.

Textual Analysis

Orphaned as a teenager, the precocious Victor Frankenstein hires a tutor, Paul Krempe, to indulge his passion for science. Over the years, their research leads them to the study of life itself, and, after they successfully reanimate a dead dog, Victor insists that they use their knowledge to create a living human being. Paul reluctantly goes along with the plan but his doubts grow, especially following the arrival of Victor's betrothed cousin, Elizabeth. Realising that Victor is becoming increasingly unbalanced, Paul tries to convince Elizabeth to leave but she refuses. Requiring only a suitable brain to complete his creation, Victor arranges for the brilliant scientist Professor Bernstein to visit. Paul is unable to stop Victor killing the professor and raiding the crypt, but during a struggle the professor's brain is damaged. Victor perseveres, transplanting the brain and bringing his creature to life. It attacks Victor, escaping and killing an old man and his grandson before being shot in the head by Paul. The creature apparently dead, Paul announces that he is leaving, not knowing that Victor has dug up the creature's corpse and returned it to his laboratory, and to life. The housemaid Justine, with whom Victor has been having an affair, attempts to blackmail him, but she is locked in the laboratory with the creature and killed. On the eve of his wedding to Elizabeth, Victor re-introduces Paul to the creature, now able to obey simple commands. Paul is disgusted and leaves, followed by Victor. Elizabeth goes to the laboratory as the creature escapes its chains, making its way to the roof. Following a confrontation with Victor the creature is set alight and falls into the laboratory's vat of acid. Jailed for his creation's murders and unable to convince a visiting priest of his innocence, Victor is led to his execution, watched by Paul and Elizabeth.

Hammer's first fully-fledged horror film opens with a scene-setting title card in Gothic script. Referring to a 'legend still told with horror the world over', its wording acknowledges the audience's inherent knowledge of the Frankenstein story (or at least the popularised version of it). However, any thoughts the viewer may have about seeing the same old monster movie are quickly dispelled. Whereas Universal chose to open their classic horror films to the sedate strains of Swan Lake and the like, Hammer signal their intentions with an ominous orchestral crash over a screen bathed in crimson. From the outset, the studio's literal 'blood and thunder' approach to the genre sought to distance their horror films from what had gone before, and the result could easily have become an exercise in lurid exploitation. But despite the director's pronouncements on the power of graphic scares, *Curse* emerges as an impressively restrained production, using both visual and audio cues to work the audience's imagination.

The distinctive musical scores by composer James Bernard, already heard in both *The Quatermass Xperiment* and *X The Unknown*, were to be an important feature of Hammer's horror films through to the mid-1970s. Here, the music first works to build anticipation and tension through the credits sequence, introducing the signature theme for Frankenstein that would continue throughout the numerous sequels. But Bernard's more sedate moments, such as in the early scene where young Victor meets with his aunt and cousin Elizabeth, are equally worthy of note. Coupled with the detailed yet economical set design that Hammer's horror films would become famous for, sequences such as this give the impression of a classic British melodrama. One can imagine audiences weaned on Ealing comedies and Gainsborough costume dramas being lulled into a false sense of security, making the violence and horror when it arrives all the more shocking.

Visually, a similar effect is achieved through Fisher's use of colour. Following the opening credits, much of the palette of *Curse* is subdued, consisting of low-key greys and browns. It is a washed-out canvas that serves to highlight and intensify the blood and gore when it comes, exemplified by the scene in which Paul and Victor find the creature following its murder of the child and grandfather. Here the gouts of crimson that spurt from the gunshot wound in the creature's head contrast sharply with the muted greens and browns of the forest backdrop for shock effect. In *Curse*, as in much of Fisher's later work for Hammer, there are numerous setups where otherwise dull palettes are set off with splashes of bright red. These begin with the fire buckets in Victor's gaol cell, and continue through the bubbling demijohns in the baron's laboratory, Elizabeth's dress, decanters of red wine, and so on. Such highlighting can draw the viewer's eye to a particular area of the shot, such as those around the head of the corpse as it lies in the laboratory, foreshadowing its off-screen decapitation. The use of colour spots for dramatic effect is a common tactic across all cinematic genres, and Nicolas Roeg's British horror film *Don't Look Now* is particularly well known for its striking use of red highlights.

Whilst Fisher's attitude to visual horror meant that he wasn't afraid to document the surgical details of Frankenstein's experiments, many of the more explicit moments are obscured through careful camera positioning. When Paul removes the sheet from the stolen corpse's head, the tracking movement of the camera affords the audience a teasing glimpse of the dead face before it slides out of shot. It is left to Paul to describe the effect of hungry birds on the head, and the viewer's imagination to fill in the gaps: 'The eyes... half the head's eaten away!' Again there is the briefest glimpse of the corpse's face as Frankenstein disposes of the head in the laboratory's vat of acid, replacing the Universal films' ubiquitous sulphur pit. Similarly, while the death of Justine the housemaid occurs off-screen, her blood-curdling screams give the audience a good idea of what's happening in the laboratory, with Frankenstein's smile making the sequence all the more chilling. Also worthy of note is Professor Bernstein's death which, although bloodless, seems particularly shocking. After Victor sends him falling from the balcony there is no expected cut away; like Frankenstein, the camera looks on impassively as the professor's body falls, his head thudding against the floor below.

Much of the film's running time is spent on the preparation and lead-up to the introduction of the monster. Whereas Whale's 1931 adaptation sufficed with the stealing of a body in the opening scene followed by the acquisition of an unfortunately criminal brain, here we see the baron gathering the various body parts in some detail. The acquisition of the creature's eyes, in particular, is worthy of note. The sequence begins with a shot of the baron walking along a darkened street carrying a surgeon's bag, angled so that only his legs and the bag are visible. This was to be a recurring image throughout the Hammer Frankenstein series, signalling to the audience that the baron was on the prowl and that some new body part would soon be in his possession. The exchange that follows, between the baron and the charnel house worker, is shot so that neither man's face is visible, highlighting the anonymity of the transaction. Cushing frequently stated that he based his interpretation of Frankenstein on the real-life surgeon Robert Knox, who in the nineteenth century paid grave robbers (and murderers) Burke and Hare to supply him with fresh corpses for dissection, no questions asked. Just as Frankenstein doesn't care where the eyes came from, so the charnel house worker isn't concerned as to the use they are to be put - as long as he is paid.

The shot that follows, of the baron examining one of the disembodied eyeballs in a pair of tweezers, is particularly well known. Framed with the eyeball in the foreground, Cushing's own eye is behind a large magnifying glass, making it appear enlarged and distorted (see Fig 4.1). An iconic image, it can be seen again in various films, such as the Cushing/Lee vehicles *The Skull* (Freddie Francis, 1965) and *The Creeping Flesh* (Freddie Francis, 1972) as well as *Frankenstein and the Monster From*

Figure 4.1

Hell (Terence Fisher, 1973), and was brilliantly parodied in the spoof *Top Secret!* (Jim Abrahams, David Zucker & Jerry Zucker, 1984) where Cushing removes the magnifying glass to reveal that his eye really is that large. Eyes (and damage done to them) remain an enduring motif in horror films. Whether punctured by wood splinters, injected with hypodermic needles, sliced open with a razor, popped out of a head in 3D or pinned open with needles or fish hooks, audiences are guaranteed to squirm when they see any kind of trauma to this most delicate of organs.

Of course, the highlight in terms of shock value, and the source of much anticipation in any Frankenstein film, is the first appearance of his creation. Mindful of the audience recognition that existed for Universal's iconic monster, the studio's resident make-up expert Phil Leakey was tasked with delivering a completely new look for their creature. Keen to stay away from anything mechanical, the result is a hand-stitched monstrosity, undoubtedly more visually disturbing than any previous incarnation and a blood-spattered yardstick against which all subsequent versions would be measured. Terence Fisher masterfully builds the suspense prior to its introduction, ensuring the audience knows that the creature is alive while Victor and Paul are arguing downstairs. Frankenstein returns to the laboratory, rushing to the door and flinging it open, with the camera following close behind. As the music shrieks, he steps aside to reveal a figure standing centre frame, the tension becoming almost unbearable as it jerkily reaches for the bandages that cover its face. The music reaching a crescendo, it rips the bandages off and the camera swoops in so that the creature's horrific face fills the screen. Fixing its gaze on Frankenstein, its mouth turns into a ferocious snarl before lunging forward to grab him by the neck. It remains a powerful sequence today, and one can only imagine the effect that it had on cinema audiences at the time of the film's release. Although the actual reveal recalls that of Karloff in 1931 (with a speeded-up dolly replacing James Whale's repeated jump cuts), the effect is altogether more terrifying.

Born as a murderous, mindless brute, the product of Frankenstein's experiments is far from the thoughtful creation of the novel or even the pathetic creature of the early Universal films (Fig 4.2). Its first instinct is to destroy, immediately trying to throttle its creator before escaping and killing two characters, a blind grandfather and a small child, who are guaranteed to elicit audience sympathy. Yet by the time the creature is introduced, well into the second half of the film, the real villain has already been established. It is primarily in the characterisation of Frankenstein himself as the 'bad guy' that Hammer's interpretation of the story differs from what had gone before. By turns utterly charming and downright

Figure 4.2

sadistic, Cushing's Frankenstein displays the classic attributes of a sociopath. Far from being merely a misguided scientist looking to further human knowledge, he is a ruthless, cold-blooded murderer (and, later in the series, violent rapist), willing to go to any lengths to realise his obsession.

More so than *Der Golem*, in this film (and the sequels that followed) we can see the typical 'overreacher' plot in action, with Frankenstein's reckless thirst for power consuming him and endangering those around him. Unlike Rabbi Low, Frankenstein's experiments are purely for his own personal gain and satisfaction, rather than for the benefit of the wider community. This distinction is first demonstrated in *Curse* following the revival of a dead dog, where Paul's excitement with what they have achieved contrasts with the baron's cold and calculating demeanour. What Paul sees as the pinnacle of their achievements, a suspended animation technique that will save hundreds of lives during surgery, Frankenstein regards as merely the first step towards his ultimate goal of emulating God: 'we've opened the door, now we need to go through it!' Determined that they will not publish their work until he has achieved this goal, Frankenstein becomes agitated, pacing back and forth and frequently staring off into space with wide eyes. It is the first sign of the madness that would overcome him as the series progressed.

With the prison warder describing him as 'dangerous' and 'raving mad', Frankenstein's character is quickly set up in the film's opening sequence. As becomes obvious, the baron is not a spiritual man, yet has asked for a priest to hear his story because of the influence such a person commands. Frankenstein seeks to use him as a tool to secure his release, and the baron's manipulation and use of others for his own ends is a trait that is evident throughout *Curse*. Paul, Justine and Professor Bernstein are all (mis)used before being cast aside, and he is equally dismissive of his family. In the sequence following his mother's funeral, the absence of any sense of loss in Cushing's voice-over, or in the acting of Melvyn Hayes as the young Victor, give an indication of the character's lack of compassion and casual disregard for human life, even as he is single-minded in his desire to (re)create it. When his cousin Elizabeth tells him that she would like to help with his work, he suggests that perhaps she will, '…one day'. The clear implication from the glint in his eye is that he sees her as a potential subject of, or donor for, future experiments. He is also more than willing to use her safety to force Paul into helping with his work, threatening to introduce her to the world of science, 'and see how she likes it'.

Making Frankenstein a member of nobility was one narrative invention that Hammer did carry over from earlier adaptations. This works well with Jimmy Sangster's decision to make him the villain of the piece, reinforcing the character's air of arrogance, self-obsession and ruthlessness. The approach also played to the growing anti-authoritarianism of the younger 1950s audience, something that, as we will see in subsequent chapters, would be exploited more obviously in the genre over the following decades. Extremely well spoken, Peter Cushing undoubtedly lends Frankenstein an air of authority and educated gentility, and his first appearance may come as something of a shock. In the dank prison cell furnished with a scattering of straw, a dejected Frankenstein is slumped in a corner; it is a sequence that foreshadows one later in the film, when the creature sits obediently behind a locked door in the laboratory. Wearing what were obviously very good clothes that are now dusty and torn, he appears dirty and dishevelled, his hair wild and unkempt, with the beginnings of an untrimmed beard. The audience's interest is immediately piqued: what could have happened to such a man to put him not only in this physical state but in a prison cell? As in the source novel, Sangster employs a narrative framing device; but whereas Shelley uses letters and diaries to add an air of verisimilitude to the proceedings, Sangster's flashback structure serves to imbue the remainder of the film with an air of fateful tragedy.

Hammer's horror films are typically short (under 90 minutes), with later productions frequently released as double-bills, and can rarely be described as boring. When dealing with existing source material the stories were routinely stripped back to the bare bones, with *The Quatermass Xperiment* cut down from six half-hour television episodes to a little over 80 minutes. For *Curse*, Jimmy Sangster returned to the original novel for his adaptation, albeit significantly paring down the story, and stripping out or consolidating many of the extraneous characters, scenes and locations. In a concession to the film's brevity (and budget), rather than attending university Victor employs Paul Krempe as a private tutor immediately following his mother's funeral. In Cushing's portrayal, Frankenstein does not exhibit any hint of self-doubt about the morality or wisdom of his experiments that are evident in the Universal films (particularly *Bride of Frankenstein*). Instead, these traits are trans-posed onto Paul, who occupies a much more prominent role than that given him in the novel. His introduction brings another display of Frankenstein's self-confidence and manipulation when it is revealed that Victor has been corresponding with his prospective teacher under the guise of his own (long-dead) father.

Although he proves himself 'an admirable tutor' it is obvious from the following passage-of-time montage that Paul's quest for knowledge is no match for that of the baron. Having learnt all he had to teach within two years, it is now Frankenstein at the blackboard while Paul looks on. They have also moved on from chemistry to electronics, certainly ahead of their time in the early to mid-nineteenth century, though as an indicator of the direction of their research an anatomical study of the human body still hangs by the blackboard. Throughout the film, Paul is posi-tioned as the audience's empathy figure and the voice of reason. Although he ini-tially agrees to go along with Frankenstein's experiments he becomes increasingly concerned about what he sees as 'a revolt against nature'. However, Paul's stance against the experiments only really comes about following the arrival of Elizabeth, the baron's betrothed cousin. Elizabeth is naïve and vulnerable, and the audience fears for her in the same way as Paul does because they know what is happening in the laboratory, whilst she remains oblivious. Her indebtedness to Victor and his family means that she can never leave him, something Paul is unable to understand.

The character of Elizabeth is underwritten, a fact acknowledged by Jimmy Sang-ster himself (Sangster 2001: 31, 58), and as such her relevance to the narrative is often underestimated. As the virginal heroine, betrothed to a mysterious elder and sent to live in an imposing house with a secret behind a locked door, there are a number of Gothic and Romantic conventions at work. The script's adherence to this aspect of the original novel marks an important distinction between *Curse* and many of the Hammer horror films that followed. Beginning with 1958's *Dracula*, and especially from 1959's *The Mummy* onwards, the films would take more of a classical Hollywood plot structure. In practically all of the subsequent Hammer horrors, the villain/monster would disrupt the lives of a young couple, who would then spend the duration of the film attempting to free themselves and the commu-nity from the clutches of evil. Although the heroine in particular would be directly threatened, the climax inevitably featured the couple in an embrace, the monster finally defeated (until the next sequel).[2] In *Curse*, this relationship is complicated by the fact that the heroine is betrothed to the villain, although by the end of the story we find Elizabeth in the arms of Paul as Victor is led to his execution. Hammer's horror films (especially those directed by Fisher, who was devoutly religious) have a strict moral code, in which right and wrong, good and evil, are very clearly delineated. Characters are either very good or very bad; there is little of the ambiguity seen in, for example, Expressionist cinema. As such, throughout *Curse* Frankenstein grows more ruthless and single-mindedly evil, while Paul becomes more determined to stop the experiment, or at least to get Elizabeth as far away from it as possible.

Paul's concern for the safety of Elizabeth, but not for that of the housemaid Justine, demonstrates an aspect of class politics at work in Sangster's narrative. The dark-haired Justine is portrayed as brazen and sexually-charged, unlike the prim and proper (and blonde) Elizabeth. If Elizabeth and Paul represent the sexual repression of Victorian society, Frankenstein's

Figure 4.3

expression of sexual energy through his relationship with the lower-class Justine is a further example of his transgression of accepted boundaries. Regarded as another object that he can use and dispose of as he sees fit, Justine's submissive relationship with the baron is underscored numerous times in Fisher's shot composition, most noticeably when she reveals that she is pregnant and attempts to blackmail him (see Fig 4.3).

Frankenstein's eventual disposal of Justine, locking her in the laboratory with his murderous creation, is a particularly shocking scene that leads into one of the most famous moments of the film. Having listened to her terrified screams, we cut to Victor sitting at the breakfast table with Elizabeth. Victor butters some toast, and calmly asks Elizabeth to 'pass the marmalade'. Working to break the tension from the previous scene, the juxtaposition of cold-blooded murder and domesticity verges on the ridiculous, as does his subsequent comment that Justine 'always was a romantic little thing'. Brilliantly understated in this instance, such comic moments would become more blatant, and frequent, in future Hammer Frankenstein films.

Thematically and stylistically, the Hammer horror films of the 1950s, 60s and 70s form a distinctive and coherent body of work, bringing a recognisable style to the genre and introducing what would become standard generic codes conventions. If Universal introduced to the horror film images of cobweb-filled crypts, moonlit graveyards, creaking coffins, ruined castles and torch-bearing villagers, Hammer augmented them with nightdress-clad virgins in mist-shrouded forests, overtly sexual and religious imagery, and village taverns run by comedic landlords (usually played by character actor Michael Ripper). *Curse*'s opening sequence of a lone traveller on a remote mountain pass, church bells tolling ominously in the distance, would be used again and again by the studio with little variation, whilst the closing image of a young heterosexual couple embracing, the evil defeated (for now) and order restored was a convention that the studio stubbornly stuck with, even as it became increasingly anachronistic. Looking back, therefore, the film's climax is somewhat predictable: the creature destroyed in a bath of acid, an unrepentant Frankenstein is led to the guillotine for his crimes while Paul and Elizabeth look on. The evil is destroyed, good triumphs, and the curtain falls on what Hammer hoped would be another successful big-screen adaptation.

Reception and Aftermath

When *The Curse of Frankenstein* was released in early 1957 it was immediately savaged by critics, particularly in Britain, where it was almost universally loathed. Described as 'repugnant' and 'repulsive', one reviewer (for the *Financial Times*, no less) called for the introduction of a new rating – 'SO', for Sadists Only (all Cooper 2016: 52). Perhaps as much as the blood and violence, critics were concerned with the style of Fisher's direction in relation to the horror films that had gone before. There are no overt fantasy elements, no dream sequences or supernatural occurrences that would tell the audience that they were watching nothing more than a macabre fairy tale. Instead, Fisher sought to present the story in as straightforward and realistic a way as possible, albeit within a fundamentally fantastical diegesis. Frankenstein's laboratory, its cramped design a world away from the grand castle towers of the early Universal films, looks like something that Victor and Paul would have built up over years of research. Similarly, the monster resembled something actually created on the surgeon's table; what had eventually become a figure of fun in the hands of Universal was a source of fear once again.

British critics also seemed shocked that such films could be produced in their own country, and it was in part the very 'Britishness' of the Hammer films that caused outrage in their homeland. Unsurprisingly, Hammer bosses welcomed the fierce criticism the film produced as free publicity, and revelled in their reputation as the disreputable side of British cinema. *Curse* broke box-office records around the world, and was the biggest money-maker of all films released by British studios in 1957. Critics and pressure groups were appalled, but the worldwide box-office returns of *Curse* and the films that followed ensured that they would continue. Over the next few years Gothic horror saw a major resurgence, primarily in Britain through the prolific output of Hammer, but also with film-makers such as Roger Corman (whose loose adaptations of the work of Edgar Allen Poe made a genre icon of Vincent Price) in the US and Mario Bava (with *Black Sunday* [1960] and

Black Sabbath [1964], amongst others) in continental Europe. The genre had entered a bloody new phase and was about to become more popular than ever.

Following the commercial success of *Curse*, Hollywood studios were falling over themselves to engage Hammer in deals for co-productions and distribution, with Warner Bros., Columbia and Universal Pictures all claiming a stake in the British studio's success. It was the relationship with Universal that proved most significant, beginning with a deal to handle the release of Hammer's next horror film, a remake of *Dracula* starring Christopher Lee as the count. When this turned out to be even more financially successful (and critically reviled) than *Curse*, the Hollywood studio handed over all remake rights for their classic horror films in return for lucrative distribution deals. As such, 1959 saw Hammer's version of *The Mummy* while *The Curse of the Werewolf* appeared in 1961 and *The Phantom of the Opera* in 1962, all directed by Terence Fisher. The single Universal remake from this period that failed both critically and commercially was *The Old Dark House* (William Castle, 1963), where the over-the-top antics of American comedian Tom Poston undoubtedly alienated the traditional Hammer horror audience.

Aside from this, the relationship with Universal provided a healthy supply of material. Although *The Mummy* is ostensibly a remake of the Boris Karloff original, its narrative contains a number of elements freely taken from its 1940s sequels, and by 1964 Universal was happy for Hammer to use a Karloff-like design for the monster in *The Evil of Frankenstein* (dir. Freddie Francis), although Cushing's baron remained the star of the show. With the only major Universal monster not to appear in a Hammer film being the invisible man (although there were plans for such a project), the company began introducing their own monsters in one-off films such as *The Gorgon* (Terence Fisher, 1964), *The Reptile* (John Gilling, 1966), and *The Plague of the Zombies* (John Gilling, 1966) with varying degrees of success. They also produced three variations on the story of Jekyll and Hyde, including the exploitative but entertaining *Dr Jekyll and Sister Hyde* (Roy Ward Baker, 1971) as well as a twist on the Jack the Ripper story, *Hands of the Ripper* (Peter Sasdy, 1971).

But it was Baron Frankenstein and Count Dracula who became Hammer's most popular characters, appearing in fourteen films between them and making the actors who portrayed them genre icons. *Curse*'s pairing of Cushing and Lee was repeated in *Dracula* and *The Mummy*, as well as Hammer's 1959 remake of *The Hound of the Baskervilles* (dir. Terence Fisher), and the actors went on to star in literally dozens of horror films throughout the 1960s and 70s, frequently together, and for a variety of British and European studios. A mixture of Lee's reluctance to be typecast and Hammer's doubts about his acting ability meant that he wasn't as prolific as Cushing in their subsequent productions. In the role of Dracula, however, he became the studio's most reliable money-spinner, and (much to Lee's dismay) Hammer's scriptwriters were not averse to inventing their own vampire mythology to enable his numerous resurrections.

Hammer of the 1960s was perhaps the closest that the British film industry came to the Hollywood studio system of the 1920s and 30s. With a consistent stable of actors, writers, directors and other technicians, Hammer was a well-oiled machine, manufacturing popular genre product (although they did make other types of films throughout this period none were as successful or are as well known as their horror output). Whilst their budgets may have been verging on Poverty Row, for the most part the quality and success of the product put the studio almost on a par with the Hollywood majors. Certainly throughout much of the 1960s they were the premier producers of horror cinema, in the UK and around the world, receiving the Queens' Award for Industry in 1968 in recognition of their overseas success.

But as Universal had discovered twenty-five years earlier, there is a limit to how much of the same formula horror audiences will take. By the late 1960s the rise of independent film-makers in the US, as well as competition from British studios such as Amicus and Tigon, who mixed Gothic themes and style with modern narratives, was taking its toll on Hammer. They responded by increasing their rate of production and turning to their most bankable assets, churning out more Dracula and Frankenstein sequels. Unfortunately after more than a decade their brand of period Gothic was looking tired, and Hammer was finding it difficult to appeal to younger audiences. Under the directorship of Michael Carreras, who had taken over the company from his father James in 1970, Hammer experimented with updated storylines. Psychological thrillers such as *Fear in the Night* (Jimmy Sangster, 1972) and *Straight on Till Morning*[3] opened to mixed reviews and generally poor box office, whilst *Dracula AD 1972* (Alan Gibson, 1972) and *The Satanic Rites of Dracula* (Alan Gibson, 1973), which see the vampire resurrected in contemporary 'swinging' London, are universally regarded as failures and remained sources of acute embarrassment for Christopher Lee throughout the remainder of his highly successful career.

Other attempts at 'rebooting' their most successful franchises met with similar results. *The Horror of Frankenstein* (Jimmy Sangster, 1970), a campy, tongue-in-cheek reworking of *Curse* featured the much younger Ralph Bates in the role of the baron. With a relaxation of censorship in the late 1960s, and the revision of the UK ratings system (the age limit for viewing 'X' rated films was raised to 18, and the new 'AA' rating was introduced for viewers aged 14 and over), Hammer became more daring in their depiction of violence, gore and sex. In particular, the studio earned something of a dubious reputation with a trilogy of exploitative lesbian vampire films, loosely based around Sheridan LeFanu's 'Carmilla': *The Vampire Lovers* (Roy

Ward Baker, 1970), *Lust for a Vampire* (Jimmy Sangster, 1971) and *Twins of Evil* (John Hough, 1971). Any appeal to the 'dirty mac brigade' was short-lived, however, with the arrival of more mainstream British sex comedies, which culminated in the highly successful *Confessions of...* series (which, like Hammer, was dependent on US studio funding, in this case Columbia Pictures).

Returning to their roots, Hammer's biggest successes at this time were film adaptations of popular British television comedy series such as *On The Buses* (Harry Booth, 1971), *Love Thy Neighbour* (John Robins, 1973) and *Man About The House* (John Robins, 1974). Indeed, the first *Buses* film became the studio's biggest money-spinner ever, leading to two sequels and plans for a third. But by the mid-1970s Hammer Films was a spent force; its final horror production, *To The Devil A Daughter* (Peter Sykes, 1976), was a commercial and critical failure. An adaptation of a Dennis Wheatley novel from the 1960s, the film was a belated attempt to ride the coattails of the worldwide success of 1973's *The Exorcist*. As we will see in later chapters, by the mid-1970s horror was big business, and a small British studio was unable to compete with the resurgent Hollywood majors. Aside from a brief resurfacing in the early 1980s with two series of one-hour television productions, Hammer Films would be dormant for the next thirty years. Over the previous two decades, however, Hammer and horror had become synonymous, and it is difficult to over-estimate the impact that the studio had on the genre, and the popularity that their films still enjoy today.

The next ten to twenty years were difficult for the horror genre in Britain, with Amicus, Tigon and the rest of Hammer's rivals similarly petering out by the late 1970s. Following the backlash against the genre during the video nasties scare of the early 1980s (discussed in more detail in Chapter 9), horror films from all countries received a particularly rough ride from the BBFC, and British film-makers were reluctant to invest time and money in product that would struggle to see the light of day. Nevertheless there were some success stories during this period, most notably British novelist Clive Barker's modern Gothic *Hellraiser*, which continues to spawn (American) sequels of varying quality. Other notable British productions which harked back to the Gothic tradition include Neil Jordan's visually stunning The *Company of Wolves*, Ken Russell's *Gothic* (1986) and *The Lair of the White Worm* (1988), and Bernard Rose's *Paperhouse* (1988), although none of these were particularly successful at the box office.

Since the turn of the century, British film-makers have had some success in combining traditional Gothic tropes with modern day narratives in well-received films such as *28 Days Later* (Danny Boyle, 2002) (and its sequel), *Dog Soldiers* (Neil Marshall, 2002), *The Descent* (Neil Marshall, 2006) (and its sequel) and 2008's *Eden Lake*, whilst the phenomenal worldwide success of *Shaun of the Dead* (Edgar Wright, 2004) finally proved that horror and comedy could actually work together. Of most interest to fans of classic British horror, however, was the revival of the Hammer Films brand in 2007, following a takeover by a Dutch private equity firm. The company has since produced a number of genre films, including *Let Me In* (Matt Reeves, 2010) (a remake of our case study *Let The Right One In*), *The Resident* (Antii Jokinen, 2011) a contemporary woman-in-peril tale featuring Christopher Lee, and the supernatural period chiller *The Woman in Black* (James Watkins, 2012). Benefitting from the presence of leading man Daniel Radcliffe, fresh from his adventures as Harry Potter, this latter film returned a handsome profit of over $100 million.[4] Although the much-anticipated sequel *Woman in Black 2: Angel of Death* (Tom Harper, 2015) fell well short of the original's success, the canny recruitment of *Goodnight Mommy* (2014) directors Veronika Franz and Severin Fiala for the 2019 release *The Lodge* bodes well for Hammer's continued involvement in the genre that it helped to shape over half a century ago.

Bibliography

Buscombe, Edward 'Sound and Colour'. In Nichols, Bill (ed.) (1985) *Movies and Methods Volume II: An Anthology*. pp. 83-91. Berkeley: University of California Press.

Conrich, Ian 'Horrific films and 1930s British cinema'. In Chibnall, Steve and Petley, Julian (eds) (2002) *British Horror Cinema*. pp. 58-70. London: Routledge.

Cooper, Ian (2016) *Frightmares: A History of British Horror Cinema*. Leighton Buzzard: Auteur.

Harmes, Marcus K. (2015) *The Curse of Frankenstein* (Devil's Advocates). Leighton Buzzard. Auteur.

Kinsey, Wayne (2002) *Hammer Films: The Bray Studio Years*. Richmond, Reynolds & Hearn Ltd.

Mathews, Tome Dewe (1994) *Censored: The History of Film Censorship in Britain*. London, Chatto & Windus Ltd.

Petley, Julian 'FILM: Horror Films'. In Jones, Derek (ed.) (2002) *Censorship: A World Encyclopedia*. pp. 812-815. London: Routledge.

Pirie, David (1973) *A Heritage of Horror: The English Gothic Cinema 1946-1972*. Gordon Fraser, London.

Rose, James (2009) *Beyond Hammer: British Horror Cinema Since 1970*. Leighton Buzzard, Auteur.

Sangster, Jimmy (2001) *Inside Hammer*. Richmond, Reynolds & Hearn Ltd.

Walden, Victoria Grace (2016) *Studying Hammer Horror*. Leighton Buzzard: Auteur.

Endnotes

1. This film disappeared soon after its release and was considered lost for many years.

2. The most obvious exception to this is the mean-spirited *Frankenstein Must Be Destroyed!* (Terence Fisher, 1969), in which both hero and heroine are despatched by the baron, and only after the virginal heroine has been brutally raped.

3. Throughout the 1960s, Hammer had experimented with the psycho-thriller genre, releasing a number of (usually Jimmy Sangster-scripted) films inspired by *Les Diaboliques* and, to a lesser extent, Alfred Hitchcock's *Psycho*. Films such as *Paranoiac* (Freddie Francis, 1963) and *Hysteria* (Freddie Francis, 1965) are rarely mentioned alongside the studio's Gothic horrors.

4. Unless otherwise noted, all box office figures in this book are taken from Box Office Mojo (www.boxofficemojo.com).

Chapter 5

The Birth of Modern Horror

Psycho
Alfred Hitchcock, US 1960

Recommended viewing
The Lodger (Alfred Hitchcock, 1927)
Les Diaboliques (Henri-Georges Clouzot, 1955)
Peeping Tom (Michael Powell, 1960)
Frenzy (Alfred Hitchcock, 1972)
Psycho II (Richard Franklin, 1983)

Introduction

The horror genre is ultimately concerned with the battle between good and evil. As we saw in the previous chapter, at times this can be very clearly delineated, but in real life this is not always the case. As *Psycho*'s Norman Bates says, 'we all go a little mad sometimes'. Evil can lurk anywhere and in anyone, and that is what is really scary. You don't need man-made monsters, cat people or haunted houses; in the here and now there are very real horrors, and it is this idea that still forms the basis of many of the horror films produced today. At the time of its release, Alfred Hitchcock's *Psycho* was truly ground-breaking in its approach to horror in everyday life. Shocking and controversial, it was initially denounced by critics yet became a worldwide box-office sensation and set the direction of the genre for the next fifty years.

One of the most analysed and discussed films in cinema history, and arguably the single most influential film in the evolution of the horror genre, entire books have been written about every aspect of *Psycho*'s production, reception and lasting influence. By contextualising the film in the environment of a Hollywood that found itself under mounting pressures, in this chapter we examine how Hitchcock's low-budget film changed the face of horror forever.

Background

Perhaps the most well known director in twentieth-century cinema, Alfred Joseph Hitchcock was born in London in 1899, the son of a greengrocer. His film career began at the Islington studios of Paramount's Famous Players-Lasky at the age of twenty-one. From designing title cards in the art department, he moved to production design and scriptwriting before taking his first steps in directing with the comedy *Always Tell Your Wife* (1923). When Paramount began to gradually wind down its British operation, Hitchcock moved to Gainsborough Productions, a company formed in 1924 by Michael Balcon. Balcon, a producer who had worked with Hitchcock during his time at Famous Players-Lasky, would go on to be an important figure in the British film industry over the next forty years, primarily through his work at Ealing Studios, which included the first British post-war horror film, *Dead of Night*.

Following his move to Gainsborough, Hitchcock continued as scriptwriter, production designer and assistant director and was sent to Berlin to write and design the first of many co-productions between Gainsborough and Ufa, *The Blackguard* (Graham Cutts, 1925). While at Ufa, he was able to watch directors such as Murnau and Lang at work, and would later respond to any questions about his stylistic influences with the simple reply 'the Germans'. The first film fully directed by Hitchcock, the melodrama *The Pleasure Garden* (1926), was another co-production, with Munchener Lichtspielkunst (MLK), an independent production company set up in Munich in 1918. Certainly, the Germanic influence is visible in this first film, through its use of canted camera angles, chiaroscuro lighting and subjective shots. It was Hitchcock's third film (following the now-lost *The Mountain Eagle* [1926]), that began the association with suspense for which the director is remembered today. *The Lodger*, from 1927, based on a 1913 Jack the Ripper-inspired novel by Marie Belloc Lowndes, introduces a number of elements which would become standard in Hitchcock's later thrillers, such as the innocent hero being suspected of a crime, the attractive blonde heroine, and of course sequences of almost unbearable tension.

By the time he arrived in America at the end of the 1930s, Hitchcock's reputation as a successful thriller director had been cemented with productions such as *The Man Who Knew Too Much* (1934), *The 39 Steps* (1935) and *Sabotage* (1936). His Hollywood adaptation of Daphne duMaurier's *Rebecca* (1940) was the first of several films the director made under contract to producer David O. Selznick at Selznick International. Following *Rebecca*, Hitchcock was loaned out to a number of studios, including RKO, Universal and 20th Century Fox, and by the end of the 1950s the director had also made films for Warner Bros. and Paramount.

Hitchcock's relationship with Selznick in the 1940s was symptomatic of the political and managerial changes occurring in Hollywood throughout that decade and into the 50s. During this period, the 'producer-unit' system of production, discussed in Chapter 3, was gradually replaced by what would become known as the 'package-unit'. With the continuing financial strains being placed on studios, they found it difficult to maintain the amount of talent (actors, actresses, directors and writers) they had on their books, and many contracts were dropped. Films began to be seen as discrete products, rather than as part of a production-line system, and the role of the producer became more powerful. Although they would still oversee films' development, they would often work independently, putting together a 'package' (including a script, stars and director) that could then be sold to a studio. Once an agreement had been made to buy and distribute the finished product, the producer would utilise that studio's facilities and personnel to make the film.

Whilst the studios would continue to produce their own features, these were increasingly outnumbered by the externally-produced films being bought in. This marked the beginning of the end of the classic Hollywood studio system, as power shifted to independent producers and production companies. At the same time, Hollywood began to face stiff competition following the arrival of television, and found it increasingly difficult to draw audiences away from their homes and into cinemas. The majors invested heavily in expensive technological experiments to combat the new medium, including more lavish colour photography, wider screens, and, briefly, 3D. During this period, independent studios such as United Artists as well as new production companies flourished. Lacking the overheads of the big studios (particularly the large backlots, which were becoming increasingly redundant due to a move towards location filming), they were able to produce films on very low budgets. These could either be sold to the major studios for an instant profit, or released through independent distribution companies to cinemas or drive-ins.

Although they had been in operation since the 1930s, drive-in theatres reached the height of their popularity in the 1950s and 60s. 'Baby boomers' who sprang from the marriages and unions of GIs returning from the Second World War, were the teenagers of the late 1950s and early 60s. Benefitting from an increase in disposable income, and keen for the privacy that the venues afforded, teenage audiences fuelled the growth of drive-ins. With the major Hollywood studios cutting back on production, smaller studios and independents stepped in to meet the demand for product. Unsurprisingly, the majority of the productions that filled the demand were geared towards exploiting the teenage market. Emerging during the 1950s, many of these early films were made to cash in on the popularity of science-fiction, but they also included films about car racing, beach parties and anything else the producers thought would interest teenage audiences. Because these films were made so quickly and cheaply, and marketed so strongly, they were able to be topical and react to changing social and cultural environments.

The introduction of television hit cinema audience numbers hard, but the medium also proved to be a lucrative source of income for the more established Hollywood studios. With hundreds of stations across the country desperate for pre-recorded content, studios began selling their film back-catalogues for television broadcast. This was a win-win situation both for the studios and the television stations. Apart from the occasional re-issue of a particularly popular title, most films would rarely be seen again once their initial cinema run had ended. By selling these older films to television, the studios were able to make money without any outlay as well as increasing awareness of their product. The sale of Universal's original monster movies to a nationwide network in the late 1950s was a major development in the resurgence of the horror genre's popularity. On television, the films were often introduced by so-called 'horror hosts', made up as vampires, ghouls and the like, with names such as Vampira and Zacherley. The hosts' jokey introductions to, and interruptions of, the films particularly appealed to younger viewers, and their popularity helped cement the Universal monsters in American popular culture.

The screenings coincided with the enormous success of Hammer's *The Curse of*

Frankenstein (see Chapter 4), and sparked an interest in the horror genre amongst younger audiences. Although the major studios did not see the genre as worthy of big-budget productions, exploitation film-makers were quickly churning out horror films designed to appeal to the new demographic, with titles such as *I Was a Teenage Werewolf* (Gene Fowler, Jr., 1957), *I Was a Teenage Frankenstein* (Herbert L. Strock, 1957) and *Teenage Caveman* (Roger Corman, 1958). Responsible for these three films was AIP (American International Pictures), a studio that would go on to play an important role in the development of the horror genre throughout the 1960s. Realising that teenagers represented the only sustainable market, in the 1950s AIP directed practically all of its resources into making exploitation films for the youth demographic. Playing on the new-found popularity of the old Universal stars, AIP gained a reputation for producing popular horror films featuring Karloff, Peter Lorre, Basil Rathbone and Vincent Price. Although Price had appeared in a number of Universal's later horror films including *The Invisible Man Returns* (Joe May, 1940), he became best known for starring roles in AIP's Roger Corman-directed adaptations of Edgar Allen Poe stories in the 1960s. Along with Peter Cushing and Christopher Lee, Price would be an iconic figure in mainstream horror cinema throughout the 1960s and 70s, his unique serio-comic persona ultimately finding its natural home in campy British horror films such as *The Abominable Dr Phibes* (Robert Fuest, 1971) and *Theatre of Blood* (Douglas Hickox, 1973).

In addition, Price made a number of notable horror films with William Castle, a producer and director who would also be important in the genre over the following decade. At one time a theatre director, Castle had directed Bela Lugosi in a revival of *Dracula* in the 1930s. Moving to cinema in the mid-1940s, Castle tackled everything from crime dramas to adventure, Westerns and comedy, depending on what was in vogue at the time. The success of the Hammer horror films and the *Teenage...* monster films drew him to a genre that was ideally suited to his showmanship approach, and he became well known for the gimmicks surrounding his films. During screenings of *The House on Haunted Hill* (Castle, 1959), a skeleton would seemingly emerge from the cinema screen and fly over the heads of the audience, while the audience's seats were wired to to give selected viewers mild electric jolts during *The Tingler* (Castle, 1959; both of these films starring Price). As well as directing Hammer's remake of *The Old Dark House*, Castle would be instrumental in the making of our case study for Chapter 8, *Rosemary's Baby*. We will further discuss his work, as well as AIP and other independent horror producers during this time, in Chapters 7 and 8.

Alongside the independents, another rich source of drive-in material were the foreign markets, many of whom were enjoying something of a renaissance following Hollywood's cutbacks. One film that was enormously successful in the US was the tense thriller *Les Diaboliques*, already mentioned in our previous chapter. Based on a book by Pierre Boileau and Thomas Narcejac, the film was universally well received, with director Henri-Georges Clouzot touted internationally as the 'new master of suspense'. No doubt offended by the French upstart, Alfred Hitchcock subsequently bought the rights to another of Boileau and Narcejac's books, *D'Entre les Morts*, which he turned into the big-budget Hollywood film *Vertigo* (1958). Although now acknowledged as a classic, Hitchcock's film was originally disliked both by critics and audiences, and was a rare box-office disappointment. Whilst darker and more fatalistic than his previous films, *Vertigo* had none of the shocks that had made *Les Diaboliques* so effective. The success of Clouzot's film remained a deep concern to Hitchcock and, determined to reclaim his title, he began looking for suitable source material with which to emulate the French film.

Les Diaboliques would later be cited as a major influence by Robert Bloch, an American novelist and short-story writer. From penning H.P. Lovecraft-inspired fantasy tales in the 1930s, Bloch's career had taken an important step in a different direction with his celebrated 1943 psychological short story 'Yours Truly, Jack the Ripper'. Real-life villains were a constant source of inspiration to Bloch (Jack the Ripper and the Marquis de Sade appear in a number of his later stories), and his artistic interest was piqued when he heard of a gruesome discovery in 1957. Investigating the disappearance of Bernice Worden, a young shop assistant in Plainfield, Wisconsin, police had searched the farmhouse of local handyman Ed Gein. Inside they found large numbers of human body parts, including ten heads and furniture made from human skin and bone, with the disembowelled and decapitated body of Worden strung up in the woodshed. It later emerged that Gein had a fixation with his dead mother, and had exhumed and mutilated the bodies of middle-aged women who he thought resembled her, before turning to murder. Gein, nicknamed 'the butcher of Plainfield', would go on to be the direct inspiration for a number of famous cinematic serial killers, including Leatherface in the *Texas Chain Saw Massacre* films and Buffalo Bill in *The Silence of the Lambs* (Jonathan Demme, 1991). However, it was his incarnation as Norman Bates in Bloch's 1959 novel *Psycho* that would have the most profound effect on the horror genre, when Alfred Hitchcock chose the book as the basis for his most shocking and controversial film.

Textual Analysis

Following a lunchtime tryst with her long-distance lover Sam, secretary Marion Crane returns to work and is asked to deposit a $40,000 cash payment into the bank. Seeing an opportunity to pay Sam's debts and enable them to marry, she takes the rest of the afternoon off and absconds with the money. During the drive from Phoenix to Sam's hardware store in Fairvale, California, a storm forces Marion to pull into a neglected roadside motel run by Norman Bates and his domineering mother. After sharing a meal with Norman, Marion resolves to head back to Arizona and return the money. However, as she is taking a shower, an intruder enters the bathroom and viciously stabs her to death. Believing that his mother carried out the murder, Norman cleans up the bathroom and disposes of Marion's car, containing her body as well as the $40,000, in a nearby swamp. Concerned by Marion's disappearance, her sister Lila travels to Fairvale to see Sam, closely followed by Arbogast, a private detective hired to track down the $40,000. Tracing Marion's movements to the Bates Motel, Arbogast calls Lila and tells her that he's going to try and question Norman's mother. He surreptitiously enters the old house behind the motel, and as he climbs the staircase the figure of an old woman rushes out from one of the bedrooms and stabs him to death. With Arbogast missing, Sam and Lila approach the local sheriff, who tells them that Norman's mother committed suicide years earlier and that Norman lives alone at the house. The two check into the motel as guests, and while Sam keeps Norman occupied Lila goes to the house to find the truth. Opening the door to the fruit cellar, Lila discovers the mummified corpse of Mrs Bates just as Norman runs in, dressed in his mother's dress and a wig. As he prepares to attack Lila with a large knife, Sam arrives and wrestles him to the floor, ripping off the disguise and disarming him. Now in the hands of the authorities, a psychiatrist explains how Norman suffered from a split personality, believing at times that he was the mother who he himself had killed. The psychiatrist suggests that if the police drain the swamp they will find more victims.

Although his previous films had included horrific moments or situations, as well as a number of serial murderers, *Psycho* was Hitchcock's first (and arguably only, with the possible exception of *The Birds*) true horror film. As 'the Master of Suspense', his earlier films had been pre-occupied with making audiences tense; with *Psycho* his aim was to terrify and shock. In Hitchcock's view, suspense and shock (or 'surprise' as he often called it) are two very different, and mutually exclusive, cinematic effects. Suspense is generated when the audience has knowledge of a dangerous situation that is denied the characters in the film. One example that Hitchcock frequently cited was that of a group of people sitting round a table playing cards while (unbeknownst to them, but known to the audience) there is a bomb under the table ready to go off. As the card game continues and the bomb's timer ticks down, suspense increases. In the case of shock, the audience knows only as much as the characters on the screen: when an exploding bomb interrupts a card game without warning, we share the characters' surprise at the event. Hitchcock's view was that a prolonged period of suspense should never culminate in a surprise, and always regretted a sequence in *Sabotage*, where a young boy unwittingly carries a bomb onto a London bus (suspense) that is subsequently blown apart by the blast (surprise!).

Psycho's most famous and celebrated sequences are all instances of shock, preceded by little, if any, suspense: the murder of Marion in the shower; the killing on the stairs of the detective Arbogast; and the discovery of Mother's body in the cellar. For the purposes of textual analysis, we will concentrate on these three scenes. However to more fully appreciate the power of *Psycho* we also need to examine its *con*textual elements of surprise. To do this we need to understand the relative positions of Hitchcock and Hollywood cinema in 1960.

While working on the Hollywood remake of *The Man Who Knew Too Much* (1956), Hitchcock agreed to be involved in a series of half-hour television dramas under the title *Alfred Hitchcock Presents*. As well as directing a number of episodes, Hitchcock would appear at the beginning and end of each tale to present darkly comic monologues to the audience. Made for Universal, the series' funding was minimal yet it proved an instant success, making Hitchcock a familiar face in millions of American homes and a celebrity in his own right. At the same time, he was at the height of his popularity with cinema audiences and studios, turning out big-budget, glossy thrillers such as *Rear Window* and *North by Northwest*. Nevertheless, Hitchcock understood the changing demographics of the movie-going public, and was acutely aware of the success being enjoyed by exploitation film-makers such as William Castle, and the teen films that played the drive-in circuits. *Alfred Hitchcock Presents* had demonstrated that it was possible to produce quality entertainment quickly and cheaply, and it was an approach that Hitchcock was keen to implement on the big screen.

Although *Psycho* contains many of the narrative and thematic elements commonly regarded as 'quintessential Hitchcock', the film can in many ways be viewed more as an extension of the television series than an integral part of his cinematic work. From the outset the production was viewed as an experiment, an attempt to emulate the success being reaped by the American exploitation films and, of course, *Les Diaboliques*. The slim source material would perhaps have appeared more suited to a half-hour television episode, and indeed Hitchcock stated that the only thing that drew him to the novel was the early murder of the apparent heroine. Everything else, he said, was secondary. Around this single moment of surprise, Hitchcock and his scriptwriter, Joseph Stefano, built a film aimed solely at manipulating its audience. From the first reading of the novel to getting the film to theatres, Hitchcock moved extremely quickly, purchasing the screen rights to the book himself for $9500. His power in Hollywood meant that at this point Hitchcock could pick and choose his own projects, putting packages together and selling them to the studio.

The director planned for *Psycho* to be a low-budget production unlike anything he had done before, and pitched the idea to Paramount executives as such.

As it turned out, the story department at Paramount had already rejected filming the book, viewing the possibility of getting it past the censors as very slim indeed. At the time, the studio's bosses were keen to move towards releasing more family-friendly films, particularly musicals, which were proving popular with audiences. They were unwilling to allow Hitchcock to make a potentially problematic film that could draw negative publicity to the studio. However, with the director pushing on with the project, and investing almost a million dollars of his own money into it, Paramount eventually drew up a deal whereby they would distribute the film if Hitchcock would shoot it at Universal, on the backlot used for his television series. Informed by Paramount that many of his usual technicians would not be available for the production, Hitchcock utilised a number of his television staff, including director of photography John L. Russell. His techniques carried over from the television series, such as using multiple camera setups, cut production time, with most of the actual shooting taking place over four and a half weeks – short for a studio feature and nowhere near the time spent on Hitchcock's preceding American films – with a full quarter of that devoted to the shower scene.

In his series of famous interviews with Francois Truffaut, Hitchcock described *Psycho* as 'a film for film-makers'. In classical Hollywood cinema, it is the strands of narrative that ultimately tie up neatly, every plot point leading logically to the next and every character's action logically motivated. In the 'pure cinema' of *Psycho,* plot is secondary to the form of the film itself, and the meanings and messages conveyed through image and sound form a distinct and coherent whole. The work's emotional impact on the audience comes as much from the film-making techniques used as its actual narrative content. Although much of that impact can still be felt today, it is important to appreciate the particular effects on audiences watching the film at the time of its initial release. These come primarily from the film's disregard of the classical Hollywood model.

The introduction of the film as 'Alfred Hitchcock's *Psycho*', signifies the director's level of control but also appeals to the audience's knowledge of Hitchcock's television persona, and of his previous film work. However anyone attending *Psycho* expecting either a typical Hitchcock thriller or a quirky tale of the unexpected were certainly in for a surprise. The opening credits' horizontal and vertical black and white bars, constantly moving and splitting, foreshadow the film's themes of good and evil, split personality, duplicity and deception.[1] What the audience does not know is that the majority of the film's deception will be played on them, by Hitchcock himself. Throughout the film he frustrates audience expectation at every turn, manipulating their emotions until they are incapable of knowing what will happen next. Hitchcock manages this through the subversion of three primary tenets of Hollywood cinema at that time: plot, characterisation and generic convention.

Figure 5.1

The film's opening shot sets out one of its key themes: voyeurism, a common element throughout Hitchcock's work, most explicitly in *Rear Window*, and the horror film in general. The camera leisurely drifts across the skyline of Phoenix, Arizona before beginning a slow zoom in, settling on a particular apartment block and closing in on a single window, its blind almost completely down. As the darkness dissolves into light, there is another reference to the horizontal and vertical, black and white, as we see Marion lying on the bed in her white underwear, Sam standing beside her in black trousers (see Fig 5.1). The dialogue between the couple in the opening scene encapsulates many of the themes of the film: sex; guilt; family; the power of the dead over the living. Listening to these opening exchanges, it seems like a typical classical Hollywood set-up: a young couple are in love but kept apart by obstacles outside of their control. They have a clearly defined goal of making enough money to pay off Sam's debts and allow them to marry, and when the opportunity arises through the appearance of the $40,000 a standard cause-and-effect chain is set in motion.

Those unfamiliar with *Psycho* would reasonably assume that the $40,000 plays an important role in the rest of the film. In actual fact the money is an example of what Hitchcock referred to as a 'MacGuffin', a narrative element that at first appears to be important but is merely a device to set the main plot in motion. Here, the $40,000 is the catalyst that brings Marion to the Bates Motel and whose significance is quickly forgotten as the story takes off in a completely different direction. It is through the money, and the crime of stealing it, that audience sympathy with Marion is fostered. By making the character of Cassidy so obnoxious, we're glad when Marion takes the money from him, and we want to see her succeed and use it to make a life with Sam. In fact, audience identification with Marion had already been initiated through standard Hollywood methods; from the opening scene in the hotel room the camera has been unwaveringly trained on her. The change from Bloch's novel, which begins with Norman at the motel, confirms Hitchcock's intentions in this regard. Audience identification is continually reinforced during Marion's drive towards Fairvale, culminating in the POV shots and inner monologue we hear as she drives through the rain.

The traffic cop that Marion meets en route, nominally a good guy, is made to appear menacing behind dark glasses and a surly demeanour. His arrival again fosters our sympathy with Marion; we don't want him to find out about the stolen money, and we are as relieved as she when he stops following. The exchanges between Marion and the traffic cop blur the line between good and bad, right and wrong in the mind of the viewer. In direct opposition to Terence Fisher's characterisations in the Hammer horror films, and indeed the majority of classical Hollywood cinema, in *Psycho*, everyone has the capacity to both be good and bad; Norman obviously through his split personality, but also Marion in stealing the money and the deception that follows. The moral change is purposefully reflected in her changing from wearing white underwear to wearing black. Again in his interviews with Truffaut, Hitchcock revealed that he was mindful of the more youthful audience the film would attract. In discussing whether Marion should be wearing white or black underwear during her hotel session with Sam, he remarked that the audience would not see a sexual relationship between an unmarried couple as particularly 'bad', certainly compared to the stealing of $40,000.

When Marion eventually arrives and checks in at the Bates motel as Marie Samuels, the reception mirror that stands beside her highlights her duplicity and double identity. It is but one of many uses of mirrors in the film, all of which reinforce the film's concerns of split personality, and represent a move from the clear-cut psychological profiles of classical Hollywood cinema back to the ambiguity of the Expressionists. Following Marion's murder, the audience suddenly finds itself without an identification character and has no option but to shift its sympathies to Norman. As Hitchcock says in the trailer for the film, 'you had to feel sorry for him', living in the shadow of such a domineering mother. As we watch him cleaning up after the murder, our empathy quickly grows, such that when he is caught in the headlights of a passing car carrying a bloodied mop and bucket, we catch our breath. A few minutes later, as Norman nervously watches Marion's car slowly sink into the swamp, we can't help but hope that it disappears without a trace. Without realising it, the audience's emotions have been expertly manipulated, and their sympathies switched from victim to murderer (although we don't yet know this).

An important element in this manipulation is Hitchcock's use of the Hollywood star system. In Chapter 2 we discussed how the star system associated actors and actresses with particular types of films or roles. Hitchcock had made frequent use of the star system in his more conventional films, casting actors such as James Stewart and Cary Grant as essentially 'good guys' caught up in dangerous situations outside of their control, with well-known 'bad guys' such as Peter Lorre against them. As the natural beneficiaries of audience sympathy, Stewart and Grant could be expected to emerge safe and triumphant by the film's end. Although by 1960 the Hollywood star system was approaching its end, both Anthony Perkins and Janet Leigh enjoyed a high level of positive publicity courtesy of the studios. Perkins, in fact a closet homosexual, was promoted as an all-American boy, with studios releasing photos of him on dinner dates with their up-and-coming young actresses. Leigh had received star billing in her films for over a decade, appearing in sympathetic roles across a number of genres including comedies and musicals, and could reasonably be assumed to survive to the film's end. With *Psycho*, Hitchcock used the audience recognition of the actors and their perceived real-life personalities to increase the surprise factor. Any doubts that the audience may have had about transferring their empathy to a voyeur with a nervous twitch and a penchant for taxidermy was offset by their (perceived) knowledge of Perkins's persona.

Hitchcock's final subversion of Hollywood norms is *Psycho*'s use of generic codes and conventions. Since its release, there has been much debate about what genre *Psycho* actually belongs to: is it a horror, thriller, or detective story? Certainly it contains elements of all three genres, but its appropriation of the codes and conventions of the horror film, not to mention its effect on the evolution of that genre, ensure its inclusion in this book. Although Hitchcock is quoted as saying that he did not want the Bates house to be a 'typical old dark house', it's difficult to see how it could appear anything but. He chose an already existing building on the Universal backlot, and for the interiors used a soundstage originally constructed for Chaney's *Phantom of the Opera*. During the film's trailer, it is referred to as 'sinister' a number of times, and its silhouette is frequently shown with time-lapsed clouds drifting behind it, giving an otherworldly look. Always shot from a low angle, two lit windows shining like watching eyes, the house represents the power that its occupant (mother) holds over Norman (and everyone else), and that the past holds over the present – another theme common in the horror film and Hitchcock's work in general. Again, though, Hitchcock uses their assumed knowledge to deceive the audience and increase the shock effect. Presenting them with a scary old house on a hill, he relocates the film's most horrific sequence to a gleaming white, modern bathroom. The message is clear: you don't need to be in an old dark house to feel frightened, horror is all around us, and what happens to Marion can happen to anyone, anywhere.

With *Psycho*, Hitchcock wanted realism, but stopped short of the documentary-style filming of the Italian Neo-realists, or the later horror films we will discuss in Chapter 7. We mentioned in the previous chapter how early colour film was seen by many in the industry as detracting from realism, so the use of black and white was logical. Patricia Hitchcock, the director's daughter, claimed that it was her mother Alma, Hitchcock's wife and assistant, who originally suggested that the film be shot in black and white as it was the only way it would get past the censors. Anthony Perkins, however, has suggested that Hitchcock wanted to emulate the look of *Les Diaboliques*, and would frequently screen Clouzot's film for the cast and crew. Whatever the reasoning, the rich black-and-white, deep-focus photography of *Psycho* is exceptional, and completely rejected the contemporary Hollywood norm of bright Technicolor and faded backgrounds. The opening captions, giving us a forensically precise time and place, reinforce the impression that we are watching actual events. Although the film has brief moments of Expressionism (for example the camera shooting from beneath Perkins' face, making him look like a bird of prey), they do not detract from the naturalistic feel of the film.

Now that we understand the tactics that Hitchcock used to manipulate audience reaction to *Psycho*, we can more fully appreciate the power of its 'shock' sequences, identified at the beginning of the chapter. With the possible exception of the Odessa Steps scene of Eisenstein's *Battleship Potemkin*, the shower scene of *Psycho* is probably the most analysed sequence in film history. To anyone who has not seen the film before (and to a great many who have), the sequence still has the power to shock and horrify, well over fifty years after it was made. In Robert Bloch's novel, Marion is beheaded with one fell swoop of the knife. This would certainly have been a shock, or surprise, in the film, but would it have been as effective as the excruciating murder that Hitchcock executed?

Returning to Hitchcock's view on suspense and surprise, referenced at the start of the chapter, to say that the shower sequence occurs without any build-up of suspense would not be entirely true. The ominous music that begins when Marion retires to her room after supper with Norman is a warning that all is not well. Watching Norman peeping on Marion through

Figure 5.2

a hole in the wall generates audience discomfort, and the rising music builds suspense. Then the music fades as Norman returns to the house. We might assume that Marion is safe, for now, yet the cinematography and editing of the following sequence makes us even more uncomfortable. The framing of Norman as he sits in the kitchen, tightly enclosed between the walls and doors of the house, represents both his physical and psychological entrapment (see Fig 5.2).

Back in the motel room, when Marion enters the shower we know that she has decided to return the money, and that the water is acting as a symbolic soul-cleansing agent. However, the deliberately-timed, alternating shots of Marion and the shower head suggests that *something* is going to happen, but we don't know what. Through the shower curtain we see a silhouette enter the bathroom and wonder who it could be. Although we fear for the safety of Marion at this point, what actually happens to her is more shocking than anything we could have anticipated. As we see the raised knife, the screaming violins of Bernard Herrman's score work to give the audience an extra jolt. The suspense that has been generated does not detract from the shock, simply because the event itself is still so unexpected. Had we previously seen the killer entering Marion's motel room carrying a large knife then it would have been the equivalent of *Sabotage*'s exploding bus, and Hitchcock's suspense/surprise rule would have been broken.

Although it would have remained a shocking sequence even without the music (as Hitchcock had originally intended), the frantic strings combine with the visuals to produce total sensory overload. As in Eisenstein's film, Hitchcock uses montage to emphasise speed and brutality. In a sequence lasting under a minute, there are over fifty cuts, alternating between Marion and the plunging knife. Although the weapon is never actually seen to enter her body, the use of montage creates the *impression* of seeing a brutally violent murder. Already shocked by the suddenness of the attack, the rapid editing and shrieking music heightens audience disorientation. Only when Marion slumps down, the pace of editing drops and the music recedes can we begin to reflect on what we have actually seen.

The build-up of suspense before the murder of Arbogast, although much shorter than that preceding the shower scene, works in a similar fashion. Had this been a straightforward detective film, the audience would expect Arbogast to eventually get to the bottom of things, find Marion's killer and return the $40,000. However, by this stage much of our identification has been shifted to Norman, particularly following his questioning by the unsympathetic detective. When Arbogast enters the house surreptitiously, the audience again suspects that something is going to happen but not what. As he slowly climbs the staircase we wonder, will he find out about Marion's murder? Will he get to question Mrs Bates and discover the truth? The movement of the camera to a high overhead shot momentarily disorientates us, and again the suddenness of the attack takes us by surprise. Our reaction is mirrored in the stunned face of Arbogast as he reaches out before toppling backwards down the stairs. With the apparent heroine and the investigating detective both dead, audiences anxiously wonder who will survive to the film's end, and what could possibly happen next.

The final sequence we will examine is a more conventional horror set-piece, although embellished by more of Hitchcock's shock tactics. Hiding from Norman, who has knocked out the ineffectual Sam and raced up to the house, Lila ventures into the fruit cellar. Had we been listening to dialogue between Norman and his mother earlier, we would know that that is where Mother has been hidden, and suspense is once again heightened through the rising soundtrack. This scene also features more recognisable horror lighting and Expressionist-styled shot composition. The frequent point-of-view shots that follow put us in the position of Lila as she slowly approaches who we assume is Mrs Bates, sitting in a chair turned away from us. As we get closer, we are fearful for Lila's safety, both from Mrs Bates and her son, but yet again the shock that Hitchcock produces is so unexpected and so horrific that it is not undermined by the preceding suspense. As seen in previous case studies, the use of a slow reveal followed by a jump cut heightens the horror effect, as we are confronted with Mother's grinning, mummified skull (see Fig 5.3).

Figure 5.3

Once again we are disoriented and wondering what is happening: if this is Mother, then who is the killer? Immediately our question is answered by Norman appearing in the doorway, brandishing the carving knife. It is yet another shock, compounded by the fact that he's dressed in his mother's clothes and wig. However, what is perhaps more shocking for the audience is the realisation that for the past hour they have been empathising with a psychotic (and cross-dressing) killer. As Norman is disarmed and dragged to the floor by Sam, Hitchcock cuts back to the head of the mummified Mrs Bates, now caught in the light of a swinging bulb. As the hollows of the eyes and mouth alternate between light and dark the head appears to be alive – laughing, or screaming.

As horrific as the sight of Mrs Bates' skull is in this sequence, its later appearance is even more disturbing. After his condition has been rather glibly explained away by a psychiatrist, we see Norman sitting alone in the police cell. As the camera slowly tracks in we can hear Mother's voice, obviously inside his head and encouraging us to again identify with him. Now in close-up, Norman looks into the camera, at the viewer, and grins. It is a direct breaking of the fourth wall, connecting character with audience, and brings the film full circle; again the audience are voyeurs, only this time Norman knows that he is being watched. Not only do we hear his thoughts, we also see both sides of his personality simultaneously, as Mother's grinning skull is superimposed over his face. For the ending of a Hollywood film of the period, it is surprisingly downbeat.

Reception and Aftermath

Marketed as the film that you should see 'from the beginning or not at all', *Psycho* was not only revolutionary in its making, but also in its exhibition. In 1960, movie-goers were accustomed to arriving at the cinema at any point during a film and taking their seats. They would routinely watch the remainder of the film, and then stay for the following showing and watch up to the point at which they arrived, a practice that seems absurd in the age of online booking and designated seating. For *Psycho*, Hitchcock was adamant that this should not be allowed. He insisted that anyone arriving once the film had begun would have to queue outside for the next showing. (The resulting queues that stretched around the block for popular films is one possible source for the term 'blockbuster'.) It was a tactic that had previously been used with *Les Diaboliques* and, less successfully, *Vertigo*. In the case of *Psycho*, Hitchcock's insistence was entirely understandable; walking into a showing half way through would dilute, if not completely ruin, many of the twists and surprises it contains.

Another blockbuster tactic, utilised with *Psycho* but which developed throughout the 1960s and flourished in the 70s, was its simultaneous release at hundreds of first-run cinemas across the US. Such a release pattern ensures that maximum income is generated as soon as possible, and in the case of Hitchcock's film meant that audiences all over the country could get to see it before the plot was given away. In fact, such was the popularity of the film that it continued playing for weeks or even months at the first-run cinemas while extra prints were struck for showing in smaller venues. It became the second highest grossing film of 1960 (after MGM's epic remake of *Ben Hur* [William Wyler, 1959]), yet *Psycho* was savaged by the majority of critics, who could not see how the director of such a 'respectable' film as *North by Northwest* could follow it up with what they saw as cheap, exploitative junk. His cause wasn't helped by not allowing preview screenings for reviewers, which meant that they had to queue up alongside regular audiences.

Despite, or perhaps because of, the critical backlash against the film, *Psycho* proved phenomenally successful at the box office, particularly with the booming youth market. Hitchcock had always valued the views of audiences much more highly than those of critics, who he accused of taking this particular film far too seriously. The director saw *Psycho* as a black comedy, and the film's advertising played on his darkly humorous TV persona. As the major investor, Hitchcock had the luxury of almost complete control over the promotion of the film, and its famous trailer consists of a guided tour of the motel and the Bates house, conducted by Hitchcock himself and featuring whimsical music and mischievous comments. Of course, it gives very little warning of the level of horror the film contains. Hitchcock had insisted on secrecy from members of his cast and crew, and during filming had given little detail to reporters. Despite the posters advertising 'Alfred Hitchcock's Greatest Shocker', very few would have known what to expect when they first queued up to see it.

Whereas the films we have examined so far may be seen as dated and having lost much of their power to scare, the same cannot be said for *Psycho*. Hitchcock stripped away the genre's foreign or period trappings and depicted horror as a product of modern-day American society. It represented a graphic transition from Gothic horror (the old dark house on the hill) to modern horror (the everyday of a motel bathroom). It was a watershed for the genre, and the effect on audiences was profound. In one incident Hitchcock received a letter from a concerned mother whose daughter had been affected by viewing his film. Having previously been scared to take a bath after seeing *Les Diaboliques* (which features one particularly disturbing scene involving a bathtub), she was now equally afraid of taking a shower. What was a mother to do? Hitchcock's advice was to 'have her dry-cleaned'.

In his book on the first fifteen years of the modern American horror film (which he dates as starting in 1960), Charles Derry positions *Psycho* as the first entry in what he calls the 'horror-of-personality' subgenre. He identifies the main traits of this subgenre as an emphasis on insanity, as well as an ambiguity in the characterisation of the film's 'villain'. Whilst some horror films had previously depicted 'monsters' as sympathetic characters (think of Irena in *Cat People*, or many of the Universal films), *Psycho* was the first to make the audience *identify* with the villain, albeit unwittingly. Unsurprisingly, the tactic of having an audience identify with a serial killing Peeping Tom has made *Psycho* the target of attacks from a number of feminist critics. In particular, Laura Mulvey sees much of Hitchcock's work as symptomatic of a patriarchal Hollywood system that treats actresses as one-dimensional objects of what she terms the 'male gaze' (see Mulvey 1989). Is *Psycho* a morality tale about the dangers of growing up without a strong father figure? Does it show what happens when a strong woman has ideas above her station and gets her comeuppance? Is it just a cheap exploitation film that appeals to a (male) audience's basest instincts? Feminist opposition to some aspects of the horror film, and the 'slasher' film in particular, is a topic that we will return to in our chapter on Mario Bava's *Bay of Blood*.

Widely regarded as the first 'modern' horror film, *Psycho* was produced as the classical Hollywood era was drawing to a close and was certainly ahead of its time. Despite making over $8.5 million on its release, the film did little to change the majors' attitudes towards the horror genre, and it would remain in the hands of independent film-makers for much of the following decade. The success of *Ben Hur* ensured that the big studios' pre-occupation with epic films continued into the 1960s with films such as *Spartacus* (Stanley Kubrick, 1960) and *Lawrence of Arabia* (David Lean, 1962), ending only when the disastrously over-budget *Cleopatra* (Joseph L. Mankiewicz, 1963) took 20th Century Fox to the brink of bankruptcy and hastened the studios' move towards what would become known as 'New Hollywood'. *Psycho*'s disregard for conventional narrative, its focus on technique, and the presence of psychologically complex protagonists would become standard features of New Hollywood film-making. Similarly, the level of control Hitchcock had as director, unusual during the studio era, would be *de riguer* for the new wave of American film-makers that followed, such as Francis Ford Coppola, Martin Scorsese (both of whom would start their careers at AIP) and Steven Spielberg. We will discuss the New Hollywood movement in more detail in our chapter on Roman Polanski's *Rosemary's Baby*.

In the years since its release *Psycho* has become firmly entrenched in popular culture like no other film; even those who have not seen it themselves are aware of the significance of a screeching violin and a shower. This scene in particular has been referenced in countless films, from horror (*The Funhouse* [Tobe Hooper, 1981], amongst many others) to comedy (*High Anxiety* [Mel Brooks, 1977], *Phantom of the Paradise* [Brian De Palma, 1974]), while Brian De Palma's thriller *Dressed to Kill* (1980) is practically an *homage* to the entire film in both narrative and form. Arguably the high point of Hitchcock's distinguished career, *Psycho* is not just a perfect example of 'pure cinema', but a piece of work that rode the wave of social and cultural changes that would shape the future of the film industry. Although *The Birds* confirmed his new tag as 'Master of Terror', his subsequent productions such as *Marnie* (1964), *Torn Curtain* (1966) and *Topaz* (1969) are generally acknowledged to be disappointing in comparison to those up to and including *Psycho* (although *Marnie* has its fervent admirers). Extremely successful within the Hollywood studio system, Hitchcock seemed to lose his way without the stability of his regular team of contracted writers, technicians and actors. His penultimate film, 1972's *Frenzy*, is the story of a London serial killer labelled the 'Necktie Murderer'. Taking advantage of more relaxed censorship, Hitchcock revels in showing the sex and horror that had merely been hinted at in *Psycho*, and the film foreshadows the more graph-ic 'slasher' films of the late 1970s and early 80s.

Following Hitchcock's death in 1980, Norman Bates was resurrected both in print and on film. Robert Bloch's novel *Psycho 2* (1982) tells of his escape from a mental institution and an exploitative Hollywood production of the events of the original book. At the same time Universal produced an entirely unrelated film, *Psycho II*, in which Norman is declared sane and released back into society. His return to the Bates Motel coincides with a spate of murders for which he may or may not be responsible. Along with Anthony Perkins, Vera Miles returns as Lila in what is actually a highly creditable sequel to the Hitchcock original. The series continued with *Psycho III* (Anthony Perkins, 1986) and the TV movie *Psycho IV – The Beginning* (Mick Garris, 1990), followed by Gus van Sant's ill-judged and needless remake of the original in 1998. The arrival in 2013 of the television series *Bates Motel*, which focused on the relationship between the teenage Norman and his mother, is testa-ment to *Psycho*'s enduring popularity.

Bibliography

Derry, Charles (1977) *Dark Dreams: The Horror Film from* Psycho *to* Jaws. London: Thomas Yoseloff Ltd.

McGilligan, Patrick (2003) *Alfred Hitchcock: A Life in Darkness and Light*. London: Harper Collins.

Mulvey, Laura (1973) 'Visual Pleasure and Narrative Cinema'. In Mulvey, Laura (1989) *Visual and Other Pleasures*, pp. 14-28. New York: Palgrave.

Ray, Robert B. (1985) *A Certain Tendency of the Hollywood Cinema, 1930-1980*. Chapter 6, pp. 153-174. New Jersey: Princeton University Press.

Taylor, John Russell (1978) *Hitch: The Authorised Biography of Alfred Hitchcock*. London: Faber & Faber.

Wells, Amanda Sheahan (2001) *Ultimate Film Guides:* Psycho. London: York Press.

Endnotes

1. Saul Bass, the influential graphic designer who created the titles for *Psycho, Vertigo* and a number of other Hitchcock films, storyboarded much of the film for Hitchcock. Following the director's death, Bass claimed that he took an active part in directing the famous shower scene, something refuted by a number of the film's cast.

Chapter 6

Asian Horror

Kaidan (Kwaidan)
Masaki Kobayashi, Japan 1964

Recommended viewing

Ugetsu Monogatari (Kenji Mizoguchi, 1953)
Onibaba (Kaneto Shindô, 1964)
Ringu (Hideo Nakata, 1998)
Ju-On (Takashi Shimizu, 2002)
The Eye (Pang Brothers, 2002)

Introduction

The mid-1990s saw a substantial increase in the number of horror films being produced in Asian countries, and in particular Japan and Korea. At the same time, globalisation and the introduction of worldwide distribution channels meant that such films became much more accessible to western audiences, with the surprise success of Hideo Nakata's 1998 *Ringu* bringing Japanese horror into the mainstream of western cinema. Hollywood cashed in with some big-budget remakes, inviting directors such as Nakata and Takashi Shimizu in an attempt to capture their original, and specifically Japanese, approach to ghostly tales. Often used to describe genre films from across Asia, so-called 'J-Horror' is now a recognised sub-genre in the west, with a number of scholarly books dedicated to its analysis.

Although many of the more recent films feature modern trappings and a preoccupation with technology, they draw heavily from Japan's long tradition of folklore and ghost stories, while stylistically referencing the aesthetics of traditional Japanese theatre. In this chapter we study one of the first Japanese horror films to gain recognition in the west, one that foreshadows many of the ideas and images used in the more recent exports. We also trace the evolution of Japan's unique national film industry, and examine how cultural differences can affect genre production and consumption.

Background

Introduced at the turn of the twentieth century, early cinema proved extremely popular in Japan, particularly in major cities such as Tokyo and Kyoto. It came at a time when the country was in the midst of a period of modernisation and increased 'westernisation', as it attempted to make its presence felt on the world stage. As such, the (western) technological innovation of cinema was of great interest to the Japanese people. As had been the case in America and Europe, when Japan began producing its own cinema it was heavily influenced by theatre. Here, however, the traditional theatrical forms of Noh and Kabuki were far removed from the realist approach of most western theatre, with an emphasis on fantastic themes and an exaggerated acting and visual style. This being the case, it is hardly surprising that early Japanese movie-goers were particularly excited by the work of the German Expressionists, and when commercial Japanese film production began in earnest, it was torn between the exaggerated style of the Expressionists and the more naturalistic 'Hollywood' style.

In the 1920s and 30s, the 'Big Two' studios in Japan were Shochiku and Nikkatsu (formed in 1912 by the merger of four production studios and a theatre chain, it introduced a studio system pre-dating that of Hollywood), who between them controlled the vast majority of cinema screens in the country through vertical integration. As in the US, genre and star systems developed, with individual studios associated with their own style and type of film. Shochiku produced western-style films, and used only film-makers who had been trained in America. The studio was also responsible for introducing female film stars (as in kabuki theatre, many female roles in early productions were filled by men). Their films were generally more modern than those of Nikkatsu, whose output tended towards traditional and historical subjects. Again, as in Hollywood, the top actors, directors and writers were kept under contract by the big studios, and actors associated with historical dramas were considered the country's biggest stars.

For all their similarities, the Japanese industry differed from that of Hollywood in a number of important ways. The major studios provided individual directors with much more freedom, both in choice of material and in cast and crew. As such, the director was always accorded higher status in Japan, where his role as primary author of the work was more readily recognised. Culturally, Japanese films of the silent era were very different to those of America and Europe, which often struggled to gain exposure in Japanese cinemas once a national industry was established. A common feature of exhibition in Japan was the use of the *benshi* (sometimes known as *katsudou-benshi* or *katsuben*). This was a commentator who would sit by the screen and explain to the audience what was happening in terms of the plot, like a storyteller. While not unknown outside of Japan, the presence of the orator came to be an extremely important feature of the Japanese cinema-going experience. As such, silent film remained popular well into the 1930s. At this time, the big two studios were joined by a third, Toho, formed from the merger of various film processing, production and theatre companies. With a formidable array of stars and directors, Toho quickly came to dominate the Japanese industry.

In similar fashion to Germany during World War One, throughout the Second World War the Japanese government oversaw the consolidation of the nation's film industry, in this case around three major studios, with Shochiku and Toho joined by Daei (a project formed by a merger of Nikkatsu with two smaller studios, Shinko and Daito). Whilst film production declined dramatically during the war, the years following were unprecedented. A massive influx of Hollywood films brought box-office takings into the studios (through their ownership of the theatre chains), which was pumped straight into domestic production. During the post-war occupation, films that dwelt on Japan's feudal history (including the traditional ghost story) were frowned upon, and domestic product at this time was heavily geared towards contemporary films (*gendaigeki*) in the Hollywood style.

Following the end of occupation in 1952, the Japanese film industry went from strength to strength. Toho, who had suffered during the previous decade, quickly returned to a position of dominance. They established the long-running 'giant monster' genre (*daikaigu eiga*) with *Gojira* (aka *Godzilla*, Ishirō Hondo, 1954, inspired by *The Beast From 20,000 Fathoms*) and its many sequels and spin-offs. Post-war horror films were a reflection of and reaction to the fears of a country that found itself in the midst of major upheaval and modernisation, as its past values were being swept aside by the invasion of western ideology and values. The legacy of the atomic bombing of Hiroshima and Nagasaki at the end of World War Two was obvious in early iterations of the giant monster genre. Such films later became important in attempts to maintain cinema audiences through the 1960s, though with a shift in theme towards monsters that defended Japan against foreign invaders.

Period cinema (*jidaigeki*) also returned after the war, with Kenzi Mizugochi's 1953 film *Ugetsu Monogatari* (aka *Tales of Ugetsu*) being one of the first Japanese productions to be widely distributed internationally. The film was heavily based on Ueda Akinari's eighteenth-century collection of nine supernatural tales from Chinese and Japanese folklore, *Ugetsu Monogatarai* (*Tales of Moonlight and Rain*, 1776). Ghost stories have proven popular throughout Japanese history, thriving in that country's cultural traditions of oral storytelling and theatre. When the introduction of printing presses in the early seventeenth century enabled the dissemination of literature, collections of short stories based on Japanese and Chinese folklore and Buddhist teachings were particularly sought after. These anthologies often featured dozens of tales, with supernatural stories (*kaidan*), from which overriding religious themes and moral lessons were generally removed, mixing freely with more traditional entries. The popularity of *kaidan* increased enormously during the mid- to late eighteenth century, when they became part of the reaction against the strict reforms placed on the country during the reign of Shogun Tokugawa Yoshimune, who died in 1751. In Mizugochi's imagining of *Ugetsu*, the story of two wronged women who return as spirits is used to explore a conflict between the values of 'traditional' Japan and a more modern focus on individual actions. As we will see, there are parallels with the first tale of *Kaidan*, in that a wayward husband returns to his loyal wife only to find that she is in fact a ghost.

Between 1957 and 1961, as Hollywood struggled with the fallout of the Paramount Decision, Japan became the world's largest producer of films. The Japanese industry peaked in 1958, with well over 500 films produced and a billion local cinemagoers. With the decline of the American studio system and the loosening of Hollywood's stranglehold on cinema worldwide, alternatives to the classical Hollywood form began to gain recognition in the west. The arrival of independent 'art-house' cinemas in American cities and campus towns from the mid-1950s onwards gave audiences access to films from around the world that would previously have struggled to find an exhibitor. We will discuss the effects of the art-house movement on Hollywood in our next two chapters, but suffice to say that the period saw the biggest influx of foreign film into American cinemas since the 1920s.

Film-makers such as Akira Kurasawa and Kon Ichikawa regularly had their work screened at film festivals around the world, and in 1962 Masaki Kobayashi's *Harakiri* became the first Japanese film to win the Grand Jury prize at the Cannes film festival. Born in 1916, Kobayashi had been working at the Shochiku studio for only a few months when he was drafted into the Japanese army and despatched to Manchuria in 1942. Released from a prisoner-of-war camp four years later, he returned to film-making, first as assistant to Keisuke Kinoshita and then as a writer and director. Determined to expose the social injustice, corruption and crime he saw as prevalent in Japan, Kobayashi earned a reputation for producing hard-hitting realist dramas such as *I Will Buy You* (1956, dealing with corruption in sport) and the politically controversial *The Thick-Walled Room* (1953, about Japanese war criminals and based on the diaries of real prisoners of war). His best-received work in this vein was the epic, almost 10-hour trilogy *The Human Condition* (1959-1961), which tells the story of Kaji, a pacifist living through World War Two Japan. Following his international breakthrough with *Harakiri*, a historical samurai drama, Kobayashi felt that he had done all he could with realist film-making.

Keen to explore more stylised, expressionistic visuals, and spiritual rather than realist social themes, Kobayashi found an ideal source in the supernatural short stories of Patrick Lafcadio Hearn. Born in 1850 to Irish parents on the Greek island of Lefkada, Hearn was raised in Dublin, before leaving for America at the age of 19. Having gained a reputation as a sensationalist newspaper reporter, he moved to Japan in 1890, where he took citizenship and the name Koizumi Yakumo. Working as a journalist and teacher, he became fascinated by Japanese myths and legends. He wrote a number of books on the subject, of which *Kwaidan: Stories and Studies of Strange Things* was one of the last, though by far his most popular and best known. It's worth noting that only two of the stories which feature in Kobayashi's portmanteau film were taken from Hearn's *Kwaidan* volume: 'Kurokami' was based on a tale anthologised in *Shadowings* (1900) and 'In a Cup of Tea' was adapted from an entry in *Kotto: Being Japanese Curios, with Sundry Cobwebs* (1902). Originally written to introduce Japanese folklore to westerners, Hearn's tales have continued to inform the J-Horror sub-genre, with the cursed kimono of 'Furisode', for example, being an early blueprint for the videotapes and mobile phones of *Ringu, One Missed Call* (Takashi Miike, 2003) and the rest.

Prior to the release of *Kaidan* the only notable entry in portmanteau horror cinema was the Ealing Studios production *Dead of Night*. However, it was a format that would reach the height of its popularity in western cinema over the next ten years. Amicus – Hammer Films' prime rivals in the production of British horror – would specialise in such films, beginning with *Dr Terror's House of Horrors* (Freddie Francis, 1964), starring Peter Cushing and Christopher Lee.[1] No doubt aware of the success being enjoyed by companies such as Hammer and AIP, Kobayashi may have seen so-called 'Edo Gothic' as a vehicle for furthering his international profile. Reluctant to describe his work as horror, his stated aims were to 'convey the sheer beauty of traditional Japan' and to 'create a drama which dealt directly with the spiritual importance of our lives'. At the time the most expensive Japanese film ever made at the cost of some 350 million yen, *Kaidan* was an extremely ambitious project. The fact that Kobayashi deliberately chose to use Hearn's westernised treatments of traditional Japanese folklore suggests that it was conceived with at least one eye on the international market.

Textual Analysis

The film consists of four vignettes:

Episode 1: Kurokami: The Black Hair

Driven by poverty and boredom, a samurai leaves his wife, moves away, and marries into a well-to-do family. Although prosperous in his new life, he is unhappy; his new bride proves selfish, his marriage is loveless, and he is constantly haunted by the memory of the wife he left behind. Years later, wracked by guilt, he returns to his old home and finds it in a dilapidated state, but with his first wife exactly as when he had left. Spending the night together, he awakes in the morning to discover her decaying corpse beside him. Her long black hair seemingly comes to life and attacks him. As the samurai tries to escape, the house disintegrates around him and he ages rapidly to match the appearance of his long-dead wife.

Episode 2: Yuki Onna: The Woman of the Snow

An ageing woodcutter and his apprentice Minokichi are caught in a ferocious snowstorm and take refuge in a forest cabin. After falling asleep from exhaustion, Minokichi wakens to find a beautiful snow demon knelt over the old man, killing him with her icy breath. She tells Minokichi that he will be spared as long as he never tells anyone about what he has seen. Years later, happily married to a loving wife and with three young children, Minokichi is reminded of that night and tells his wife the story of what happened. She reveals that she is in fact the demon, but will spare him once again for the sake of their children. She leaves, threatening that she will return to kill him if he ever hurts their children.

Episode 3: Hoichi The Earless

Hoichi, a blind young minstrel, lives and works at a temple built to commemorate samurais killed in a famous sea battle. Well known for his skills at musically reciting the story of this battle, he is approached one night by a stranger who tells him that his lord is staying nearby and would like to hear a recital. Hoichi is led away to play for his unseen hosts. Sworn to secrecy, his mysterious disappearance from the temple becomes a nightly occurrence and two of his co-workers are sent by the priest to follow him. Finding him playing to the ghosts of the fallen samurais, they report back to the priest who decides that Hoichi is in grave danger and must not be led away again. He transcribes prayers all over Hoichi's body, believing it will make him invisible to the ghosts. That night the ghost returns, but can only see Hoichi's ears, which the priest neglected to protect. Determined to follow his lord's instructions, the spirit rips the ears from Hoichi's head and leaves. Hoichi survives, is never visited by the ghost again, and becomes rich and famous from his recitals.

Episode 4: In a Cup of Tea

In a Meiji-era village, a writer struggles to finish a story, set 200 years earlier. In it, a guard named Konnai sees a mysterious man reflected in his cup of water. Unable to fathom how to get rid of the reflection, the guard drinks the water. That night, when on duty, the man from the reflection appears in person and introduces himself as Shikibu Heinai. The guard attacks and apparently wounds the apparition, only to see him disappear through the wall. Upon returning home, the guard is visited by three retainers of Heinai, who tell him that their master will come to take his revenge for the wound inflicted. The guard attacks the three men, becoming increasingly manic as they seem to disappear in front of his eyes. Back in the Meiji era, a publisher pays a visit to the writer but he has disappeared. There is a shriek from the writer's wife and when the publisher investigates he finds the writer, or his soul, trapped in a pot of water.

In contrast to *Dead of Night* and the portmanteau horrors produced by Amicus, the four supernatural tales in *Kaidan* have no unifying narrative or framing story. Instead, the common thread is the male narrator (serving as the *benshi* of early Japanese cinema), who effectively adopts Patrick Hearn's narrative voice. Although each tale of *Kaidan* stands alone, there are shared narrative themes and cinematic styling that lend coherence to the film. In terms of the narrative, each vignette positions male characters as the victims of ghostly apparitions, usually as a result of their own character failings. The samurai of the first episode pursues wealth and personal gain at the expense of true love; the young hero of 'Yuki-Onna' is unable to keep his promise; Hoichi's pride leads him to dangerous nightly audiences with the dead; and the main character of the final story is driven to madness after foolishly swallowing a samurai's soul (though this final tale is the most ambivalent in its message). As in so many ghost stories, the supernatural provides a means of reflecting on very real, human strengths and weaknesses; while the main protagonist of each story may appear broken and weeping by the end (albeit temporarily in the case of Hoichi), it is their own human folly that has proved their downfall.

In the first three tales, these characters are victims of female spirits, seeking or threatening some kind of vengeance. The figure of the female avenging ghost (*onryou*) is a centuries-old motif of Japanese folklore, long pre-dating Hearn, which continues to have resonance in modern Japanese horror cinema and literature. It can also be found in a number of what we term 'mainstream' supernatural horror films, discussed in our final chapter, such as *Mama* (Andy Muschietti, 2013) and *Lights Out* (David F. Sandberg, 2016). 'Kurokami', adapted from Hearn's story 'The Reconciliation', depicts the avenging spirit of a wronged wife of a samurai. In Kobayashi's version, the hair of the wife's corpse appears possessed and attacks the samurai; he attempts to flee but, as he tries to free himself, ages hideously. The image of long, black hair has a long tradition in Japanese theatre, often used to symbolise demonic women. Kobayashi's visually striking representation of the dead wife and the possessed black hair expands on these traditional tropes to bring a more explicitly horrific supernatural edge to Hearn's tale. For modern viewers, the device of the black hair in particular has become familiar through films such as *Ringu* and *Ju-On* and their respective sequels and remakes. Sadako's unkempt hair, obscuring her face as she emerges from the television screen in *Ringu*, is one of the most terrifying and instantly recognisable images of the J-Horror cycle. Plot-wise, 'Kurokami' is a typical twist-in-the-tail story, much used in the anthology horror film (and in written short horror fiction), and serves as a fine opening to Kobayashi's film.

The second and third instalments of *Kaidan* also feature female spirits exerting a powerful influence over the human world. In 'Yuki-Onna', the snow demon is a terrifyingly uncanny but beautiful figure. When she adopts a human form in or-

Figure 6.1

der to marry the handsome young man she maintains her beauty; as with the wife in 'Kurokami', she seems forever young. It is this very beauty that reminds Minokichi of his earlier encounter and leads him to break his promise. Although angry, Yuki does not carry out her threat to kill, seemingly for the sake of her children. Like the wronged wife of the first tale, Yuki is essentially faithful even when confronted with the weakness of her husband, and Kobayashi generally maintains the beauty and dignity of these avenging women (see Fig 6.1). In contrast, more recent J-Horror films present female spirits who could be characterised more explicitly as what feminist theorist Barbara Creed terms the 'monstrous-feminine', carrying the physical trauma of their earthly demise for shock effect.

The spirit women of the third story are of a very different social standing, being the elite of the defeated Heike who collectively commit suicide when their clan lose the battle of Dan-no-ura. Lady Nii fearlessly leads the way, with the words, 'Woman though I am … I will escort the Emperor to the next world.' As tragic figures they have much in common with Lady Wakasa of *Ugetsu*, who commands a strong and ultimately dangerous influence over the wayward samurai. These are similarly powerful women of status, speaking on behalf of the child emperor. Whilst it is a male retainer who summons Hoichi every evening, it is women's voices commanding him to play. Again, the Heiki women are part of a broader avenging spirit tradition, though their vengeance has been tamed through the building of a temple in their honour. Although they do not seem to wish Hoichi any particular harm, their insistence on his nightly narration saps him of life. Associating with the dead is fraught with danger, as the priest warns Hoichi: 'They'd have destroyed you sooner or later.' In this tale, however, the most violent sequence is in the attack on Hoichi by the male retainer, who tears off the minstrel's ears to take them as evidence he has fulfilled his mission. In contrast to the other stories, the domestic world Hoichi is part of, and in which he is cared for, is an entirely male one.

In the final instalment, 'In a Cup of Tea', the female characters are marginal figures, with the unsettling figure of Shikibu Heinai and his three retainers the ghostly focus of the tale. Apart from their ability to appear and disappear, there is little exposition as to their spirit nature, and it is not made clear why Shikibu would mark this particular guard as the target for vengeance. As such, Shikibu is by far the most malevolent spirit of the four episodes. He has not been betrayed or abandoned like the wife of the first tale, nor is he a victim of war, like the brave but tragic ghosts of the Hoichi story. He is not inclined to be merciful like Yuki Onna. His anger seems related to being 'wounded' by Kannai, when the guard apparently drank his soul. Kannai's actions, meanwhile, are understandable, if foolhardy: he is unnerved to find the spirit in his cup at first, and later views the man as an intruder to be stopped. The story is left entirely unresolved, with the author himself seemingly transformed into a trapped spirit.

Although in general the film is extremely faithful to its source material, frequently using Hearn's exact dialogue, Kobayashi does alter plot, character and imagery to enhance the cinematic impact of the texts, and frequently to ramp up the horror. In the written version of 'Kurokami', for example, when the samurai discovers the corpse of his wife beside him he stumbles outside and questions his neighbours. They tell him that his wife died soon after he left, and that he returned on the anniversary of her death. In the film, the narrator describes the samurai returning home at midnight on September 10th, but the relevance of that date is left unexplained. In its original form, the story is more like that of *Ugetsu Monogatari*, and it could well be that Kobayashi wanted to outdo the horror of the earlier film. As such, rather than being given any sense of rational explanation, the viewer is left to contemplate the freeze-frame horror of the samurai's tortured expression.

One important, though seemingly minor, plot addition to 'Hoichi' is the death of a local fisherman. Apparently the latest in a recent spate, the villagers link the deaths to the presence of a ghost-ship and to the Heiki spirits – a clear sign that all is not well. This sub-plot brings a palpable sense of the physical danger posed by the Heiki spirits, as well as serving to round out the world of the characters beyond the immediate environs of the temple and graveyard. When the body is found, one local man lifts the sheet that covers the corpse; his exaggerated expression of repulsion suggests the horrific state of the body, which is left to the viewer's imagination. The priest's warning to Hoichi that the spirits will 'tear him to shreds' is lent further credence through the obviously violent death of the fisherman. Finally, the funeral of the fisherman is included by Kobayashi as a plot device, used to draw the priest away from the temple to administer last rites prior to sending the body out to sea.

Kobayashi's alterations to the original stories are not all made in the service of horror, however. The servants at the temple in 'Hoichi' and, to a lesser extent, the peasant women of 'Yuki-Onna', bring some welcome moments of comic relief to these dark tales. The two servants reluctantly heading out into the rain to search for Hoichi provide some pure slapstick as they frighten each other when skulking around in the night. The comically-exaggerated expressions of the servants, and of some of the villagers, serve to provide contrast to the ever-serious Hoichi. In the final scenes of the story, the juxtaposition of the temple workers, trembling under their blanket as night approaches, enhances the calm dignity and courage of Hoichi. Comedy in the midst of horror is not unique to Kobayashi of course, as we have already noted in relation to the conventional comic landlord of Hammer's Gothic productions, and the dark humour of James Whale. Such moments of flippancy can indeed heighten the effect of the darker moments of the film, and in *Kaidan* these comic characters bring a very human dimension to the otherwise ethereal atmosphere.

The concept of time is also a more explicit consideration in this film than it had been in the original source material. Where Hearn was interested in documenting, preserving and interpreting folk traditions, for Kobayashi the relationship between past and present is more fraught. There is an awareness of time in each story, and although Kobayashi leaves out the significance of that one specific date in 'Black Hair', he introduces the passing and effects of time as an important motif. Both the samurai and his first wife are ageless until the final scenes, though we are aware of the passage of many years. This enhances the shock when the samurai wakes to see the bones of his wife and her thick, matted hair. The wife's references to time hint at her own awareness that they will only have one night together: 'I don't want to sleep so I can keep you forever.' When he awakens, the samurai seems to move in and out of real time as the hair first appears black, then grey, then black again. Similarly, the red kimono they have been sleeping under suddenly turns to rags, and the samurai in the final moments rapidly moves beyond his natural age, turning his face into a horrific grey death mask.

In the final tale, Kobayashi adds the opening and closing sections set in the Meiji era (1899), when Hearn himself would have been living in Japan. The director juxtaposes the young girls in pretty red kimonos with an older woman in westernised dress. In the background it is just possible to spot a black bowler hat, very different to the traditional Japanese clothes we have seen thus far. Following these brief hints at a modernising Japan, Kobayashi takes us back another 220 years in time, closer to the period of his other stories. The final moments of the film then return to 1899 and the author's unexplained demise, as Kobayashi transports his audience to an era when the ghost story itself had achieved renewed popularity. He thus positions his film as a commentary on authorship and the nature of creativity, and on the ghost story genre, rather than as a straightforward ghost story for its own sake. (Such self-reflexivity within the horror film will be discussed more fully in Chapter 11.)

Ghost stories emanating from Japan are constructed according to specific beliefs particular to that region, passed down through centuries of legend, theatre and literature. In comparison to, say, Robert Wise's *The Haunting*, the approach of Kobayashi's film demonstrates a distinctly eastern perspective on ghosts and spirits. Whereas the narrative of a western ghost film would typically seek some kind of logical explanation for supernatural events, eastern culture fosters a belief in and reverence for ghosts. Thus in Japanese horror films the existence of a spirit world is generally taken as a matter of fact. In Japanese culture the worlds of the living and the dead co-exist, and anyone can meet a ghost, anywhere, at any time (although this certainly does not diminish the fear of meeting one). Whereas *The Haunting* never reveals the spirits who terrorise the human inhabitants of the house (Wise doesn't open the bulging door), Kobayashi's spirits appear in human form and are often indistinguishable from the other characters.

Like *Ugetsu*, in which the ghost of the wife continues to appear on screen, naturalistically completing her household chores even as her husband sleeps, Kobayashi creates an environment in which the stories' ghosts are just as real as their flesh-and-blood characters. This is particularly apparent in the final tale. Konnai is unable to recognise his attackers for the ghosts that they are and treats them as humans who can be fought, ultimately driving himself insane. The apparently mundane cup of tea of the title also serves to locate this odd tale in the everyday world. From the opening tableaux of village and domestic life in the early Meiji era to the scenes at the compound, Kobayashi depicts a realist *mise-en-scène*, with special effects limited to the reflection of Heinai's face in the liquid and the disappearing act of the spirit and his retainers. Similarly, 'Kurokami' is a measured prelude to the more overtly supernatural tales that follow. Only when the doomed samurai returns home are we introduced to the world of the spirit. Yet despite its realism, Kobayashi makes use of stylised *mise-en-scène* to subtly convey atmosphere and detail. When the samurai is leaving his first wife the shots of him walking out of the house are filled with vertical lines, black pillars and frames, representing his feeling of imprisonment and desire to escape his mundane life. Notice also the murky colour scheme of his first home compared with the bright creams and reds at the home of the second wife's family, contrasting the apparently boring and lifeless world of the first marriage with that of the second.

While the opening and closing episodes of the film are essentially realist in style, for the second and third tales Kobayashi purposely evokes an altogether more dream-like atmosphere. The middle two stories were shot almost entirely on indoor sets, located in an abandoned aircraft hangar due to the lack of sufficiently large sound stages. Here, Kobayashi had complete control over the set design and was able to indulge in highly stylised film-making, employing an art cinema aesthetic. This is apparent from the opening of 'Yuki Onna', which features a perfectly symmetrical shot of a forest landscape.

Figure 6.2

It is an ordered world that soon turns to disorder following the harsh north wind that blows in and covers the trees with snow. The sky turns white, and, as a giant painted eye looks down from above, it is apparent that this is no natural snowstorm. Obviously an artistic representation on the part of the director rather than a view as seen through the eyes of the characters, the impression given is that Minokichi and the woodcutter are actually being watched from a higher level (see Fig 6.2). Indeed, throughout the film there are a number of overhead shots looking down on the characters; like the narrator (and the denizens of the spirit world), the viewer is granted a degree of omniscience. Later, when the hero Minokichi meets Yuki in her human form, a giant pair of lips hangs in a warm sky. This then turns black as they continue walking through the forest, while the landscape becomes red, then grey. Such *mise-en-scène* demands interior filming, and recalls the use of painted sets by the German Expressionists.

Although Kobayashi denied it was a horror film, previous works of the genre undoubtedly informed many of *Kaidan*'s visuals. In the opening of 'Kurokami', as the camera glides around the outside of the samurai's house like a spirit on the prowl, doors creak and sheets and shutters swing in the night-time wind. It is a traditional horror film opening, showing the house and its surroundings as a place of dread, and aptly sums up the unhappy lives of its inhabitants. In 'Yuki Onna', when Yuki and the children visit the grave of Minokichi's mother, the camera pulls back to reveal a landscape of scattered, bare trees silhouetted against the sky. This scene in particular reminds us of the expressionistic graveyards seen in films such as James Whale's *Frankenstein*.

The visual difference between *Kaidan* and the early Universal horror films is of course Kobayashi's use of vibrant colour. Given his mastery of the palette throughout each of the stories, it is hard to believe that this was Kobayashi's first experiment in colour film-making. The sky in 'Yuki-Onna' and the giant impassive eyes looking down from it, span an impressive range of colours. As in the other stories, vivid red objects appear throughout, here made even more striking against the stark white backdrop of the snow. In particular, the red cloth that hangs outside the hut at the start of the tale, and the red sandals Minokichi makes for Yuki, represent the contrast between the living and the dead. In 'Hoichi' the reds and oranges of the backdrops are a stark contrast to the cool blues and whites of the previous tale, with highlights used effectively in the scenes at the cemetery. When Hoichi is dragged away from his performance, there is a cut to a shot of damaged red cloth landing on water, a visual reminder of the suicide of the Heiki women and of the blood shed in battle. The tale of Hoichi as a whole lends itself beautifully to Kobayashi's cinematic treatment, with its extended poetic battle scenes and musical performances to a grand audience of spirits. The scene in which Hoichi's body is painted with kanji is never rushed, as we witness the priests painting the palms of his hands and the backs of his legs. Again the use of red, this time for key kanji characters, is striking. Although used sparingly in the palette of the final tale the colour is a feature at key moments: from the kimonos of the young girls playing bat and ball, to the film's final shot of the cup in the centre of the screen.

The use of lighting effects, facilitated by the studio setting, is particularly strong in the story of 'Yuki Onna'. When Minokichi is reminded of the events of the night of the snow demon, blue-white light suffuses the scene, evoking the freezing temperatures of that evening and the whiteness of Yuki herself. The transformation of Yuki from human to angry snow demon is also achieved through a clever use of lighting (in a similar style to Irene's transformation in *Cat People*). Yuki advances towards Minokichi through a series of cuts as she transforms from human to spirit. This sudden transformation from happy domesticity to a terrifying encounter with the spirit world is the climax of the second vignette. Years later, *Ringu*'s Sadako frightened audiences by creeping towards the viewer in similar fashion through jerky jump cuts. However, like his themes, Hideo Nakata's palette of colours is altogether darker.

The final tale plays around with light and dark through the use of shadows. There are no colourful skies or expressionistic settings, leaving us wondering how much of this is in Kannai's imagination. When Heinai appears to Kannai during the latter's night watch, he materialises in the depth of the shadows and a light mysteriously appears behind him. He then steps forward into the light and the area behind him darkens. His face is brightly lit, giving him a ghostly white complexion in contrast to the more ruddy face of Kannai. When Heinai leaves, he seems to exit through the shadow of the clock against the wall (another reference to time, past and present). Shadows are also crucial to the final fight scene, as Kannai does battle with the dark shadows of the three retainers. Here Kobayashi employs a range of techniques to enhance the sense of Kannai's descent into madness. The slow motion view of Kan-

Figure 6.3

nai advancing towards the camera cuts to a point of view shot from Kannai himself, showing the tip of his weapon levelled against the three retainers, who are arranged symmetrically before him. The canted camera angles in the balletic fight scene are disorienting and the careful choreography of this one-sided battle sequence gives it a fittingly surreal quality (see Fig 6.3). In the final moments, Kannai's own face greys, recalling the deathly complexion of the samurai in 'Kurokami'.

Complementing the haunting visuals in generating an otherworldly atmosphere is the score by composer Toru Takemitsu. Given the lack of dialogue throughout much of the film, but especially so in the first episode, diegetic and non-diegetic sound takes on a particularly important role. Rather than having a musical score that would dilute tension, the composer has said that he wanted to generate the effect of quietly creeping up on someone, before jumping out to scare them. As a result, silence helps to build tension so that sound effects, when they do occur, jolt the viewer. For 'Black Hair', Takemitsu wanted all of the sounds to be like wood, splitting, ripping or cracking. These natural sounds are rendered unnatural through electronic amplification and distortion. In the final scenes of the story, as the samurai attempts to flee, the sounds of breaking wood as he falls through the floor occur just a moment after the action. This measured spacing between action and sound is disorienting and very deliberate – the empty space that is left is an effect known in Japanese as 'ma'. Such naturalistic sound effects, though eerily detached from their realistic origins, would have been strikingly different at the time of the film's release to the musical scores of western horror.

The three other tales each use sound in similar but distinct ways, as suited to their particular setting and theme. The soundtrack of 'Yuki-Onna' builds atmosphere from its opening, with howling winds accompanied by animal-like screams and deep, ominous chords. As in the first tale, sound effects are rooted in the world of the story, rather than being musical accompaniments. 'In a Cup of Tea' is similarly naturalistic in tone. The pervading silence is unnerving, particularly when Kannai is left alone with the ghosts. Stark sound effects punctuate the final battle scenes, often, as before, a beat behind the action. In 'Hoichi', with its set-piece opening, music still emanates from the tale itself. Prominence is given to the song of the battle, as performed by Hoichi and accompanied by the stringed biwa. Aside from scenes where Hoichi is performing (either on- or off-screen), the dialogue is generally unaccompanied by any other soundtrack. However, Takemitsu's technique of simple sounds is used to great effect in the horrific moment when the samurai tears off Hoichi's ears. Hoichi is thrown around with force, a sharp sound coming just a moment after he collides with a wall or with the ground. The audience does not see the moment when the ears are ripped from his head as the samurai blocks our view, but we flinch with each sound.

As previously noted, Kobayashi makes use throughout the film of an orator. Although a traditional technique from the early days of Japanese cinema, the device is used inventively, varying for each of *Kaidan*'s four segments. In 'Black Hair' we hear a fairly standard story narrator and there is minimal dialogue from the characters. 'Yuki Onna' adopts a typical male omniscient narrator at the start, though the narrator's duties are subsequently taken over by other characters. The mother and village women, for example, each take on an orator role, providing key details that explain the story to the audience. 'Hoichi' and 'Cup of Tea' both feature stories within stories. Hoichi opens with the staging of a battle scene and it emerges that Hoichi himself is our orator for this segment through his song. 'Cup of Tea' introduces the writer as orator, describing his own predicament before narrating the story that we see played out.

The presence of an orator in some form enhances our sense that these are folk stories being retold and reimagined through the medium of cinema. Oral and written story-telling are key features of *Kaidan*, making the nature of folk tradition itself a central theme. Narratives and folk-tales, according to this film, are powerful devices in society (something that we will discuss further in Chapter 11). There are multiple levels of textuality at work throughout: from the overt reference to folk stories and story-telling, to the use of Hearn's text (referenced in the title), to Hearn and Kobayashi's own reinterpretations of long-standing folk-tales. Even the credits sequence, with its patterns of swirling coloured ink, foreshadows this focus on text and story. In 'Yuki Onna', the hero is sworn to secrecy but eventually cannot resist re-telling the story of his own ghostly encounter. In 'Hoichi', his own ability as a story-teller brings him to the attention of the ghosts, who yearn to hear their own legend, and later brings him great fame. Written text inscribed on his body also saves him from the ghosts, though only partially. The fate of the writer in the final tale is more disturbing and suggests a connection to the destabilising peril of unfinished stories. This element did not appear at all in Hearn's original version. Whether planned or not, the tale of a writer unable to complete his ghostly tale speaks to the challenges Kobayashi faced during the making of *Kaidan* and following its release.

Reception and Aftermath

Shot in extremely wide-screen 'TohoScope', *Kaidan* was trailed as a 'revolution in cinematic technique'. However, Japanese audiences were unimpressed, finding the film slow and stylistically too far removed from Kobayashi's earlier work. Locally it was a commercial failure, exacerbating tensions between the director and the studio over the budget that had already surfaced during production; the final instalment

'In a Cup of Tea', wherein the ghost story is left unfinished and its author is cast out, is often interpreted through this lens. Kobayashi would make one more film for Toho, the historical *Jōi-uchi: Hairyō tsuma shimatsu* (aka *Samurai Rebellion*, 1967), before the director and studio parted ways. By then, however, *Kaidan* (renamed *Kwaidan* in the west to link more clearly to Hearn's tales) had received an international release and been met with overwhelming critical acclaim. Oscar nominated for Best Foreign Language Film, it claimed the 1965 Grand Jury Prize at Cannes, repeating Kobayashi's earlier success with *Harakiri*. For its western release, 'Yuki Onna' – arguably the most atmospheric and haunting episode in the film – had been removed. Kobayashi himself made this decision, thinking that the film was too long for western audiences to enjoy and wanting it closer to a more manageable two-hour running time. The full film runs just over 3 hours, and students are encouraged to seek out this version, widely available on DVD.

Impressionistic films such as *Kaidan*, popular as they were at Cannes and on the art-house circuit, did not inspire any direct foreign imitations. In terms of theme, atmosphere and style, one notable film that comes close is Mario Bava's portmanteau *Black Sabbath* (1964), which took European legends of ghosts and the supernatural as its premise and made use of similarly stylised sets. Conversely, western horror films continued to achieve success with Japanese audiences, influencing local productions such as Shochiku's *Goke: Bodysnatcher From Hell* (Hajime Sato, 1968) and a trilogy of Hammer-inspired vampire films directed by Michio Yamamoto for Toho in the early 1970s: *Chi o Suu Ningyou* (aka *Blood-Sucking Doll*, 1970), *Chi o Suu Me* (aka *Lake of Dracula*, 1971) and *Chi o suu bara* (aka *Evil of Dracula*, 1974). In general, however, this period was one of struggle for the larger Japanese studios, with Daiei going bankrupt and the remainder cutting back on production in the face of dwindling audiences.

Independent film-makers, on the other hand, flourished. The Japanese 'New Wave' had emerged in the late 1950s, with directors such as Nagisa Oshima following the lead of the French *nouvelle vague*. Working outside of the established studio system, their films were often funded by the exhibition chain Arts Theatre Guild (ATG), set up in 1961 specifically to distribute experimental and 'art' cinema from around the world. Films of the Japanese new wave generally catered to the youth market and often featured healthy doses of sex and violence. The so-called 'pink cinema' genre (effectively softcore pornography) was extremely successful, and played a large part in keeping the Japanese film industry alive during this period. In 1968 director Teruo Ishii made the first of what would be a series of eight films chronicling the country's history of torture, *Shogun's Joys of Torture* (aka *Criminal Women*). Extremely popular within Japan, but rarely seen outside of that country, the films featured protracted sequences of semi-naked women being tortured, with little in the way of conventional narrative. An offshoot of pink cinema, *ero guro* ('erotic grotesque') films with titles such as *Sadistic Violence to Ten Women* (1968), *Grotesque Perverted Slaughter* (Giichi Nishihara, 1976) and *Entrails of a Virgin* (Kazuo Komizu, 1986), formed a highly popular and profitable sub-genre in Japan that still thrives today.

Unsurprisingly, given the success of *ero-guro*, Japanese audiences have gained something of a reputation for enjoying more extreme fare than most. It has long been rumoured that more explicit versions (in terms of both sex and violence) of the later Hammer horror films were specially made for Japanese release, while controversial films such as *Faces of Death* (Conan Le Cilaire, 1978) and 1979's *Cannibal Holocaust* have enjoyed extended periods at the top of Japanese box-office charts. In terms of exports, the introduction of videocassettes meant that later entries in the *ero-guro* sub-genre became better known outside of Japan, particularly the notorious *Guinea Pig* series of the 1980s. More recent examples include *Audition* (Takashi Miike, 1999) (a more mainstream entry that received a worldwide cinematic release), *Strange Circus* (Sion Sono, 2005) and *Grotesque* (Kôji Shiraishi, 2009). Films such as these were a major influence on the makers of so-called 'torture porn' American films of the 2000s, typified by the extremely successful *Saw* and *Hostel* series. In particular, the elaborate and deadly traps of *Shiryou no wana* (aka *Evil Dead Trap*, Toshihara Ikeda, 1988), itself inspired by the Italian *giallo* and American slasher films of the 1970s and 80s (see Chapter 9), foreshadow the ingenious methods used to despatch the victims of *Saw* and its sequels.

Whilst many of these films saw limited exposure outside of Japan, it was the breakout success of Hideo Nakata's *Ringu* in 1998 that sparked the explosion of western interest in Japanese and other Asian horror films. Thanks in part to the arrival of multi-region DVD and Internet distribution, Nakata's terrifying but far less gory horror aesthetic was able to find a much broader audience than had the *ero-guro* films. Based on the 1991 novel of the same name by Suzuki Koji, Nakata's adaptation is generally regarded as the first in a school of films known collectively as J-Horror. The success of *Ringu* (and to a lesser extent the controversially violent *Battle Royale* [Kinji Fukasaku, 2000]) in the west led to an increased interest in Japanese horror films at the turn of the millenium, which in turn led to increased production and export of such films under the J-Horror banner. Generally taken as a blanket moniker for horror films emanating from Japan or Asia in general, some have argued that the term 'J-Horror' instead describes a set of films with specific characteristics. According to David Kalet in his 'definitive guide' to the genre, these characteristics include a focus on childhood trauma and dysfunctional families, with modern women featuring as threats to social order. As such, the term can be applied not only to original Japanese productions such as *Ringu*, *Ju-On* and *Dark Water* (Hideo Nakata, 2002), but also to their American remakes, which retain the underlying themes and iconography while losing much of the cultural and ideological background (see Kalet 2007).

There is no simple trajectory to be drawn from *Kaidan* to the later J-Horror successes; Kobayashi's film belongs to a very particular moment in Japanese film history. Nevertheless, while contemporary Japanese horror directors draw from a range of cultural influences, including the ubiquitous manga comic (see especially the *Tomie* series of films [1999-2011]), there are elements of *Kaidan* that should feel familiar to viewers of more modern Asian horror. The influence of folk-tales, so crucial to *Kaidan*, is evident in both the form and content of the J-Horror cycle, with the figure of the avenging spirit in particular a recurring motif. But whereas Kobayashi detailed its effect on individual characters, in contemporary Japanese horror vengeance is rarely contained, often spreading in the form of a curse or disease to claim innocent victims. The past's incursion into the present, another major theme in Kobayashi's film, also persists. Reflecting Japan's pre-occupation with modernity, in more recent films this incursion will frequently be felt through the manipulation of modern technology, such as a cursed videotape (*Ringu*), mobile phones (*Phone* [2002], *One Missed Call*) or the Internet (*Kairo* [aka *Pulse*, 2001]).

In comparison to much of the J-Horror cycle, and certainly when compared to *ero-guro*, the thrills of *Kaidan* can seem very tame indeed. Kobayashi's film relies on atmosphere, sound and subtle chills to provide its scares. Along with the deliberate pacing and sheer running length this can make for a somewhat tiring viewing experience nowadays, and it seems that the film has returned to partial obscurity. However, *Kaidan* represents an outstanding example of an art-house horror film, itself a rare beast, and a critically successful one to boot. Spearheaded by the New Waves of France, Japan and elsewhere, the art cinema movement of the 1950s and 60s would come to have an enormous effect on mainstream Hollywood cinema towards the end of that period. These effects will be examined in more detail in the next two chapters, as we look at two American productions from 1968.

Bibliography

Balmain, Colette (2008) *Introduction to Japanese Horror Film*. Edinburgh University Press.

Creed, Barbara (1986) 'Horror and the Monstrous-Feminine: An Imaginary Abjection'. In 'Screen' (27) 1, pp. 44-71.

Hayes, Marisa C. (2017) *Ju-on: The Grudge (Devil's Advocates)*. Leighton Buzzard: Auteur.

Hunter, Jack (1998) *Eros in Hell: Sex, Blood and Madness in Japanese Cinema*. np: Creation Books.

Jones, Steve (2013) *Torture Porn: Popular Horror After* Saw. New York: Palgrave.

Kalat, David (2007) *J-Horror: The Definitive Guide to The Ring, The Grudge and Beyond*. New York: Vertical.

Mes, Tom and Sharp, Jasper (2005) *The Midnight Eye Guide to New Japanese Cinema*. Berkeley: Stone Bridge Press.

Richie, Donald (2005) *A Hundred Years of Japanese Film*. Revised Edition. Tokyo: Kodansha International.

Schlegel, Nicholas (2009) 'Identity Crisis: Imperialist Vampires in Japan?' in John Edgar Browning and Caroline Joan (Kay) Picart, eds, *Dracula, Vampires, and other Undead Forms: Essays on Gender, Race and Culture*. Plymouth: Scarecrow Press, Inc.

Wee, Valerie (2013) *Japanese Horror Films and their American Remakes*. Abingdon: Routledge.

Endnotes

1 The publications of EC Comics provided titles and stories for two of the Amicus films, *Tales From The Crypt* (Freddie Francis, 1972) and *The Vault of Horror* (Roy Ward Baker, 1973), and we will discuss the output of EC Comics and its influence on the horror film further in our chapter on George Romero's *Night of the Living Dead*.

2 As an acknowledgement of this debt, writer/director Eli Roth gave Takashi Miike a cameo role in his first *Hostel* instalment.

Chapter 7

American Independent Horror

Night of the Living Dead

George A. Romero, US 1968

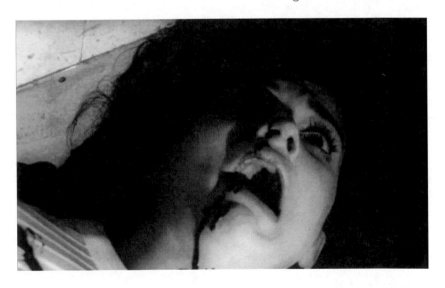

Recommended viewing

Blood Feast (H G Lewis, 1963)

The Texas Chain Saw Massacre (Tobe Hooper, 1974)

The Hills Have Eyes (Wes Craven, 1977)

Dawn of the Dead (George A. Romero, 1978)

The Evil Dead (Sam Raimi, 1982)

Introduction

By the mid-1960s, the traditional Hollywood studio system was responsible for only around 20 per cent of America's film production (Cook 1996: 512). The remainder came from independent film-makers and from films made outside of the US, where labour and locations were cheaper. Not only were audience numbers still dwindling, but demand for American films had been outstripped by that for foreign productions, from nations whose own industries were now flourishing. The 'New Wave' movements in countries such as Japan, France, Britain and Czechoslovakia introduced new styles of film-making to American cinemagoers, who found them an attractive alternative to the classical Hollywood feature film. As such, the late 1960s saw enormous changes in American cinema, including within the horror genre. Influenced by social, political and cultural upheavals occurring in the country at the time, 1968 is often cited as the dawn of the 'modern American horror film'.

Across the following two chapters we discuss a pair of seemingly very different horror films released in this year, and examine their origins, reception and lasting influence. In this chapter we look at how political and social turmoil in America led to a growing number of independent film-makers actively working against the industry establishment, taking advantage of the heavily diminished influence of the major studios, and producing films which rejected Hollywood conservatism and deliberately pushed the boundaries of acceptability. In the next chapter we look at how the major studios fought back against both independent American film-makers and the rise in popularity of art-house and counter-cinema from around the world. We also examine the concept of 'family horror', introduced in *Psycho* but which grew throughout the 1960s and flourished in the 1970s in films such as *Last House on the Left*, *The Texas Chain Saw Massacre*, *The Exorcist* and *The Hills Have Eyes* (Wes Craven, 1977).

Background

When we left the American film industry in Chapter 5, the major studios were in poor shape. The Paramount Decree had drastically cut the power that the majors could wield over the cinemas that showed their films, and the arrival of television had led to shrinking audiences. The audiences that remained were getting younger yet the studios steadfastly refused to move with the times, remaining committed to attracting older movie-goers and families, who would only venture out for 'must-see' films such as *The Sound of Music* (Robert Wise, 1965). The critical and commercial success of Wise's film (which made over $70 million and rescued 20th Century Fox from the disaster that was *Cleopatra*) served only to strengthen Hollywood's block-buster mentality, with studios assigning huge budgets in an effort to chase the next big box-office spectacular. Ticket prices at first-run cinemas rocketed, masking the dwindling audience numbers. As the majors grew more and more desperate to find a winning formula, their staid, conventional product alienated younger and more sophisticated audiences. It was during this period that alternatives to the traditional Hollywood cinema really began to make an impression on the American social and cultural landscape. These films came from the New Waves of Europe and Japan, and from America itself.

The rise of independent American film companies that began in the late 1950s continued apace throughout the 1960s, and they brought with them an approach to film-making and marketing quite different from those of mainstream Holly-wood. Although the term was popularised in the 1950s, 'exploitation films' (those that seek to capitalise on popular trends and use extravagant or sensational mar-keting to entice an audience) had been around since the early days of cinema. The fledgling Universal Studios, which did so much to establish the horror genre in Hollywood in the 1930s, produced what is generally considered to be the first exploitation feature film, *Traffic in Souls* (dir. George Loane Tucker), in 1913. Pur-portedly exposing the trade in young immigrant women by a New York prostitution ring, the film promised much in its publicity ('A Powerful Photo-Drama of Today – Six Reels of Thrilling Realities!') but actually delivered very little. Still, its box-of-fice return of almost half a million dollars on a $25,000 budget did much to help set up Universal as one of early Hollywood's major players.

The horror films released by the Poverty Row studios during the 1930s and 40s, although foregoing much of the marketing ballyhoo later associated with the term, can still be considered exploitation films. Their promotion of familiar names such as Bela Lugosi (who appeared in many such films during the 1940s and 50s) and the promise of thrills and chills unavailable elsewhere attracted a genre audience no longer catered for by the bigger studios. During the 1950s and 60s exploitation film-making began to be associated with less-reputable productions trading on the promise of controversial content, primarily sex, violence and drug use. Whereas previous films such as the 'sex hygiene' production *Mom and Dad* (aka *The Family Sto-ry*, William Beaudine, 1945) had managed to avoid censorship problems by passing themselves off as educational (or 'cautionary') films, by the late 1950s films featur-ing nudity and mild sex scenes were being widely released purely as entertainment, outside of mainstream Hollywood distribution.

The 1954 film *Garden of Eden* (Max Nosseck), set in a nudist colony, opened the floodgates following a lengthy court battle that saw the film's labelling as obscene overturned (see Schaefer 1999: 329). For a while nudist colonies remained the setting of choice for many exploitation film-makers, who endeavoured to keep up the appearance of educational value in their productions. However, the turn of the decade saw the arrival of the so-called 'nudie cuties', beginning with *The Immoral Mr Teas* (Russ Meyer, 1959). Abandoning all pretence of educational content, these films built their flimsy comedy plots around showing as much naked (female) flesh as possible. 'Sexploitation', as it came to be known, was a highly profitable area for independent film-makers in the early 1960s. Like the horror genre in the 1940s and early 50s, there was a ready audience whose viewing needs were not being met elsewhere. As they did not comply with the Production Code and so were generally not shown in mainstream cinemas, these films found homes in drive-ins and the more disreputable 'grindhouse' theatres.[1] Nevertheless, given their shoestring budgets, this was usually more than enough to turn a handsome profit.

One prolific American director in the 'Sexploitation' field was Herschel Gordon Lewis, who, with producer David F. Friedman, had made early nudie films with titles such as *Nature's Playmates* (1962) and *Goldilocks and the Three Bares* (1963). By 1963, however, their profits were falling, and Lewis and Friedman realised that the market for such films was becoming saturated and their audience jaded. They began looking for newer and more sensational thrills and found inspiration in, of all places, a Parisian theatre. Founded in 1894 and operating until 1962, *Théâtre du Grand-Guignol* specialised in explicitly gory horror productions revolving around scenes of murder, rape and torture. Aimed at the lower classes of theatre-goer, such shows were alternated with comedy productions for heightened shock effect, and proved extremely popular. It was to the graphic horror of the *Grand-Guignol* that Lewis and Friedman turned.

Just as their earlier films had consisted of stripped-down plots which did nothing more than link one scene of gratuitous nudity to the next, so *Blood Feast* (Herschel Gordon Lewis, 1963) offered little more than a collection of crude, yet shockingly explicit, scenes of murder and mutilation. Nevertheless, this was enough; universally credited as being the first 'splatter' film, *Blood Feast*'s commercial success was nothing less than sensational. With graphic sequences showing leg and tongue amputation, decapitated torsos and smashed-in skulls in glorious EastmanColor, the film pushed the boundaries of what was acceptable on screen. Lewis's subsequent films, beginning with *Two Thousand Maniacs!* (1964) and continuing into the 1970s, cemented his reputation as 'The Godfather of Gore'. The plots of these films are often ridiculous, and instantly forgettable. They exist purely to showcase as much gore as the budget will afford, and can be seen as forerunners of the more recent 'torture porn' sub-genre.

Whereas Lewis's films often included comedy to lighten the proceedings somewhat, another offshoot of the nudie cutie film that took a decidedly more downbeat approach was the so-called 'roughies'. With titles such as *Olga's House of Shame* (Joseph P Mawra, 1964), these low-budget productions revelled in the torture and beating of scantily-clad young women, usually in a bondage environment. Often adapted from men's pulp magazines, they were calculated to appeal to the basest instincts of their intended audience. The emergence and popularity of such films reflected changing attitudes in American society. The assassination of John F. Kennedy in November 1963 marked the beginning of one of the most tumultuous periods in that country's history. Violent protests over civil rights and the rise of organisations such as the Black Panthers, the assassinations of Malcolm X, Martin Luther King and Robert Kennedy, the hippie counterculture fuelled by the arrival of LSD, student activism and opposition to the Vietnam War, and the murder of actress Sharon Tate and others by the Manson 'family' all had a lasting effect on American society. Culminating in the August 1974 resignation of President Richard Nixon in the wake of the Watergate scandal, it was an era that cultivated a general distrust of authority within much of the American public.

One of the more notable successes of this period was a film that had remained practically unseen for thirty years. Tod Browning's controversial 1932 film *Freaks* (see Chapter 2) resurfaced in American drive-ins in the 1950s under the misleading (though enticing) title of *Forbidden Love*. Shown in its original version at the 1962 Venice Film Festival, *Freaks* was subsequently picked up by the American art-house circuit and quickly gained a reputation as something of an avant-garde classic, lauded for its realistic *cinema vérité* style. The film's central theme of the repressed rising against the established order also appealed to young American audiences, reflecting their disillusionment with, and active rejection of, the wisdom and rules of the older generation. These tensions would form the basis of a new wave of horror films, beginning with the case study for this chapter, George A. Romero's *Night of the Living Dead*.

Born in New York City in 1940, Romero was the son of a Cuban father and Lithuanian-American mother, and from an early age was an avid reader of the EC (Entertaining Comics) horror publications. Titles such as *Tales From the Crypt* and *The Vault of Horror* were bi-monthly comics full of tales of graphic violence and bloodshed. The extremely grim stories, heavy in irony and moralistic in tone, were leavened somewhat by the presence of a supernatural storyteller who would contribute suitably pithy comments at the beginning and end of each tale. Extremely popular amongst younger age groups, the comics were the cause of much consternation amongst parents and religious bodies, and were the subject of a study by psychiatrist

Fredric Wertham, published in 1954 as *The Seduction of the Innocent*. In it, Wertham blamed much of the rise in juvenile delinquency on the influence of violent comics, and he was instrumental in the adoption by the comics industry of the self-regulatory Comics Code Authority. Unable to conform to the code's restrictions, EC had ceased publication of all of their horror titles by 1955. However, the narratives, themes and imagery of the EC horror comics would be displayed throughout Romero's cinematic work, beginning with our case study and including a direct *homage* in the form of *Creepshow* (1982), featuring five EC-style short stories written by Stephen King.

As a teenager, Romero was bitten by the film-making bug when he was given an 8mm movie camera as a birthday present. After finishing high school, he moved to Pittsburgh to attend the Carnegie Institute of Technology, studying art, design and theatre, and graduated in 1961. His professional directing career began with commercials and industrial films in the Pittsburgh area, where together with John Russo he set up an advertising company, The Latent Image, in 1963. Inspired by the work of other independent film-makers, by 1967 they were eager to make their first feature film. They gathered ten investors each willing to put $600 into the production, many of them staff from The Latent Image, and formed Image Ten Productions. Investments from other sources would eventually total $114,000 (a fraction of the budget for an average major studio release), and the decision was made to produce a low-budget exploitation film, provisionally entitled *Monster Flick*. Basing his idea for the film's plot on the Richard Matheson novel *I Am Legend* (1954), Romero eventually settled on the more exploitable title *Night of the Flesh Eaters*. Filming would take place around their day jobs, on evenings and weekends, much of it in a rented farmhouse earmarked for demolition. All of the original investors were keen to help out behind the scenes or in front of the camera, and only two of the cast, Duane Jones and Judith O'Dea (who play Ben and Barbra), had any previous acting experience. Whilst the film would obviously lack the polish of a Hollywood studio production, Image Ten were confident that it would find a home in the drive-in market and at least return their financial investment.

Textual Analysis

Present day Pennsylvania. During a visit to their father's grave, a strange man attacks Johnny and his sister Barbra. Johnny is killed, and the stranger pursues Barbra to an isolated farmhouse where she meets Ben, a truck driver. As Johnny's killer is joined outside by more strange-looking figures, Ben barricades the doors and windows. They learn from radio reports that the country is experiencing an epidemic of mass murders, and that the killers are partially eating their victims. Two men, Harry and Tom, emerge from the farmhouse basement where they had taken refuge with Tom's girlfriend, Judy, Harry's wife Helen and their injured daughter, Karen. Further news reports reveal that the killers are in fact the recent dead who have returned to life, although there is no clear explanation how or why. A plan to refuel Ben's truck goes wrong and Tom and Judy are burned to death in an explosion, their bodies eaten by the ghouls that now surround the building. A power cut precipitates another attack on the house, and Harry is shot dead during a fight with Ben. Helen retreats to the cellar where she discovers Karen has died and turned into a ghoul. After partially eating her father's body, Karen kills her mother with a trowel. Upstairs, Barbra is dragged away by the ghoul that was Johnny as the house is quickly overrun. Karen attacks Ben but he manages to throw her off and retreat to the cellar, barricading the door behind him. The bodies of Harry and Helen return to life and Ben shoots them in the head. Next morning the ghouls have gone and Ben ventures upstairs as a posse approaches the house. Mistaking Ben for a ghoul they shoot him in the head and drag his body to a funeral pyre.

Night of the Living Dead is generally regarded as having evolved from 1950s science-fiction films, typified by *The Thing* (Christian Nyby, 1951) and *Them!* (Gordon Douglas, 1954), in which society battles against an inhuman force capable of destroying civilisation. Stemming from anxieties over the power of the atomic bomb to annihilate the planet (and later the threat of Communist infiltration), these films invariably ended with the immediate threat being defeated, but with a stark warning to remain alert, to 'keep watching the skies'. This sub-genre, which Charles Derry describes as the 'horror-of-Armageddon', took a significant step forward in 1963 with Alfred Hitchcock's *The Birds*. Based on a Daphne du Maurier short story, Hitchcock's film tells of a sleepy American coastal town, Bodega Bay, whose population of birds suddenly and inexplicably turn against humanity. Along with its lack of any meaningful explanation for the birds' behaviour, the downbeat ending of the film, in which the surviving humans slowly make their way out of the town as the amassed birds look on, marked an explicit departure from the science-fiction films of the 1950s. Like *Psycho* before it, with *The Birds* Hitchcock brought horror to everyday life, yet in this case there were no spooky houses in the background, or pat explanations from a psychiatrist.

Night shares a number of thematic elements with *The Birds*, most obviously in its disparate group of survivors who barricade themselves against a seemingly unstoppable and inexplicable attack. However, the level of horror and the sense of hopelessness far outdo anything that had gone before; if Hitchcock's film is downbeat, Romero's is positively nihilistic. From the opening graveyard scene, the institutions of modern American society are mercilessly pulled down and destroyed. It is a no-holds-barred, unremittingly grim horror film that sets out to terrify, disgust and essentially torture its audience, and it undoubtedly succeeds.

We have previously noted how the effectiveness of a horror film can depend on its ability to make the audience believe the events that it depicts, and *Night* accomplishes this by taking the appearance of a contemporary news report or television documentary. The fact that the film is in black and white rather than colour helps in this respect, as does the choice of film stock; *Night* was one of the last feature films to be shot in Academy Ratio, which roughly equates to the display of standard (at the time) 4:3 television screens. Although colour televisions were commonplace in America by the late 1960s, news reports were still routinely filmed and broadcast in black and white. Opening with long, steady shots designed to lull the audience into a false sense of security, subsequent sequences, beginning with the first attack on Barbra and Johnny in the graveyard, utilise hand-held, jerky and unsteady camerawork. This sudden switch projects an air of immediacy, evoking contemporary news reports showing scenes of escalating violence from both Vietnam and the streets of America itself. When moments of horror and violence occur, this style of camerawork immediately transports us 'to the scene', and the distance between the viewer and the events in the film is removed.

Night seeks to present a naturalistic image of a world no longer ordered or predictable, one in which random acts of violence are commonplace, and in doing so Romero delivers his personal view of American society at the time. Whilst the style of the film can be described as 'realist', it is worth remembering that, as with any film, the director has chosen to construct it in a particular way; camera angles, lighting and so on are deliberately chosen in order to convey specific meanings and cultural or political viewpoints. This is as true of news reports and documentaries as it is of fiction films. That society has been programmed to believe implicitly what they see in news reports is something that Romero comments on a number of times throughout *Night*. One explicit example is when Tom reassures Judy that all they need to do to survive is listen to what the television tells them. Less obviously, when everyone stops and gathers round the television set to see the latest on-the-scene news reports (even though the event is happening right outside the door), reaction shots of the group are from low, canted angles whereas shots of the television screen are perfectly balanced and symmet-

Figure 7.1

rical (see Fig 7.1). In a world that has gone mad, the television remains as true and reliable as ever. With juxtapositions such as this, Romero draws attention to film-making processes that classical Hollywood films strove to conceal.

Conscious rejection of the classic Hollywood aesthetic is something we have discussed previously in regards to the Expressionist and Poetic Realist movements, yet neither of these sought to depict the type of 'realism' for which *Night* is famous. Romero's approach instead recalls the work of Italian directors such as Roberto Rossellini and Luchino Visconti, proponents of the post-war Neo-realist movement. Under Mussolini the Italian film industry of the 1930s and early 40s was primarily government-funded, with the state also controlling all film distribution and exhibition. With the import of American films banned for the duration of the Second World War, film-makers utilised a massive studio complex known as Cinecitta to churn out predominantly feel-good Hollywood-style productions. Whilst the films proved enormously popular, the Neo-realists rallied against the artificiality of what they saw as little more than diversionary entertainments. They took their cameras out of the studios and into the bombed-out streets of Rome. Projecting a depressing 'slice of life', films such as *Rome: Open City* (Roberto Rossellini, 1945) and *La Terra Trema* (Luchino Visconti, 1948) forewent conventional narrative structure, usually consisting of episodic, meandering plots hinging on chance occurrences, and ambiguous, often downbeat, endings.

Aesthetically, Neo-realism diverged from the classic Hollywood film in featuring hand-held camerawork, natural lighting and non-professional actors, and would often be shot silent, with sound added during post-production. Cheaper newsreel film was frequently used, giving the films a gritty quality. Distinctly Italian in theme, the films were nevertheless designed to project a realistic image of the country to audiences around the world. Although the movement was relatively short-lived, it foreshadowed the emergence of other national cinemas, and marked the beginning of European art cinema as a recognised film form. During the 1950s and 60s, the anti-narrative aspect of Neo-realism was embraced by the French New Wave (which will be discussed in the next chapter), while its aesthetics and subject matter informed British social realist ('kitchen sink') dramas such as *Room at the Top* (Jack Clayton, 1959) and *Saturday Night and Sunday Morning* (Karel Reisz, 1960).

Although he has claimed to be more influenced by his academic background in painting and design than any particular film movement or style of cinematography, Romero is not averse to using traditional horror lighting and framing to effect scares from the audience. This is particularly noticeable when Barbra first enters the farmhouse (which is undoubtedly a conventional 'old, dark house') and makes her way from room to room, surrounded by darkness and potential danger, and again when

Helen ventures down into the cellar after her husband is shot. In these sequences, rather than indulging in complex lighting setups, Romero used opaque cloth, with cut-outs generating the required patterns of light and shadow. Canted camera angles are used throughout to represent Barbra's unstable state of mind, and her discovery of the decomposing body at the top of the stairs recalls *Psycho*'s reveal of Mrs Bates' grinning skull in terms of both technique and content. More obvious jumps are generated when figures (whether ghouls or 'good guys') enter shot unexpectedly, or grasping undead hands punch through barricaded doors and windows.

From its opening sequence, the film projects an air of ambiguity and dislocation. Although what we see appears to be relatively benign (the daytime journey of a car along a quiet road) what we hear on the soundtrack tells us otherwise. *Night*'s score consists of a selection of stock library music, much of which had been used previously in low-budget science-fiction productions in the 1950s. However, rather than using the music as originally recorded, the film-makers added electronic effects to turn the familiar into something uncanny and slightly disorienting. Visually, the film's neglect of classical conventions such as the 180-degree rule (most obviously during the sequence when Harry and Ben argue about the benefits of retreating to the cellar or staying above ground) and eye-line matching, as well as the use of jump cuts, add to the air of instability.

Editing techniques also work to subconsciously increase audience tension, such as having the individual shots becoming shorter as the film progresses. Also, when Barbra runs from the first ghoul, she does not seem to put much distance between herself and it. This is a much-used technique in horror films, where the pursuer is still able to catch the victim despite moving at a much more deliberate pace. In what is known as 'nightmare logic', no matter how fast you run and no matter how slowly the threat is approaching, you can't escape. Another film worth mentioning at this point, which in many ways foreshadows *Night* (although Romero never acknowledged its influence) is the low budget *Carnival of Souls* (Herk Harvey, 1962), in which a young woman (not dissimilar to Barbra in appearance) finds herself stalked by ghoul-like figures following her involvement in a car crash. The film contains a number of disturbing scenes, and shares *Night*'s fatalistic atmosphere and striking black and white cinematography. Although its shock twist-in-the-tail is now a little passé, *Carnival of Souls* is highly recommended and well worth tracking down.

In narrative terms, *Night*'s use of the cemetery and the approaching thunderstorm evokes memories of horror films from an earlier age, along with the familiar science-fiction device of electronic malfunction (in this case the car radio) signalling trouble ahead. However, Johnny's mocking impersonation of Boris Karloff as he attempts to scare his sister marks a deliberate shift away from the traditional horror film. The Karloff parody works to place the characters in the same reality as the young audience; like them, Johnny and Barbra have grown up with the television screenings of the Universal monster movies and watching campy horror sitcoms such as *The Munsters* and *The Addams Family*. Times had changed, and where once the graveyard was the realm of mad scientists and cloaked vampires, it was now the site of random acts of violence by strangers. Furthermore, this is not one of the fog-drenched, studio-bound graveyards familiar from the Gothic productions of Hammer and AIP, but a real modern-day location. One year before the release of *Night*, Peter Bogdanovich's *Targets* (1967, produced by Roger Corman) brilliantly juxtaposed the fantasy of the classic Hollywood horror film with the violent reality of contemporary America. In it, Karloff himself takes a semi-autobiographical role as retiring horror star Byron Orlok,[2] making a personal appearance at a drive-in theatre that subsequently comes under attack from a spree-killing sniper.

Night dispenses with any supernatural basis for the dead returning to life, and in fact does not provide any definitive explanation at all for the phenomenon. In line with the film's sci-fi roots, there is a suggestion that it may be caused by radiation from a space probe returning from Venus, but this is never confirmed. This ambiguity is just one of many ways in which the film diverges from classical convention (both generic and cinematic), and through which *Night* reveals a modernist approach. However, the hints that it is in some way related to the US space program adds to the theme of technological breakdown, as well as implicating the government in the unfolding chaos. News reports showing generals and scientists bickering over what to do is an explicit move away from the science-fiction films of the 1950s, in which decisive scientific or military action was sufficient to halt the menace. In reflecting the turmoil that America was enduring in the latter half of the 1960s, Romero's film depicts a society on the verge of collapse, in which the so-called experts are as ineffective as the individual. As an audience we have no more idea than the characters about what is happening, deducing what we can from snippets of radio, television, and garbled back-stories, which, in the case of Barbra's at least, we know are unreliable.

As mentioned, *The Birds* was undoubtedly an influence on *Night*, but whilst Hitchcock's film presents the audience with a number of empathetic characters (in particular Melanie, played by Tippi Hedren, who we follow from the film's opening scene), Romero provides no such luxury. The opening sequence at first seems to present two identification figures for the intended audience in Johnny and Barbra. Johnny's cynicism and lack of respect for his parents (and religion) would have appealed to much of the 60s generation, but he is killed within five minutes. His sister, to whom audience identification is then transferred, manages to escape but spends much of the remainder of the film in a state of almost catatonic shock. Johnny's actions in trying to protect his sister from the graveyard ghoul are a rare display of selflessness in the film. Whereas Hitchcock's characters show genuine concern for each other, and work together to survive the onslaught, the occupants of *Night*'s farmhouse generally display nothing but negativity, jealousy and hate, and are arguably more dangerous to each other than are the ghouls outside. Johnny and Barbra's testy conversation in the graveyard is a gentle introduction to the film's overriding theme of conflict; centrally and most obviously between the living and the dead, but tensions also run along familial, generational and, although perhaps not intentionally, racial lines.

The battle of wills between Ben and Harry Cooper is particularly bitter, and the source of much of the film's perceived racial message. The Cooper character is often described as a racist, but the film's script makes no mention of Ben being black, and the fact that he is came about solely because Duane Jones was the best actor for the part. But even without the film having to mention it, it is impossible to watch the exchanges between Harry and Ben and not think of the racial implications, particularly in the context of what was happening in America at the time of the film's release. As the no-nonsense blue-collar worker, not afraid to stand up to the ruthless, yet ultimately cowardly, white-collar Harry Cooper, Ben becomes the audience's identification figure, yet he too has misguided trust in the authorities, assuring everyone that 'they'll tell us what to do'. In one of the film's many ironies, had Ben not refused to listen to Harry's suggestion of retreating to the cellar and waiting it out, most of the occupants would probably have survived.

Figure 7.2

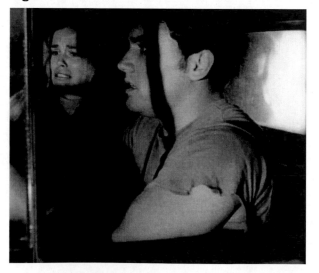

The idealistic young lovers, Tom and Judy, are recognisable characters from the science-fiction films of the previous decade (see Fig 7.2). By convention a teenage couple would be responsible for discovering and alerting the authorities to whatever deadly threat had arrived, and it was their ultimate survival that represented the continuation of the human race. In *Night*, the pair are portrayed as mawkishly sentimental, their characters barely fleshed out in a heart-to-heart that seems deliberately ponderous. A rare slowdown in the film's frantic pace, the dialogue scene between Tom and Judy before their ill-fated escape attempt affords the audience a brief respite, a chance to reflect on what they've seen so far and think about what may be to come. Romero spends time letting the audience get to know these characters only to kill them off in brutal fashion, and then prolongs the shock with graphic images of the living dead feasting on their charred remains. Their fate preys on a youthful audience's fear of untimely death; certainly before *Night* it was highly unusual (outside of the H.G. Lewis productions) for young, innocent teenagers to be killed off in a horror film. In the decades that followed, such an occurrence would become *de rigeur*.

Unhappily married Harry and Helen Cooper are united only in the concern they have for their infected daughter. The fact that this concern is repaid by Karen ripping the flesh from her father's body and stabbing her mother to death represents Romero's most explicit comment on the breakdown of the American family unit. The brutal murder of Helen by her own daughter is perhaps still one of the most contentious sequences in the film, and at the time of its release certainly the most shocking. It's difficult to forget the sight of Karen kneeling over her father's body, her chin covered in blood as she feasts on a lump of his flesh, before picking up the trowel and slowly advancing on her mother. The staging is similar to *Psycho*'s shower murder, and although more explicit the scene is horrifying more for what it represents than what is actually shown on screen.

Following Karen's killing of her mother in the basement, the theme continues upstairs. Barbra, who has now broken out of her near-catatonic state, is trying to help Ben barricade the farmhouse against the advancing ghouls. As the door breaks open she is confronted with the resurrected corpse of her brother Johnny, who drags her out of the house to her death. If *Psycho* had brought the source of horror into the everyday here and now, *Night* brought it even closer, into the home and the family. It was a theme that would be continued throughout a number of important independent horror films of the 1970s, including *Last House on the Left*, *The Texas Chain Saw Massacre* and *The Hills Have Eyes*. Cannibalism, a topic that had remained largely taboo in the horror film before the release of *Night*, would also feature heavily in the latter two of these. In the image of the undead Karen we can see an early incarnation of the monstrous children that would soon appear in films such as *It's Alive* (Larry Cohen, 1974), *The Exorcist*, *The Omen* (Richard Donner, 1976) and their numerous sequels and lookalikes.

As the horrors mount and the film careers towards its conclusion, for the audience the worst is yet to come. Whereas the classic horror film had provided the viewer

with some kind of catharsis, a release following the suspense and shocks that they
had experienced, the modern horror
films would supply none of this. Watching *Night* is a gruelling experience and it
does not relent; there is no release and
no happy ending. Our nerves have been
stretched to breaking point, but with the
dawn comes a brief glimmer of hope for
the character we have followed for much

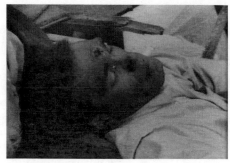

Figure 7.3

of the film. To have Ben killed in such a fashion leaves us with a sense of shock but
also pointlessness; even in the wave of horror films that followed it was unusual to
have such a bleak conclusion. It has to be said that American audiences were not
completely unaccustomed to having identification figures killed in the final reel. A
year earlier, Arthur Penn's revolutionary *Bonnie and Clyde* (1967), had ended with the
brutal slaughter of its main characters, although their ultimate fate is hardly unexpected. Whereas the aesthetic beauty of the climax of Penn's film served to raise its
anti-establishment 'heroes' to the level of martyrs, the killing of Ben in *Night* leaves
the audience with an empty feeling of hopelessness. The still photographs of Ben's
body being dragged to the funeral pyre recall the all-too-real scenes of violence
that were being reported daily in the nation's newspapers (see Fig 7.3).

Although neither would have affected Ben's fate, two alternate endings were considered for the film during production. In the first, following the shooting of Ben
the posse would enter the farmhouse and discover Barbra alive but hysterical in
the basement. In the second, the final shot would show Karen watching as the
posse drives off, signifying that the threat had not been contained and the dead still
walked. Both of these have their merits; certainly the first would have given some
kind of catharsis for the audience following Ben's demise, but lessened the film's
overall effect. If it were being made today, then the second alternative would almost certainly be used – it is now practically convention that an epilogue will reveal
that danger still exists. Yet in the case of *Night* it would have undercut Romero's
message that it is not the zombies we need to be afraid of. We're told at the end of
the film that 'everything is under control'; the world has been saved. The question
Romero asks us is whether it is a world in which we would want to live.

Reception and Aftermath

With the film completed in early 1968, the first stumbling block came in the form
a lawyer's letter from another production company who were also releasing a film

with *Flesh Eaters* in the title. The letter suggested that to avoid confusion Image Ten should rename theirs, which duly became *Night of Anubis*, referencing an ancient Egyptian god of the dead. It was under this title that they began approaching distributors, practically all of whom pointed them in the direction of AIP. Already well-known in the genre for their Edgar Allen Poe adaptations, AIP were at the time enjoying great success handling the US release of the violent British horror *Witchfinder General* (Michael Reeves, 1968). The company were interested, but insisted that Romero change the ending so that Ben survives. The director refused, and the search for a distributor continued. Columbia Pictures then showed an interest but eventually passed on it, primarily because it was in black and white and unlikely to attract audiences away from their television sets. Unlike AIP however, Columbia had no qualms with the downbeat ending, as evidenced by their release of *Easy Rider* (Dennis Hopper, 1969) the following year.

The film was eventually picked up by Continental Pictures, a small independent distribution company that saw drive-in potential with younger audiences. The company had a reputation for handling controversial films including *Room at the Top*, and Continental's owner, Walter Reade, also ran a successful chain of art-house cinemas. Like the bosses at Columbia, Reade was happy to keep the ending, and even asked the film-makers to cut out dialogue-heavy scenes and add more zombies. Reluctantly Romero took out sequences of character development and exposition and inserted more close-ups of ghouls munching on flesh. Reade's other request was a title change to something more audience-friendly and exploitable: *Night of the Living Dead*. Although seemingly a sensible move, it was a change that was ultimately to have dire consequences for the film's investors.

Night was released in the US in October 1968, one month before the arrival of the MPAA's new ratings system and two years after the wholesale revision (and effective abandonment) of the Production Code. As such it went out unrated, available to audiences of all ages, and on its initial run was double-billed with the BBC TV series spin-off *Dr Who and the Daleks* (Gordon Flemyng, 1965).[3] The fact that many parents unwittingly left their children at weekend matinees under the impression they would be seeing a harmless 'creature feature' double-bill added to the furious outcry that accompanied the film's release. Questions were again raised over the effects of horror films on children, recalling the furore over EC comics in the previous decade.

The majority of the early reviews were dismissive, criticising the film's amateurish acting, the level of gore and that ending. Trade paper *Variety* described it as an 'unrelieved orgy of sadism' (a quote that was subsequently plastered across the film's publicity materials, in the best traditions of exploitation), going on to comment that 'on no level is the unrelieved grossness of "Night of the Living Dead" disguised by a feeble attempt at art or significance' (Russell 2005: 65). All of this, of course, served to increase audience curiosity, and *Night* broke box-office records wherever it played. However, it was here that Image Ten discovered the main drawback with going through a small distribution company. Lack of funds meant that they were unable to produce enough prints of the film to meet demand, so whilst it played to full houses, these were in smaller, cheaper theatres and drive-ins. As well as the teenage demographic, the African American cinema audience had been growing throughout the 1960s, and while it would be a few years before the arrival of the 'Blaxploitation' sub-genre, Continental were canny enough to gear at least some of the film's marketing to black audiences.

Although relatively successful at the box-office, *Night* was still regarded by the majority of critics as an amateurish, nasty piece of low-budget trash. However, in 1969 the film reached European cinemas and everything changed. There, it was regarded by critics and audiences as an 'art film', and became the continent's highest-grossing film of the year. This recognition led to a major reappraisal in the US. Championed by Andy Warhol, among others, it found a home in art-cinemas and college campuses, with Romero invited to introduce a screening at the Museum of Modern Art. Reviewers who had previously dismissed it suddenly saw it in a new light; what once was 'amateurish' was now 'realist'. As the film's popularity grew, Continental again struggled to keep up with demand. Extra prints that were struck tended to be of poor quality, using cheap film stock and low quality processing, yet in a way this made the whole thing even more gritty and disturbing.

Night achieved mainstream success through art-house recognition, yet despite it's eventual success (by the mid-1970s it had become the most financially successful independent horror film ever made), the makers were to see very little return on their investments. Continental proved to be reluctant to reveal the actual profits generated by the film, and were painfully slow at releasing any of that income, which led to a number of legal wrangles between Walter Reade and Image Ten. However, more long-term damage had been done before the film was even released. Under its original title of *Night of the Flesh Eaters*, the title card had included a copyright notice. When the title was changed to *Night of the Living Dead*, the copyright notice was omitted (Romero claimed that this was done deliberately by Continental). As a result, the film has been in the public domain, available for anyone to copy and distribute without any payment to the makers, ever since its release. Over the years, audiences have grown accustomed to seeing the film only in a washed-out, grainy bootleg form that robs it of much of its aesthetic power, and for this reason it is highly recommended that viewers ensure they locate a legitimate and authorised version of the original film.[4]

It is difficult to overestimate the effect that *Night of the Living Dead* had on the horror genre, and its influence continues to be felt, perhaps now more than ever. In his introduction to *Nightmare Movies*, a study of the contemporary horror film, Kim Newman suggested that the book was 'entirely about' the influence of George Romero and this film in particular. Of course, the most enduring aspect of Romero's film when talking about its influence on the horror genre is in his vision of the walking dead. Nowhere in the film is there any mention of the term 'zombie', yet nowadays that phrase evokes images of the shambling cannibalistic corpses first introduced in *Night*. Instead, the living dead are referred to here as 'ghouls', a word used in folklore to describe creatures that frequent graveyards and eat human flesh. Certainly this would appear a more accurate term, particularly given the circumstances of Johnny and Barbra's first encounter. The monsters of *Night* share characteristics with the traditional vampire – they are neither living nor dead, they feed on humans, they spread contagion through their bite, and they have an aversion to flame and bright light. In terms of appearance, if not actions, precursors to Romero's walking dead appear in the already-mentioned *Carnival of Souls*, as well as the science-fiction films *Invasion of the Body Snatchers* (Don Siegel, 1956) and particularly *Invisible Invaders* (Edward L. Cahn, 1959).

It was only in *Night*'s first sequel, *Dawn of the Dead* (George A. Romero, 1978) that the term 'zombie' was used to describe this particular brand of walking dead. Prior to their popularisation in Romero's films, zombies had been associated almost exclusively with Caribbean voodoo practices, with William Seabrook's 1929 Haitian travelogue *The Magic Island*, introducing the concept to western culture. The first film to deal with the subject, *White Zombie* (Victor Halperin, 1932), was a low-budget independent production heavily influenced by both Seabrook's book and a successful stage play of the same year. Starring Bela Lugosi as the villain, the film made effective use of Universal Pictures' sets from *The Hunchback of Notre Dame*, *Dracula* and *Frankenstein*. The central idea in all of these texts, that of a villainous witch doctor figure raising the dead for their own ends, formed the basis of subsequent films such as the Val Lewton production *I Walked With a Zombie* and Hammer's *The Plague of the Zombies*, which transplanted the living dead from the Carribean to nineteenth-century Cornwall.

The Spanish/Italian *Living Dead at the Manchester Morgue* (Jorge Grau, 1974), filmed in England's picturesque Peak District, was the first zombie film to be directly influenced by Romero's debut, but it was with *Dawn of the Dead* that the cannibalistic zombie industry really took off. Released in continental Europe in a shorter version, re-edited by Italian director Dario Argento under the title *Zombi*, it proved extremely popular and sparked something of a cottage industry in Italy. Beginning with the unofficial follow-up *Zombi 2* (aka *Zombie Flesh Eaters*, Lucio Fulci, 1979), the Italian zombie cycle produced dozens of films, including *Zombie Creeping Flesh* (Bruno Mattei, 1980) and *Zombies Lake* (Jean Rollin, 1981), with a number of them caught up in the 'video nasties' controversy of the early 1980s. These films took the mythology that Romero had created for his films and added their own twists, with Lucio Fulci combining elements of H. P. Lovecraft and atmospheric Gothic horror in his 'trilogy' *City of the Living Dead* (1980), *The Beyond* and *The House by the Cemetery* (1981).

The convention of having re-animated corpses that crave human flesh and can only be killed by a shot to the head is one that seems to be increasingly popular. Some of the most noteworthy recent examples are the *[Rec]* (Jaume Balaguero and Paco Plaza, 2007–) films (and their American remakes), *Splinter* (Toby Wilkins, 2008), *La Horde* (Yannick Dahan and Benjamin Rocher, 2009), and the hugely popular television series *The Walking Dead*. It has informed video games, such as *House of the Dead* and *Resident Evil* (both of which have spawned film series) and been parodied in *Shaun of the Dead* and *Zombieland* (Ruben Fleischer, 2009). With the success of the best-selling novel *Pride and Prejudice and Zombies* (though not so much the 2016 film adaptation), the appeal and versatility of Romero's creations appears limitless. At the time of his death in 2017, George Romero himself had written and directed no fewer than six films in the original series, following *Dawn of the Dead* with *Day of the Dead* (1985), *Land of the Dead* (2005), *Diary of the Dead* (2007) and *Survival of the Dead* (2009), and was in the process of preparing a seventh. In addition, *Night of the Living Dead* was remade in 1990, *Dawn of the Dead* in 2004 and *Day of the Dead* twice, in 2008 and 2018. *Night*'s original co-writer John Russo wrote a follow-up novel *Return of the Living Dead*, with a 1985 film version itself spawning four sequels.

Night was also influential outside of the zombie sub-genre. It was the first horror film ever seen by writer-director Wes Craven, and inspired him to make *Last House on the Left*, one of the most controversial horror films of the 1970s. Like *Night*, *Last House* deliberately uses shaky hand-held, documentary-style camerawork in the most violent and explicit scenes to make the horror more 'real'. Whilst *Night* at least presented a threat from outside, *Last House* and many of the horror films produced by the independents over the next ten years would concentrate on man's inhumanity towards man. These include some of the most vicious and downbeat entries in the genre such as *The Hills Have Eyes*, *The Texas Chain Saw Massacre* and *I Spit on Your Grave* (Meir Zarchi, 1978), all of which have gone on to achieve cult status and been the subject of Hollywood remakes. It has been suggested that 1970s horror films such as these (as well as more mainstream studio films including *Death Wish* [Michael Winner, 1974] and *Taxi Driver* [Martin Scorsese , 1976]) reflected a perceived powerlessness of society, and use outbursts of physical violence as a substitute for social action. Whatever their motivation, the arrival of young directors such as Romero, Craven and Hooper revolutionised the horror film, and in a genre that has traditionally attracted little support from the major film studios, the role of independent American film-makers cannot be overstated. With *Night*, and through such ground-breaking films as Sam Raimi's *The Evil Dead*, *The Blair Witch Project* and *Paranormal Activity*, the low-budget efforts of enthusiastic teams of film-makers have continually succeeded in re-inventing and re-energising the genre.

Bibliography

Cook, David A. (1996). *A History of Narrative Film – Third Edition*. London: W. W. Norton & Company Ltd.

Hervey, Ben (2008). *Night of the Living Dead (BFI Film Classics)*. Basingstoke: Palgrave Macmillan.

Kane, Joe (2010). Night of the Living Dead: *Behind the Scenes of the Most Terrifying Zombie Movie Ever*. London: Aurum Press.

Newman, Kim (1988). *Nightmare Movies: A Critical Guide to Contemporary Horror Films*. New York: Harmony Books.

Russell, Jamie (2005). *Book of the Dead: The Complete History of Zombie Cinema*. Godalming: FAB Press.

Schaefer, Eric (1999) *"Bold! Daring! Shocking! True!": A History of Exploitation Films, 1919-1959*. Durham, Duke University Press.

Thrower, Stephen (2007). *Nightmare USA: The Untold Story of the Exploitation Independents*. Godalming: FAB Press.

Waller, Gregory A. (ed.) (1987). *Essays on the Modern American Horror Film*. University of Illinois Press.

Williams, Tony (2003). *The Cinema of George A. Romero: Knight of the Living Dead*. London: Wallflower Press.

Endnotes

1. As with the demise of the Hays Code in the 1920s, the number of films being released that did not adhere to the Production Code rose steadily throughout the 1960s, until its eventual dissolution in 1966. Amongst these were more explicit foreign (usually Scandinavian) films, which played the art-house circuit.

2   The character is named after Count Orlok, the vampire of Murnau's *Nosferatu*.

3   The Dr Who film and its 1966 sequel were co-written by Milton Subotsky, and starred Peter Cushing as The Doctor.

4   The copyright problems have led to a number of ploys by the makers to gain some level of financial control, including the release of a 'colourised' version and a '30th anniversary' version that includes new material directed by John Russo.

Chapter 8

New Hollywood Horror

Rosemary's Baby
Roman Polanski, US 1968

Recommended viewing

Repulsion (Roman Polanski, 1965)
Don't Look Now (Nicolas Roeg, 1973)
The Exorcist (William Friedkin, 1973)
Carrie (Brian De Palma, 1976)
The Omen (Richard Donner, 1976)
The Shining (Stanley Kubrick, 1980)

Introduction

For a genre so thematically grounded in the battle between good and evil, the figure of Satan would seem an obvious attraction for horror film-makers. Certainly, the early decades of cinema saw numerous appearances by 'the horned one', from the trick films of George Méliès through countless re-workings of the Faust legend. Yet, when it comes to serious works of the genre concerning Satanism or witchcraft, it is surprising how underexplored this area was, at least until the 1960s. Examples prior to that decade are few and far between, the most notable being the Scandinavian semi-documentary *Haxan: Witchcraft Through the Ages* (Benjamin Christensen, 1922), which was banned or heavily censored in most countries at the time of its release; *The Seventh Victim* (Mark Robson, 1943), a Val Lewton RKO production; and the British *Night of the Demon* by *Cat People* director Jacques Tourneur. However, beginning with *Night of the Eagle* (Sidney Hayers, 1962), the 1960s saw a steady stream of noteworthy entries. These included Hammer Films' *The Witches* (Cyril Frankel, 1966) and *The Devil Rides Out* (Terence Fisher, 1968), the latter adapted from a book by British author Dennis Wheatley, who had been writing popular witchcraft tales since the 1930s.

The production of such films was fuelled by a growing public interest in magic, witchcraft and the occult in general. In the US in particular, the counterculture movement championed alternative spiritual experiences while rejecting mainstream organised religion. As such the so-called Church of Satan, established in San Francisco in 1966, quickly gained tens of thousands of followers while membership of the Catholic Church fell precipitously. It was against this backdrop that Ira Levin's novel *Rosemary's Baby* (published 1967) managed to capture the mood and resonate with a society in a state of transition. Whilst the story also plays on the distrust of the older generational establishment, so much a feature of the youth counterculture of the 1960s, its themes of alienation and loss of personal control go back to the dawn of horror cinema and our first case study. Its arrival also came at a time when Hollywood found itself facing some of its greatest challenges in terms of market forces and changing demographics. We saw in the previous chapter how independent film-makers were able to exploit changes in the industry to differentiate their product from that of classical Hollywood. In this chapter we look at how the major studios reacted to this, assimilating new approaches to film-making while retaining much of their influence and power, albeit under new ownership.

Background

Away from the horror genre, the 1960s saw an unprecedented boom in film-making outside of North America – across Asia, South America, the Middle East, and especially in Europe. These were the 'new wave' films, from directors such as Jean Luc Godard and François Truffaut (France), Frederico Fellini and Bernardo Bertolucci (Italy), Miklós Jancsó (Hungary), Tony Richardson and John Schlesinger (UK) and Jiří Menzel (Czechoslovakia). While all provided an alternative approach to conventional film-making to some degree, the French New Wave in particular sought to deliberately distance itself from traditional French (and by extension Hollywood) cinema. Whereas the 'invisible' editing techniques of classical Hollywood strove to make the viewer forget they were watching a film, the French New Wave went out of its way to draw attention to the film-making process. Classical narrative and aesthetic forms such as establishing shots were dispensed with, and non-standard editing techniques, for example jump cuts and mismatched eye-lines, were deliberately foregrounded. The chronology of the narrative was often jumbled, set in unglamorous locations and populated by non-professional, plain-looking actors.

The international new wave films were an important feature of what became known as art-house cinema. Art-houses were independently run theatres that ignored major releases and instead screened foreign or independent films for smaller and more discerning audiences. First appearing in America in the second half of the 1950s, the movement was in part economically motivated. With the outlawing of block-booking, Hollywood studios began charging more for cinemas to show their films, leading exhibitors to look for cheaper alternatives to fill their screens. As mainstream audiences dwindled, the number of art-house cinemas in the US steadily grew, with well over five thousand in operation by the end of the 1960s. At the same time, in the twenty years to 1970 the ratio of films shown in American cinemas that had been produced overseas was estimated to have increased from 19 per cent to 70 (see Toeplitz 1974:38). The demographics of those going out to watch movies was also changing. With university film courses and film societies springing up on American campuses, audiences were increasingly young, educated white-collar workers and students who sought more cerebral (and liberal) entertainment.

While independent exploitation producers such as William Castle had experimented with various cheap gimmicks to draw audiences in (skeletons flying out of the screen and across audiences' heads, electric buzzers in patrons' seats, and so on) the big studios reacted the only way they knew how. The number of productions decreased but the budgets skyrocketed as Hollywood invested heavily in family-friendly epics, projected in lavish colour on ever-widening screens. It was a dangerous game. For every *Ben Hur* and *The Sound of Music* that brought in the millions there was a *Cleopatra* and *Doctor Dolittle* (Richard Fleischer, 1967) that threw even more away. The out-of-control spending and poor commercial reception of films such as these sent a number of the big studios to the brink of bankruptcy. Back-lots were sold off to developers by the hundreds of acres, and by 1970 MGM was auctioning off the entire collection of props and costumes it had amassed over the previous four decades. These struggling studios became targets for larger companies keen to extend their investments into the entertainment industry. It was a trend that began in 1962, when Universal was bought by MCA (Music Corporation of America), and by the end of the decade Paramount, United Artists, Warner Bros. and MGM, as well as a number of smaller studios, had become assets of much larger corporations (see Toeplitz, 1974).

Gulf+Western was a multinational conglomerate, initially involved in oil and car accessories but which diversified heavily throughout the 1960s and 70s under the chairmanship of Charles Bluhdorn. Bluhdorn's decision to acquire Paramount Pictures in 1966 was an astute one. With advertisers willing to pay the studios ridiculous sums for a single screening,[1] Paramount at that time owned Hollywood's most valuable library of films not yet sold to television. Given the relative sizes of Gulf+Western and Paramount,[2] Bluhdorn was willing to take chances. Even so, his decision to hire the relatively inexperienced Robert Evans as the studio's head of production, at first for Europe but soon after worldwide, stunned the industry. Beginning his film career as an actor in the 1950s (most notably in the role of Irving Thalberg in the Lon Chaney biopic *Man of a Thousand Faces* [Joseph Pevney, 1957]), Evans was never convinced of his own acting abilities and was more comfortable behind the scenes. In 1966 he put together a package as an independent producer for Paramount, buying the film rights for a little-known novel entitled *The Detective*, and signing Frank Sinatra in the title role (film version directed by Gordon Douglas, 1968). Evans saw potential in bringing contemporary novels to the screen, and began aggressively buying up the film rights to novels before they even hit the shelves.

With many of the studios' screenwriters, producers and directors having been around since the 1930s, it seemed obvious to Evans and others in the industry that the traditional Hollywood way of doing things was no longer working. The 'old guard' moguls, those who had established the major studios half a century earlier, were leaving the business through retirement, deposition or death. Younger production heads were being brought in, more receptive to change and eager to succeed. They began to look at what was happening in Europe, and what was proving popular in these thriving independent cinemas. Embracing the idea of the *auteur* (a term popularised by Truffaut which implied that the director was the true 'author' of the film), studios began hiring directors to make more personal and individualistic films. Encouraged to take creative (if not yet financial) risks, these directors were given the freedom to work autonomously, as if outside of the studio system. Film school graduates such as Martin Scorcese, Francis Ford Coppola and George Lucas were early leaders in what became known as the 'New Hollywood', which essentially lasted from the late 1960s to the early 1980s. Having studied the work of Truffaut, Rosellini, Gance and the rest, as well as classical Hollywood and television, they were able to produce distinctive films that seamlessly married the themes and aesthetics of European art-house with the narrative structure of the conventional Hollywood model. Although there were certainly successful independent New Hollywood films (for example, 1969's *Easy Rider*), the vast majority were made and funded by established studios, the thinking being better these talented film-makers and their ideas were brought into the studio system, rather than work independently against it.

The beginning of the New Hollywood movement also coincided with major changes in the US ratings system. The Production Code that had been in place since the early 1930s was revised in 1966, replacing its lengthy list of rules and regulations with more generalised guidelines. More significant was the introduction of the SMA (Suggested for Mature Audiences) label, which allowed more adult-themed films to be released with a Production Code seal of approval. Effectively a stop-gap prior to the introduction of a formal ratings system in 1968, the changes gave studios and film-makers more creative freedom to depict adult themes as never before. Early New Hollywood films such as *Bonnie and Clyde* and *The Graduate* (Mike Nichols, 1967) introduced new levels of violence and sexual frankness to studio-produced and distributed movies. The critical and financial success of these films encouraged the studios to produce more films that would appeal to the younger audiences who made these two of the highest grossing releases of 1967 and 1968.[3]

With all of the changes affecting the industry, one of Paramount's more experienced employees was also looking to move with the times. Keen to distance himself from the gimmicky films he had been associated with over the previous decade, William Castle was actively seeking more mainstream projects. After a couple of minor hits with Columbia he had switched to Paramount, but managed to produce only two unsuccessful comedies. As he began to lose hope of ever being involved in serious film-making, Castle received a pre-release copy of *Rosemary's Baby*, the second novel by playwright Ira Levin, from the author's agent (another copy had been sent to Alfred Hitchcock). After reading it, he saw it as the ideal vehicle to make his name as a 'real' film-maker. He bought the film rights for an initial fee of $100,000 plus a percentage of the film's profits, and took it to Robert Evans with the intention of producing and directing, with long-time collaborator Vincent Price in a starring role. Bluhdorn agreed to take on the project, paying Castle $250,000 plus 50% of the film's net profits to produce (Castle 1976: 192). But when it came to the question of directing, Bluhdorn insisted that Castle meet with Evans' preferred choice, Roman Polanski.

Born in Paris to Polish Jews in 1933, Polanski's childhood was a turbulent one. Having returned to Poland in 1936, his family were sent to the Krakow ghetto following the German invasion of 1939. His parents and sister were subsequently interned in separate concentration camps, his mother killed in Auschwitz. Between the ages of seven and twelve Polanski wandered the Polish countryside, fending for himself and taking refuge with a number of different families. Eventually reunited with his father following the end of the Second World War, his traumatic experiences would remain with him and influence much of his later work. Attending film school in Lodz, Poland, he found work as an actor before directing several short films. His debut feature, *Knife in the Water* (1962) contains dramatic elements that would recur again and again in his subsequent films, such as claustrophobic settings, intense psychological conflict and an ambiguous or open-ended conclusion. Polanski followed *Knife* with the British psychological horror *Repulsion* (1965), the story of a young woman, alone and isolated in her London flat, slowly descending into madness. With events increasingly shown from the protagonist's point of view, the audience is unsure as to whether what they are seeing is real or the figment of her imagination, a feeling enhanced by the film's art-house aesthetics. Featuring a number of motifs and narrative elements that would reappear in *Rosemary*, *Repulsion* is often described as the first entry in Polanski's 'apartment trilogy', followed by *Rosemary* and *The Tenant* (1976).

The director remained in Europe for his next two films, *Cul-de-Sac* (1966), another British psychological horror, and *Dance of the Vampires* (1967) (re-edited and released by MGM in the US as *The Fearless Vampire Killers, or Pardon Me But Your Teeth Are in My Neck*), an enjoyably affectionate, albeit commercially unsuccessful, parody of Hammer's Gothic horror films. It was *Repulsion*, though, that brought Polanski to the attention of the Hollywood studios and of Robert Evans, who was well aware of the success that European film-makers were having with younger audiences. The screenplay for *Bonnie and Clyde*, arguably the first of the New Hollywood films, had been written specifically as a vehicle to bring Truffaut and the French New Wave to Hollywood. Despite initial interest, however, both Truffaut and later Jean Luc Godard declined the project and it fell to established American television director Arthur Penn. Polanski was more amenable to Hollywood's advances, however, as an ambitious young director keen to make it big in America. Summoned to a meeting with William Castle in Los Angeles, Polanski's understanding of the novel and ideas for the film overcame the producer's initial doubts. After assuring Castle that he would avoid the more artistic excesses of the European new waves, he was hired to write and direct.

Handed a $3.2 million budget (almost thirty times what Romero had for *Night of the Living Dead*, but quite reasonable for a major studio production at the time), Polanski began putting together a stellar cast to bring Levin's story to life. Although he originally wanted Tuesday Weld for the role of Rosemary, both Evans and Castle suggested Mia Farrow. The actress was well known in America for her recent high-profile marriage to Frank Sinatra,[4] and her regular appearances in the popular daytime soap *Peyton Place*. As soon as he met her Polanski realised that she would bring the character a fragility and vulnerability not apparent in the novel. In addition, viewers familiar with her likeable television role would have had little difficulty in transferring its attractive traits to Rosemary and quickly attaching themselves to the character. For the role of Guy, both Polanski and Evans wanted Robert Redford, already a respected theatre, television and film actor. Unable to hire him due to studio politics (he was in the process of being sued by Paramount for walking out on a previous film), the part instead went to prolific television actor John Cassavetes. Also an independent film-maker heavily into the avant-garde, Cassavetes used the money from his acting work to fund his own unique films, which were often improvised and shot using hand-held cameras in the French New Wave style.

For many of the supporting roles Polanski cast well-known character actors from the studio era who were familiar faces to contemporary television audiences. Following performances as likeable characters in successful films such as the screwball comedy *His Girl Friday* (Howard Hawks, 1940), in the 1950s and 60s Ralph Bellamy had become a regular in television drama series, game shows and comedy programmes. Sidney Blackmer had been acting for over fifty years when he took the role of coven leader Roman Castavet. Making his television debut in 1949, over the next twenty years he had appeared in dozens of television series and dramas, as well as a number of high profile movies, including *High Society* (Charles Walters, 1956) alongside Frank Sinatra. Ruth Gordon's performance as Minnie Castavet in *Rosemary* would spark a resurgent career in film and television, most notably starring as Maude in the romantic comedy *Harold and Maude* (Hal Ashby, 1971). In the small but memorable role of Mr Nicklas was Elisha Cook Jr., a stalwart of Hollywood crime and horror films including William Castle's *House on Haunted Hill*. Although the project would go over schedule and budget, both Castle and Robert Evans stood by the young director. As far as Evans was concerned, with Levin's story, Castle's genre experience, Polanski's fresh approach and the cast he had assembled, there was little chance that the film would fail.

Textual Analysis

New York City, 1965. Struggling actor Guy Woodhouse and his wife Rosemary take out a rental in The Bramford, an imposing old tenement block in Manhattan with a history of supernatural events. Following the apparent suicide of a young woman in their care, elderly neighbours Minnie and Roman Castavet take Guy and Rosemary under their wing. As his acting career begins to take off, Guy suggests that he and Rosemary try for a baby. On the designated 'baby night', however, Rosemary collapses and dreams that she is taking part in a Satanic ritual during which she is raped by a demonic creature. Guy confesses that he had sex with her while she was unconscious, and Rosemary subsequently discovers that she is pregnant. The Castavets arrange for her to see their choice of obstetrician, Abe Sapirstein, and increasingly take control of her life, as Guy becomes more and more distant, and Rosemary experiences growing paranoia about her neighbours' intentions. When her friend Hutch dies mysteriously and she reads a book on witchcraft bequeathed to her, she comes to the conclusion that her neighbours, as well as Dr Sapirstein, are part of a witches' coven. She believes that Guy has been indoctrinated and has agreed to give them her baby in return for advancing his acting career. As she reaches full term, Rosemary returns to her previous doctor, and tries to tell him what is happening. Despite his reassurances, he turns her over to Guy and Sapirstein, who take her back to the apartment. Waking after the birth, she is told that the baby has died. However, she follows the sounds of a crying child to the Castavets' apartment and finds her baby, its cradle surrounded by the coven. At first horrified to discover that the baby is in fact the son of Satan, she is persuaded by Roman to nurture it.

Rosemary's Baby marks a return to the realm of the fantastic: are we watching an innocent young woman drawn into a sinister plot by a coven of witches, or merely the paranoid and confused thoughts of a 'country girl at heart', struggling with life in the big city and a traumatic first pregnancy? Although for the most part Polanski's screenplay remains incredibly faithful to Ira Levin's novel, with long passages of dialogue lifted verbatim from the page, the film is much more ambiguous than its source. Whereas Levin leaves little doubt that Rosemary's body is being used as a vessel to bring the Antichrist into the world, Polanski's own agnosticism made him reluctant to suggest that the Devil (and therefore God) could actually exist. Even the film's climax, in which Rosemary follows the cries of her supposedly stillborn child into her neighbours' apartment to discover the horrific truth, could be read as the feverish nightmare of a mother traumatised by the loss of her child.

For the purposes of our analysis, however, we will assume that Rosemary's suspicions are correct, and that she is indeed the victim of a Satanist plot. Although this is a film about the supernatural, its realistic approach is completely different to that of, for example, *Kaidan*, with that film's overt depiction of ghosts and spirits. More than any of our other case studies, *Rosemary* relies on the skill of its makers to unsettle the audience – not through graphic shocks or jumps (although even today the 'dream rape' can be disturbing), but through atmosphere, situation, and the gradual realisation of what is, or what appears to be, happening. As with *Repulsion*, the horror comes from a sense of doom that builds as the story progresses towards its fatalistic climax. The source of our unease is the uncanny feeling that something is 'not quite right', be it about Guy, the neighbours, the tenement building itself, or the pregnancy. The film's ambiguity and psychological emphasis is true to the Gothic tradition, as is the general storyline, in which an overbearing husband takes a naïve young woman to live in a foreboding house with a dark history.[5]

The film's opening, a slow pan across the contemporary New York skyline before shifting down to the incongruous Bramford, references yet another standard Gothic trope – that of evil lurking beneath the surface of everyday normality. With dark towers reminiscent of a Hammer horror castle, it's entirely fitting that Ira Levin named the tenement building after *Dracula* author Bram Stoker. The power of the Bramford is emphasised in this shot, looking down on the tiny, vulnerable figures of Guy and Rosemary on the sidewalk. As they enter its mouth-like lobby, little do they know that they are about to be swallowed up by the building and the machinations of its eccentric residents. In real life the apartment block was the Dakota, at the time on its way to becoming one of the most prestigious addresses in the city. It would later become infamous when one of its residents, ex-Beatle John Lennon, was shot dead outside the lobby in 1980.

While the Dakota served as the exterior of the Bramford the interior scenes were shot on Paramount sets, with Polanski and his set designers having complete control over layout and decor. His use of wide-angle lenses for interior filming makes the apartments and corridors seem vast and cavernous, while at the same time isolating central characters and instilling feelings of paranoia. With a wide-angle lens, depth and perspective are lost and the perception of movement towards or away from the camera is heightened. These effects are particularly noticeable in the scene where Guy and Rosemary first enter the apartment following their meal with Hutch; compared to what they have left behind, the apartment seems cold, empty and unwelcoming. Although Rosemary will attempt to put her own stamp on the apartment with new wallpaper, curtains and furniture, we are constantly aware that it's always just a door away from the coven.

The building plays an important part in generating the film's atmosphere of dread, and like the Femm family home of *The Old Dark House* is a character in its own right. Indeed, it seems to have more of a back-story than any of its inhabitants, as introduced over Guy and Rosemary's 'last supper' with Hutch. In Levin's novel this conversation takes place in a German restaurant, and Hutch is much more serious and forceful in his efforts to dissuade the pair from moving to the Bramford. Here, he seems to take great delight in reciting tales of ritual sacrifice and baby-eating (he later, sarcastically, refers to the building as 'Happy House'), while jovially carving up a home-cooked roast. The opening of this scene also serves to set up the dynamic between the three characters, Hutch and Rosemary framed together smiling happily while Guy stands away, passively watching. We soon learn that Guy has little time for Hutch, describing him as a 'professional crepehanger', criticising the 'Boys Own' adventures that he writes, and, once indoctrinated, having no qualms in stealing one of his gloves for use in a ritual against him. Taking the role of 'knowledgeable expert', Hutch's inquisitive nature is quickly identified as a threat to the coven, and he ultimately provides Rosemary with the book that reveals Roman Castavet's true identity.

Given that we see everything from Rosemary's point of view (she is present in every scene, and almost every shot), a lot of the credit for the film's success in drawing the audience in should go to Mia Farrow. Her dedication to the role was admirable, from eating rare steak and raw offal despite being a committed vegetarian to wandering into the path of New York traffic on Polanski's instruction ('no-one will hit a pregnant woman', the director assured her). Rosemary's innocence and good nature is in such contrast to practically all of the characters around her that an audience cannot help but feel not just empathy but a need to protect her. Late in the film, when it seems that Dr Hill may provide an escape route to the safety of the hospital, the audience shares Rosemary's relief. Such is our attachment that when Hill subsequently leads Guy and Sapirstein to her we immediately assume that he is in league with the coven, rather than merely doing what he thinks best for a confused and deluded young mother-to-be. After all, he did seem to act suspiciously when he requested that second blood sample...

While her brief friendship with Terry (played under a pseudonym by Victoria Vetri, the actress who Rosemary mistakes her for) remains, a number of scenes in the book featuring Rosemary's interaction with parents or more innocent neighbours were cut for the screenplay. This has the effect of leaving the character more isolated and vulnerable. Also missing from the film is much of Rosemary's religious angst, in part due to Polanski's lack of personal beliefs, but also because he was concerned that Rosemary's internal conflicts would detract from the central narrative. Certainly, there is no real need for a lot of back-story; her dreams are enough to reveal that whilst she tells the Castavets that she's no longer a Catholic, she is actually still attached to, and struggling with, the faith. Instead, her emotional journey in the film is from naïve country girl ('there are no witches, not really') to a paranoid wreck, unable to trust anyone ('there *are* plots against people, aren't there?' and 'all of them witches!'), and her faith is essentially irrelevant.

Rosemary's mental breakdown is matched by an obvious physical deterioration during much of the pregnancy. Given what we learn at the film's conclusion, one can assume that the baby is voraciously feeding on her from the inside, drawing its strength and power like a vampire. Rather than blossoming she loses weight and grows pale, prompting the otherwise faithful and supportive Hutch to describe her as resembling 'a piece of chalk'. Unsurprisingly given his personal circumstances, Polanski chose not to include dialogue from the novel where one of Rosemary's friends likens her appearance to that of a concentration camp victim. Guy, on the other hand, typically ignores her health issues and is more concerned by the severe haircut she suffers at the hands of Vidal Sassoon. For a film released at the height of the women's liberation movement, Rosemary seems remarkably content in her life as dutiful wife, homemaker and prospective mother, and even when Guy admits to having rough sex with her while she was unconscious she doesn't seem overly upset. As such, her impromptu suggestion to make love on their first night in the apartment, not present in the novel, seems out of place given her passivity through-out much of the film. Could it be the first sign of the Bramford's unholy influence?

Judging by how keenly she watches his TV appearances, and how proudly she reels off his acting roles to anyone who'll listen, Rosemary is obviously very much in love with Guy. However, despite the playfulness between them in the film's opening scenes, his general demeanour makes it difficult to understand why this should be the case. Regardless of whether he has actually made a pact with the Devil, he constantly comes across as cynical, self-centred and mean-spirited, and his attitude towards Rosemary throughout most of the film is terrible. He frequently resorts to making her feel guilty to get his own way, such as when she doesn't wear the 'tannis root' charm or complains about the chocolate mousse, or when she suggests going to Dr Hill for a second opinion. Guy's response in refusing to pay for two doctors also demonstrates Rosemary's financial dependence on her husband, a situation that serves to compound her overall powerlessness.

When discussing his character, the effect of the events on Guy – his concern dur-ing the dream sequence, his shock when Baumgart is blinded (a demonstration of the coven's power, used to persuade him that the pact is real) and the fear when he feels the baby moving inside Rosemary – is often overlooked. It's interesting here to consider what effect Polanski's preferred casting for the role would have had on the film. Robert Redford's image throughout much of his career was that of a clean-cut 'all-American boy', and whilst audiences would not have expected his character to be in league with the Devil, the change in Guy's demeanour once indoctrinated would almost certainly have been more noticeable. By contrast, John Cassavetes's moody performance and 'bad boy' reputation lends a greater sense of ambiguity, meaning that, when Rosemary tells Hutch that Guy is more distant and self-absorbed than usual, we can't tell if this is really the case or just the beginning of her paranoia.

Despite some early clues (both narrative and aesthetic) that all is not as it seems at the Bramford, Polanski draws the audience in with an upbeat opening: a seemingly happily-married young couple move into an apartment overlooking Central Park, begin decorating it in warm colours, and plan to start a family. This first section has been likened to a 'Doris Day movie' rather than a horror film, and when he first read the novel Polanski himself described it as a 'soap opera' (fitting, given Farrow's previous acting experience). While the opening panoramic shot to locate our protagonists is similar to that of *Psycho*, the frantic music and visuals of Hitchcock's film are here replaced by Mia Farrow's mournful lullaby and bright pink titles. The viewer is eased into the film, giving them time to get to know the characters and lulling them into a false sense of security. Things begin to change, however, when we reach the fifteen-minute mark. Strange chanting is heard in the next apartment, the ominous music rises, the ticking clock is heard for the first time, and Rosemary's dreams begin.

Rosemary's first inkling that something is not quite right with her neighbours comes when she notices that Roman has a pierced ear, and the film makes a deliberate point of this (at the time it would have been unusual for a man of Roman's age to have pierced ears). However, there are more subtle hints throughout the film, which may be missed on first viewing. Minnie is unusually inquisitive about the fertility of Rosemary's family, and following their first meal together deliberately takes her time washing up, presumably to give Roman a chance to sound Guy out about the pact. Perhaps the most blatant narrative pointer as to the Castavets' beliefs, which Rosemary doesn't appear to pick up on, occurs during the New Year's Eve. As the clock strikes midnight, Roman raises his glass and toasts 1966 as 'Year One', something that would be more relevant to contemporary audiences than it is today; Anton LaVey, flamboyant founder of the Church of Satan, famously declared 1966 as 'Year One, Anno Satanis'.[6]

As well as the narrative clues, Polanski uses other cinematic techniques to raise audience suspicion and paranoia. The most obvious example occurs after the Castavets have been told about the pregnancy and persuade Rosemary to see their friend Dr Sapirstein. When Minnie goes to the bedroom to telephone Sapirstein, the film cuts to a shot of the bedroom doorway. As she makes the call, we can see that she is sitting on the bed but the door hides her face. Although we can hear everything that she is saying, we get the impression that something is going on 'behind the scenes' because we can't see the top half of her body. We get suspicious, because there seems to be no reason for us not to see her on the telephone, other than Polanski's choice of camera angle. Obviously, we think, there is more going on here than meets the eye, and Polanski was apparently delighted at an early screening of the film when members of the audience craned their necks in an attempt to see what was happening behind the door.

Later in the film, when Rosemary has realised the truth about Sapirstein and fled from his surgery, there is a short sequence where Polanski plays with the audience's perceptions to great effect. As Rosemary telephones Dr Hill to arrange a meeting, a figure appears outside the booth, facing away. From the back it looks like Sapirstein, and Rosemary and the audience take an anxious gasp (helped by the discordant music). Rosemary closes her eyes and the figure moves out of shot before returning. When she opens her eyes, he turns to reveal it is not Sapirstein but a friendly stranger (actually William Castle, chomping on his trademark cigar). However, here Polanski tricked the audience – the first figure, with his back to the booth, actually *was* Ralph Bellamy. We subconsciously share Rosemary's fear in thinking the figure outside is Sapirstein, because it is.

Polanski's casting decisions for the supporting players, as well as demonstrating the director's affection for classical Hollywood, allows him to play with the star system in a similar fashion to Hitchcock's approach in *Psycho*. The most obvious example of this is Ralph Bellamy, who as Dr Sapirstein would have exuded warmth and familiarity to contemporary audiences. Appearance-wise, his grey hair, beard and glasses lend him an air of authority, especially in comparison to the young and less experienced Dr Hill. Within the narrative, the fact that he delivered two of Hutch's grandchildren would have also helped raise him above suspicion. The revelation that he is in fact part of the coven is one of the most shocking scenes of the film, and marks the beginning of the final act. It's also worth mentioning that, whether by accident or design, the casting of Maurice Evans as Hutch was another example of playing against type. Instantly recognisable to television audiences at the time, Evans regularly appeared as the father of Samantha, the housewife witch in the extremely popular supernatural sitcom *Bewitched* (1964-72). As Samantha's father his character was, of course, a warlock.

Bewitched, and films such as *The Wizard of Oz* and *Snow White and the Seven Dwarfs* (1937) had popularised images of witches that *Rosemary's Baby* goes against completely. There are no hook-nosed crones in pointed hats flying around on broomsticks here, and not a cauldron or a black cat to be seen. Instead there is the highly respected doctor, the local dentist, and of course the nosey neighbours. As the eccentric Minnie Castavet, Ruth Gordon's grotesquely exaggerated acting style (and make-up) recalls the camp, so-called 'hag horror' productions of the early 1960s, such as the Bette Davis-Joan Crawford vehicle *Whatever Happened to Baby Jane?* (Robert Aldrich, 1963) and William Castle's own *Strait Jacket* (1964). Loud costumes rein-

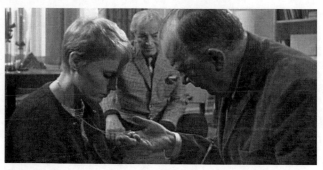

Figure 8.1

force her larger-than-life personality. By contrast, from his first appearance at the scene of Terry's death, Minnie's husband Roman projects an air of refinement, reserved authority and confidence. These qualities are particularly apparent in the scene where Roman is introduced to Hutch, the camera angles emphasising Hutch's vulnerability and Roman's power as he literally towers over him. Once introduced, Roman sits centre frame, slightly out of focus in the background, yet his piercing stare (later remarked on by Hutch, and used by Rosemary to identify him as Adrian Mercato's son) makes him the focus of the shot, and his presence dominates the scene (see Fig 8.1).

Similarly, when Rosemary and Guy sit having drinks with him before dinner, Roman holds forth in his chair, set apart and lit dramatically by a large lamp. Here the red of Roman's sweater stands out against the earthy cream and brown of the décor, and from this point in the film the colour red begins to appear more frequently. Typically of course red signifies danger, and it is interesting to note that Rosemary, associated with the soft, innocent and pure colours of white and yellow throughout the vast majority of the film, wears a set of bright red pyjamas on 'baby night'. Polanski was very particular about the use of colour in the film, as demonstrated by an incident at the scene of Hutch's funeral. When a red taxi arrived to pick up Rosemary the director immediately sent it back and insisted that a yellow one be used. Polanski's use of standard 'studio' colour attracted some criticism on its release, with commentators questioning whether horror films 'worked' in colour. Comparing this approach to that of George Romero in the previous chapter we can see the differences in thinking between the two directors. Whereas Romero sought realism through the use of handheld cameras and grainy newsreel-format footage, Polanski presented his film in the style of a classical studio melodrama that audiences would recognise, though not associate with a horror picture. As much as it deals with fantastical events, he wanted the appearance of the film to be grounded in mainstream cinematic 'reality', and these criticisms were exactly what he was aiming for.

Although identified as a key work of the New Hollywood movement and coming from a European film-maker, Polanski presented the film very much in the classical tradition. He avoids the anti-narrative and aesthetic excesses of the French New

Wave, and outside of the dream sequences (which he claimed were based on his own frequent LSD experiences) is remarkably restrained. Granted, there are certain scenes, such as those on the streets of New York, with passers-by obviously

Figure 8.2

watching the actors and looking into the camera, which have a distinct new wave quality, but these are few and far between. In this film distorted shapes and obtuse camera angles are primarily used to reflect (literally) Rosemary's confused state of mind. The most obvious examples of this are her reflection in the silver sheen of the toaster (an effect repeated from *Repulsion*) when she feels compelled to eat the raw meat (see Fig 8.2), and those of Rosemary, Sapirstein and Guy in the glass of the Bramford's lobby on the final return from Dr Hill's surgery. The discordant music by Christopher Komeda that accompanies both of these sequences heightens their sense of disorientation and panic. Although William Castle was no doubt pleased that Polanski remained true to the promise he had made before filming, John Cassavetes resented what he saw as Polanski's slavish imitation of and *homage* to classical Hollywood. This led to frequent tensions on set, including the threat of physical violence, and in the years following the film's release they were each dismissive of the other's work on it.

Given the realist approach to the rest of the film, the final revelation that an assortment of eccentric pensioners has brought forth the Devil's child, witnessed by an over-eager Japanese photographer, seems somewhat surreal. This of course raises the question of whether we are actually witnessing another of Rosemary's dreams. The fact that the scene begins with the sound of a ticking clock, used previously in the film to introduce Rosemary's dream sequences, suggests that this may indeed be the case. This ticking clock motif, which also featured heavily in Polanski's *Repulsion* to signal the psychological deterioration of its protagonist, highlights one of this film's key themes. Throughout *Rosemary* the audience is acutely aware of the passage of time, something that becomes more apparent once Rosemary is pregnant. We are given constant cues as to the current date, whether from the calendar that Rosemary keeps on the wall, Rosemary writing Christmas cards, events such as the New Year's Eve party thrown by the Castavets, or dialogue references: Minnie tells Rosemary that there are two weeks to Christmas; Rosemary tells Guy that the party for their 'young' friends will be in two weeks; when she packs her hospital suitcase, Guy tells her that she still has three weeks before the baby is due. More subtly, the passing time is marked by the improving skills of the piano player, whose practising can be heard drifting through the Bramford's corridors (and is yet another reference to Polanski's earlier film). All of these things remind us of the in-exorable countdown to the birth, which we presume will be the climax of the film.

Figure 8.3

The film's other dominant theme, that of imprisonment, is fore-shadowed in the opening shot of Rosemary and Guy's arrival at the Bramford with its barred gate and guard-like doorman. As soon as they move in the coven quickly begins to assume control over prac-tically every aspect of Rosemary's life, and once pregnant she is rarely allowed out of the apartment save for her weekly visit to Sapirstein. This situation is graphically alluded to in the scenes immediately following the rape: left alone in the apartment Rosemary sits at the kitchen table, framed by the doorway, the wide-angle lens emphasising the isolation and feeling of entrapment (see Fig 8.3). It is a shot almost identical to one discussed in our chapter on *Psycho*, where Norman sits alone in the Bates house just prior to Marion's murder. The brief scene that follows, a head-and-shoulders shot of Rose-mary in the shower against the stark brick-tiles and the vertical stripes of the wall-paper and shower curtain, reinforces the message by deliberately evoking a prison setting. Another reading of this scene is that she is unable to 'wash away' the events of the night before, and is condemned from that point to carry the Devil's child.

Like the novel, the film references real-life events from the period to generate an air of verisimilitude. Instances of this include the televised mass by the Pope at Yankee Stadium, which would indeed have occurred on 'baby night' given Levin's choice of birth date (June 25th 1966 – 6/66, and six months exactly from Christmas Day). The copy of *Time* magazine that Rosemary looks at in Sapirstein's waiting room, with its 'Is God Dead?' cover was a famous issue from April 1966. Towards the end of the film, when Guy mentions that he bought a shirt that he'd seen in the *New Yorker*, Polanski contacted Levin to try and find out exactly which issue he was referring to in the novel. At the same time, events and names are mentioned as if they are well known but are in fact an invention, such as Hutch and Guy cryptically discussing 'the Keith Kennedy business' that went on at the Bramford. This merging of fact and fiction affects the audience's perception of reality, and lends an authenticity to the film's more fantastic aspects. It is these fantastic aspects, the appearance of the Devil, the ability of the coven to remotely affect its enemies through rituals, which ultimately place the film in the horror genre. Without them, it could easily be classed as a psychological drama like *Repulsion* or a Hitchcockian persecution thriller.

Outside of the 'dream rape' sequence there are no scenes of graphic horror; Polanski eschewed traditional horror movie scares and dark shadows, he wanted everything out in the open, in bright light and colourful, everyday surroundings. When Polanski decided very early on that the baby itself would not be shown, William Castle argued that an audience who had sat through the whole film and then didn't get to see the baby would feel cheated. The director disagreed, and said that not only would viewers' imaginations conjure something more terrifying than they could possibly show, they would believe that they had actually seen the baby. The director was proved correct, with a number of early reviews describing images of a baby that was not there.

Polanski's decision not to show the baby underlines the fact that the film is less about the birth of the Antichrist than about more earthly fears, specifically that of losing control over your own life, and your own body. Its depiction of pervasive infiltration is shared with 1950s science-fiction films such as *Invasion of the Body Snatchers* and *Invaders from Mars* (William Cameron Menzies, 1953), and even *Night of the Living Dead*. But whereas Romero's film is an apocalyptic view of civilisation crumbling at the hands of marauding zombies, *Rosemary* is a story of personal disintegration. The horror comes not so much from the possibility of a coven existing in New York (their existence at the time was common knowledge, though none apparently succeeded in conjuring up Satan himself), but from Rosemary's personal predicament. For female viewers in particular (the younger demographic of which made up a large percentage of its original audience), the film preys on their fear of something going wrong with their pregnancy, or something untoward happening to their unborn child, losing it or having it taken away from them. The effects of Thalidomide were very much fresh in the minds of the population; launched in 1962 to keep morning sickness at bay, the drug had horrendous side-effects that resulted in the births of tens of thousands of physically disabled children.

It's worth remembering that at the time of the film's release, for viewers who had not read the book the revelation that Rosemary had borne the son of Satan would have come as something of a shock. Throughout the film Polanski sets the viewer (and Rosemary herself) up to believe that her baby is to be used in some nefarious act by the coven. Hutch's history of the Bramford plants the idea that babies are used in rituals or for sacrifice – eaten, or found dead and wrapped in newspaper, while his book states that the most powerful blood for rituals is baby's blood. When

Rosemary discovers the existence of the coven she understandably assumes that they are planning to use the baby for sacrifice, and tries to get away from them in order to protect it. The publicity tagline for the film, 'Pray for Rosemary's Baby', was a message designed to encourage audiences to believe the same. As such, the final revelation that the child she has been protecting all along is in fact the son of the Devil does come as a shock, and we share Rosemary's confusion and horror. This technique of holding back information and having everything fall into place to surprise the viewer at the film's climax is quite a common one in the horror genre. Its practice goes back at least to *Dead of Night* and of course *Psycho*, with more recent examples being *The Sixth Sense* (M. Night Shyamalan, 1999) and various entries in the *Saw* franchise (2004-2010; rebooted 2017).

Polanski has stated that he hates happy endings, and with *Rosemary* there is still one more 'gotcha'. In agreeing to take on the role of mother to the Antichrist, Rosemary's final action represents a total victory of evil over good. No other mainstream production to that point had ended on such a downbeat note, but it was a feature that would become increasingly common in American cinema, and not just within the horror genre.

Reception and Aftermath

Rosemary's Baby was released in the US in June 1968, four months before *Night of the Living Dead*. Whereas Romero's film played at drive-ins and cheaply-run cinemas in poorer areas, *Rosemary* had full studio backing and was treated as a major cinematic event. In a notable departure from Hollywood tradition, though one that would quickly become the norm, the task of publicising the film was handed to an external marketing company. Gulf+Western used specialised marketing companies for every other commodity, so why should film be any different? In what was one of the first cases of saturation publicity for a film, posters, badges and graffiti as well as television and radio ads, were used to get the message out. It was also one of the first non-musical films with a heavily-publicised commercial soundtrack release, providing an additional income stream as well as stimulating interest and generating extra exposure. By the time of the film's release, Ira Levin's novel was already a best-seller, providing a ready-made audience keen to see Polanski's adaptation. Playing on the director's European credentials, as well as the literary cachet, its first venues included some of the more prestigious art-house cinemas, where it proved extremely popular. More importantly financially, it was just as popular in neighbourhood theatres and drive-ins, and finished 1968 as one of the ten top grossing films of the year.

The film was a watershed for Hollywood horror, delivering Paramount an Academy Award (for Ruth Gordon, with Polanski's adapted screenplay also nominated) and box-office success, and went some way to making the genre 'respectable' in the eyes of the major studios. It's ironic that William Castle, who had spent almost two decades working against the majors with his schlock films and showman's tricks, was largely responsible for bringing horror back to Hollywood. It wasn't without controversy, however. Castle himself received numerous death threats for his involvement in bringing such blasphemy to the screen. The National Catholic Office for Motion Pictures (formerly the National Legion of Decency), an influential religious pressure group, was incensed by 'the perverted use which the film makes of fundamental Christian beliefs and its mockery of religious persons and practices' and classified the film as Condemned. Although there was already a stream of such productions, following the success of *Rosemary*, the number of films about witchcraft intensified through the 1970s.

During filming, the MPAA had urged Castle to tone down the nudity in Rosemary's dream sequence but Polanski resisted (although some shots were removed for its UK release). He wanted realism in every aspect of the film, and this included its use of dialogue; *Rosemary* was the first major studio production to feature the word 'shit', uttered by Guy when Minnie arrives with the chocolate mousse during the 'baby night' dinner. In response to Castle's concerns, Polanski told him that there was 'a new Hollywood' on the way, and soon all this and more would be commonplace in mainstream cinema. He was right, of course. November 1968 saw the introduction of the MPAA's first ever ratings system, with certificates G (General Audiences), M (Mature Audiences), R (Restricted) and X (Adults Only). Although G, M and R were ratings officially granted by the MPAA, X could be self-imposed by any distributor not wanting to go through the ratings system, to denote adult content. Although some mainstream films were released with an X (MGM's *Midnight Cowboy* [John Schlesinger, 1969] won three Academy Awards, including Best Picture and Best Director), it was most commonly used for the distribution of hardcore pornography, which became big business with films such as *Deep Throat* (Gerard Damiano, 1972) and *The Devil in Miss Jones* (Gerard Damiano, 1973). As such, X-rated films were generally frowned upon, with many exhibitors refusing to handle them and newspapers turning away advertising. The X rating was replaced by NC-17 (No Children Under 17 Admitted) in 1990, although a reluctance to advertise or exhibit films with this rating still remains. As such, the vast majority of horror films released theatrically in the US are R-rated, nowadays often with more violent or graphic material held back for an 'unrated' DVD release.

Rosemary marked the beginning of an incredibly successful run for Paramount, and under the stewardship of Bluhdorn and Evans the studio rose from number 9 in

1966's studio rankings to number 1 in 1974. During this time Evans green-lit classic films such as *True Grit* (Henry Hathaway, 1969), *Love Story* (Arthur Hiller, 1970), *The Godfather* (Francis Ford Coppola, 1972) and *The Conversation* (Francis Ford Coppola, 1974), before leaving Paramount to set up his own production company. The first release from Robert Evans Productions was Roman Polanski's neo-noir classic *Chinatown* (1974). In 1976, Paramount produced a forgettable television movie sequel, *Look What's Happened to Rosemary's Baby* (Sam O'Steen), with Ruth Gordon the only returning cast member. Ira Levin's official sequel, the novel *Son of Rosemary* appeared in 1997, with a circular plotline that seems to imply the events of the first novel were indeed a dream on the part of Rosemary. More recently, a 2014 US television remake moved the story's setting from Manhattan to Paris. On the topic of location, it's worth noting that the horrors in Polanski's film are primarily restricted to within the Bramford, with bustling New York City depicted for the most part as a welcome escape for Rosemary. This is a reversal of the view of contemporary New Yorkers, and a far cry from the gritty representations of New York that would soon become standard in films of the 1970s such as *Panic in Needle Park* (Jerry Schatzberg, 1971) and the previously-mentioned *Death Wish* and *Taxi Driver*, where the city itself becomes the source of horror and depravity.

In 1969, one year after the release of *Rosemary*, Polanski found himself involved in real-life horror when his wife Sharon Tate was brutally murdered in their Beverly Hills home (along with the couple's unborn baby and four of their friends) at the age of 26, by members of Charles Manson's 'family'. Outspoken against media stories that attempted to link him to the crimes (drawing on the macabre subject matter of his films), Polanski came under intense criticism shortly afterwards when he was paid by *Life* magazine to allow a photo-shoot at the house. This included infamous pictures of him posing beside the back door of the property; the word 'PIG', scrawled on it in Tate's blood by one of the Manson family, was still clearly visible. The killings shocked America and cast a shadow over Hollywood that still endures, forming the basis for Quentin Tarantino's 2019 film *Once Upon a Time In Hollywood*. For many it marked the end of the 1960s and any hopes of peace and love that decade had promised.

Rosemary, along with *Psycho* and *Night of the Living Dead*, is an example of 'modern horror'. All of these films bring the monstrous into the everyday here and now, the home and the family. Polanski's film contains a number of themes that would feature in horror films throughout the 1970s, including the destruction or corruption of the younger generation by their elders, the family (particularly children) as the source of horror, and the ultimate inability of good to overcome evil. Satanism (and demonic children) became big business with major studio franchises such as *The Exorcist* and

The Omen, as well as independent horror films like *The Other* (Robert Mulligan, 1972) and *It's Alive!*. The broader theme of familial breakdown and/or conflict would also feature heavily in many other important horror films of the 1970s, amongst them *Don't Look Now*, *The Texas Chain Saw Massacre*, *Carrie* (Brian De Palma, 1974), *The Hills Have Eyes*, *The Amityville Horror* (Stuart Rosenberg, 1979) and *The Shining*.

The major studios' appropriation of best-selling novels was a hallmark of the 1970s, with *Airport* (George Seaton, 1970), *The French Connection* (William Friedkin, 1971), *The Godfather* and *Jaws* (Steven Spielberg, 1975) typifying much of the output of the Hollywood studios at this time. This coincided with the rise of popular horror novelists, such as Stephen King, Dean Koontz and the British writer James Herbert. King in particular provided the source material for numerous horror films from the 1970s onwards, beginning with *Carrie*, the TV-movie *Salem's Lot* (Tobe Hooper, 1978) and the archetypal New Hollywood horror, Stanley Kubrick's *The Shining* (see Chapter 13). However, it was Warner Bros. adaptation of William Peter Blatty's *The Exorcist* that provided horror cinema with its first 'blockbuster'. A phenomenal critical and commercial success around the world, it heralded a sea change in the genre. When H.G. Lewis watched *The Exorcist*, he realised that his gore films had gone the way of his nudie cuties. The major studios were now producing films every bit as horrific and explicit as those he had been peddling for the previous ten years. *The Wizard of Gore* (1973) was his last horror film. On the other side of the Atlantic, Hammer Films' final theatrical release was an adaptation of a Dennis Wheatley novel about the satanic possession of a young girl, *To the Devil a Daughter*. Unashamedly trying to cash in on the success of *The Exorcist* it was a critical and commercial disaster, and signalled the end of Hammer as a film studio until the resurrection of the brand in 2007.

Hollywood had rediscovered and re-appropriated the horror film, and the genre was about to experience its most prolific and controversial period. Whilst films such as *Rosemary's Baby* and *The Exorcist* had brought critical acclaim and Academy Awards, the next stage in the evolution of the horror film would represent for many the lowest point of the genre's history in the form of the 'slasher'. Although its roots can arguably be traced back to Hitchcock's *Psycho*, the cycle of films which proliferated between 1978 and 1983 was heavily influenced by what had been emerging from Europe over the previous decade, and the work of one film-maker in particular – Italian director Mario Bava.

Bibliography

Castle, William (1976) *Step Right Up! I'm Gonna Scare the Pants off America*. New York, Putnam.

Derry, Charles (1977) *Dark Dreams*. London, Thomas Yoseloff Ltd.

Harris, Mark (2007) *Scenes from a Revolution: The Birth of the New Hollywood*. London, Canongate.

Hefferman, (2004) *Ghouls, Gimmicks & Gold*. London, Duke University Press.

Hutchings, Peter. *By The Book: American Horror Cinema and Horror Literature of the Late 1960s and 1970s* in Nowell, Richard (ed.) (2014) *Merchants of Menace: The Business of Horror Cinema*. London, Bloomsbury.

Kiernan, Thomas (1981) *Repulsion: The Life and Times of Roman Polanski*. London, New English Library.

Langford, Barry (2010) *Post-Classical Hollywood: Film Industry, Style and Ideology Since 1945*. Edinburgh University Press.

Polanski, Roman (1984) *Roman*. New York, William Morrow & Co.

Toeplitz, Jerzy (1974) *Hollywood and After: The Changing Face of Movies in America*. Regnery, Chicago.

Waller, Gregory A. (ed.) (1987) *Essays on the Modern American Horror Film*. University of Illinois Press.

Zinoman, Jason (2011) *Shock Value: How a Few Eccentric Outsiders Gave Us Nightmares, Conquered Hollywood, and Invented Modern Horror*. New York, The Penguin Press.

Endnotes

1. In 1966, the Ford Motor Company paid Columbia $1.2 million for the rights to show their advertisements during a single ABC TV screening of *The Bridge on the River Kwai* (David Lean, 1957).

2. For a number of years following the takeover, Paramount generated only around 5 per cent of the conglomerate's income

3. 48 per cent of American cinemagoers in 1968 were aged 16-24.

4. Their marriage would end during the filming of *Rosemary*, when Farrow refused to abandon the over-schedule production to star with Sinatra in *The Detective*.

5. The actual narrative has distinct echoes of the 1943 Val Lewton production *The Seventh Victim*. In this earlier film a naïve young woman travels to New York to investigate her sister's disappearance, only to discover that she is the victim of a secretive cult of Satanists.

6. Rumours have persisted since the film's release that LaVey played the part of the Devil in Rosemary's dream, but this is unlikely to be true. However, LaVey is credited as technical advisor (and played a small part) in a later witchcraft film, *The Devil's Rain* (Robert Fuest, 1975).

Chapter 9

The Slasher Film

Bay of Blood
Mario Bava, Italy 1971

Recommended viewing
Blood and Black Lace (Mario Bava, 1964)
Black Christmas (Bob Clark, 1974)
Deep Red (Dario Argento, 1975)
Halloween (John Carpenter, 1978)
Friday the 13th (Sean S. Cunningham, 1980)

Introduction

Of all the horror genre's many strands and variations, the original 'slasher' cycle of the 1970s and early 80s remains the most disreputable and critically vilified, yet its commercial popularity and lasting influence are unquestionable. Between 1978 and 1983, scores of films were produced, primarily in the United States and Canada, in which groups of unsuspecting teens were stalked and viciously slain by a mysterious killer. Whilst rarely making out-and-out slashers themselves, major Hollywood studios cashed in by buying finished films from their independent producers, giving the makers an instant profit and the studios a cheap marketable film virtually guaranteed an audience of teenagers. With the arrival of home video in the 1980s, low-budget film-makers were able to market their films to a much larger audience than available through cinema exhibition, and even the most poorly-produced films, those unable to attract a studio buyer, were able to turn a profit.

Our case study is a film frequently cited as a forerunner of the slasher, one heavily influenced by the Italian *giallo* genre of crime fiction. In diverging from the established conventions of the *giallo*, Mario Bava's *Bay of Blood* introduced a number of narrative and aesthetic features found in many of the slasher films that followed. In this chapter we also examine the influence of the video industry on the evolution of the horror genre (and vice versa), and take our final in-depth look at the issue of censorship, as we examine the British 'video nasties' scare of the early 1980s.

Background

The American horror film suffered something of a split personality throughout much of the 1970s. On the one hand, low-budget independent productions filled drive-ins and grindhouses, with films such as *Last House on the Left*, *The Texas Chain Saw Massacre* and *The Hills Have Eyes* following in the footsteps of *Night of the Living Dead* in bringing audiences ever more harrowing experiences. At the same time, with films based on best-selling novels, such as *The Exorcist*, *The Omen* and *Carrie*, the major studios succeeded in taking horror to the masses. However, with the emergence of the blockbuster mentality following the unprecedented success of *Jaws* and *Star Wars* (George Lucas, 1977) (coupled with the disastrous reception of big budget genre entries such as *Exorcist II: The Heretic* [John Boorman, 1977] and *The Fury* [Brian De Palma, 1978]), the major studios once again drifted away from horror film production. Back in the hands of the independents, two young film-makers in particular laid the groundwork for what was to be one of the most prolific periods in the history of the genre. Writer and director John Carpenter had enjoyed a degree of critical success with the science-fiction comedy *Dark Star* (1974) and the thriller *Assault on Precinct 13* (1976) before making his horror debut with *Halloween* in 1978. It quickly became the most profitable independent film ever, of any genre, earning $80 million from its $320,000 budget. The following year Sean S. Cunningham, producer of *Last House on the Left*, took the basic formula of Carpenter's film (nubile teenagers being stalked by a mysterious killer) and increased the violence and gore. Picked up for distribution by Paramount,[1] *Friday the 13th* was an instant box-office success, and demonstrated how easy (and cheap) it was to reproduce *Halloween*'s winning formula, if not its style and mood. The floodgates were opened.

Although it is widely acknowledged that the commercial success of *Halloween* and *Friday the 13th* sparked the slasher cycle of this period, there is constant debate around the sub-genre's ultimate origins. In heralding the birth of the modern horror film, *Psycho* has been described as 'the grandfather of the slasher film' (and it is worth noting that it was only with the arrival of the slashers that *Psycho* came to be regarded as a true horror film, rather than a thriller or crime movie). Although certainly not the first film to feature a serial killer, *Psycho*'s pre-occupation with voyeurism, putting the viewer in the shoes of its deranged murderer, foreshadows one of the fundamental aspects of the sub-genre. Similarly, Michael Powell's *Peeping Tom* (1960), a psychological study of a serial killer, features narrative and stylistic elements that would become standard in the slasher film. Venturing back even further, Robert Siodmak's *The Spiral Staircase* (1945) similarly contains a number of elements that will be discussed in this chapter. Another frequently mentioned forerunner, Bob Clark's *Black Christmas* (1974) tells the story of the members of a sorority house who are killed one by one by a psychopath living in their attic. This last film was certainly an influence on early slashers, with Clark claiming that following its release he discussed his idea for a sequel with John Carpenter. Involving a psychopath who escapes from an asylum and terrorises babysitters in the course of a Halloween night, the proposed plot is essentially that of *Halloween* (see Leeder 2014: 27).

For our case study, however, we will look at an Italian film that was made some three years before *Black Christmas*, and seven years before *Halloween*. The interesting thing about Mario Bava's *Bay of Blood* is that what is commonly regarded as the 'proto-slasher' component (the arrival and murders of the four teenagers) takes up only around a quarter of the film's running time, yet the film as a whole contains many of the requisite elements of the sub-genre as it was to later develop. Before examining the film itself, it is worth looking at the social and cultural circumstances from which it emerged.

The Italian film industry has long had a reputation for jumping on bandwagons and recycling whatever the latest hot property from Hollywood (or anywhere else) happens to be. The Gothic horror of Hammer and AIP, *Jaws*, *The Exorcist* and *Dawn of the Dead*, have (along with James Bond, *Star Wars* and numerous other non-horror successes) all formed the basis of Italian mini film industries. During the 1960s, however, there emerged two types of film native to Italy that are of particular interest to students of horror cinema. The first of these is the so-called 'mondo' film, a genre that began with *Mondo Cane* (Gualtiero Jacopetti & Franco Prosperi, 1962) and still continues in various forms today.[2] Essentially a feature-length documentary, *Cane* focuses on the more extreme aspects of human and animal existence, featuring scenes of death and disaster, bizarre rituals, drug addicts, and so on. Such was the success of the film (including a 1964 Academy Award nomination for Best Song) that a sequel and many imitations followed, each seeking to out-do what had gone before in terms of graphic violence and suffering. Real-life animal killings became a feature of the Italian cannibal movies, which flourished briefly in the late 1970s, most notoriously in *Cannibal Holocaust* (itself a powerful critique of the ethics of mondo film-making) and *Cannibal Ferox* (Umberto Lenzi, 1980).[3] Meanwhile the fascination with human death and suffering continued in films such as *Africa Addio* (Jacopetti & Prospero, 1966), inspiring the American *Faces of Death* (John Alan Schwartz, 1979) and its many follow-ups and lookalikes. The aesthetics of these (and in particular Deodato's entry) continue to inform the 'found footage' style of film, which began in earnest with *The Blair Witch Project*. Although the non-fiction aspect of the mondo film places it outside the scope of this study, interested students are directed to David Kerekes and David Slater's excellent book, *Killing for Culture*.

The second interesting branch of Italy's home-grown product, and the starting point for this chapter, is the *giallo*. Meaning 'yellow', the genre's name derives from the standard colour of the covers used by Italian publishers for written crime fiction. Beginning with the output of Milan-based publisher Mondadori in the late 1920s, and still extremely popular today, *gialli* are essentially murder mysteries. Original publications included translations of novels by well-known English language authors such as Agatha Christie and Edgar Wallace, but the field has since become increasingly dominated by Italian writers. The transition from literature to film occurred in the early 1960s, with Mario Bava's *The Girl Who Knew Too Much* (1963). The first in a series of Italian productions funded by AIP for US distribution to the teenage drive-in market, it is widely accepted as the first cinematic *giallo*. In it, an American tourist visiting Rome becomes embroiled in a series of murders carried out by the mysterious 'Alphabet Killer' (an acknowledgement of Agatha Christie's book *The Alphabet Murders*). Titled as *homage* to Alfred Hitchcock's *The Man Who Knew Too Much*, the film features rich black and white photography reminiscent of *Psycho* and *Les Diaboliques*, along with effective use of canted camera angles and Gothic locations. Co-written by Franco Prosperi (responsible for *Mondo Cane* and several of its follow-ups), *Girl* introduced a narrative structure that was repeated largely unaltered throughout the sub-genre entries which followed: a violent murder is witnessed by an amateur detective, usually, as in this case, a foreign visitor; the witness embarks on their own investigation during which the killer's victims mount up; the witness discovers a clue or remembers a crucial fact which sheds new light on the original crime; the witness is earmarked as the next victim; witness and killer meet in a final showdown during which the killer is unmasked.

Born in 1914, Mario Bava began his film career as a cinematographer working on shorts and documentaries in the early 1940s, before moving onto feature films. Included in these are *I Vampiri* (Riccardo Freda, 1956), credited as the first Italian vampire film and one that anticipates the Hammer films that were soon to follow. As a director, Bava's best-known films are the period Gothic *Black Sunday* – his debut and a film which was refused even an X certificate in the UK for eight years – and the portmanteau *Black Sabbath*, starring Boris Karloff in one episode as a vampire-like 'Wurdalak'. Although frequently compared to the output of Hammer at that time, Bava's films tend to have a much more dreamlike and disturbing quality and are heavily influenced by his early training as a painter. In this respect parallels can be drawn with the work of fellow artist Kobayashi; Bava's films were a major departure from the documentary-style Neo-realism of the 1940s and 50s, and helped signal the arrival of the 'New Italian cinema'. Throughout the 1960s directors such as Michelangelo Antonioni, Frederico Fellini and Bernardo Bertolucci created highly personal films, worlds away from the tales of poverty and depression to which Italian audiences had become accustomed.

Following *The Girl Who Knew Too Much*, Bava returned to *giallo* a number of times with varying degrees of success. His second such film, *Blood and Black Lace* (1964), was hugely influential stylistically, introducing the cinematic *giallo* killer's iconic costume of black coat, wide-brimmed hat and leather gloves.[4] *Lace* also featured explicit violence and sexual imagery, and elaborately staged 'set-piece' murders that would become typical of the genre. Although commercially successful, *Lace* was criticised at the time of its release for being an exercise in style over substance, effectively eschewing a meaningful narrative and relying on its (usually bloody) visuals to keep the audience's interest. Looking back, and considering many of the films that have followed in its path, such criticism is harsh; whilst undoubtedly stylish, the film follows the standard *giallo* plot structure and remains a very efficient murder mystery.

Now regarded as one of Europe's most important horror directors, Bava is cited as an influence by popular modern film-makers such as Quentin Tarantino, Martin Scorsese and Tim Burton. *Planet of the Vampires* (1965), another of Bava's AIP-financed films, was acknowledged as a major influence on Ridley Scott's blockbuster *Alien* (1979).[5] John Harrington, the protagonist of *Hatchet for the Honeymoon* (1970), is an early blueprint for Patrick Bateman of *American Psycho* (Mary Harron, 2000), and the opening scenes of both films are strikingly similar. Although Bava's output spanned a number of genres, including the sword-and-sandal epic *Hercules in the Haunted World* (1961), with Christopher Lee, and the James Bond spoof *Dr Goldfoot and the Girl Bombs* (1966),[6] it was to the horror genre that he always returned. By the early 1970s, however, Bava found it a constant struggle to secure financing or distribution for his projects. As such, *Bay of Blood* was filmed on a shoestring budget and an extremely tight schedule, and is a far cry from the sumptuous *mise-en-scène* of *Black Sunday, Black Sabbath* or even *Blood and Black Lace*. With much of the filming taking place around the producer's beach house, tight framing in the outdoor sequences hid the lack of greenery, which mostly consisted of a few tree branches waved in front of the camera by off-screen 'technicians'. However, despite its many limitations *Bay* is an extremely important film in the evolution of the horror genre. The first production since *The Girl Who Knew Too Much* that Bava both directed and photographed, it combines familiar narrative and stylistic features of the *giallo* with those of the traditional horror film while at the same time introducing a number of new elements that would become standard in the modern horror film as it developed throughout the 1970s and into the 80s.

Textual Analysis

Modern-day Italy. In their bayside mansion, Filippo Donatti murders his wife, the wealthy countess Frederica, before himself being stabbed to death by an unseen attacker. The Countess's death is ruled a suicide and Filippo is declared missing. Estate agent Frank Ventura, who already owns a neighbouring cottage, travels to the bay, ostensibly to try and meet with Filippo in order to buy the rest of the estate. Meanwhile, four teenagers arrive at the bay, and after exploring the surroundings break into Ventura's cottage. Following the discovery of Filippo's decomposing body in the water, an unseen killer murders the teenagers one by one. That night sees the arrival of Donatti's estranged daughter, Renata, along with her husband Albert and their two young children. Assuming that she will inherit the bay, they are shocked to discover that Renata has a brother, local fisherman Simon, who is the rightful heir. It is revealed that Ventura's lover, Laura, persuaded Filippo to kill his wife, whilst Simon killed Filippo after Ventura promised him the proceeds of the sale of his parents' estate. Over the course of the night, bodies pile up as various interested parties try to clear the way to inherit the bay. Neighbours Anna and Paolo are killed after witnessing Renata apparently stab Ventura to death. Simon strangles Laura before being speared to a wall by Albert, who also kills the wounded Ventura. The following morning, Renata and Albert congratulate themselves and prepare to return home to await news of their inheritance. However, in a final twist their young children pick up a shotgun and shoot them both dead before skipping down to the bay.

One year prior to shooting *Bay of Blood*, Mario Bava had made an unofficial *giallo* version of Agatha Christie's 1939 novel *Ten Little Indians* (aka *And Then There Were None*) under the title *Five Dolls for an August Moon* (1970). Following *Five Dolls*, for which he was very much a director-for-hire without any input on casting or script, with *Bay* Bava had complete control, albeit subject to strict financial limitations. In terms of the narrative, *Bay of Blood*'s (at the time) excessive list of victims and impossible-to-guess plot can be read as a parody, both of Christie's 'whodunit' format and of the *giallo* in general. The premise of the film is undeniably absurd, and Bava's tongue-in-cheek approach is evident from the opening post-credits shot: the camera tracks a buzzing fly before its lifeless body drops mid-flight into the water of the bay with an exaggerated 'plop', its untimely and sudden demise foreshadowing those of the film's characters who will literally drop like flies. Bava's style and tone in *Bay* consistently undermine any pretension to realism, and with a palette rich in primary colours of reds, greens and blues its cartoon violence is certainly not to be taken seriously.[7]

On the face of it, *Bay*'s scenario may look like a typical *giallo* set-up: a wealthy countess, seemingly alone in her opulent home, is brutally killed by an unseen, black-gloved murderer. Isa Miranda, who played the countess, was a famous actress from the 1930s onwards (including a short Hollywood contract with Paramount), and would have been a familiar face to Italian audiences of the time. Certainly she was the film's biggest name star, and despite the brief screen time her character is arguably the most sympathetic and rounded in the film. Like Polanski with the Bramford building in *Rosemary's Baby*, Bava uses wide-angle lenses and deep focus to convey the vastness of the mansion, and the countess's loneliness within it. As thunder rolls in the distance, an angst-ridden piano theme symbolises her troubled state of mind. That she harbours some dark secret is apparent when she is unable to look at herself in the mirror, something Bava highlights with a quick zoom-in. Heavy use of the zoom was a trait of many European directors of the time, and it is particularly apparent in this film. In this instance it draws attention to something that we will later realise is significant to the plot: Simon, whose shack she can see from the window, is the countess's illegitimate son, kept there, Anna later suggests, as 'a constant reminder of her weak flesh'.

Positioning the camera at her lower eye level throughout the opening sequence encourages the viewer to invest a degree of empathy with the countess; when it suddenly switches to a more usual vantage point and she looks up in shock, we re-alise that she is not alone. Reminiscent of the *Psycho* shower scene, her murder begins with a musical crash followed by a series of quick cuts, as a noose is tightened around her neck and the wheelchair kicked away. Whilst nowhere near the shock levels of Janet Leigh's murder, the killing of the film's star in the opening few minutes would still have held a measure of surprise. And it is here that Bava appears to break one of the main rules of the *giallo*. From a cut to the killer's shoes, the camera moves up to reveal the now-familiar black leather gloves being removed. The camera then continues upwards until it shows Fillipo Donati's face, revealing the killer's identity. The audience is surprised, but they are quickly distracted by a standard horror film convention. Fillipo is disturbed by a noise outside and goes to investigate, only to find it apparently caused by a gate flapping in the wind. Characters venturing into the darkness to investigate strange noises is a suspense-building tactic used again and again in the modern horror film. They walk slowly, ominous music ratcheting up the tension, and whilst the actual noise they are investigating is invariably a false alarm, it is usually one that, as here, hides something more sinister: a second killer is now in the house, waiting to attack when Fillipo re-enters. Fillipo's murder is much more bloody and violent than that of his wife, with fleeting shots of the plunging knife inevitably recalling *Psycho*. In comparison, however, it is presented in a very matter-of-fact fashion, with no music or other non-diegetic effects. Having had no time to make any connection with the character, the audience is emotionally unaffected by his death other than by the graphic nature of it.

This opening sets the film's tone with not one but two elaborately staged murders, pulling the rug out from under the audience with a double shock and suggesting that this is no ordinary *giallo*. Indeed, it is debatable whether *Bay of Blood* could be classed as a *giallo* at all, given that it is missing several key conventional elements. These omissions, which relate to narrative, setting and character, place the film much closer to the slasher sub-genre as it was to develop, and it is within the context of 'proto-slasher' that the remainder of this analysis will operate. The slasher cycle of 1978 to 1983 is universally recognised as the most formulaic of all strands of horror cinema, employing a set of rules that remain remarkably consistent from film to film. Vera Dika's excellent book *Games of Terror* (1990) describes the common narrative and stylistic elements of the films she sees as the purest form of the slasher sub-genre, the 'stalker' film, which includes *Halloween* and the first two chapters of the *Friday the 13th* series.

In Bava's film, we can detect the generic slasher formula in its embryonic state, in the way that it introduces standard features while at the same time rejecting those of the earlier *gialli*. Conventionally, slashers open with a prologue detailing an occurrence in the past, a death or other traumatic event that will serve as a catalyst for a series of murders that occur in the present. These murders are triggered by an anniversary of the original event, the re-opening of the event's location, the escape or release of the person responsible, or combinations of any of these. Once the present-day murders begin they are concentrated in a small geographical area and a very short time frame, frequently a single night. The opening sequence of *Bay* could certainly be read as a prologue, hinting at past misdeeds that are later discovered and which explain the reasoning behind the killings. Following the murders of the countess and her husband the bulk of the film's action occurs one week later, over the space of a single day and night. There is no time to develop a standard *giallo* investigation narrative due to the rapidity with which the bodies pile up, and this is a marked departure from the films that had gone before.

Whereas the traditional *giallo* is invariably set in an urban locale (often Rome), the action of *Bay* takes place in a small, isolated, rural location. The credits sequence consists of landscape shots showing the bay of the title as an empty and isolated space, its swirling waters tinged red from the setting sun. Although it may well represent 'nature's innate sense of beauty' in daylight, the bay is depicted here as dangerous, frightening, and unmistakeably a bad place. The brewing storm foreshadows the horrors to come, while the simplistic music, full of primeval drums and discordant strings, creates an atmosphere of foreboding that continues into the film's opening scene. In conventional slashers the location is similarly isolated, either geographically or socially (favoured spots are summer camps, remote cabins, fraternity or sorority houses, and sleepovers), ensuring that the threatened parties (invariably teenagers,) are away from anyone who could possibly help them. Even when the victims are in apparently safe surroundings, for example the leafy suburban neighbourhood of *Halloween*, parents and guardians will inevitably be kept busy elsewhere. In any case, the speed at which the murders occur means that there is little time for them to respond. A conservative extension of the modern horror film's depiction of the powerlessness of authority figures, in the slasher film they are simply oblivious to the threat.

In *Bay* there is talk of a previous attempt to bring tourism to the bay and the misfortunes that followed, and of Fillipo trying to open a nightclub with disastrous consequences. Conventionally, the area in which the murders occur is often regarded as cursed or unlucky, and the victims are urged not to go there by community elders whose warnings fall on deaf ears. Oftentimes there will be an eccentric individual who claims to have insight into what is happening and attempts (usually unsuccessfully) to warn the other characters. A variant of the 'knowledgeable expert' of the traditional horror film, examples of this would be Dr Loomis in the *Halloween* franchise and Crazy Ralph in the first two *Friday the 13th* entries. In Bava's film this role is taken by Anna, the alcoholic fortune-teller whose dire prediction that 'the sickle of death is about to strike' is laughed off by her husband. Horror films in general and slashers in particular are often criticised for their characters' lack of intelligence: they wander off into the woods by themselves, go out to investigate noises in the middle of the night, or break in to Norman Bates' fruit cellar to have sex (as in *Psycho II*). Anna provides a prime example of this when, despite her apparent insight and having just been told that Filippo's body has been found in Simon's boat, she decides to head down to the boathouse alone and in the dark. But the viewer shouldn't be too critical; the films' simplistic narratives require their characters to behave with a degree of stupidity in order to generate suspense, and to allow the killer to pick them off. There wouldn't be much of a story if the intended victims simply barricaded themselves in a secure room and called the authorities.

The characters in Bava's film are often ambiguous, with the narratives examining the innate evil or capacity that lies within all of us, waiting for occasion to break out. In *Bay* that capacity is graphically demonstrated by practically everyone, and there is no real identification figure that we can support throughout. In fact, outside of the doomed countess there are no sympathetic characters at all. In any case, none of the characters seem to last long enough for audience identification to take place. The question that we need to ask therefore is, what enjoyment can the audience get from watching nothing more than a series of bloody murders? In the eyes of the majority of critics, the answer would be very little. We do not identify with any of the characters, and are happy to observe coldly from a distance in voyeuristic fashion, as they receive their just desserts. This is most apparent in the fifteen-minute section for which the film has become most famous, the introduction and brutal murders of the four holidaying teenagers. The arrival of these characters seems to be nothing more than an excuse to insert gratuitous doses of sex and violence, and forms a condensed blueprint for the films that would follow.

Yet another moniker attached to the slasher sub-genre is the 'have-sex-and-die movie', referring to the frequency with which fornicating couples are swiftly punished for their misdeeds by death. Similarly those who take drugs or drink alcohol are unlikely to survive until the end of the film. The teens in Bava's film are unequivocally portrayed as 'bad' – disrupting the peace and quiet of the bay, trespassing on Ventura's property, drinking alcohol, skinny-dipping and having sex. Whilst in this case their short screen time doesn't afford any real opportunity for characterisation, a typical slasher cast would include a predictable selection of teen characters: at least one heterosexual couple keen to get to a secluded spot; the nerdy outsider; the annoying joker; the promiscuous cheerleader; the jock; and the aloof, straight-laced girl who will generally, through their intelligence and in-genuity, make it to the final showdown with the killer. This 'final girl', a phrase introduced by Carol Clover in her influential book *Men, Women and Chain Saws*, is one of the mainstays of the early slasher sub-genre.[8] Quickly marked out as the character to foster audience empathy, she incorporates traditional female traits, is sexually passive, non-threatening (until cornered by the killer) and depicted more sympathetically than the rest of the characters.

The 'final girl' is a progression from the main characters in traditional *gialli* who unwittingly find themselves involved in the series of murders and are eventually tar-geted by the killer. However, in dispensing with the traditional *giallo* investigation ele-ment, as well as any audience identification figures, *Bay* doesn't really present us with a prototypical 'final girl' as such. Much more successful in representing this transition is Sergio Martino's *I Corpi Presentano Tracce di Violenza Carnale* (aka *Torso*, 1973), which begins as a standard *giallo* and turns into a full-blooded proto-slasher, with British actress Suzy Kendall in the role of final girl (although admittedly she does have to be rescued by her boyfriend at the film's climax).[9] Probably the closest equivalent in *Bay* is the cold-hearted Renata, the latest in a long line of strong (or positively menacing) female characters in Bava's work. One common theme throughout his films is the power that women (alive, dead or undead) hold over men, and this is apparent early in *Bay* during the first exchange between Laura and Ventura following the opening murders; he thinks he is keeping her in her place, but Bava's framing tells us other-wise. The balance of sexual power is much more explicit in the relationship between Renata and her 'weak' husband, while the two male teenagers who turn up at the bay seem perpetually in thrall of their blonde female companion, Denise.

Stylistically, the trademark cinematic technique of the slasher film is the previ-ously-mentioned POV (point-of-view) shot, and it is worth discussing this in some depth. In the slasher these shots are signified by unstable, hand-held camerawork, and/or the deliberate positioning of the camera as if peering at the action from be-hind foregrounded objects. Generally taken to represent the viewpoint of the killer, a POV shot can also be used as a red herring to build suspense, or to distract the viewer (if they think the killer is watching from a distance, they will be surprised to see him strike from another part of the frame). Bava makes much use of the tech-nique in this film, beginning in the opening scene. As the countess gasps her last breath and the wheel of her chair gradually slows to a stop, the POV shot puts us in the place of the killer as he slowly walks towards her hanging body. There is an-other shot prior to this, with the camera positioned behind the piano, which gives the impression that she is being watched from the shadows. In the slasher film the prowling POV camera is often accompanied by laboured breathing, and this too is evident in Bava's film, in the shot looking out of the derelict nightclub window immediately following Fillipo's murder (although it's never made clear in this case who is doing the breathing).

More recognisable use of the POV as it would appear in later films comes with the stalking and murder of Brunhilda and its aftermath. As she runs to the bay for a spot of skinny-dipping, apparently subjective POV shots signify that she is marked as the next victim. We, like the killer, voyeuristically watch her undress from behind the bushes, the camera following her dress as it drops to the floor. Bava then cuts to another angle, from behind a tree and again seemingly subjective, as she pulls off her underwear and runs to the jetty. And then there's yet another cut to a different vantage point, hidden by branches, as she prepares to jump into the water. Obviously all three angles cannot represent the position of the killer (although it may be an acknowledgement of the film's multiplicity of killers), but again the general impression we get is that Brunhilda is being watched. Once the audience is aware of this, suspense is generated in wondering how, when and from where the killer will strike. As discussed previously, suspense occurs when the audience knows more than the characters in the film; in this case we know that there's a killer on the loose at the bay, and, through various shots of a watching eye, that the teenagers are being stalked (see Fig 9.1).

Figure 9.1

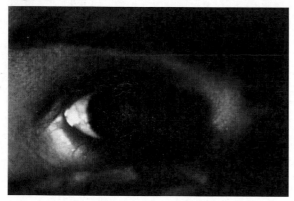

Having Brunhilda naked, as well as providing some titillation for the audience, ensures that she is at her most vulnerable, and the viewer is more fearful for her safety. The lead up to Brunhilda's death is drawn out, consisting of a chase through the woods, around the abandoned nightclub and towards Ventura's house. The changing camera positions are repeated as she runs back from the water, but it's interesting to note that the only time a true cinematic POV shot is used in the chase towards the house is through the eyes of Brunhilda herself. Only when she reaches the abandoned nightclub is it made explicit that she's actually being stalked, by way of a fleeting shadow across its walls. When her murder does come, however, it is swift and extremely violent, a sickle ripping through and chopping at her neck. Barely giving the audience a chance to recover from the shock, another POV reveals the killer approaching the house and knocking a plant pot off the windowsill.

Of course Bobby comes out alone to investigate the noise, only to receive a sickle in the face for his trouble.

Although certainly not a new technique, nor one restricted to the horror genre, slashers draw particular criticism for the POV's apparently explicit invitation to identify with their psychopathic villains. Critics (and in particular feminist critics whose views are expanded on later in this chapter) suggest that it panders to audiences who, whether consciously or subconsciously, want to commit violent acts, allowing viewers to fantasise that they themselves are doing the killing and mutilating. However, as we discussed in relation to *Psycho*, without any kind of empathy for the killer, such identification is difficult. Certainly, there are films where the audience is invited to feel a certain empathy and identification with the killer, but such films (for example *Maniac* [William Lustig, 1980] and *The Fan* [Ed Bianchi, 1981]) were generally unsuccessful commercially. The fact is that the POV shot is simply another weapon in the director's arsenal when it comes to generating suspense. Through it we know that someone is watching, but because they are off-screen we don't know who they are: they could be the killer, or a harmless prankster. In general the POV shot builds and prolongs suspense more effectively than what would otherwise involve showing a rustling bush, or a fleeting shadow, or whatever. Victims are rarely afforded POV shots, except to show that they are oblivious to whatever menace is lurking, and with good reason. As in the traditional *giallo*, many slashers are whodunits, and a more informative shot from the victim's point of view would no doubt reveal the identity of the killer.[10]

While the POV holds the audience in a state of suspense, Bava brings this to release using other techniques that would soon become familiar. The dramatic discovery of previous victims in some hidden place, or having them suddenly fall from a tree or out of a cupboard is a standard convention of the slasher, usually occurring when the final survivor is attempting to outrun the killer. Similarly, characters

Figure 9.2

looking into a bathroom mirror will spot something, or someone, lurking in the semi-darkness behind them. Renata's discovery of the teenagers' bodies in Ventura's bathroom encompasses both of these, along with Bava's enthusiastic use of the zoom (see Fig. 9.2). Bava frequently uses the zoom as an in-camera replacement for a shock cut, whether zooming out, as in this case, or zooming in on a gory kill, as in the decapitation of Anna. While such use of the zoom is a particularly Italian trait, slashers in general tend to rely heavily on shock cuts accompanied by audio stings to make audiences jump. Anna's beheading is also a good example of Bava's 'shot matching' technique, cutting from the close-up of the bloody stump of Anna's neck to the smashed pottery head in the caravan. Practically every transition from one scene to the next consists of a shot match, and alludes to one of Bava's favoured titles for the film, *Chain Reaction*. The narrative is a cause-and-effect chain that exists solely to ensure that all of the characters meet a grisly death.

Bay of Blood, like the majority of the slashers that followed, features no supernatural elements. Although the killer in these films would often appear unstoppable, they were generally no more nor less than a homicidal maniac on the loose, with any apparent superhuman powers added merely for dramatic effect. In the climactic fight of Bava's film, for example, Ventura appears remarkably active despite being stabbed in the hip earlier. (Incidentally, Bava's ploy of having the killer and prospective hero fight in the shadows, with only an unidentifiable silhouette emerging at the end of it, would feature in a number of early slasher films.) Any killer who had apparently returned from the grave for revenge would usually turn out to be that person's son, brother or other relation. This villain is generally disguised, wearing a mask or full costume (many slasher films take place during holidays, parties or other such occasions). Sometimes the mask will hide a deformity (as in the *Friday the 13th* sequels), or the character will be monstrous because of his deformed appearance (as in *The Burning* [Tony Maylam, 1981]). The killer is generally male, and their weapon of choice is a knife, machete, axe or other manual implement, though for variety they may also find an imaginative use for power tools.

Devoid of any supernatural aspect, what makes *Bay* a horror film rather than a thriller or mystery is the presentation of horrific imagery, such as the squid crawling over Fillipo's face, or his decomposing body floating inexorably towards the naked Brunhilda, and, of course, its focus on bloody violence and death. As in the slasher films that were to come, Bava takes great delight in showing the effect of blades ripping through or being plunged into soft young flesh. For many slasher fans the death scenes are the highlight of the film, with plot and characterisation very much secondary considerations, and film-makers were subsequently required to produce ever more in-

Figure 9.3

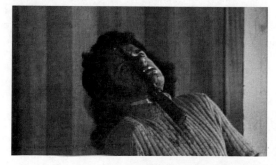

ventive ways of killing off their victims. In this respect Bava does not disappoint, and *Bay*'s pre-occupation is with the murders themselves, set up as stylised set-pieces graphically and gorily executed. Although Sean Cunningham has denied being influenced by the film, the build up and execution of *Bay*'s sickle-in-the-face murder (see Fig 9.3) and the later axe-in-the-head are remarkably similar to the axe murder in his *Friday the 13th*, while the entire dual murder by spear sequence is reproduced practically shot-for-shot in *Friday the 13th Part 2* (Steve Miner, 1981).

Although the thirteen murders in Bava's film may seem high, this was not unusual for some of the later slashers. Also known as the 'body count movie', the average number of victims per film rose steadily as the cycle progressed, reaching as many as 22 (or one death every four minutes) in *Friday the 13th Part V* (Danny Steinmann, 1985). Undoubtedly an attempt to keep bloodthirsty audiences satisfied, too often the constant parade of killings masked film-makers' inability to generate suspense. The fact that Steinmann's mean-spirited film was one of the worst received by fans of the franchise tells us something about the slasher audience. While critics would portray them as latent psychopaths, fans of the sub-genre generally need some kind of light relief from the constant parade of murder and mayhem. Bava's approach with *Bay* shows that he understood this; the shot of the smiley-faced buggy, immediately following the teenagers' gruesome deaths, is a typical example of his tongue-in-cheek winks to the audience. At the turn of the 1980s, when the original slasher cycle was at its height, juvenile comedy films such as *Porky's* (Bob Clark, 1981), *Screwballs* (Rafal Zielinski, 1983) and their sequels appealed to largely the same demographic. Three notorious films in particular which boast excellent (and frequent) gory special effects, *Don't Go in the House* (Joseph Ellison, 1979), *Maniac* and *The New York Ripper* (Lucio Fulci, 1982) are unremittingly grim, feature an older cast, are set in sleazy, naturalistic surroundings, and were unsuccessful at the box-office.

When discussing the violent content of these films, it's also important to note that the spectacle of elaborate death scenes wasn't restricted to low budget slashers – 20th Century Fox's *The Omen* and its two sequels, for example, were famous for their inventive death set-ups. With the increase in on-screen violence across the genre as a whole throughout the 1970s and into the 80s, the work of the make-up or special effects artist was to become more and more important in the horror film. This will be discussed in greater detail in the next chapter, but it's worth noting that for *Bay of Blood* Bava secured the services of one of the best in the Italian film business, Carlo Rambaldi. Soon after this, Rambaldi would relocate to Hollywood to work on big-budget studio productions such as *King Kong* (John Guillermin, 1976), *Alien* and *ET* (Steven Spielberg, 1982).[11] With the limited budget at his disposal, the fact that Bava sought out Rambaldi for the effects work demonstrates the importance that the director placed on this aspect of the film.

Although the influence of Bava's film on the horror genre is difficult to overstate, it would be wrong to assign the birth of the slasher sub-genre to a single source. The movement away from the classic horror film had begun in 1960 with *Psycho*, and the levels of violence and explicit gore had been rising steadily as the Production Code became increasingly irrelevant. However, it is safe to say that in bringing together so many elements that would soon become standard, *Bay of Blood* is an extremely important film in the modern horror genre. Whatever his motivation, whether he thought he had taken the *giallo* as far as he could or just wanted to make an absurdly tongue-in-cheek 'splatter movie', Bava's film foreshadowed a sea-change in the evolution of the genre.

Reception and Aftermath

If critics had bemoaned the violence and apparent lack of narrative in *Blood and Black Lace*, it was as nothing compared to the backlash that followed the release of *Bay of Blood*. During its premiere at the 1971 Avoriaz Film Festival (under Bava's preferred title *Twitch of the Death Nerve*) genre icon Christopher Lee walked out, describing the film as 'revolting'. Although it won the festival's award for Best Make-Up and Special Effects, mainstream and genre critics alike were appalled by what they saw as a film devoid of any plot whatsoever, and merely an excuse for the depiction of a series of gruesome and explicit murders. A 1975 review in fantasy magazine *Cinefantastique* described it as Bava's 'most complete failure to date, heaping graphic violence onto one of his more ridiculous scripts'. Little did they know how the horror genre was to evolve over the next few years, and how much of an influence Bava's film was to have on its development. What the director himself thought of the film is up for debate, with quotes ranging from 'satisfactory' to 'a piece of shit'.

Bay of Blood was not a commercial success in Italy or anywhere else, returning around half of its budget during its initial release. Despite making profits with both *Black Sunday* and *Black Sabbath* (in a severely edited form), AIP had decided not to distribute *Blood and Black Lace* in the US, considering its murder sequences too strong for younger audiences. Not surprisingly they gave *Bay of Blood* an even wider berth, and it was instead picked up and released by Hallmark – exploitation experts who had previously distributed Wes Craven and Sean Cunningham's controversial *Last House on the Left*. Bava's film remained in circulation around American drive-ins and grindhouse theatres for a number of years, doing steady business under a dizzying array of alternate titles, including *Last House on the Left Part II*. Bava himself made only a handful of further films before his death in 1980, although the *giallo* sub-genre remained popular in Italy well into the 1970s and beyond. Dario Argento took up Bava's mantle with excellent films such as *Bird with the Crystal Plumage* (1970) and *Profondo Rosso* (*Deep Red*, 1975), through *Tenebrae* (1982) to *Giallo* (2009). The latter combines standard narrative conventions with the 'torture-porn' aesthetics of more recent films such as *Hostel*. Interviewed shortly after the release of *Halloween*, John Carpenter revealed that he was a great fan of Dario Argento, and some of Argento's later work, for example *Tenebrae*, is much closer to the conventional slasher film than the *giallo*, indicating a circularity of influences.

Despite changes to the UK certification system in 1970, that raised the age limit for viewers of X-rated material to eighteen, *Bay of Blood* was refused a certificate by the BBFC. Ordinarily this would have ensured that the film remained unseen by British audiences, yet by the end of the decade this and scores of other films that had either been banned or heavily censored were freely available in the UK. The introduction of affordable home video technology to the UK in the late 1970s brought with it unfettered access to previously unavailable material through high street video rental stores, who could legally loan uncertificated films to viewers of any age. Unsurprisingly, the British public took full advantage, with horror, sex and general exploitation titles proving extremely popular. The popularity of the slasher film, along with (primarily Italian) cannibal and zombie films, coincided with the birth of the home video market, and it is not unreasonable to suggest that graphic horror films of the 1980s and the burgeoning home video industry served to fuel each other's success. The result was an explosion of interest in the horror genre, quickly followed by cries of outrage and a classic 'moral panic' directed at the producers and distributors of such unsavoury entertainment.

Following orchestrated campaigns by moral crusaders such as Mary Whitehouse, between 1981 and 1983 the BBFC and the British Videogram Association (the video industry trade body) negotiated a self-regulatory code of practice, under which video distribution companies would voluntarily submit their films to the BBFC for classification. Video shops were encouraged to only stock titles that had received a classification, with police raids on shops supplying unclassified films resulting in confiscation of stock and in some cases charges under the Obscene Publications Act. Many such charges were overturned on appeal, however, and the police found themselves in a situation where films successfully prosecuted in one area were failing in another. In an effort to put an end to the confusion, in August 1984 the Director of Public Prosecution drew up a list of 62 so-called 'video nasties', horror and exploitation films that were classed as obscene and liable for prosecution as such. The vast majority of the films were from either the US or Italy, and included almost all of the Italian cannibal and zombie films, as well as *Bay of Blood* (under the title *Bloodbath*). Unsurprisingly, given their popularity (one of the titles on the list, *The Evil Dead* [Sam Raimi, 1982], had been the UK's top rental of 1983), this did not stop video shops stocking the titles, and obscenity charges brought against them were still successfully overturned. Continuing public concern about this state of affairs, enthusiastically stoked by the media (especially the *Daily Mail* newspaper), led to parliament drawing up the Video Recordings Bill, which was eventually introduced in 1985. The bill decreed that all films released on video must carry BBFC certification by law, and that it would be illegal for anyone to supply a video to a customer younger than the age specified.

The arrival of the slasher sub-genre also coincided with the emergence of feminist film criticism, which questioned both the role of women in the film industry and their representation on screen. Chief amongst these critics was Laura Mulvey, whose highly influential, politically-charged essay 'Visual Pleasure and Narrative Cinema', first appeared in the periodical *Screen* in 1975. In it, Mulvey uses psychoanalytic theory to attempt to show how cinema in general, and classical Hollywood in particular, functions to satisfy male voyeurism and fetishism through the exploitation of women. Perpetuating a patriarchal order, Mulvey suggested, characters and events are viewed from the perspective of a heterosexual male audience, through what she terms cinema's 'male gaze'. As such, women in film are presented as objects merely to be looked at (by both the audience and the male characters) whilst fulfilling no meaningful narrative purpose. Supporters of Mulvey's theory found plenty of ammunition in the new breed of horror film that developed in the wake of *Halloween*. In the view of feminist critics, the slasher film was the ultimate insult: not only did the subjective camerawork implicate the viewer in the actions of the (usually male) killer, but the women on screen existed only to be killed in ever more horrific ways. Dario Argento's infamous quote that he would much rather see a beautiful woman killed than an ugly man did little to endear him to such critics. From Lon Chaney's *Phantom of the Opera* onwards, the horror film has been fascinated with the female gaze but generally only insofar as it reflects back male perspectives. Cutting from a female face to an object of horror, the horror film is compelled to cut back to view her terrified reaction.

Dressed to Kill, Brian De Palma's X-rated Hitchcock *homage* with Michael Caine in a Norman Bates-style role, found itself the target of a number of feminist groups, who picketed cinemas showing it in both America and the UK. Featuring explicit and highly sexualised violence against women, the fact that it was distributed by a major studio (MGM) was a particular source of anger. While it's true to say that the majors were reluctant to produce slasher films themselves, they were often more than happy to acquire and distribute them for a slice of the action. Independent film-makers would often sell their finished film to the majors at a healthy profit, without the hassle of having to market or distribute the film themselves, with the studio then taking all of the box office. So, MGM, Columbia (*Happy Birthday To Me* [J. Lee Thompson, 1981]), 20th Century Fox (*Terror Train* [Roger Spottiswood, 1980], *Visiting Hours* [Jean Claude Lord, 1982]) and Paramount (*My Bloody Valentine* [George Mihalka, 1981], *Friday the 13th* and its sequels) were able to cash in on the early popularity of the slasher without having to get their own hands dirty with their production. With the popularity of horror films in the booming home video market, extremely low budget films could also be released direct to video, bypassing cinema, and still turn a quick and healthy profit. Such was the dominance of the sub-genre that by 1981 *Variety* was reporting that slasher films accounted for 60 per cent of all domestic (US and Canadian) film production, and placed twenty-five of these among the year's fifty top-grossing pictures.

Two years later, with the proliferation of violent 'adult thrillers' such as *Sudden Impact* (Clint Eastwood, 1983) and *Tightrope* (Clint Eastwood, 1984), over half of all new films being made in America still owed some debt to the slasher. While the sub-genre itself was quickly fading, Hollywood appropriated the slasher narrative and aesthetic in films like *Jagged Edge* (Richard Marquand, 1985) and *Fatal Attraction* (Adrian Lyne, 1987). Introducing a police procedural aspect to further distance them from their unwholesome origins, big-budget and prestige productions such as *The Silence of the Lambs*, *Basic Instinct* (Paul Verhoeven, 1992) and *Se7en* (David Fincher, 1995), whilst arguably no less gruesome than their predecessors, were marketed purely as thrillers. Indeed, when the slasher returned to prominence after more than a decade with 1996's *Scream* it was advertised as 'the new thriller by Wes Craven'. Whatever the marketing department claimed, *Scream* was an unmistakeable throwback to the original slasher cycle (albeit with a postmodern, self-referential twist), and resulted in huge box office takings and general critical acclaim. Craven's film was followed by two immediate sequels and a slew of similar productions such as *I Know What You Did Last Summer* (Jim Gillespie, 1997), *Urban Legend* (Jamie Blanks, 1998), and their respective follow-ups. Keen to cash in on the nostalgia factor generated by these, the late 1990s and early 2000s saw a flurry of remakes of horror films from the 1970s and 80s, including a number of slashers such as *Halloween*, *Black Christmas*, *Friday the 13th*, *My Bloody Valentine* and *Prom Night* (Paul Lynch, 1980). Unlike the original cycle, these were glossy productions, featuring relatively well-known casts of 'teens' and aimed squarely at the MTV crowd. While performing respectably at the box office, the new versions were generally regarded as watered down, sanitised pap by the majority of true slasher fans.

The demise of the original slasher cycle by the mid-1980s can be attributed to a number of factors. A victim of its own success and of technological advancement in the shape of home video, the market quickly found itself oversaturated with poor quality productions. Moreover, increased censorship in the wake of the video nasties controversy meant that much of the appeal of the films ended up on the cutting room floor, with already-censored cinema versions being further cut by distributors as well as the BBFC for home video release. Facing a backlash against graphic violence, horror film-makers sought a new avenue for the advancements in special effects that had been made in the previous decade, far away from the nihilistic realism of *Maniac* and *New York Ripper*. Spearheading the movement was a softly-spoken Canadian writer-director who had been perfecting his own particular brand of horror for well over a decade: David Cronenberg.

Bibliography

Bracke, Peter M. (2005) *Crystal Lake Memories*. Los Angeles: Sparkplug Press.

Clover, Carol J. (1992) *Men, Women and Chain Saws: Gender in the Modern Horror Film*. London: BFI.

Conterio, Martyn (2015) *Black Sunday (Devil's Advocates)*. Leighton Buzzard: Auteur.

Dika, Vera (1990) *Games of Terror:* Halloween, Friday the 13th, *and the Films of the Stalker Cycle*. London: Associated University Presses.

Harper, Kim (2004) *Legacy of Blood: A Comprehensive Guide to Slasher Movies*. Manchester: Headpress.

Kerekes, David and Slater, David (1995) *Killing for Culture*. np: Creation Books.

Kerekes, David And Slater, David (2000) *See No Evil: Banned Films and Video Controversy*. Manchester: Headpress.

Koven, Mikel J. (2006) *La Dolce Morte: Vernacular Cinema and the Italian Giallo Film*. Maryland: Scarecrow Press.

Leeder, Murray (2014) *Halloween (Devil's Advocates)*. Leighton Buzzard: Auteur.

Martin, John (1993) *The Seduction of the Gullible*. Nottingham: Procrustes Press.

Rockoff, Adam (2002) *Going to Pieces: The Rise and Fall of the Slasher Film, 1978-1986*. Jefferson: McFarlane & Co.

Endnotes

1. Warner Bros. distributed the film outside of the US.

2. As noted in Chapter 5, Japan has consistently been one of the biggest consumers of 'mondo' film, with its own homegrown versions also beginning in 1962 with *Japan By Night* (Kelzo Ohno). Still a thriving genre today, Japanese mondo films tend to be extremely graphic and are rarely seen outside of their home country.

3. The premise and aesthetics of Deodato's film informed the phenomenally successful *Blair Witch Project*, and its influence can still be felt in the proliferation of 'found-footage' films that continue to be a major part of the horror genre.

4. This disguise had been used previously in Siodmak's *The Spiral Staircase*, which foreshadows a number of elements (in both narrative and style) that would become associated with the *giallo* and slasher sub-genres. These include the close-up of a watching eye, as used heavily in *Bay of Blood*.

5. Scott's film also features a number of elements from the cycle of films that followed *Bay of Blood*, and has frequently been described as a 'slasher in space'.

6. Featuring the tag-line 'Meet the girls with the thermo-nuclear navels!' this is undoubtedly one of Bava's worst films and a career low for its star Vincent Price.

7. The film has also been subjected to some very poor video and DVD releases over the years, but recent versions have restored much of the colour and sharpness, as well as the gory killings.

8. In later entries, and in particular the remakes of the early 2000s, it became common for a heterosexual couple to survive to the end, in a return to the more conservative stance of earlier genre cycles.

9. Also worthy of note in respect to this is Robert Fuest's excellent British thriller *And Soon the Darkness* (1970).

10. The fact that POV shots are present in films where the identity of the killer is known (for example the *Halloween* films and the *Friday the 13th* sequels) points to their necessity as a slasher convention.

11. It is worth noting that Bava himself was an accomplished special effects artist, and was also approached to work on the 1976 version of *King Kong* but declined the offer.

Chapter 10

Body Horror

The Fly
David Cronenberg, US 1986

Recommended viewing
Shivers (David Cronenberg, 1975)
Rabid (David Cronenberg, 1977)
The Thing (John Carpenter, 1982)
Videodrome (David Cronenberg, 1983)
Society (Brian Yuzna, 1989)

Introduction

In the field of film studies, the term *'auteur'* is used to describe a director whose body of work, within or across genres, can be seen as the development of a particular personal vision. Championed by the French journal *Cahiers du cinema* in the 1950s, *auteur* theory posits that truly great directors are able to stamp their individual outlook, or 'world view', on each of their films, regardless of who else was involved in the writing, production or financing. Whilst a number of the directors already covered in our case studies have been the subjects of *auteur* study (Hitchcock in particular was revered by the writers of *Cahiers*), one of the most highly regarded *auteurs* within the horror genre is the Canadian film-maker David Cronenberg. During the 1970s and 80s, from low-budget independents to high-profile studio productions, the viewing of a 'David Cronenberg film' usually promised horror audiences a unique and disturbing experience.

Coinciding with advances in make-up and special effects, and the rise in popularity of the artists who created them, Cronenberg's films spearheaded one of the most popular sub-genres of the 1980s in the form of 'body horror'. In this chapter we look at how and why this sub-genre emerged, a product of technological, commercial and cultural changes in the industry, and how it relates to the 'transformation' films that had gone previously. We also examine how such a distinctive director as Cronenberg was able to produce a successful mainstream horror film while remaining true to his own world view, and the lasting influence of his work on the genre as a whole.

Background

When the failure of Michael Cimino's epic western *Heaven's Gate* (1980) single-handedly brought down United Artists, it ended the Hollywood studios' appetite for giving creative freedom and unlimited budgets to brilliant but unpredictable directors. In truth, it was just the excuse the studios needed to wrest control back from the film-makers, and triggered wide-ranging changes in the culture and practices of Hollywood. Following the spectacular commercial success of films such as *Jaws*, *Star Wars* and *Superman* (Richard Donner, 1978) (all of which would spawn several sequels) in the latter half of the 1970s, huge sums began to be invested in making and promoting so-called 'tent-pole' releases. These were high-profile films calculated to deliver maximum revenue and offset losses made in other areas of the studio. Dubbed the decade of excess, average budgets in 1980s Hollywood rocketed from $9 million to $23 million. With so much riding on a small number of films, audience recognition was paramount, and at a time when 'high-concept'

film-making meant that tens of millions of dollars could be pledged on the flimsi-
est of pitches ('it's *Top Gun*, with cars!'), simply adding a number to the title of last
year's box office success seemed a sure-fire winner.

In the wake of *Star Wars* in particular, the studios came to recognise the lucrative
potential of merchandising, with box-office takings supplemented (or even eclipsed)
by sales of licensed toys, novels, comics, video games, T-shirts, mugs, lunch boxes
and anything else large enough to hold a film's logo. The emergence and rise of
MTV also led to the cross-marketing of soundtrack albums: heavily-rotated music
videos acted as free advertising for the film, which in turn featured the songs during
memorable scenes.[1] For an example in the horror genre look no further than *The
Lost Boys* (Joel Schumacher, 1987), which is essentially a feature-length music video.
Hollywood's tent-pole approach and its pre-occupation with pre-sold blockbusters,
remakes and sequels continues today, with the Marvel and DC Comics superhero
franchises, and *Jurassic Park* (Steven Spielberg, 1993) and *Star Wars* sequels and spin-
offs guaranteeing regular billion-dollar box office and merchandise returns.

The increased commercialisation of Hollywood cinema in the 1980s saw the majors cutting back on horror film investment. The genre didn't produce sufficient
box-office revenue to warrant the spiralling budgets, and opportunities for merchandising were limited. Of course, as we saw in the previous chapter, this didn't
stop the appropriation of the slasher template for use in more mainstream films,
and these continued through the decade. Whilst independent horror films continued to be made, the backlash against the slasher film and increased censorship in
the wake of the video nasties controversy ensured that by the mid-1980s the majority of special effects were ending up on the cutting room floor. With the exception
of the *Friday the 13th* franchise, the popularity of which was increasingly based on
the character of Jason Voorhees rather than the heavily-edited killings, the slasher
sub-genre quickly faded.

As horror films turned away from a realist approach and towards something more
fantastical, the advancements in latex and mechanical effects responsible for frequent and bloody cinematic violence throughout the 1970s found a new outlet.
Labelled 'body horror', these new films depicted mutation and transformation in
place of mutilation and murder. Just as slasher films were accused of being nothing
more than a collection of graphic death scenes connected by a slim or non-existent
storyline, many films of the body horror sub-genre arguably exist solely to showcase the abilities of their special effects artists. The arrival of body horror fuelled
the popularity of genre magazines such as *Cinefex* and *Fangoria*, which gave readers
access to behind-the-scenes photo-shoots showing the effects artists at work, along
with interviews and how-to guides. Such publications often ranked the effects art-

ists' importance to a film higher than its writer or director, and in some ways that wasn't far from the truth. Narratives could be shaped to provide a showcase for the latest special effects, with lighting and camerawork used to best highlight the gruesome results.

When Rick Baker won the Academy Award for Best Makeup in 1982,[2] it was Hollywood's first official recognition of the special effects artists who were now so important in the industry. Baker's work on *An American Werewolf in London* (John Landis, 1981) included an elaborate transformation scene in which the actor's body stretched, snapped and popped in every direction. It was a vivid demonstration of how the genre had developed in the forty years since Lon Chaney Jr's metamorphosis into *The Wolf Man*. While previous films in the horror genre had dealt with bodily transformation (for example, the original *Cat People*), the films that appeared throughout the 1980s took a very different approach. Rather than hiding the transformations off-screen or in deep shadow, body horror films made sure that every visceral detail was shown in brightly lit close-up. Make-up artists continually sought to outdo what had gone before in the gross-out stakes, with films pushing the boundaries of what was considered 'bad taste'.

In what was undoubtedly a case of technology driving the direction of the genre, during the 1980s body horror informed much of Hollywood's horror output. As part of this movement the period saw a number of remakes of earlier films that used special effects to present a vastly different version. The most notable of these were updates of popular 1950s science-fiction films, among them *Invasion of the Body Snatchers* (Philip Kaufman, 1978), John Carpenter's *The Thing*, and *The Fly*. *The Thing* in particular, in its original version, had relied on what was unseen to generate tension and fear. In the remake, disgust and horror are generated through showing absolutely everything, courtesy of Rob Bottin's still-incredible special effects. Although Carpenter's film is often credited with starting the body horror cycle, in fact the sub-genre had its genesis almost a decade earlier in the work of Canadian writer and director David Cronenberg.

Born in Toronto in 1943, Cronenberg had grown up as a fan of science fiction and fantasy, and dreamt of becoming a novelist.[3] While studying English at the University of Toronto (he had originally enrolled in biochemistry), he discovered an interest in film after watching the work of one of his fellow students, and effectively taught himself film-making through the production of a number of short films. From the very beginning Cronenberg's unique vision and 'world view' was apparent. Short films such as *Stereo* (1969) and *Crimes of the Future* (1970) revolve around ideas of science out of control, and physical and mental transformation, themes that would recur throughout his career. Unlike his contemporaries who had attended film school, Cronenberg was less influenced by the work of other directors, and felt free to develop his own ideas and film-making methods. When it came to producing his first commercial feature, however, his lack of formal training was in part responsible for American producers and distributors such as AIP turning away his approaches for financial backing. Like many countries in the mid-1970s, the Canadian film industry was heavily reliant on government funding, and when Cronenberg finally found a backer, Cinepix, it was in collaboration with the government-funded Canadian Film Development Corporation.

Cronenberg has described his horror films as 'body conscious', and has demonstrated a particular interest in bodily transformation and mutation, as well as in mortality and bodily decay. His first commercial feature, *Shivers* (1975), was in part *homage* to Romero's *Night of the Living Dead* – more apparent in its working title, *Orgy of the Blood Parasites*. Another of *Shivers*'s alternate titles, *They Came From Within*, highlights the director's approach to these themes. In his films the source of the horror is generally internal, with a repressed or latent Otherness making its presence known through a physical emergence from or disruption of the body. None of Cronenberg's horror films feature supernatural elements, they are all grounded in his ideas of scientific 'reality'. Showing how the occupants of an apartment block are turned into sex-crazed psychopaths by strange parasites, passed from person to person through various orifices, *Shivers* unsurprisingly caused something of a stir on its release.

Questions were asked in Canada's parliament about whether taxpayers' money should be used to fund such an objectionable film. The fact that it returned a healthy profit seemed irrelevant – it was in fact the first CFDC-backed film to make any return on their investment, according to Cronenberg (Grundberg 2006: 41) – and the controversy resulted in the production of his next film, *Rabid*, being delayed. Although the funding bodies acknowledged that he was a bankable film-maker, they didn't want to be seen to support a film that was just as objectionable as his first. In *Rabid*, hardcore porn actress Marilyn Chambers[4] stars as a woman whose experimental surgery results in a penis-like growth in her armpit that not only has an insatiable appetite for blood, but also spreads a virus that turns much of the population of Montreal into psychotic flesh-eaters. Eventually a deal was struck to fund *Rabid* as part of a package with other, less controversial, films, and the Corporation received an even greater return on its investment than it had with *Shivers*. *The Brood* (1979), Cronenberg's third horror film (following the drag racing-themed *Fast Company* [1979]), was financed by both government and private backers and marked his first production with 'name' performers in the shape of Oliver Reed and Samantha Eggar.

In common with many genre films of the late 1960s and into the 70s, Cronenberg's first three features play on the theme of 'family horror', with *Shivers* featuring scenes of incest as well as intra-family killing. The tag-line for *Rabid* highlighted the closeness of the source of horror: 'You can't trust your mother, you can't trust your neighbor, you can't trust your best friend. One minute they're normal, the next RABID.'[5] Cronenberg has described *The Brood*, which depicts monstrously deformed (and psychotic) children produced as a by-product of rage, as his version of the 1979 Robert Benton-directed divorce tug-of-war film *Kramer vs Kramer* ('but more realistic').[6] The idea of effecting physical change through the projection of thought was highlighted again in *Scanners* (1981). Make-up legend Dick Smith's infamous 'exploding head' effect, which was used heavily in the promotion of the film, went a long way to gaining Cronenberg recognition outside of Canada. Often described as his masterpiece, his next film *Videodrome* (1983) sees its protagonist's mind taken over by transmissions from a rogue television station, and his body transforming and mutating in strange, surrealist ways. Whether the transformations are real or hallucination is never made clear, as the film explores the character's tortured psyche.

Following *Videodrome*, Cronenberg made his first film based on another writer's material. An adaptation of a Stephen King novel, *The Dead Zone* (1983) was a relatively high budget production financed by Dino De Laurentiis, starring big-name actors Martin Sheen and Christopher Walken. Whilst his input on the script was limited,[7] many elements in the story chimed with his own interests: in particular, the use of ESP and telepathy, and a protagonist undergoing both mental and physical changes who is ostracised by society for what appears a blessing but turns out to be a curse. Undoubtedly helped by the King association, *The Dead Zone* was a mainstream critical and commercial success, and led to a number of offers from the major studios, including for such iconic 80s movies as *Beverly Hills Cop* (Martin Brest, 1984) and *Top Gun* (Tony Scott, 1986). None of these appealed and he chose instead to work again with De Laurentiis on an adaptation of science-fiction author Phillip K Dick's short story 'We Can Remember It For You Wholesale', under the title *Total Recall*.

Cronenberg was writing *Total Recall* when he was first approached to direct a remake of *The Fly*, from an already-written script by Charles Edward Pogue. He turned it down. Although he had enjoyed the original film as a child, he felt that there were too many problems that had to be overcome with the story, and it was passed to another director, Robert Bierman. When Bierman's daughter was tragically killed in a plane crash during pre-production, and the *Total Recall* project fell through, Cronenberg was again approached to direct. The company behind *The*

Fly was Brooksfilms, set up by writer, actor and director Mel Brooks, whose comedy films Cronenberg had admired a great deal. Likewise, Brooks was impressed with Cronenberg's previous productions, and had no qualms about working with a director still seen by many as 'leftfield'. In 1980 Brooksfilms had scored a major critical success with *The Elephant Man* directed by David Lynch, an underground film-maker whose only previous feature was the disturbing, surrealist *Eraserhead* (1977). Following his big break with *Elephant Man*, Lynch would go on to make major films such as *Dune* (1984) and *Mulholland Drive* (2001), as well as creating the *Twin Peaks* television series.

Given Cronenberg's pre-occupation with science and bodily transformation, *The Fly* would have seemed a perfect fit for the director, but he still had problems with Pogue's script. Struggling financially, he eventually agreed to make the film on condition that he was allowed to rewrite it completely to reflect his own personal vision. Mel Brooks was more than happy to give him such artistic freedom.

Textual Analysis

Modern-day Toronto, Canada. Veronica Quaife, a journalist working for *Particle* magazine, is covering a scientific exhibition being held by the Bartok Organisation. There she meets and is attracted to Seth Brundle, a reclusive scientist who invites her home to witness his new invention. He demonstrates a teleportation system, capable of transmitting inanimate objects across a room from one telepod device to another. When her editor and ex-lover Stathis Borans refuses to believe the story, Brundle offers Veronica the chance to document his work and to write a book on it once he has succeeded in teleporting a human being. His initial experiment involving the teleportation of a baboon ends in disaster, and it is only when Veronica and Brundle become lovers that he begins to understand why the system has issues with living flesh. In a drunken state and driven by jealousy, Brundle teleports himself, unaware that a fly has entered the telepod with him. He emerges seemingly unscathed, but soon discovers that he has gained tremendous stamina and agility. However, when his personality and body begin to deteriorate, he pushes Veronica away and becomes a recluse. Discovering she is pregnant, Veronica and Borans arrange for an abortion, but Brundle, now an unrecognisable creature, arrives at the clinic, kidnaps her and takes her back to the laboratory. As he prepares to fuse himself with Veronica and the unborn baby through the use of a third telepod, Borans shoots the cable connecting Veronica's telepod to the system, resulting in the fusion of Brundle with his own telepod. With Brundle now a pathetic creature barely able to move, Veronica tearfully shoots him dead.

The Fly is an ideal case study through which to examine David Cronenberg's unique approach, given the potential for comparison with both the 1958 version and Pogue's initial rewrite. In putting together his own vision for the film, the director has stated that he retained only one line of Pogue's dialogue and none of his characters. Nevertheless, he has readily acknowledged that many of the seemingly Cronenbergian aspects of *The Fly* were already present in the script, and insisted that the screenwriter receive a credit on the finished film.[8] In particular, Pogue's rethinking of the original human-fly transformation, having it occur gradually and at a molecular level, opened the story up to a number of new possibilities. In the 1958 film the teleportation experiment resulted in the scientist and fly swapping heads and 'arms', something that Cronenberg, even when watching as a child, found laughable and unconvincing ('Where did the extra molecules and atoms come from to create the giant fly head?', he had wondered). Cronenberg felt that Pogue's approach was much more believable, especially with growing public awareness of scientific concepts such as DNA, and it chimed with his own interest in insects and their capacity for metamorphosis.

As would be expected, Cronenberg's rewrite paid particular attention to the visualisation of the human-fly transformation, but also made key changes to character, plot and theme. While drawing on science-fiction and transformation horror traditions, his version explores, through a distinctly Cronenbergian lens, the all too human fears of loneliness, disease, degeneration and death. In discussing the themes of his films, Cronenberg frequently mentions the idea of being able to 'hide behind' genre. Essentially *The Fly* is a tragic tale of two people who meet and fall in love, and when one of them contracts a hideously disfiguring and terminal disease the other must watch them suffer before finally assisting their suicide. As a conventional drama such a film would be unremittingly grim (see Michael Haneke's *Amour* [2014]), but in a science-fiction-horror story such a tragic outcome is somehow more acceptable, though perhaps no less disturbing. By facing up to such issues directly, Cronenberg sees horror films as more true to life than, for example, escapist soap operas. *The Fly* is an excellent example of how the genre can be used as a vehicle to examine more general fears, and provide catharsis from issues that may otherwise go unaddressed in popular entertainment.

Much of the power of the film comes from the care taken in creating sympathetic, articulate characters. This renders scenes depicting the fly-human hybrid and its actions all the more grotesque and compelling. The character of Seth Brundle is very different to the scientist in the original film, being a charming though eccentric bachelor as opposed to a family man with a loving wife and child. This immediately makes for a less predictable narrative (especially given that the 1958 version works backwards from the premise that the loyal wife has just killed her husband).

Jeff Goldblum brings a particular presence to the role, with the actor's physical and intellectual attractiveness crucial to Cronenberg's exposition on the relationship between body and mind. Goldblum is matched by Geena Davis as Veronica, a powerful female lead depicted as a strong career woman and more than capable of fending off her ex-lover's unwanted advances. However, she is also the emotional heart of the film, guiding Brundle through an emotional and sexual awakening and attempting to make him more human, even before he begins his physical transformation. It is obvious from Veronica's agonised response to her final actions that she still loves Brundle, even in his hideously altered state. This consistency in her affections and her courage in pulling the trigger to end the nightmare make her the true hero of the piece.

As we discuss in more detail later, the differences between male and female sensibilities are a typical Cronenberg concern. These are highlighted a number of times during the film, in both its narrative and style. When he and Veronica are discussing technical issues, such as the workings of the teleportation system, Brundle is shot from a low angle, emphasising the power of his knowledge, whereas during conversations about their relationship the angles are reversed.[9] Veronica describes herself at one point as 'lazy and disorganised', the exact opposite of Brundle, whose neatly-racked sets of identical clothes allow him not to waste effort on deciding what to wear. The soft, golden glow of Veronica's apartment is in stark contrast to his grey, soulless living space, and of course once his transformation is underway Brundle's physical deterioration only highlights Veronica's beauty. This is particularly evident in the scene where she arrives at the laboratory as Brundle is attempting to drag his one-night stand Tawny into the telepod. 'You look bad, you smell bad,' Veronica tells him, while she herself is exquisitely dressed and made up despite the early hour (Fig 10.1).

Figure 10.1

The third character in the film's love triangle is Stathis Borans, Veronica's boss, ex-tutor and ex-lover, whose advances towards her are often threatening and occasionally downright creepy. Although there are moments when he reveals vulnerability in his attempts to keep her in his life (his display in the shopping centre is particularly pathetic), for much of the film Stathis comes across as a domineering bully with a penchant for pithy one-liners. Even Brundle's ultimate descent into madness, when he kidnaps and threatens to kill the woman who loves him, fails to install Stathis as the male hero in the eye of the viewer. A number of alternative epilogues for the film, all showing Veronica and Stathis back together, did not meet with the approval of test audiences. Instead his actions throughout the film only serve to increase audience sympathy for the two leads, and as such he can be seen as the notional villain of the piece. Interestingly, Cronenberg claimed that a true villain figure, the head of the Bartok Organisation, was quickly written out of his version of the screenplay. This character's presence would have given *The Fly* even more of a Cronenbergian slant; in the universe of his films, big businesses or shadowy organisations often have a controlling influence over the characters and events. It seems that for this film the director was determined to have a more intimate story, with everything revolving around the relationships of the three main characters.

The doctors and scientists in Cronenberg's films up to this point had been obsessed with the mental or physical improvement of the human race, through assisting or diverting the path of evolution. In many ways Seth Brundle is a continuation of these characters, whose commitment and enthusiastic experimentations with Nature have disastrous consequences. But whereas his enigmatic predecessors, such as Hal Raglan in *The Brood*, or Emil Hobbes in *Shivers*, appeared unconventional and even sinister, Brundle is charismatic and likeable. The other difference, of course, is that in this film Brundle is both the instigator and the victim of his own experiments. Although his attempts to improve the lives of humans are through the advancement of technology rather than physical or mental change, his experiments in teleportation can be seen as a potential cure for his own very human limitation of travel sickness. And, as we will see, it is due to his human failings that Brundle ends up personally evolving in the most horrific way.

In Cronenberg's horror films, problems are not created by technology running out of control, but by Nature doing whatever it needs to in order to survive and evolve. As such, Cronenberg's main problem with Pogue's script was its anti-technology stance, something that had been present in both the original film and George Langelaan's short story on which it was based. Generally, science-fiction in the 1950s reflected the emotional shock waves from the dropping of the atomic bomb, and the tangible fear of the damage such new science could wreak in the event the Cold War became hot. Whereas the 'mad doctors' of the 1930s and 40s had often conducted their experiments with explicitly evil (or at least dubious) intent, the scientists of the 50s were simply misguided in their efforts. The overriding view of science-fiction film-makers at the time was that it was science itself, and atomic science in particular, that should be blamed for unleashing all kinds of ills onto the world. In the face of such technology scientists quickly found themselves out of their depth, with the physical strength of the military usually required to combat whatever evil the latest experiment had created.

In line with this thinking, Helene, the female lead in the 1958 version of *The Fly*, is terrified of what is loosely termed 'progress'. She is ultimately vindicated as her husband destroys all of his work, his equipment and formulae, before asking her to destroy what he has become. By contrast, Cronenberg's view is that there is no such thing as 'bad science', or things that Man is not meant to know. The idea that in some sense the telepod was evil and needed to be destroyed, just because a single experiment went awry, to him seemed ludicrous. His rewrite ensures that science is not blamed for what happened; it is Brundle's jealous nature and inebriated condition that instigates the ill-fated experiment, and his lack of due care and attention that allows the fly to enter the telepod. Regardless of the technology used to fuse scientist and fly, it is the insect's natural instinct to survive, and its ability to mutate, that results in horrific consequences for the characters in the film.

The swapping of heads in the original film had rendered the scientist suddenly unknowable. For the most part hiding his transformed features under a cloth, he was unable to communicate with those around him other than through typed notes and table-banging. Though not as dramatic a change, Pogue's script had the Brundle character losing his voice early in the story, something that Cronenberg again felt would not have worked. For him, it was important that Brundle be able to articulate his thoughts and feelings to Veronica and the audience throughout his degeneration, in order to retain their sympathy and to fully explore the effects of the disease. By the time Brundle is talking directly to the audience via Veronica's video camera, demonstrating his newly acquired eating habits, we are unsure whether to react with revulsion or sadness. Here the director successfully draws together the various strands of audience interaction with the horror film – we are fearful for what might happen to the characters but we are also made fearful for what we ourselves may be presented with on screen. While the violent horror films that appeared in the wake of Romero's *Night of the Living Dead* present us with graphic and disgusting imagery that invokes a visceral physical reaction, rarely does a film-maker succeed as well as Cronenberg in making an audience invest physically, emotionally, and indeed intellectually.

There are two well-known sequences that Cronenberg filmed and removed from the second half of the film (both of which had been retained from Pogue's storyline): the partially-transformed Brundle's murder of a homeless woman, and an experiment involving the joint teleportation of a cat and baboon, the results of which he beats to death with a lead pipe. In both of these cases the director felt that audience sympathy for the character would be removed too early; he wanted that to continue as long as possible. Drawing on the experience of watching his father slowly dying from cancer, Cronenberg wanted to ensure that the audience didn't lose sight of the human being behind the horrific effects of disease. In his manic speech on insect politics, Brundle warns Veronica that his human traits – compassion, self-awareness – are disappearing, and that he will soon become a danger to her. The device of having the scientist's computer be voice-activated is particularly clever; once the computer fails to recognise his commands, Brundle and the audience know that he has irreversibly become something 'Other'. At this point our allegiance begins to move to Veronica, and the film becomes more of a traditional monster movie – even down to the transformed Brundle carrying her off into the night.

While the transformation story has been a staple of horror cinema, and before that literature and folklore, the 1980s saw a particular revival in werewolf films, due in no small part to the advances in special effects that allowed increasingly complex transformation scenes. In films such as *The Howling* (Joe Dante, 1980), *An American Werewolf in London* and *The Company of Wolves*, much of the physical horror came from the transformation process itself, rather than the resultant creature. A werewolf may well be savage and dangerous, but it is not in itself disgusting. A housefly, on the other hand, is for many people one of the basest and most repugnant of creatures. They gather where there is rotting food, animal waste or death; to have them buzzing around you, or landing on your body or food, is both annoying and unpleasant.[10] *The Amityville Horror*, amongst others, uses swarms of houseflies to represent the presence of evil, and in *The Fly* Cronenberg uses the low buzzing of an unseen fly on the soundtrack to invoke a feeling of foreboding or danger. The mere thought of being fused with such a creature is already enough to generate a feeling of disgust, even before any outward effects are apparent. Brundle's mimicking of a fly's method of eating (vomiting digestive liquid onto its food before ingesting it) is for many viewers the most uncomfortable part of the film. It is in stark contrast to the 1958 version, where the human-fly hybrid eats discretely with its head hidden under a cloth.

The opening third of the film offers little warning of the horrific scenes to come, focusing instead on the developing relationship between Brundle and Veronica. Only at the close of the first act do we get a glimpse of the terrors in store, when we witness the aftermath of the first baboon teleportation, but it delivers a suitably visceral punch. The bloodied hand on the telepod window would have been sufficient to convey that the experiment has failed but, this being a David Cronenberg film, the camera unflinchingly takes us inside to view the full extent of the horror. The creature, still alive, has literally been turned inside out (Fig 10.2). This breaking down of bodily borders, of biological order, is absolutely central to the body horror

Figure 10.2

genre, and is something Cronenberg excels at, here and in his other works. He is unflinching in depicting gruesome scenes, claiming that the sometimes bizarre images he needs to convey simply could not be imagined by audiences if they happened off-screen. Nowadays, such visions would no doubt be provided by CGI, but physical effects artists in the 1980s were adept at creating such abject horrors.

Before discussing the film's visual effects in more depth, it is worth pointing out some of the more generic devices that Cronenberg uses to create suspense and shock. If we take Hitchcock's concept of suspense, discussed in Chapter 5, it is generated when the audience has more information than the protagonist about an impending threat. The most obvious example of this in *The Fly* occurs when Brundle makes the decision to enter the telepod himself. He is oblivious of the fly that enters with him, whereas we see it settling on the inside of the porthole window as Brundle kneels behind it. There follows a series of cuts, to a close-up of the fly, to the telepod door locking, to the timer counting down, to Brundle reaching out towards the inquisitive baboon. The fly leaves its resting place and starts buzzing around – will Brundle notice it in time? Or will he spot it when it's too late to do anything about it? As the countdown continues, the chances of Brundle seeing the fly and being able to halt the experiment diminish, and we resign ourselves to the fact, if we didn't know already, that this experiment is not going to go to plan.

When the teleportation finally occurs, the camera tracks in slowly to the door of the second telepod as it opens, and a plume of white smoke appears. This leads us to a question: why do the receiving telepods produce such a thick fog when an object is teleported? There is no narrative reason for it to behave in this way – in the original film there was a brilliant flash of light but no smoke. Obviously Cronenberg added this for aesthetic effect, and its purpose is to build tension as we wait to see what is revealed when it clears. After witnessing the result of the ill-fated baboon experiment, our imagination works overtime on what could possibly emerge following Brundle's teleportation with the fly (the film's poster featured a human arm and a wholly misleading fly's leg emerging from the telepod smoke). The tension is increased by the film's score, which drops down to a single ominous chord. When a seemingly normal Brundle steps out of the smoke we can breathe a sigh of relief, the low camera angles implying that, if anything, he has emerged with increased power. Of course, the telepod smoke also allows Cronenberg to make the audience jump with a good traditional shock effect, when the first baboon's bloody palm slams against the window. A similar but more spectacular shock occurs towards the film's climax, when the almost fully transformed Brundle smashes through the glass wall of the abortion clinic to kidnap Veronica and their unborn child.

These calculated jumps aside, as in Cronenberg's other genre films much of *The Fly*'s horror comes from visual effects that are designed to repulse, whether it be the inside-out baboon, the maggot-baby in the dream sequence, Borans' melting flesh, or the numerous stages of Brundle's transformation. Purposefully highlighting the importance of its special effects, the first credit to appear at the close of the film reads 'THE FLY CREATED AND DESIGNED BY CHRIS WALAS, INC.' Best known at the time for designing and building the creatures in *Gremlins* (Joe Dante, 1984), Walas had earlier been an assistant to Dick Smith on Cronenberg's *Scanners*. Whilst not as well known as some of his contemporaries, Walas's effects work here is truly exceptional and provides the film with much of its lasting power. As well as handling the various stages of the creature itself, Walas and his team of over thirty assistants were responsible for the rest of the film's gory effects, including a number that didn't make it to the final cut.

In order to keep audience attachment with Brundle going as long as possible, Cronenberg wanted him to be portrayed by an actor right up to the film's climax, and only then introduce something which is completely inhuman. Although for the most part the transition is a gradual metamorphosis, to get from actor to the final creature required a transformation scene. Walas has said that he wanted this to be unlike the transformation scenes that had gone before in films such as *An American Werewolf In London*, *The Howling* and Paul Schrader's 1982 remake of *Cat People*. He didn't want to have the character's body stretch and burst through the use of bladders, which by this time had become heavily over-used in the genre.[11] He wanted the transformation to be like a reptile shedding its skin, or an insect breaking free of a cocoon. The creature has been using Brundle's rotting body as a host, and it emerges once there is no more energy to consume. Although Walas ultimately designed all stages of the creature, one thing that Cronenberg was adamant about was that he didn't want the scientist to turn into a giant fly. He wanted something new, as Brundle puts it, 'something that never existed before': Brundlefly.

Brundlefly was, in Walas's designs, the sixth stage of the transformation. Prior to this the effects ranged from blotchy and discoloured skin in stage one, through to a full body suit, magnified contact lenses and dentures for stage five. A mechanised head was used for the sequence in which the creature vomits acid onto Stathis Borans' hand and ankle. We have noted previously how some actors have a reluctance to appear under too much heavy make-up, as it can limit their performing abilities and make them unrecognisable to audiences. As well, with special effects and make-up becoming more complex, they can be forced to spend hours in the make-up chair before appearing on set. Jeff Goldblum had no such qualms, and saw acting under layers of make-up as a challenge.[12] For the later stages of the transformation it would take up to five hours to have his suit and make-up applied, during which Geena Davis (his real-life partner at the time) read or sang to him. It is testament to Goldblum's abilities that he is able to keep audience sympathy for his character alive while acting under increasingly constricting layers of make-up.

By the film's climax, eight operators were required to work the mechanical puppet that represents the final fusion of Brundle, fly and telepod, a creation that Walas termed 'Brundlebooth'. Some critics suggest that by this point special effects had well and truly taken over as the driving force behind the narrative, yet in a Cronenberg film the confronting scenes of biological horror are never there simply to shock, nor to impress us with technical brilliance, but rather to make an intellectual point. Cronenberg takes his film-making very seriously, likening *The Fly* to works of metaphysical poetry such as John Donne's 'The Flea', which describes human love through imagery of one of nature's basest creatures. In Cronenberg's hands this translates into a modern romance story combined with a horrific tale of physical mutation involving a housefly. The director's choice of rousing, classical-style music for the score and his later production with composer Howard Shore of an opera based on the story — reflects his conviction that this is more than just a throwaway horror picture.

Cronenberg's previous films used sex and reproduction as a source of horror: in *Shivers*, the disease is created as an aphrodisiac and spread during intimacy; in *Rabid*, Rose has to get her victims into a compromising position in order to get their blood; in *The Brood*, the monsters are the result of immaculate conception caused by their mother's inner rage; in *Scanners*, the telepathic powers are the result of their mother's use of Ephemerol, a fertility drug, in the period leading to conception. Reproduction is seen as a disease in these films. Similarly, we can take Brundle's condition as being the result of an unholy union between fly and human, made possible through technology: 'It mated us … we hadn't even been properly introduced.' Brundle's condition has frequently been referred to as a metaphor for AIDS, the film being released at a time when public awareness of the disease was at its height.[13] Cronenberg himself has fought against any attempt to draw such parallels: in his view such a reductive reading would suggest that Brundle contracted the disease through his sexual relationship with Veronica.

Refuting the connection to any specific disease, Cronenberg instead suggests that Brundle merely suffers the ageing and bodily decay that everyone must go through ('the disease of being finite'), albeit at a greatly increased rate. His condition embodies universal fears of ageing and death, exemplified by the scene where he confronts the physical signs of his own mortality in the bathroom mirror. He is unable to shave due to the coarse hairs that have appeared on his body, and when he bites his fingernails in anxiety they begin to fall off: 'What's happening to me?' he asks himself. 'Am I dying?' Although he jokes about his condition, when his ear comes away in his hand he finally admits to Veronica that he's scared. The fact that he is aware of what is happening to him, and is able to articulate this, makes it more tragic and affecting for the viewer. For her part, Veronica is able to see past the disease to the man she still loves. She comforts him even as she is disgusted by what he is becoming.

As previously mentioned, the distinction between male and female is a recurring preoccupation of Cronenberg. He has expressed a keen interest in how biological differences could diminish through mutation, producing what he has termed 'omnisexuality' and leaving only male and female 'sensibilities'. In *The Fly*, when parts of his body begin falling off, Brundle's detached penis is one of the first appendages to be glimpsed in his 'museum of natural history'. Max Renn, the protagonist of *Videodrome*, develops a vagina-like slit in his stomach that acts as a receptacle for mind-controlling videotapes as well as his own phallic 'hand-gun', while Rabid's protagonist develops a penis-like appendage in her armpit that spreads disease through its 'bite'. In Cronenberg's universe, as physical differences between males and females are elided, omnisexual humans would develop new organs for pleasure, unrelated to sex or procreation. This idea is hinted at in Brundle's rambling speech, when he tells Veronica: 'I'm not just talking about sex and penetration, I'm talking about penetration beyond the veil of the flesh.'

Whilst the physical aspect of the theme is underplayed in comparison to some of Cronenberg's other works, 'sexual sensibility' is a key concept that arguably drives the narrative of the film as a whole. It is Veronica's female sensibility, her understanding of the flesh, which gives Brundle the insight to reprogram the system to handle living organisms (although how he instructs the computer to 'be made crazy by the flesh' is never explained). In effect, she completes him, filling in the gaps of his male sensibility and allowing him to make the necessary intellectual leap. His plan at the film's climax is to fuse himself with both Veronica and their unborn child (of unknown gender), so creating a true sexual hybrid. The introduction of Veronica's pregnancy intensifies the horror of the situation, as well as allowing an arguably gratuitous nightmare scene (with the director himself on gynaecologist duties). Here Cronenberg introduces the still-controversial issue of abortion, both in the nightmare, where Veronica begs to keep the baby, and in her desperate late-night visit to the doctor, when she threatens to 'do it myself if I have to'.

When Brundle initially tells Veronica that his invention will 'end all concepts of transport, borders and frontiers', little does he know what form this will take. At its core, body horror is about breaking down boundaries – between internal and external, self and other, human and non-human (be it animal, alien or machine). In *The Fly*, even the borders between species are permeable: 'I was an insect who dreamt he was a man, and loved it. But now the dream is over, and the insect is awake.' Cronenberg's *Videodrome* manifesto for the 'New Flesh', a hybrid of human and technology, re-emerges in *The Fly*. In true Cronenberg tradition Brundle is (re)born of the New Flesh, crouching naked in a foetal position within the womb-like pod. His diatribe on society's 'sick fear of the flesh' hints at his reimagining of human flesh through scientific experiment. At the film's climax, Brundle is 'mated' with the telepod itself. Rather than a powerful fusion of technology and human, as in the absorption of a gun into Max Renn's hand, the result is a pitiful sight. Although by this time any vestiges of humanity had disappeared from the creature, Cronenberg wanted to present a 'pathetic' creature, whose silent plea for Veronica to kill it gives a final tug at the audience's heartstrings (Fig 10.3).

Figure 10.3

Reception and Aftermath

The Fly featured heavily in horror and science-fiction genre magazines leading up to and immediately following its release in 1986. *Fangoria* in particular devoted numerous pages across several issues to behind-the-scenes photographs of Brundle in various stages of his transformation, alongside interviews with Cronenberg and Chris Walas. Fans who were perhaps disappointed by the relatively bloodless *Dead Zone* looked forward to a return to form from the 'King of Venereal Horror'. Distributed by 20th Century Fox (who had made the 1958 original), the film benefited from an extremely effective marketing campaign, with the ominous tag-line 'Be afraid... Be very afraid' tapping into the audience's perverse desire to be frightened. Spoken by Veronica in the film, this quote has since become an oft-used phrase within and outside of the genre. On its release the film topped the US box office charts for two weeks, becoming by far the most commercially successful of Brooks-films' productions, and of Cronenberg himself. Featuring in the top 25 grossing films of the year, it was the highest placed horror film with worldwide takings of over $60 million. Critically, the film received acclaim both from genre publications and the wider press. Cronenberg, Goldblum and Chris Walas were singled out for praise, with Walas taking the 1987 Academy Award for Best Make-Up.

While the gruesome effects more than satisfied the traditional horror film fan, it was the strength of the human story, played out by charismatic actors, which enabled the film to achieve mainstream success. Its box office performance meant that the inevitable follow-up would soon appear, and Cronenberg was approached to write and direct. However, Mel Brooks thought the idea he proposed was too far removed from the first film, telling the director that he wanted 'more of the same'. Cronenberg demurred, and *The Fly II* (1989) became the directorial debut of Chris Walas from a script by Frank Darabont, a prolific writer now better known for directing *The Shawshank Redemption* (1994) and developing the television series *The Walking Dead*. Apart from Veronica's brief appearance in a prologue (played by a different actress), in which she dies giving birth, Stathis Borans is the only character to return. The story revolves around Brundle's son, who discovers his father's identity while undergoing his own physical transformation. Despite the attraction of Walas's excellent special effects, including a more elaborate transformation, *The Fly II* is generally considered a disappointing sequel, and marked the end of the cinematic franchise.

By the time the sequel arrived, the body horror sub-genre was waning, at least in Hollywood. Perhaps the final word on that particular phase was *Society* (1989), directed by Brian Yuzna, who had produced the body horror/mad-scientist movies *Re-Animator* (Stuart Gordon, 1985) and *From Beyond* (Stuart Gordon, 1986). For his directorial debut Yuzna pulled out all the stops to present some of horror cinema's most surreal and disturbing images of bodily mutation and distortion (albeit with tongue firmly in cheek). It was a last hurrah for practical special effects artists. By the early 1990s their work was increasingly being replaced by CGI, a development initiated by the success of films such as *The Abyss* (James Cameron, 1989), *Terminator 2: Judgment Day* (James Cameron, 1991) and *Jurassic Park*. With computer effects becoming ever more realistic and affordable to film-makers, the move from physical effects to CGI is a trend that would be difficult to reverse. Nevertheless, you would be hard pressed to find a serious horror fan who believes that the digital effects in the 2011 prequel *The Thing* (Matthijs van Heijningen, Jr) are superior to the prosthetic work in John Carpenter's 1982 'original'.

Outside of the US, one of the most successful markets for body horror was Japan.

The sub-genre informed a wave of Japanese horror films that emerged from the end of the 1980s through the early 90s. *The Evil Dead Trap* (1988) may have its roots in the western slasher films of earlier in the decade but it culminates in a Cronenbergian body horror climax. Featuring a number of scenes of torture and bodily mutilation, the film remained largely unseen outside of Japan until quite recently. It was followed by a number of sequels, and its influence can be traced through the controversial *Guinea Pig* series (1985–1988), *Audition* (Takashi Miike, 1999) and the more recent 'torture porn' sub-genre. Closer in spirit to Cronenberg's early work is the controversial *Naked Blood* (Sato Hisayasu, 1995), in which a drug makes its users experience pleasure through pain, resulting in graphic scenes of self-mutilation. More well-known in the west are Shinya Tsukamoto's *Tetsuo: The Iron Man* (1989) and *Tetsuo II: Body Hammer* (1992), the first of which won top prize at the 1989 Fantastic Film Festival in Rome and effectively re-ignited western interest in contemporary Japanese cinema. Concentrating on the fusion of body with machine, the film highlights the Japanese pre-occupation with technology and modernity.

Although the vast majority of his early films were in the horror genre, Cronenberg's 1991 quasi-adaptation of William S Burrough's *Naked Lunch*, possibly the most surreal of his films, marked something of a turning point in the director's career. Following this he has moved progressively more mainstream, with successful (and occasionally controversial) films such as *Crash* (1996), *A History of Violence* (2005) and *Eastern Promises* (2007), together with not-so-successful experiments like *ExistenZ* (1999) and *Spider* (2002). As well as his writing and directing work, Cronenberg has also had acting roles in a number of films, most notably Clive Barker's *Nightbreed* (1990) and the ninth *Friday the 13th* sequel, *Jason X* (James Isaac, 2001). In 2008, Cronenberg and Howard Shore, who had composed the music for many of the director's films, collaborated on an operatic version of *The Fly*. With short runs in Paris and Los Angeles, the production was unfortunately not well received at either location. Obviously Cronenberg's attraction to the subject matter survived, as in 2011 he announced that he had written a sequel to *The Fly*, based on the proposal he had originally put together for *The Fly II*. 20th Century Fox expressed interest in the project (having previously discussed the possibility of a franchise 'reboot') but were ultimately unwilling to invest the required funds. The fact that the story was based more on the scientific ideas of the first film, rather than being a remake or direct sequel, may well have had the same effect on the studio as it had on Mel Brooks fifteen years earlier. The universe of Cronenberg's original film remains active, however, and 2015 saw the publication of a comic book sequel *The Fly: Outbreak*, in which the son of Brundle and Veronica continues his father's experiments.

While Cronenberg's involvement has ended for now, the influence of the sub-genre he helped create continues to be felt in the wider horror genre. Body horror's blurring of boundaries (between self and other, subject and object, normal and abnormal, reality and fantasy, internal and external, living and dead) and its surrealist imagery represents for many commentators the beginning of the so-called 'postmodern horror' movement. Although the phrase would be popularised with the arrival of the second cycle of slasher films – beginning with *Scream* and *I Know What You Did Last Summer* – its origins can be seen in films such as Cronenberg's *Videodrome*. That film's commentary on the effects of media on its audience is a major theme in our next case study, which effectively bridges the modern and postmodern horror film.

Bibliography

Campbell, Mary B. (1984) *Biological Alchemy and the Films of David Cronenberg*. In Grant, Barry Keith (ed.) *Planks of Reason: Essays on the Horror Film*. London: The Scarecrow Press.

Goldberg, Lee (1995) *The Dreamweavers: Interviews with Fantast Film-makers of the 1980s*. Jefferson: McFarland & Co.

Grunberg, Serge (2006) *David Cronenberg: Interviews with Serge Grunberg*. London: Plexus.

Mathijs, Ernest (2010) *They're Here! Special Effects in Horror Cinema of the 1970s and 1980s*. In Conrich, Ian (ed.). *Horror Zone*. London: I. B. Tauris.

McLarty, Lianne (1996) *"Beyond the Veil of the Flesh": Cronenberg and the Disembodiment of Horror*. In Grant, Barry Kieth (ed.) *The Dread of Difference*. University of Texas Press.

Rodley, Chris (ed.) (1997) *Cronenberg on Cronenberg*. London: Faber & Faber.

Browning, Mark (2007) *David Cronenberg: Author or Film-maker?* University of Chicago Press.

Emery, Robert J. (2003) The Films of David Cronenberg. In *The Directors: Take Four*. New York: Allworth Press.

Riches, Simon (ed.) (2012) *The Philosophy of David Cronenberg*. The University Press of Kentucky.

Westwood, Emma (2018) *The Fly (Devil's Advocates)*. Leighton Buzzard: Auteur.

Endnotes

1. *The Fly* wasn't immune to this phenomenon, with Bryan Ferry's single *Help Me*, featured in the arm-wrestling scene, released as a tie-in to the film.

2. The category was created in 1982 following industry complaints that Chris Tucker's groundbreaking make-up for David Lynch's *The Elephant Man* had gone unrecognised.

3. He eventually published his first novel, *Consumed*, in 2014, at the age of 70.

4. Cronenberg originally wanted Sissy Spacek, but Cinepix chief John Dunning wanted a name actress.

5. This message is echoed in the advertising for John Carpenter's *The Thing*, which suggested that you 'Look closely at your neighbour… Trust no-one… they might be THE THING!'

6. Cronenberg wrote *The Brood* when he himself was going through a particularly bitter separation and custody battle.

7. The script by Jeffrey Boam was written well before Cronenberg was brought into the project, although he, Boam and Debra Hill spent three days re-working it prior to beginning the shoot (see Goldberg 1995: 59).

8. Pogue's work was good enough for Universal to give him the job of writing *Psycho III* (Anthony Perkins, 1986).

9. Note that this is also apparent in the dynamic between Veronica and Stathis Borans. Although he is her editor (and previously her college tutor), and so in a position of power, Borans is as much in her thrall as is Brundle.

10. It is the baboon's reaction to the fly, waving and grabbing at it, which finally convinces Brundle that the animal has suffered no ill effects from the experiment. So as well as being responsible for the consequences of the experiment, the fly is ultimately the catalyst for the experiment taking place at all.

11. Pioneered by Joe Blasco in *Shivers*, bladders involved placing inflatable devices on the actor's skin under a layer of make-up. The application of air would give the impression of something moving under the surface of the flesh.

12. Prior to Cronenberg's involvement in the film, John Getz was offered a choice of the Brundle and Stathis Borans roles. He chose Borans on the basis that it involved the least make-up.

13. Similarly, the contagion spread by the characters in *Shivers* has been compared to herpes, a sexual disease of huge proportions in the late 1970s and into the 80s.

Chapter 11

Postmodern Horror

Wes Craven's New Nightmare
Wes Craven, US 1994

Recommended viewing
A Nightmare on Elm Street (Wes Craven, 1984)
Scream (Wes Craven, 1996)
I Know What You Did Last Summer (Jim Gillespie, 1997)
Scream 2 (Wes Craven, 1997)
Scary Movie (Keenan Ivory Wayans, 2000)

Introduction

Postmodern film simultaneously makes explicit and undermines generic codes and conventions. In postmodern horror cinema, the very formulaic nature of the genre becomes part of an in-joke: horror audiences are savvy, they know the rules, so why not treat them as intelligent by making the characters in the films just as knowledgeable? Wes Craven's *Scream* (1996) featured teen characters so familiar with slasher films that they were able to list the generic conventions with ease. In the memorable opening scene, a film quiz on scary movies by a mysterious caller quickly turns into a life-or-death scenario, with a gory conclusion for two of the teen characters. As the mechanics of the genre are made explicit, the safe boundaries separating reality from the frightening scenes on film are called into question and audiences can be genuinely scared all over again. Craven's film is often credited with sparking a new wave of so-called 'postmodern' horror cinema, resulting in three direct sequels, a television series and a slew of imitators, reboots and re-imaginings.

In this chapter we examine a film that Craven made two years prior to the first *Scream*, and which in many respects is closer to the concept of postmodernism as it is more broadly defined. *Wes Craven's New Nightmare* allowed the director to revisit his most famous creation with a postmodern twist, using reflexivity and circularity to adapt what had gone before and present audiences with something new. Given Craven's fascination with dreams and the overlap between the real and the imaginary, we also discuss surrealism in cinema. Finally, as we approach the end of our journey, we take a first opportunity to evaluate the cultural popularity of horror cinema, and how it affects both audiences and film-makers.

Background

Wes Craven was a relative latecomer to film-making. Dissatisfied with his career as an English professor, he followed his passion for cinema and moved to New York in his early 30s. After struggling for some years to break into the industry, he wrote and directed his first feature, *Last House on the Left* (loosely based on Ingmar Bergman's art-house classic *The Virgin Spring* [1960]) in 1972, after being inspired by a viewing of Romero's *Night of the Living Dead*. While Craven had never intended to become a 'horror' director his controversial debut, banned in Britain and heavily censored in the US and elsewhere, set him on a course he would find difficult to alter. In amongst his pseudonymous (behind-camera) involvement in a number of hardcore porn productions, *Last House* was followed by the genre entries *The Hills Have Eyes*, *Deadly Blessing* (1981) and *The Hills Have Eyes Part II* (1984). Horror also informed two TV movies he directed in this period, *Stranger in Our House* (1978) and

Invitation to Hell (1984). While occasionally branching out with more mainstream films, such as the DC Comics adaptation *Swamp Thing* (1982) and the Oscar-nominated Meryl Streep vehicle *Music of the Heart* (1999), Craven's career would remain predominantly tied to the horror and thriller genres until his death in 2015. Continually asked what he thought about the effects of horror cinema on society, he defended the films by arguing that, without them, the evil they repress would be set loose into the real world. In Craven's opinion horror films should be genuinely frightening and violent, describing them as 'honest' in comparison to action films such as *Rambo* (George P. Cosmatos, 1985), which he thought irresponsibly trivialised violence.

Both *Last House* and the first *Hills Have Eyes* are recognised as important works of modern horror, but it was a 1984 film that Craven wrote and directed with which he will forever be associated. A very personal project, it took a number of years to attract funding for *A Nightmare on Elm Street* before it came to the attention of Bob Shaye, head of New Line Cinema. At the time a small film distribution company catering to the teen market, New Line was actively looking to get involved in production and Shaye saw potential in Craven's relatively low-budget horror film. Although superficially a belated entry in the slasher cycle, *Nightmare* introduced as its killer the supernatural figure of Freddy Krueger. The spirit of a child killer burned to death by the parents of his victims, Krueger returns from the grave to exact his bloody revenge through their teenage children's dreams. The topics of child murder and vigilantism brought a dark morality to the film; as in *Last House*, the dividing line between right and wrong is muddied as 'good' people turn to murder in the pursuit of justice. Freddy himself inhabits a nightmare realm in which time, space and objects, including bodies, are malleable, stretched and distorted. This dream element allowed the serial killer character to escape the standard hack-and-slash approach and inhabit a more surreal and elastic reality. Rather than simply gutting his victims with his fingerknives, Freddy could twist and stretch his victims (and himself) in ever more bizarre and extreme ways. Also, unlike the more usual slasher villains, Freddy takes great pleasure in tormenting his victims (physically, mentally and verbally) prior to despatching them, rather than moving straight in for the kill. This aspect of the character was increasingly played for laughs in numerous sequels, with which Craven had little involvement – until *New Nightmare*.

Although the character of Freddy was drawn from his own childhood experiences, the general idea for the film came from newspaper reports of teenagers dying violently, and seemingly without reason, while asleep. A topic of particular interest to Craven, the blurring of the real and dream worlds had been referenced in his earlier work, with both *Last House* and *Deadly Blessing* featuring sequences in which the audience is unaware initially that the character they are watching is in a dream. While at college, Craven had been drawn to the work of Luis Buñuel, a Spanish-Mexican film-maker active from the 1920s until his death in 1983. Heavily involved in the Surrealist movement, Buñuel famously collaborated with Salvador Dali on the 1928 film *Un Chien andalou*. Taking dream imagery as their basis, Buñuel and Dali deliberately sought to link sequences of film that had no rational connection, foregoing any conventional narrative continuity. Like the Expressionists, Surrealists rejected conventional realist art forms, and were committed to expressing the imagination as revealed in dreams, free of the conscious control of reason and convention. The Surrealist Manifesto, issued by André Breton in 1924, highlighted what he saw as the importance of the subconscious in the advancement of the arts and sciences. Referencing the ghosts and castles of Gothic literature, Breton praised previous works of the fantastic (paying particular attention to Matthew Lewis's *The Monk*) in their ability to convincingly juxtapose the real and the unreal. He believed that the artist (indeed, man himself) should not be constrained by the logic of rationalism and should instead give free reign to his imagination, as occurs when in the dream state.

Sitting through a film that is completely surrealist can be a disorienting, even disturbing experience (see for example David Lynch's *Eraserhead*, *Carnival of Souls*, or indeed *Un Chien andalou*). Viewers have, however, become accustomed to seeing shorter surreal sequences in more mainstream cinema, such as the celebrated dream sequences in Hitchcock's *Spellbound* and *Vertigo*. The surrealist fantasy world of dreams (or more usually nightmares) has proven popular with makers of horror films, as we have seen with a number of our previous case studies. Released at the crossover point of the slasher and body horror cycles, *Nightmare* was effectively a bridge between the two and proved to be very successful at the box office, making $28 million in the US alone on a budget of $1.8 million (Muir 1998: 19). In addition, Craven created a figure in Freddy Krueger that would go on to become one of the genre's most successful and recognisable pop culture icons. Although undeniably a despicable character, Freddy was given far more personality than the silent, masked serial killers of the *Halloween* and *Friday the 13th* series. This was largely through the inspired casting of Robert Englund in the role, and the make-up by David Miller, which allowed the actor to invest Freddy with a greater range of expression. Almost as soon as the first film was released, sections of the audience began attending screenings in Freddy costume, with the instantly recognisable red and green sweater, razor glove and Fedora hat ready-made for commercial exploitation. New Line had already spotted the potential for a lucrative horror franchise, and insisted that Craven give the film an open ending.

Throughout the 1980s, *Nightmare on Elm Street* and Paramount's *Friday the 13th* franchises battled for supremacy, racking up thirteen films between them. Both received their own syndicated television series; *Freddy's Nightmares* took the *Alfred Hitchcock Presents* approach, with Freddy as the host introducing a different weird tale each week. Connections were made with the music industry, with Freddy appearing in promo videos alongside the heavy metal band Dokken ('Dream Warriors'), rappers The Fat Boys ('Are You Ready for Freddy?') and DJ Jazzy Jeff and the Fresh Prince ('A Nightmare on My Street'). Whilst held back somewhat in the vocal department, Jason Voorhees toured with rock-horror legend Alice Cooper,[1] who also contributed the theme song ('He's Back') for *Friday the 13th Part VI: Jason Lives*. These were serial killers for the MTV generation, and money was made through the sale of records, T-shirts, action figures and the rest. As the *Nightmare* films became increasingly campy, the once-disturbing character of Krueger evolved into 'America's favourite child killer', with child-size play-safe Freddy gloves promising the infant wearer that they too could be 'the bastard son of a thousand maniacs'. Craven, however, saw little by way of the profits from his creation; as part of the agreement to fund the original *Nightmare*, he had signed away all rights to the story and characters to New Line. After working on an aborted script for the third film under less than ideal conditions, he became increasingly unhappy with the company's treatment of the franchise, as well as the lack of payments and royalties he felt were his due. By 1994, the *Nightmare* movies had generated $500 million worldwide, but Craven himself had received only $400,000, less than 0.1 per cent of the earnings (Greenberg 1994).

Following what appeared to be the conclusion of the series in *Freddy's Dead: The Final Nightmare* (Rachel Talalay, 1991), Bob Shaye contacted Craven to try to mend some of the broken bridges, and after a long meeting set about straightening out the business and financial relationship to Craven's satisfaction. Shaye then asked the director if he would come back to the franchise for one last film. Giving him free rein to do whatever he wanted with the character of Freddy, Shaye regarded the new film as an apology to Craven for the way his creation had been treated since the original *Nightmare*. In those intervening years the horror genre had changed dramatically. The slasher film, the dominant sub-genre of the early 1980s had all but burnt itself out, with franchises such as *Halloween* and *Friday the 13th* limping on through films of decreasing quality and appeal. The success of *Fatal Attraction*, *Se7en* and *Silence of the Lambs* had taken the slasher mainstream, body horror had been drowned out by CGI, and the genre as a whole was again in something of a rut. Much of its independent output was low-budget, direct-to-video fare, while the major studios attempted to draw in older audiences with high-brow, big budget productions of horror classics such as *Bram Stoker's Dracula* (Francis Ford

Coppola, 1992) and *Mary Shelley's Frankenstein* (Kenneth Branagh, 1994). Although these achieved some commercial success they did little to revive the genre, and the limited appeal of horror was essentially abandoned in favour of the family-friendly blockbuster. There was no way that the genre could produce a franchise capable of bringing in $100 million per film; at least, not without a major rethink.

In preparation for the new *Nightmare* Craven watched all of the previous entries in the series, and found difficulty in following any particular story. He felt that this was due to the character of Freddy becoming so much the focus of the films. As happened in the Universal horror cycle in the 1940s, the monster had been moved from the shadows to front and centre, and in doing so had lost much of its power to scare. He wanted to take the character back to the margins, making him a lurking menace and the stuff of real nightmares. Early in the project, he arranged to have lunch with the actress Heather Langenkamp, with a view to her returning as Nancy Thompson, the ostensible 'final girl' of the original film. Having not met for some years, she told him about problems she'd been having with a stalker who was obsessed with a character she had played on television. Craven began thinking about how films can affect real life, and particularly about how the *Nightmare* franchise had affected the real world – the cast and crew, the audiences, the studio, and the genre itself. Fired up by the project, Craven began writing a script under the provisional title of *A Nightmare on Elm Street 7: The Ascension*. Just as his original *Nightmare on Elm Street* effectively bridged the slasher and the body horror film, the new film would link those two earlier sub-genres to what was to become the most popular and successful strand of horror cinema in the late 1990s and into the 2000s, so-called 'postmodern horror'.

The central ideas of postmodernism had been around for some time, and became widespread in the aftermath of the Second World War. In a world struggling to come to terms with the horrors of the Holocaust and the nuclear bomb, there was a questioning of whether advances in science, medicine and technology were in fact bringing us closer to any answers. Postmodernists argue that there is no ultimate absolute truth (either morally or scientifically), no certainty, only constant ambiguity and confusion. While modernism posits that such truth exists and can be discovered through an examination of the present, postmodernism instead attempts to describe the present in relation to, and through the use of, everything that has gone before. When postmodern architecture emerged in the 1950s and 60s, it rejected the modernist approach of producing something new and unique for the sake of it by returning to previous design patterns and creating a collage from pre-existing works. Similarly, postmodern cinema relies heavily on referencing what has gone before, using generic and other filmic conventions to reinforce or subvert audience expectations. In deliberately highlighting these conventions it overtly draws attention to the film-making process, connecting it to movements such as the French New Wave, as discussed in Chapter 8.

Craven's decision to take a self-reflexive approach to the 'final' *Nightmare* enabled him to reimagine the genre for a more informed critical viewer. While not achieving the commercial acceptance of his later *Scream* series, *New Nightmare* would prove to be the first step in taking the horror film out of its post-slasher malaise and into a more commercially attractive mainstream arena.

Textual Analysis

Los Angeles, 1994. Heather Langenkamp, Hollywood actress and star of *A Nightmare on Elm Street*, dreams that her make-up artist husband, Chase, is killed on the set of a horror film. The next day she attends a TV interview where she is reunited with Freddy Krueger actor Robert Englund to mark the tenth anniversary of the original *Nightmare*. Afterwards Heather is approached by the head of New Line Cinema, who tells her that Wes Craven is writing a new *Nightmare* film and they want her to be in it. She declines, telling him that she has an obsessive fan and no longer wants to be involved in horror films. Later that night, Chase falls asleep at the wheel of his truck and is killed, as Heather dreams of him being attacked by Freddy's razor claw. Visiting the morgue to view the body she sees what look like claw marks across his chest. Following the funeral, Heather's son Dylan's behaviour becomes erratic, reciting lines from the original film and throwing violent fits. She meets with Wes Craven, who tells her that he's been having bad dreams and is using them in a script for the new *Nightmare* film. He believes that the character of Freddy is the embodiment of an ancient evil, and while the films were being made that evil was contained. However, now that the character is no longer scary the evil is free to escape into the real world. The only way to stop it is to make another film where Heather herself finally defeats Freddy, just as Nancy had in the first film. That night she dreams that she is attacked by Freddy, and wakes up with slash marks on her arm. Rushing to the hospital where Dylan is under observation, she arrives to find his babysitter's mutilated body in his room. As dreams and reality blur, Heather finds herself outside the home of Nancy in the original film. Following a trail left by Dylan she emerges into a subterranean cavern where they battle Freddy and manage to lock him in a blazing furnace. With the evil defeated and the cavern threatening to collapse, they jump into a pool of water and arrive back in Dylan's bedroom. Finding the finished script for the new film on the floor, Heather begins reading it to her son, like a fairy story.

New Nightmare's premise, that of Freddy Krueger escaping the cinematic world of the *Nightmare on Elm Street* series into the 'real' world, had originated when Craven was approached to write *Nightmare 3* in 1986. As with many of his creative ideas, it came to him in a dream, in this case one where he was attending a party with Robert Englund. While the actor entertained the guests in full Freddy garb, Craven noticed a dark presence watching from the shadows. At the time, though, New Line Cinema found his ideas too leftfield. They knew that there was more mileage to be had from Freddy remaining the comic book villain audiences love to hate, and didn't want to mess too much with a franchise that had barely begun. By the time part seven came around, however, they'd had the big finale in the previous film and acknowledged that they would need something different to get the character back on screen for the series' tenth anniversary.

Although the limited budget meant that some of Craven's more ambitious ideas were curtailed (script rewrites were ongoing throughout the production, and the climax in Freddy's lair feels particularly rushed), the level of freedom given to the director by New Line was admirable. While the idea of evil stalking Hollywood was nothing new (the George Clooney-starring slasher parody *Return to Horror High* [Bill Froehlich, 1987] is an early precursor of the *Scream* sequels in this respect), what sets *New Nightmare* apart is the level of self-reflexivity involved in its narrative. In having Freddy Krueger menace the real-life cast and crew of Craven's original film, *New Nightmare* is an example of what is known as meta-fiction: essentially a fiction about fiction. Specifically, this film is about the next film in the *Nightmare* series, which Craven is currently writing. As it turns out, the film *is* the film he is writing. Again, the idea of a narrative telling the story of the construction of that same narrative is not new, with literary examples going back at least to Laurence Sterne's *Tristram Shandy* in the eighteenth century, and in film to Federico Fellini's *8½* (1963). Indeed, the final episode of our earlier case study *Kaidan* can be interpreted as a piece of self-reflexive meta-fiction.

It is this self-reflexivity that has come to define what is commonly referred to as the postmodern horror film. Often fragmented and non-linear in style and narrative, postmodern film in general requires what can be termed an 'active audience', one that is able to recognise references to earlier work in order to complete the cinematic jigsaw. In the *Scream* series, the active audience is anyone who is familiar with the slasher sub-genre, although the character of Randy is on hand to helpfully list the conventions for his (on- and off-screen) audience. In the case of *New Nightmare*, the active audience is restricted to those who saw and remembered the original *Nightmare on Elm Street*, though key excerpts appear on television screens to handily jog the collective memory. *New Nightmare* assumes that audiences are familiar with the characters from previous instalments, but also aware to some degree of the real lives of the actors and film-makers, who portray versions of themselves in the film. Heather Langenkamp's real-life family circumstances are reproduced on screen, albeit with actors playing the part of her young son and special effects artist husband. The characters within *New Nightmare* of course have full knowledge of the previous Freddy films, many having been involved in the making of them, with Craven himself cast in the role of knowledgeable expert. Within the context of the *New Nightmare* narrative, Craven has been having nightmares that have driven him to start work on the new script and which therefore give him insight into what is happening. The film abides by unique mythology as created by Craven; whatever he says is gospel, whatever he dreams/writes is the truth as it happens. In this film (and the film within the film) Craven is the ultimate *auteur*.

In the original *Nightmare*, Freddy derived his energy from Nancy and could only be defeated by her turning her back on him, thereby reclaiming all of the power she had given him. Here Craven extends that narrative logic, taking his cue from mythology theory and in particular the power of myth and its ability to 'capture the genie'. In general terms, as Craven explains to Heather, if we were to stop making horror films or telling scary stories then the evil contained in them would be free to express itself in other, less desirable forms. In the case of Freddy, the *Nightmare* films captured an ancient evil and kept it contained within the character. Now that the films are over and the character is no longer scary, that evil is free once more. The only way to recapture it is by confronting it and taking away its power – just as Nancy had done in the first film and Heather must do again. To defeat the evil that is Freddy she has to play the character of Nancy one last time – only this time the boundary between actress and character is not so concrete. The script that we see being written on Craven's word processor is for a film that will never be made, at least not within the universe of the film that we're watching. We can only make sense of the script that we see by stepping outside of the diegetic 'reel' world and into the 'real' world. By continually making us aware that we are watching a film by detailing the making of that very same film, Craven introduces layers of complexity and uncertainty. In postmodernism, there is no definable truth, and we can find ourselves going in circles searching for answers. This sense of spiralling uncertainty is exemplified towards the end of the film, when Heather finds a script on the floor of Freddy's lair. As she looks down at the script we experience a kaleidoscopic, or hall of mirrors, effect: we are watching her read a film script, a film script which describes her reading that same film script. It is impossible to find the one 'true' moment here; we can only see an infinite number of Heathers reading a script about reading a script.

Postmodernism thrives on repetition, eschewing any sense of a legitimate 'original' or singular 'true' version, and throughout *New Nightmare* dialogue, images and events are repeated from the original film. Whilst on one level Craven is putting in the references to the original for the benefit of the viewer, within the narrative the 'real' Freddy is using them to play with Heather's mind, reminding her that she is in part responsible for what is happening in the real world. Freddy's tongue emerging from her telephone handset is a direct lift from the first *Nightmare*, while other sequences, such as the construction of Freddy's glove and the killing of the babysitter, recall memorable scenes only to push them to more extreme levels. Julie's death restages the murder of Tina in the original, but, rather than being an unseen force emanating from the character's subconscious, here the character of Freddy himself can be seen dragging his victim across the wall and ceiling (Fig 11.1). The boundaries between the real and dream worlds are more porous, reinforcing the film's postmodern questioning of the nature of reality and truth.

Figure 11.1

The blurring of dream and reality had of course been a central feature throughout the *Nightmare* series, with the audience often sharing the characters' inability to distinguish between the two. Rarely when presenting a dream sequence would there be establishing shots showing the character asleep, or any identifiable visual or audio cues as to what we were watching. By convention the films typically opened within a main character's dream, plunging the audience straight into a nightmare scenario. *New Nightmare* is no exception. In the original *Nightmare* it was through Nancy Thompson's dream that we were introduced to the character of Freddy Krueger. We saw Freddy's hands as he fashioned his iconic leather glove, complete with razor fingernails, in a grimy boiler-room. In *New Nightmare* we observe the same scene, this time pushed to an absurd degree when the razors are affixed to a mechanical hand and wrist before Freddy (recognisable through his red and green striped sweater) lops off his own hand, presumably in preparation for the mechanical replacement. (In a self-reflexive touch, the biomechanical hand was based on artwork featured on a publicity poster for the original film.) Off-screen we hear a call for 'more blood', at which point we realise that what we are watching is no more than the making of a film within a film. The audience can breathe a sigh of relief. The bloody stump of an arm is no more than a make-up artist's prop, though at this point we are still unaware that we're watching Heather's dream.

New Nightmare's absence of opening credits acts to unsettle the audience. Although the lack of a title sequence has become more common in recent times, filmgoers in the early 1990s were still accustomed to some kind of scene- or tone-setting before launching into the film proper. In this case the lack of credits adds to its aura of realism. For all we know we could be watching a documentary about the making of a film, and when we see Langenkamp on the set, dressed in pyjamas, we assume that she is appearing as Nancy in a new Freddy production. (Given the lack of logic inherent in the previous films, the fact that Nancy was killed off in the second sequel need not concern us.) The relief we felt earlier is short-lived however, when the mechanical hand suddenly takes on a life of its own and kills two of the special effects crew before bearing down on Heather's husband. As she screams in terror, Craven finally reveals this to be a dream on the part of the actress. From the beginning, then, our sense of what is 'real', within the context of the fictional film, is repeatedly undermined, and the boundaries between the multiple layers of reality are blurred.

Heather awakens to an earthquake, a conveniently 'real world' explanation for the vivid nature of her nightmare and for the otherwise unexplainable connections between her dreams and everyday life: Chase's hand was cut on the mirror when it fell during the quake, rather than by the mechanical claw of her dream, and later aftershocks could be responsible for the TV switching on seemingly by itself. The earthquake motif again references the original film, in which Freddy's first victim, Tina, suggests that she and her friends are having nightmares because they're being affected by an upcoming quake. As well as being a useful plot device, the earthquake and aftershocks serve as a metaphor for the breaking down of the border between good/evil, reality/nightmare. They open up cracks in the earth's surface, fracturing the boundaries of 'civilised' urban society and revealing the darkness below, while the cracks in the living room wall evoke Freddy's knives and the wounds that they inflict. In a case of life imitating art, real-life earthquakes struck Los Angeles at the time of filming *New Nightmare*, and Craven despatched a second film crew to capture footage to be cut into the film. The shots depicting the earthquake's aftermath have an almost apocalyptic quality, and add to the film's sense of realism and impending doom.

Raising parallels with the character of Rosemary in *Rosemary's Baby*, Heather is the audience's identification figure and appears in practically every scene of the film. Like Rosemary, there is the nagging suspicion throughout that she's being kept in the dark, that everyone seems to know something she doesn't, and for much of the film the audience is as confused as she is. Langenkamp's acting style (she permanently seems to be in a daze) doesn't help the viewer differentiate between reality/film/dream, which works to make the film appear jumbled. Is she being driven mad by the memories of the original film and the effect that it's having on her son? Are the earthquake aftershocks real, and are they affecting her mentally? When Julie the babysitter first arrives she claims not to have felt any recent shocks, only a truck going past. This raises questions about Heather's state of mind, but also establishes the babysitter herself as a potentially untrustworthy figure (Julie remained an ambiguous character until late in the film's development). At first these fears seem to have a rational explanation – she is on edge because of the actions of a real-life stalker, and the stalker is using Freddy to scare her. Regardless of the cause of the nightmares, the opening dream sequence serves an important purpose in establishing that Heather the actress is still affected by her association with the *Nightmare* series.

These feelings are confirmed during the television interview that follows. Heather's unease at the situation is highlighted by the shadow of Freddy's glove falling across her face in slow motion, recalling the nightmare she experienced earlier. At the same time, the scenes at the television studio serve to remind the audience that the films are just that – fictional scenarios played out by actors. When the host introduces Robert Englund, he bursts onto the stage as Freddy, hamming it up with a line from the second *Nightmare* film – 'You're all my children now!' A wry Craven in-joke, the phrase takes on an extra dimension here given that the studio audience seems to be filled with actual children. From a cinematic audience perspective, if Englund is in the film as himself, then (if we were playing by the usual rules) Freddy cannot be real within the world of this film: Englund *is* Freddy, as we all know. As the familiar *Nightmare* theme plays we see, from Heather's POV, his silhouette waving his arms to the audience, the studio spotlight creating a halo effect around him (Fig 11.2). The crowd, an active audience in every sense, are chant-

Figure 11.2

ing Freddy's name and several are sporting Freddy costumes and holding signs begging for a new film. The fandom of Freddy, and its critique, is echoed in the opening of *Scream 2*, where a cinema audience dressed in *Scream* masks and waving glow-in-the-dark knives cheer the on-screen murders, even as an actual killer stalks amongst them.

While Craven deals explicitly and critically with the pop culture surrounding Freddy in this film, it is fair to say that the earlier *Nightmare* entries had also referenced the popularisation of their central character. Throughout the film series, Freddy appeared in video games, comic books and television chat shows within the dreams of his victims, mirroring the commodification that was occurring in real life. Other pop culture references would place Freddy within recognisable scenarios outwith the series. *Freddy's Dead*, for instance, opens with an *homage* to *The Wizard of Oz*, showing Freddy flying on a broomstick through a tornado a la the Wicked Witch of the West. In *Part 4* his razor fingers glide along a beach in an imitation of *Jaws'* shark fin: 'Just when you thought it was safe to get back into bed!' Craven shows himself not averse to paying *homage* to external sources in *New Nightmare*, although the reference to *Nosferatu*, in which a clawed silhouette stalks Heather, at least serves to reinforce the suggestion that the evil embodied in Freddy is timeless. As well, the director can't resist a few wry comments on the state of the franchise, such as when the limousine driver tells Heather that he thought the first film was the best (a sentiment repeated by Drew Barrymore's character in the opening sequence of *Scream*).

The inclusion of scenes at the actual New Line offices not only further the plot but offer additional commentary on the workings of the commercial horror film industry. The office of studio head Bob Shaye is filled with pictures and memorabilia of Freddy, marking him as complicit in the commodification of the character (Fig 11.3). The studio has clearly

Figure 11.3

made a lot of money from the franchise and Shaye is keen to make more by re-uniting Heather with Wes Craven in another film. He misunderstands Heather's fears about an obsessive fan, interpreting everything through the language of commercial profit and telling her that market research proves she has 'plenty of fans'. When she turns down his offer on the basis that she has a child, Shaye protests that 'kids love horror', reinforcing the images from the television studio. Although Craven became increasingly critical of the exploitation of the Freddy character, he had initially been pleased to see children taking on board the Freddy persona at one of his own TV interviews, interpreting this as a means of actively overcoming their fears rather than being harmed by them. Later in the film, Dr Heffner[2] overtly implies that Dylan is the victim of abuse at the hands of his own mother through being allowed to watch the *Nightmare* movies. While Heather insists that she wouldn't knowingly let Dylan watch the films, she tells Heffner that 'every kid knows who Freddy is. He's like Santa Claus, or King Kong'. It is an acknowledgement that

Freddy has taken on an existence beyond the bounds of the films themselves; children recognise the popular image of Freddy Krueger even though they may not have actually watched any of his films.

Aiming the film at an older audience who had seen the original ten years earlier, Craven explores how they as parents view the Freddy phenomenon and its effects on their children. While Dylan's increasingly erratic behaviour can be interpreted as a consequence of being exposed to horror films, the audience is given clues throughout that something far more disturbing is behind these episodes. After his father's funeral Dylan stands in the family sitting room, transfixed by the original movie on television, yet we see that the set is not even plugged in. When he tapes knives to his fingers and starts attacking Heather in Freddy fashion, it represents the ultimate nightmare of any film-maker and parent. However, Craven undercuts this link between films and children's behaviour by making it clear that Freddy, a source of evil no longer contained within a movie, is physically controlling Dylan in this moment. Challenging those who would assert the negative effects on children of watching horror, Craven tells Heather that such films are necessary to suppress and manage our fears and to take control over evil, in much the same manner as fairy tales. Dylan validates this when Heather suggests that Hansel & Gretel will give him nightmares, and he smiles and tells her that he likes the story. When she then tries to stop reading before the end, Dylan protests and recites the book from memory up to the point where the witch is killed. He then insists that Heather tells him how Hansel and Gretel find their way home, following the trail of bread-crumbs just as Heather will later follow Dylan's trail of sleeping pills to rescue him.

In another example of postmodern intertextuality, parallels are drawn throughout the film between the witch in Dylan's storybook and the 'real' Freddy. This underlines two of the film's central concepts; firstly that horror films are no more than updated fairy stories (a point driven home at the very end of the film, when Heather begins reading the script of the film to Dylan in his bedroom), and secondly that the evil currently occupying the Freddy character has taken on different guises throughout history. Visually, the witch wears red and green striped stockings and brandishes fingernails reminiscent of Freddy's razor claw, while at the climax of the film Freddy's face morphs to mimic that of the witch. The defeat of Freddy by pushing him into an oven is both a reference to the furnace that the Elm Street parents used to destroy the 'real' Fred Krueger and an echo of the witch's death at the hands of Hansel and Gretel. Heather reinforces the link, stating 'They're saved – the witch is dead'. When Freddy tells Dylan 'I've got some gingerbread for you,' it is an unnerving allusion both to the story and to the dangerous sweet-carrying strangers all modern children are warned about. Similarly, Freddy's claim that he could 'just eat [Dylan] up' simultaneously uses the affectionate language of parents/grandparents and makes a genuine literal threat. The relationship between Nancy and Freddy had always had an underlying sexual dimension, and given that Krueger was originally intended to be a child molester (an aspect reintroduced in the reboot) it's unsurprising that he uses Dylan to get to Heather. There is, however, little to suggest anything paedophilic other than when he cryptically tells her that he 'touched him', just prior to his tongue emerging from the telephone.

The character of Dylan echoes that of Nancy in the original - his parents are holding information back in an attempt to protect him, though he in fact understands more than they know or will admit. Certainly Heather is unwilling to accept his claims that he hears children chanting at the bottom of the bed and that his stuffed dinosaur is having nightly battles with a 'meanie man with the claws'. A common trope of the contemporary Gothic, disconnected (or plain dysfunctional) families were a standard feature throughout the *Nightmare* series. For Nancy, her alcoholic mother and absent father were unable to save her and she was left to her own resources to take on and destroy Freddy. In contrast, and despite her reluctance to believe the real reason for Dylan's behaviour, Heather proves herself a fearless mother in pursuing him to the depths of hell. She is not only the 'final girl' of this film but a powerful maternal figure who ultimately displaces the father from the Hansel and Gretel story: 'and his mother covered him with kisses and he was safe'. Surviving this traumatic experience appears to have helped Dylan to deal with the loss of his own father. This 'real-life' tragedy, for both Heather and Dylan, has been overshadowed by the immediate dangers posed by Freddy. Only the poignant playground scene, when Dylan hopes that God will take him too, suggests the depth of mourning he is experiencing.

While fulfilling the role of the conventional 'final girl', Heather (like Sidney in the *Scream* films) is hyper-aware of the scenario in which she finds herself. When John Saxon reverts to his on-screen persona of Nancy's ineffectual father, Heather realises that the only way to defeat evil, and rescue her son, is to re-enter the fictional world of the *Nightmare* films. The return to the exterior of Nancy's house at 1428 Elm Street serves once again to provide a postmodern sense of repetition and non-linearity, thrusting us back into the world of suburban Gothic. Moreover, the final showdown circles back to the opening of *New Nightmare*. Following Dylan's trail of sleeping pills, Heather finds herself in her pyjamas on the film set from her dream, except now it is not a set but the actual lair of the evil contained in Freddy.

For much of the film to this point, the 'real' Freddy has been kept off-screen: he is the disturbing voice on the phone, the evil spirit that possesses the special effects claw, the unseen demon that takes over Dylan. However, once the character moves front and centre it's difficult to divorce Freddy from the safe pop culture icon he had become. Efforts to make the character appear bulkier, and changes to the make-up and costume, are largely ineffectual, with Craven himself later expressing regret at some of the updates. As the film reaches its climax, back come the wise-cracking one-liners and elastic body-stretching familiar from the earlier films. Whilst undoubtedly disturbing, the sight of Freddy Krueger morphing into a snake, stretching his arms or tongue to ridiculous lengths, or dislocating his jaw to fulfil his promise of gobbling Dylan up, tread a fine line between horror and black comedy. As such, the climactic scenes ultimately undermine Craven's efforts to re-introduce Freddy as the genuinely scary villain he had originally envisioned.

Reception and Aftermath

Made ten years after the original, *New Nightmare* allowed Craven to reflect on the impact of his creation on horror audiences over the previous decade. A very personal and ambitious film, *New Nightmare* was an attempt to reconnect horror cinema with the telling of genuinely scary tales. But although the story benefits from having all of the other sequels (good or bad) before it, the fact that Freddy had become something bigger than the films also acted against it. Many die-hard fans didn't like what Craven did with their icon, and the level and complexity of the self-awareness was seemingly too much for many viewers. Conversely, the apparent pandering to the traditional Freddy fanbase in the final showdown disappointed those who appreciated Craven's intentions. As such the film fell between two stools and was commercially the least successful of the franchise. An interesting and ultimately influential experiment, it failed to find an immediate audience, taking just over $18 million in total at the US box office. This is some way off the almost $50 million earned by the most financially successful (at the time) fourth instalment in the series, and only just over half the takings of *Freddy's Dead* a few years earlier.

The film did achieve critical acclaim however. Following its premiere one review lauded it as 'the first postmodern horror film', though it's worth mentioning that earlier films (most notably Kubrick's *The Shining*) had received similar plaudits. Moreover, with their open-endedness, blurring of boundaries in genre and narrative, as well as the incorporation of pop culture references, it is arguable that the *Nightmare* films themselves had been postmodern for the previous ten years. What the new instalment did bring to the genre, however, was enhanced self-reflexivity. Slashers had died because they were all the same; they had become too predictable and audiences knew exactly what to expect. In *New Nightmare* self-aware characters know all about the *Nightmare* series, but because of their supernatural element are initially unwilling to accept that what is happening in 'real' life is in any way related. The border between the worlds of reality and fiction is thrown into question for both characters and audience. In terms of what was to become known as 'postmodern horror' in the late 1990s, *New Nightmare* certainly anticipates, more than anything that had come before, many of the themes and ideas that would appear in later films.

While *New Nightmare* failed to attract large audiences, this was not a problem suffered by the director's next project. Foregoing the supernatural elements of *New Nightmare*, the phenomenally successful *Scream* emerged as a new take on the classic stalk-and-slash scenario. As usual, there is a serial killer on the loose, but now the teen characters, well versed in slasher lore from *Halloween*, *Friday the 13th* and the rest, know the rules of survival according to the conventional plot. At the film's climax, after apparently despatching the killer, 'final girl' Sidney is warned that they always come back for one last scare.[3] 'Not in my movie,' she says, before calmly shooting the killer through the head as he moves to get up. In comparison to *New Nightmare*, *Scream* kept its deconstruction of the genre more firmly within the confines of its 'realistic' plot. While still reflecting directly on the slasher cycle and its production, *Scream* and its sequels maintain more stable boundaries between the 'real' and the 'film' world; the appealing teenage cast, more typical of the genre, are clearly characters in a fictional setting. Less demanding of its audience, *Scream* is a watered down, mainstream, fan-friendly (and therefore commercially attractive) take on what Craven had attempted with *New Nightmare*. It proved extremely popular commercially, bringing in over $100 million at the US box office alone and guaranteeing the start of a lucrative franchise.

Scream 2 and *Scream 3* (2000) took self-reflexivity to ever-greater heights, showing Hollywood making films based on the 'real-life' events of the first instalment. As cast and crew are killed off by a mystery stalker, characters discuss the rules for staying alive in sequels. *Scream 3* (by far the most disappointing of the series), which revolves around Hollywood's obsession with slasher franchises, has distinct echoes of *New Nightmare* and explores many of the same themes. Following the critical and commercial success of the *Scream* series, the horror genre began to thrive again, through films such as *I Know What You Did Last Summer*, *Urban Legend* and their sequels. These later films, though labelled as 'postmodern', lost much of the clever self-reflexivity of *Scream* to return to a more standard slasher format, though keeping a shift in focus away from the killer to the lives of the teenage characters. The writer of the first, second and fourth *Scream* films as well as *I Know What You Did Last Summer*, Kevin Williamson, had already enjoyed success in television writing for the teen/young adult demographic, with series such as *Dawson's Creek* (1998-2003), which he created. It was this demographic that would provide a profitable audience for the new wave of horror cinema, as film studios ramped up production of scary movies to appeal to the MTV audience.[4]

Of course, with this upsurge in horror popularity, Craven was mistaken if he thought that he had finally brought the *Nightmare* franchise to a close. By the time *New Nightmare* was produced, New Line Cinema had acquired the rights to continue the *Friday the 13th* series from Paramount. Although a potential match-up between Freddy Krueger and Jason Voorhees was hinted at in the climax of the ninth *Friday the 13th* instalment, *Jason Goes To Hell: The Final Friday*, it would take fifteen years of negotiation and development before *Freddy vs Jason* (dir. Ronny Yu) arrived in 2003. Both franchises, along with *Texas Chain Saw Massacre*, were subsequently bought by Michael Bay's Platinum Dunes production company, which resulted in relatively big-budget remakes of *Chain Saw* (Marcus Nispel, 2003), *Friday the 13th* (Marcus Nispel, 2009) and *Nightmare on Elm Street* (Samuel Bayer, 2010). Generally derided by fans of the original films, these versions were very successful financially, each returning $100 million or more at the worldwide box office. This new cycle of re-makes and reboots ensured that there was plenty of fodder for the inevitable *Scream 4* (2011), Wes Craven's last feature film before his death in 2015.

While the remakes of these and other slashers that emerged in the wake of *Scream* largely remained true to the spirit of the originals (with a few token postmodern twists on character and plot), there were a number of differences in both the narrative and style. By way of 'rebooting' the franchises, the Platinum Dunes remakes in particular featured more backstory and exposition. *Nightmare*, for instance, went back to Freddy's days as a janitor at a Springwood kindergarten and detailed his fiery fate at the hands of irate parents. In general, the new wave of slasher films were less violent and gritty than the original cycle, with a high-budget gloss and slick music video aesthetics to make them more accessible to a younger teen market. Marking a return to the conservative stance of pre-1970s genre output, the survivors of these films were more often than not a heterosexual couple, rather than the conventional 'final girl'.[5] Their cast lists were frequently littered with well-known actors and actresses, often from popular television series. Buffy the Vampire Slayer herself, Sarah Michelle Gellar, lent her celebrity status to *I Know What You Did Last Summer* and *Scream 2* and wound up dead in both. That well-known actors brought with them associations from their previous roles suited the postmodern approach of questioning boundaries and encouraging multiple readings, and, in the case of the indestructible Buffy, enabling the subversion of audience expectation.

Postmodern film, though rarely marketed as such outside of the horror genre, is so widespread nowadays that it is almost mainstream. Whilst not usually as overt as *Natural Born Killers* (Oliver Stone, 1994), which jumbles film stocks, inserts animated sequences and blurs generic codes and conventions (from gangster film, horror, Western and even sitcom) in an explicit examination of the effect of media on real life and vice versa, many films that are released today include elements of postmodernism. Where modernist film-making neatly compartmentalises film into genre, postmodernism breaks down these divisions and draws in pre-existing cinematic art, whether as reference, *homage* or pastiche. The films' message comes not so much from their narrative, but from the recognition and appropriation of external sources that are already invested with meaning. Such retro-homage is a speciality of Quentin Tarantino, as in *Pulp Fiction* (1994) and *Grindhouse* (2007). Rather than using genre expectations to help the film, postmodernist film often uses them against the audience, twisting conventions or destroying them through the film's own internal logic, or even switching genre mid-story, as in Tarantino's script for *From Dusk Til Dawn* (Robert Rodriguez, 1996). Such an approach is one pursued (in a more exaggerated form) by parody, and it is not surprising that in the wake of the postmodern horror films of the 1990s there was an upsurge in parodies, beginning with *Scary Movie* and continuing through its various sequels and spin-offs (*Date Movie*, *Epic Movie*, etc.).

Since its rise to prominence in the mid-1990s, the term 'postmodern film', and 'postmodern horror film' in particular, have often been used derogatorily to describe productions that are superficial and dumbed-down, overly derivative and uninventive, emphasising spectacle over narrative; familiar phrases that had been used to describe the genre throughout much of the previous two decades. The central tenets of postmodern thinking – rejection of objective certainty and absolute truth, acceptance that there is no reality other than that which is (re-)presented to us, perceived and constructed by us through our culture – lends itself particularly well to the horror genre as we have seen throughout this book. Indeed, it is arguable that since its inception, the horror film, and the Gothic literature that preceded it, has taken a postmodern stance. And, of course, Hitchcock did the whole 'switching genre mid-way through a film' trick with *Psycho*, three decades before Tarantino.

Very much underrated and even dismissed by fans of the genre, *New Nightmare* is an important marker in the evolution of the horror film. Just as he had reinvigorated the genre ten years earlier with *A Nightmare on Elm Street*, Craven produced something in *New Nightmare* that would inform horror cinema for the next decade and more. To the surrealist approach of the earlier films, which blurred the lines between dream and reality (within the film's universe), Craven added a postmodern self-reflexivity that would become a standard feature of horror in the late 1990s and well into the 2000s. Not only that, his ambitious approach brought critical approval back to what had become an increasingly panned franchise. Some scholars have questioned the usefulness of the term 'postmodern' to aid our interpretation of these later films, but there is no doubt that the term has come to have meaning in defining – and perhaps more importantly in marketing – a particular moment in horror cinema.

Bibliography

Conrich, Ian (2000) 'Seducing the Subject: Freddy Krueger, Popular Culture and the *Nightmare on Elm Street* Films. In Alain Silver & James Ursini (eds), *Horror Film Reader*. New Jersey: Limelight Editions.

Greenberg, James (1994) 'Freddy Krueger's Creator Breaks Out of His Genre'. *The New York Times*, 9 October, accessed 30 January 2018, <http://www.nytimes.com/1994/10/09/movies/freddy-krueger-s-creator-breaks-out-of-his-genre.html>

Mayshark, Jesse Fox (2007) *Post-Pop Cinema: The Search for Meaning in New American Film*. London: Paeger.

Muir, John Kenneth (1998) *Wes Craven: The Art of Horror*. Jefferson: McFarland & Co.

Phillips, Kendal R. (2012) *Dark Directions: Romero, Craven, Carpenter, and the Modern Horror Film*. Southern Illinois University.

Robb, Brian J. (1998) *Screams & Nightmares: The Films of Wes Craven*. London: Titan Books.

Tudor, Andrew (2002) 'From paranoia to postmodernism? The horror movie in late modern society'. In Steve Neale, ed., *Genre and Contemporary Hollywood*. London: British Film Institute, pp.105-116.

West, Steven (2019) *Scream (Devil's Advocates)*. Leighton Buzzard: Auteur.

Endnotes

1   Cooper would later appear as Freddy's father in *Freddy's Dead: The Final Nightmare*.

2   Craven is having a dig at the censors here in naming the doctor after Richard Heffner, then head of the MPAA.

3   The concept of the 'final scare' emerged from films such as *Carrie* and *Friday the 13th*. Giving the audience one last jump before the closing credits became a convention and then a cliché expected at the end of every horror film from the 1980s onwards.

4   It was hardly surprising that when the *Scream* TV series arrived in 2015 it was produced and broadcast by MTV.

5   See, for example, Michael Bay's Platinum Dunes remakes, as well as *Prom Night* (Nelson McCormick, 2008), *My Bloody Valentine* (Patrick Lussier, 2009), *I Know What You Did Last Summer* and its sequels.

Chapter 12

Modern-Day Vampires

Låt den rätte komma in (Let the Right One In)
Tomas Alfredson, Sweden 2008

Recommended viewing
Martin (George A. Romero, 1977)
Near Dark (Kathryn Bigelow, 1987)
From Dusk 'Til Dawn (Robert Rodriguez, 1996)
Afflicted (Clif Prowse and Derek Lee, 2013)
A Girl Walks Home Alone at Night (Ana Lily Amirpour, 2014)

Introduction

In his preface to *Fear Without Frontiers* (Schneider 2003), a study of horror films from around the world, Kim Newman suggests that 'the figure of the vampire has come to stand for the horror film as the figure of the cowboy does for the western, and a handy way of encapsulating the horror film in any culture is to examine its vampire movies' (Newman 2003:7). Whilst Newman may be overstating its importance somewhat, the vampire movie has undoubtedly been the most enduring sub-genre throughout the history of horror cinema. From the German Expressionism of *Nosferatu*, through the Universal and Hammer versions of *Dracula*, George A. Romero's modernist *Martin*, the genre-busting *From Dusk 'Til Dawn*, to the *Twilight* saga and beyond, they have remained popular with audiences the world over.

Once confined to the cobweb-filled cellars of nineteenth-century European castles, since the 1970s the cinematic vampire is more likely to be found in contemporary suburbia. In this chapter we take a look at the history of movie vampires, and how they have evolved to their current form. For our case study, we examine a film that takes the conventions laid down across a century of vampire cinema to produce something that still appears fresh and exciting.

Background

If the *Scream* films helped to breathe new life into the genre in the second half of the 1990s, the commercial success in 1999 of both *The Blair Witch Project* ($250 million from a budget of $60,000) and *The Sixth Sense* (over half a billion dollars on a $40 million budget) ensured that by the turn of the millennium, horror was once again hot property. However, whilst the American horror film did produce some original scares with films such as *What Lies Beneath* (Robert Zemeckis, 2000), *The Village* (M. Night Shyamalan, 2004) and *Paranormal Activity*, these were very much the exception rather than the norm. Scanning a list of the most successful horror films from Hollywood across the first decade of the twenty-first century can be a depressing read. Rather than experimenting with new avenues, the studios chose to play it safe, with franchises and remakes (primarily of American slashers and J-Horror) the order of the day.[1] Add to this the emergence of the so-called 'torture porn' cycle (discussed in our next chapter), and the American horror film industry appeared to be at a very low ebb indeed.

For now, though, we return to Europe. While Hollywood cannibalised its back catalogues with remakes and reboots, and Asia turned out ever more derivative J-Horror entries (which would culminate in the *Ring/Grudge* mash-up *Sadako vs Kayako* [Kôji Shiraishi, 2016]), something of a renaissance was going on in continental

Europe. Although the torture porn aesthetic was evident in confronting films such as the French trio of *Haute Tension* (Alexandre Aja, 2003), *Frontier(s)* (Xavier Gens, 2007) and *Martyrs* (Pascal Laugier, 2008), it was the psychological horror of *The Others* (Alejandro Amenabar, 2001) which resonated with audiences. A Spanish co-production, the film made over $200 million worldwide and marked the beginning of a highly productive and successful phase, both artistically and commercially, in that country's genre output. Following this, other important works included Guillermo del Toro's fantasy-horrors *The Devil's Backbone* (2001) and *Pan's Labyrinth* (2006), *The Orphanage* (J. A. Bayona, 2007), *[Rec]* and *Julia's Eyes* (Guillem Morales, 2010), all proving popular internationally. Del Toro's work in particular has bearing on the concept of 'mainstream' horror, as discussed in our next chapter.

In comparison to other European countries, the Scandinavian regions are not renowned for their genre output. Prior to the release of *Let the Right One In*, Sweden's main contribution to the cinematic horror genre was arguably *The Virgin Spring*. Not conspicuously a horror film in itself, its plot was the inspiration for Wes Craven's first film, the notorious *Last House on the Left*. True, there had been bona fide Swedish genre entries in the form of *Evil Ed* (Anders Jacobsson, 1995) and the vampire film *Frostbiten* (Anders Banke, 2006) amongst others, but it's safe to say that none of these had received much, if any, exposure outside of their home country. So, it is perhaps surprising that one of the most original and refreshing – and well-received – horror films released in the first decade of the twenty-first century should be a Swedish production based around one of the genre's oldest and most filmed topics.

Unlike most horror sub-genres, the vampire film is subject to an established set of rules and conventions laid down in both literary precedents and folklore. Originating in Eastern European legend, the traditional vampire was a soul or reanimated corpse, which would leave its grave by night to feed on the blood of the living. Bram Stoker introduced the more overtly religious aspects of vampirism in his 1897 novel *Dracula*, namely an aversion to crucifixes and holy water. Stoker was also responsible for numerous other now-well-known characteristics, such as the ability to crawl up walls and to transform into and control various animals ('the children of the night'), the need to sleep in the soil of their homeland and to be invited in by their intended victim, the passing of vampirism through their bite, and the stake through the heart as a preferred method of despatch. Such conventions have been added to or amended throughout the history of vampire films and literature, to suit the needs of the writer or film-maker. As an example, in Stoker's novel, Dracula is able to operate during daylight hours, albeit in a weakened state. *Nosferatu*, F.W. Murnau's 1922 unlicensed adaptation of *Dracula*, introduced the idea of the vampire being killed by sunlight in an (unsuccessful) attempt to avoid accusations of copyright infringement. It is a dramatic convention that has endured, and one that is embraced to spectacular effect in this chapter's case study.

Since that first appearance in 1922, the vampire has been a mainstay of the horror genre. Count Dracula remained the recognisable face of cinematic vampirism for the four decades to 1970, at which point the popularity of vampire films really boomed. Although there had been the occasional departure from Christopher Lee's charismatic portrayal of the count, such as *Brides of Dracula* (Terence Fisher, 1960) and *Kiss of the Vampire* (Don Sharp, 1964), at the turn of the decade Hammer Studios produced a flurry of spin-offs and vampire films derived from other sources. These were drawn from literature (the Karnstein trilogy, based on the work of Sheridan LeFanu) and legend (*Countess Dracula* [Peter Sasdy, 1971]), as well as original ideas such as *Vampire Circus* (Robert Young, 1972), *The Legend of the 7 Golden Vampires* and *Captain Kronos – Vampire Hunter* (Brian Clemens, 1974). However, in the wake of *Night of the Living Dead*, *Last House on the Left* and the like, the period trappings of Hammer's output looked increasingly dated. Witnessing the relative success of American films such as AIP's *Count Yorga, Vampire* (Bob Kelljan, 1970) and *Blacula* (William Crain, 1972), which situated vampires in modern day locales, Hammer brought their most successful character to swinging London in *Dracula AD 1972*. The fact that all three of these films spawned direct sequels demonstrated an audience appetite for contemporary vampire tales.

This period coincided with a resurgence in literary vampirism, producing novels such as Stephen King's *Salem's Lot* and Anne Rice's *Interview With the Vampire* (the first part of her 'Vampire Chronicles' series), which has continued, and intensified, ever since. The success of these works, in particular *Salem's Lot* and the 1979 TV movie version directed by Tobe Hooper, further fuelled Hollywood's interest in modern-day vampire productions. Indeed, since the mid-1970s the vast majority of vampire movies have been set in the modern era, with the only notable exceptions being retellings or 're-imaginings' of Stoker's *Dracula*. Throughout the 1980s, films such as *The Hunger* (Tony Scott, 1983), *Fright Night* (Tom Holland, 1985), *The Lost Boys* and *Near Dark* (Kathryn Bigelow, 1987) played on the idea of vampires living amongst us. The last two of these also helped introduce the concept of vampires existing as a group or family, where previously they had been depicted primarily as solitary outsiders. Alongside this, stories were frequently told from the perspective of the vampires themselves, most overtly in *Interview With the Vampire*, Chelsea Quinn Yarbro's 1978 novel *Hotel Transylvania*, and their numerous sequels.

This trend towards 'humanising' the vampire had begun over a decade earlier with the American daytime Gothic soap opera, *Dark Shadows* (1966–71). Set in contemporary New England, the premise of the series involved a young governess arriving at a mansion to take charge of a young boy. In response to poor ratings, producer Dan Curtis decided to add a ghost to the story and then, in some desperation, a vampire by the name of Barnabas Collins. Ratings went through the roof, *Dark Shadows* became a cult hit, and Collins ('the reluctant vampire') was a pop culture phenomenon. From then on, the series generated an unprecedented level of merchandising, including board games, posters, comic books, bubble gum cards and spin-off novels, as well as two feature films. The cultural popularity of vampires with television audiences would be revived in the 1990s with the long-running *Buffy the Vampire Slayer* and its spin-off *Angel*, continuing through series such as *True Blood*, *The Vampire Diaries* and *The Originals*.

For much of their literary (and indeed cinematic) history, vampires tended to be of elite or aristocratic status, rather than the undead peasants of traditional folklore. Stoker's Count Dracula is, of course, crucial in setting this trend, although the character had a precedent in the suave Lord Ruthven of Polidori's 1819 story, 'The Vampyre'. With the refined, though repugnant, nobleman Kurt Barlow, *Salem's Lot* (described by its author as an *homage* to Stoker's novel) effectively links the aristocratic vampire to its modern-day equivalent. From the 1970s onwards, class has become less of a factor in vampire cinema, and this allowed for new imaginings of the sub-genre. *Near Dark*, one of the first films to romanticise the undead-human relationship, depicts the vampire 'family' as white trash roaming the American west in a battered truck. From the same period, the antagonists of *The Lost Boys* are the delinquent children of broken homes and dysfunctional families. More generally the trend has been to integrate the vampire into everyday characters and situations, and the recent parody *What We Do in the Shadows* (Jemaine Clement and Taika Waititi, 2014) manages to wring considerable comic mileage from contrasting the traditional aristocratic vampire with this more modern incarnation.

The figure of the contemporary vampire remains enormously popular, in cinema, literature and on television. With such massive exposure, and for a sub-genre so rooted in its own ground rules and conventions, it could be easy to assume that there was nothing new that could be said on the subject. When John Ajvide Lindqvist, a former magician and stand-up comedian, decided to introduce the subject of vampirism into his first novel, he wanted to remove all romanticised notions about what it was to be a vampire. A life-long horror fan, Lindqvist has stated that he finds the vampire sub-genre the most boring and 'least rewarding' (Northlander 2008), and as we will see through our textual analysis, his story is notable more for its divergences from 'traditional' vampire fiction than for its similarities. Drawing on personal experiences of growing up in Blackeberg, a non-descript suburb of Stockholm, in the 1980s, Lindqvist wondered what it would be like for a vampire child to exist in such an environment and came to the conclusion it would be 'horrible... miserable, gross and lonely' (ibid). At the same time, he wanted to explore how the arrival of such a creature would affect the lives of the suburb's inhabitants, all of which were based on actual residents, and in particular the book's protagonist, Oskar. The character of Oskar was modelled on the author himself, who at his age also shared an apartment with his mother (following the death of his father) and suffered at the hands of school bullies. The title for the novel was taken from the lyrics of the song 'Let the Right One Slip In', a typically jangly pop effort from former The Smiths frontman Morrissey.

Although initially rejected by a number of publishers, the novel quickly became a bestseller when it hit Swedish bookstores in late 2004. A copy was gifted by a friend to Tomas Alfredson, a director who had been active in Swedish television for over twenty years, predominantly in the fields of comedy and children's entertainment. Alfredson read the novel, identified with the character of Oskar, and immediately wanted to be involved in an adaptation. Although there was enormous interest from a number of parties, Alfredson and EFTI (a small independent television and commercial production company) secured the rights for the film version on the condition that Lindqvist could write the screenplay himself. The film was awarded funding by the Swedish Film Institute, giving it a total budget of approximately $4 million. The search for the two lead actors took over a year, and although this would be their first feature film, both had previous theatre experience and were accomplished in the arts. Kåre Hedebrant (Oskar) was a member of the choir at one of Sweden's most prestigious music schools, while Lina Leandersson (Eli) was a noted dancer who had already appeared on Swedish television. With much of the film's success resting on the performances (and chemistry) of the two leads, Alfredson's previous experience working with children no doubt proved invaluable, in both the casting and the filming process.

Textual Analysis

Stockholm, 1982. From the window of his drab apartment block in a run-down Swedish suburb, 12-year-old Oskar observes two figures arrive in a taxi late at night. The pair, an older man and a young girl, Hakan and Eli, take up residence in the adjacent apartment. Oskar, a bullied loner prone to fantasising about torturing his tormentors with a knife, strikes up a friendship with the enigmatic Eli, who only emerges from her apartment during the hours of darkness. Unbeknownst to Oskar, she is a vampire who relies on her protector Hakan to bring her fresh blood for sustenance. Disturbed during the murder of a man in a nearby town, Hakan returns empty-handed, forcing Eli to go out and kill a local man, Jocke. Following another failed murder attempt, Hakan is cornered in the school and pours acid over his face to avoid being identified. At the hospital he sacrifices himself by allowing Eli to drink his blood, before falling to his death from the building. Oskar and Eli's relationship grows stronger, despite the revelation that she is a vampire. Following an attack on a local woman who subsequently dies, her husband tracks Eli down to the apartment. Oskar helps Eli to kill him, after which Eli leaves town. At school one night a gang of bullies trap Oskar in the swimming pool, holding his head under the water. As Oskar struggles, Eli arrives, slaughtering his tormentors and pulling him out of the pool. Eli and Oskar depart on a train for a new life elsewhere, she hidden in a trunk and he her new protector.

Before beginning our analysis, note that throughout this chapter the character of Eli will be referred to as female. In the novel, it is made clear quite early on that Eli is in fact a boy (or, rather, a 200-year-old man) named Elias, who was castrated when he became a vampire. This is alluded to in the film, with the brief shot of Eli's scarred pelvic area, but never made explicit. At one point she tells Oskar that she's not a girl, but does not elaborate on exactly what that means. Is she a boy? A man? A woman? Or 'just' a vampire? Whereas the book goes into great detail about Eli's background and history, practically all of this is left out of the film version. As such Eli remains an enigmatic and disturbing figure, neither young nor old, neither male nor female.[2] Although this can be seen as another example of postmodernism's rejection of binary oppositions, as discussed in our previous chapter, the androgynous nature of the vampire has been highlighted previously in films such as *Requiem for a Vampire* (Jean Rollin, 1971) and *The Hunger*, while Anne Rice's work in particular highlights a homo-erotic angle that is rarely far from the surface.

Sexuality in general has always been an important element in vampire legends around the world. According to some folklore the vampire will ravish their victim before taking their blood, or even kill them purely through sexual exhaustion. It is an angle that film-makers have been keen to exploit. During the late 1960s and early 70s in particular, the relaxation of censorship internationally meant that anyone attending vampire film screenings would be almost guaranteed plenty of nudity, heaving bosoms and overt eroticism. Of course, *Let the Right One In* features none of this. While it can be read as a coming-of-age story revolving around the relationship between a human and a vampire, it could scarcely be more different from the romantically charged films of, for example, the *Twilight* saga. Even when Eli slips naked into Oskar's bed following the death of Hakan, there is little hint of any sexual attraction between them. Oskar's feelings for Eli throughout the film are driven more by a need to connect emotionally rather than physically; the characters see in each other a kindred spirit, and experience a mutual urge to protect one other.

Outside of the 'lesbian vampire' films that flourished in the early 1970s it has been relatively rare to see female vampires as central characters. Although more recent entries such as *Byzantium* (Neil Jordan, 2012), *A Girl Walks Home Alone at Night* and the *Underworld* series have redressed the gender balance somewhat, the female of the species has traditionally been kept in the background; Dracula's 'brides' in Tod Browning's version were wraith-like figures who floated silently around the castle basement, while Hammer frequently portrayed them as blood- (and sex-) starved slaves locked or chained in cellars. In presenting the vampire as a twelve-year-old girl, *Let the Right One In* runs the risk of placing Eli alongside the demonic children of *The Omen* and *The Exorcist* in the eyes of the audience, but this never happens. Lindqvist and Alfredson (and the young actors) invest Eli and Oskar with such levels of audience sympathy and empathy that it's the characters around them who are seen as the 'bad guys'. With this in mind, it's worth contemplating how different the audience experience would be had Eli been portrayed as a 200-year-old man, grooming Oskar as his new 'companion' while encouraging him to act out violent fantasies against his classmates. It would almost certainly have resulted in a different film altogether, though probably one more aligned to the conventional horror genre we have discussed so far.

Plot-wise, *Let The Right One In* takes a premise familiar to audiences from films such as *Salem's Lot*, *The Lost Boys* and *Fright Night* – you discover there's a vampire in the neighbourhood, or even next-door, what do you do about it? Usually the protagonist must find a way to defeat the vampire and rescue the community, either single-handedly or after convincing some knowledgeable expert of their fears. In this case, however, expectations are turned on their head when Oskar joins forces with the vampire to slay his tormentors and ultimately runs away with it. This subversion of genre norms again implies a postmodernist approach, and it is one that has become increasingly common through more recent films and series such as *True Blood* and of course the *Twilight* franchise. Much of the success of the original *Buffy* television series (first broadcast at the height of *Scream*'s postmodernist influence) hinged on the long-running relationship between the eponymous heroine and her vampiric lovers, Angel and Spike. As witnessed by the popularity of *Twilight* amongst its target audience of adolescent females, the romantic relationship between the living and the undead can be an important aspect of the modern vampire story.[3]

Unlike the modern zombie sub-genre, most vampire films do not present a sense of widespread contagion, or of impending apocalypse from which the world needs to be saved.[4] In the case of *Let the Right One In*, we have little sense of how prevalent these creatures are; Eli clearly operates alone and seems unwilling to 'turn' anyone else. Like Oskar, she wants to go unnoticed, and in this respect the film conforms to the increasing trend in vampire stories to centre on the creatures' efforts to 'live' with their condition – and to consume human blood – without attracting undue attention. From the reluctant Barnabas Collins to the 'vegetarian' Cullen family, this approach constitutes part of what can be termed the 'humanisation' of the vampire. More broadly, traditional horror monsters can be seen as just another segment of increasingly diverse human societies. It is a trend that's particularly evident in the television series format; from the suburban serial killer Dexter to the undead mortician of *iZombie*, these are just characters trying to go about their daily lives. Of course, this is not an entirely new phenomenon – both the Addams Family and the Munsters enjoyed small screen success with this very topic in the 1960s.

Thus, the boundaries between good and evil, human and monster become increasingly blurred. In the 1931 film version of *Dracula*, the count's nemesis Van Helsing declares that 'the strength of the vampire is that people will not believe in him'. Yet by ignoring some of the more far-fetched aspects of vampire lore, writers and film-makers are able to situate their stories within the bounds of believability. George A. Romero's *Martin* is particularly ambiguous as to whether the titular youth, who extracts blood via razor blade and hypodermic needle, is a supernatural vampire or not. Indeed, as Anne Billson has noted, many conventional vampiric symptoms can be explained through recognised medical conditions (see Billson 2011). That such conditions can be passed through the bite of an infected person is hardly far-fetched – since the arrival of AIDS in the mid-1980s, the perception of blood as a source of viral contagion has been prominent in the public consciousness. Whilst vampirism as a metaphor for AIDS is a relatively recent development, the portrayal of vampires as carriers of disease in general has a long history. *Nosferatu* introduced the first cinematic vampire through a broader narrative of the 'Great Death', explicitly linking Count Orlok with the arrival of the plague. Following Eli's attack, when Virginia tells Lacke that the 'kid must have infected me somehow', it's safe to assume that vampirism would be well down their list of potential diseases.

Eli's powers of transformation, such as the ability to grow wings, are described at length in the novel, along with vivid descriptions of her claws and fangs. Although the viewer is in no doubt that she is a vampire in the supernatural sense, the film is much more restrained. There are a couple of allusions to Eli being able to fly, and we glimpse her scaling walls and trees, but none of this is particularly overt. While many modern vampires undergo grotesque transformations when preparing to feed (for example in *From Dusk 'Til Dawn* or TV's *Buffy*), the subtle make-up employed here ensures that Eli is almost always recognisably, and disturbingly, herself. The exceptions to this are two brief episodes where Eli (portrayed by a much older actress) displays her true age to Oskar and the audience. The most obvious is in the

Figure 12.1

den, when she drops to the floor to lap up the blood he has spilt and commands him to leave (Fig 12.1). The other is more sublim- inal, when she asks him to 'be me, for a little while'. In the novel this is a prel- ude to a telekinetic transfer of memories from Eli to Oskar, revealing Eli's past history; in the film, this history is etched into her grey, blood-stained face. The lack of any explicit transformation ensures that there is no hint of Eli suffering from a Jekyll-and-Hyde type personality disorder. Such a sug- gestion would be misleading; Eli doesn't switch between vampire and non-vampire. As evidenced throughout the film, she is capable of murder at any time.

Blood, as we have noted throughout this book, is crucial to the horror genre, and for vampires it is the key to their existence. They must consume it to survive and this aspect of vampire lore is sacrosanct. Whilst some vampires can be satiated with animal blood, for most only the human variety will do, and the use of fangs to pierce the neck of their victims has proven a remarkably efficient means of feeding. Psychoanalytical approaches to vampire cinema have explored in some depth the significance of the mouth and blood in relation to sex and sexuality. The vampire's bite is often depicted as an almost sexual act, particularly in the various adaptations of the Dracula story; Stoker's novel depicts the count very much as a sensual creature, with a hypnotic stare that women are powerless to resist. Indeed, ever since Bela Lugosi's suave turn had female audience members swooning in the aisles, the actors who have featured in that role have been chosen as much for their sex appeal as anything else. From Christopher Lee's first appearance in 1958, the busty co-stars of Hammer's Dracula series would waste no time in loosening their nightgowns and anxiously awaiting the count's arrival at their bedside (but not before they'd opened their windows wide as an explicit invitation to let him in). *Let the Right One In* diverges noticeably from this approach, in that none of the attacks are depicted as sexual or erotic, overtly or otherwise. At no point is Eli seen to have traditional vampire canines and, with the exception of that of Hakan, her kills do not involve the drawing of blood through neat puncture wounds. When she feeds it is in an animalistic frenzy; she is primal and savage and driven by an ultimately insatiable blood lust. There is certainly no attempt in this film to romanticise Eli's predicament; she often looks dishevelled, her flat is filthy and Oskar frequently comments on how bad she smells.

The film's title references the conventional rule (going back to folklore but reinforced by many works of fiction from Stoker's *Dracula* onwards) that a vampire cannot enter a dwelling without being invited to do so, by either the owner or someone who lives there. While obeying this convention, *Let the Right One In* differentiates itself from previous works by depicting exactly what happens when a vampire enters uninvited. As blood starts streaming from Eli's orifices and pores, it acts as a graphic demonstration to Oskar, and the audience, of the level of trust she has in him (see Fig 12.2). One has to ask what would happen if Oskar didn't relent; would she eventually die from exsanguination? Equally graphic, and altogether more spectacular, is the fate of Virginia, who bursts into flame when exposed to direct sunlight. While showing that these vampires adhere to this cinematic convention, it's quite an extreme reaction compared to the fate of Christopher Lee in *Dracula* (who crumbles to ash) or Nosferatu (who merely fades away). As with all works based on the vampire legend, *Let the Right One In* is selective about which elements of the myth it adopts (and how it interprets them) to suit the requirements of the narrative. Whilst it obeys the rules of invitation and sunlight, there is no mention of garlic, crucifixes, holy water or stakes through the heart, and Eli is seen to cast a reflection. In fact, Tomas Alfredson has claimed to have been completely ignorant of vampire lore, never having read or watched any vampire stories prior to Lindqvist's novel.

Figure 12.2

Like the similarly gritty *Martin*, Alfredson's film is frequently described as 'social realist'. It is a term we discussed briefly in our chapter on *The Curse of Frankenstein*, and one that references both aesthetic and narrative elements. Typified by the British 'kitchen sink' dramas in the 1950s and 60s, as well as more recent films such as *Nil by Mouth* (Gary Oldman, 1997) and *This is England* (Shane Meadows, 2006), the narratives of these films concern the struggles of lower class characters against the apparent injustices of the social system. Shot in a detached and naturalistic fashion, they employ documentary-style aesthetics to bring the viewer a (usually depressing) slice of life. Alfredson's adoption of this approach for the film certainly differentiates it from the glossiness of Hollywood vampire films such as *Twilight*, and is in direct opposition to the comic-book action of *Blade* or *Underworld*, yet it matches the subject matter perfectly. The deliberately inconspicuous *mise-en-scène* reflects the mundane and lifeless world in which the characters exist, while the ever-present snow and ice highlight the cold (both figuratively and literally) environs of a 1980s

Stockholm housing estate. Unlike our next case study, the film doesn't deliberately exploit its 1980s setting, omitting the book's references to wider fears over the Cold War, Russian incursions and the like. Despite the appearance of the Rubik's cube there is very little that ties the film's narrative to any particular year or era, instead concerning itself with the timeless personal struggles of 'the outsider'. Although in typical social realist fashion this term could apply to every member of the community (and the book provides plenty of background on the other characters), the film centres on the relationship between Eli and Oskar.

The director has said that he sees Eli and Oskar as two sides of the same character, 'with her as the dark side and he as the light' (see Vaux 2010). Such differentiation is visually evident in their physical attributes; Oskar is of typical Nordic appearance, with fair skin and blond hair, whereas Eli is dark and of indeterminate origin. Ever the outsider, the vampire is traditionally depicted as nomadic, roaming the earth restlessly over the centuries or, in more contemporary imaginings, moving on to avoid detection by the authorities. While Eli shifts location regularly there is little sense of freedom in her travels, and in her constant need to keep moving she is as trapped by circumstance as Oskar. From the first shots of him looking out from his bedroom window, Oskar is depicted as isolated, and throughout the film Alfredson frequently uses framing to highlight the space between him and the other characters. Bullied both verbally and physically, he is alienated and excluded by his peers, and effectively ignored by most of the adults around him. There can be no doubt that Oskar is the audience's identification figure, but although we empathise with him (many horror film fans can find a kinship with this emotionally fragile character), his latent psychopathic tendencies are a cause for concern. Of course, it is these tendencies that attract Eli to him. Telling him that she knows he would kill if given the chance, she positively encourages his fantasies of revenge and urges him to hit back hard against the bullies.

Given Hakan's ineffectual attempts to procure blood, it's entirely possible that Eli was on the lookout for a replacement helper long before she spotted Oskar's potential. The figure of the vampire's retainer, or familiar, often plays a significant role in the modern story; from a logistics viewpoint, being unable to operate in daylight vampires would surely require mortal assistance of some kind. In Stoker's novel, the deranged Renfield ultimately loses his life at the hands of Dracula, after turning against his master in an attempt to save Mina. More usually, the vampire's retainer is a fiercely loyal servant, willing to lay down their own lives to protect them. Devoted to their undead masters, these characters are often kept under control with the promise of eternal life that will come when they are 'turned'. Depending on the requirements of the narrative, they can play a significant role as the public face of the vampire's business – literally so, in the case of Barlow's 'business partner' Straker in *Salem's Lot*. Although the vampire undoubtedly dominates such arrangements, there is always a degree of interdependence. The relationship between Hakan and Eli is particularly strained and not as one-sided as you might expect, as evidenced by his angry chastising of her over the irresponsible killing of Jocke.

The film gives few cues as to how or why Hakan came to be associated with Eli, raising the question of why this old man is so devoted to what appears to be a twelve-year-old girl. In the novel, he is a much more sinister figure, a serial killer and paedophile who lusts for Eli even after his apparent death at the hospital. Justifying the absence of any reference to Hakan's paedophilia in the film, the director has stated on a number of occasions that its inclusion would take away from the main focus of Oskar and Eli's relationship, and that the broaching of such a subject in a genre film would be necessarily rushed and lack the required level of seriousness (ibid). While certainly not an attractive character, Hakan in the film comes across as more of a bumbling old man. Despite the meticulous preparation, his handling of the film's first murder is clumsy and almost comedic. For someone who has presumably had plenty of practice, his failed attempt at obtaining the blood that Eli craves is an early sign that he is outliving his usefulness. That we cut from the murder scene to Oskar venturing out to practice his knife skills on a tree is an early and explicit indication of the boy's eventual fate. From the film's conclusion, we may guess that Hakan was himself once like Oskar, a young boy besotted with the enigmatic Eli.[5]

As the vampire has become a more developed character in its own right, so the figure of the 'slayer' or hunter – a mainstay of vampire fiction throughout much of its history – has largely been relegated to the shadows. The ultimate 'knowledgeable expert' of the horror genre, slayers conventionally provide an insight into vampire mythology (both for the audience and the other characters in the story) and an identification figure in the fight against evil. Stoker's Abraham Van Helsing became key to screen versions of the Dracula legend, with Peter Cushing making the role his own in the Hammer films of 1958–74. More recently, Buffy Summers and her gang perfected the vampire slayer personae for contemporary popular culture, wielding wooden stakes and clever jokes in equal measure. In cinema too, the slayer has occasionally taken centre stage, most successfully in the *Blade* franchise (1998–2004). Also worthy of note are the hapless heroes of Polanski's *Dance of the Vampires*, while *Fright Night* elevates TV horror host Peter Vincent to real-life slayer when he helps out a young fan with a neighbourhood vampire problem. In the case of *Let the Right One In*, there is no knowledgeable expert who handily turns up to explain what is happening and save the townsfolk from Eli. Instead Lacke, a drunken bum, manages to put two and two together and work out that the two newcomers to the area must be behind the attacks.[6]

Of course, Lacke is unaware of exactly what he is dealing with when he breaks into Eli's apartment looking for revenge. Like all of the adult characters, he appears to be largely ignorant and uninterested in what is going on around him until he is directly affected. Following the death of Jocke, it's Lacke's self-absorbed lamenting of having 'nothing left' (while sitting right next to his girlfriend) that prompts Virginia to storm out of the restaurant and into her fateful meeting with Eli. Despite their friendships, all of the characters in the film are essentially lonely; the film's overriding theme of loneliness and connection is highlighted a number of times through shots of hands reaching out. Gosta finds companionship with his cats, while the rest congregate in the Chinese restaurant, seemingly as reliant on alcohol as Eli is on blood. Even Oskar's father, the one adult Oskar seems to have genuine affection for, and with whom his time is limited, quickly loses interest in his son once a neighbour turns up with a bottle. While his mother appears genuinely sympathetic, concerned and upset when he comes home late and sharing a laugh and a smile while brushing their teeth, they become more distant as his relationship with Eli grows. Often absent due to work, she remains unaware of her son's bullying at school and of his unhealthy preoccupation with murder and violence.

We have described the film as 'social realist', and while that may imply something of an amateur or plain approach to aesthetics, that could not be further from the truth. Although Alfredson depicts the (initially) humdrum lives of the Blackeberg masses in a leisurely, matter-of-fact fashion, his use of the frame is never boring and the film contains some truly stunning sequences, in particular, the climax at the swimming pool. Rivalling the haunting atmospherics of *Kwaidan*, where the worlds of the everyday and the supernatural meet, the effect of disembodied heads and limbs floating by Oskar in slow motion is dreamlike and almost surreal (see Fig 12.3). The cinematographer was well-known Dutch painter Hoyte van Hoytema, and Alfredson has said that they based the film's look on that of Renaissance paintings (see Badt 2009). The resultant soft lighting diffuses and mutes background colours, while allowing a dramatic foregrounding of red highlights. These include the sledge that Hakan uses to

Figure 12.3

move Jocke's body, the pole he uses to push Jocke's body under the ice and which Oskar later uses against Conny, the bag on the seat of the train in the film's closing moments, the lamp in Eli's bedroom, the table in Virginia's apartment, the plastic cowboy that Oskar plays with in the taxi – and, of course, the blood.

Despite containing a number of gory moments, the film does not glorify or linger on scenes of violence and bloodshed. Echoing Val Lewton's approach to horror, Alfredson has suggested that 'the most horrifying images are the ones you make yourself' (ibid). Rather than depict violence for the sake of it he prefers to leave much of it to the audience's imagination. Hakan's attempts at procuring blood for Eli are depicted very pragmatically, without any gratuitous shots of blades ripping flesh or the like. The first murder recalls the resurrection set-piece of Hammer's *Dracula – Prince of Darkness* (Terence Fisher, 1966), where the actions of the count's manservant and subsequent spilling of blood are melodramatically detailed to the accompaniment of James Bernard's ominously rising music. By contrast, Hakan's stringing up and slashing of his victim is filmed in a detached fashion, with limited and primarily diegetic sound, and delivers an altogether more disturbing experience. Even when showing the (CGI-enhanced) effects of acid on Hakan's face, it is out of necessity, not to deliberately shock or horrify the audience, and as such evokes more pity than disgust.

In looking beyond the surface horror and exploring the psychology of its fragile protagonists, Alfredson's film marks a distinct departure from much of the contemporaneous Hollywood output. Such an approach invites ambiguity, and this is particularly evident in the film's ending. Did Oskar drown in the swimming pool, with the rescue and subsequent train journey just a dying hallucination? (Perhaps more to the point, did Eli even exist in the first place, or was she just a manifestation of Oskar's pent up anger and pain, a schizophrenic invention to blame for his revenge killings?) The final train journey is an epilogue that does not feature in the book, but one that was retained in the American remake (see below). Of course, its purpose is to provide a more upbeat ending, leaving the viewer with hope that Oskar and Eli will find happiness together somewhere along the line.[7] The ultimate message of the film is that two disparate individuals can find companionship, regardless of their negative traits; whatever weaknesses you may have, there is a 'right one' out there waiting to be let in.

Reception and Aftermath

Released in Sweden in October 2008, *Let the Right One In* proved very popular with local audiences already familiar with the bestselling novel, and attracted universally excellent reviews. Over the following months it was screened at a number of film festivals around Europe and the US, eventually picking up over 60 awards including Best International Film at the British Independent Film Awards (a festival traditionally appreciative of social realism, with Ken Loach, Shane Meadows and *Nil By Mouth* all winners at the inaugural ceremony). The fact that Sweden did not enter the film into consideration for an Academy Award as Best Foreign Language Film has been a continuing source of incomprehension.

By the time it was released in the UK in April 2009, the film already had a reputation as something of a genre classic. Whereas a few years earlier subtitled foreign genre films would have been relegated to small independent cinemas, thanks to the relative mainstream success of films such as *Pan's Labyrinth*, *Let the Right One In* managed to obtain a wider release to multiplexes. Of course, the film appeared soon after the extremely popular first *Twilight* adaptation, and vampires were regarded as a hot property with mainstream audiences. At the same time Lindqvist's novel received its first English release, which also helped raise the profile of the film version. Although it had no hope of competing with the box-office success of *Twilight*,[8] where it did beat its better-known rival was in its critical reception. Alfredson's film quickly established itself as part of the horror canon, representing for many horror fans a welcome respite from the sanitised appeal of Hollywood's vampire output, and a return to a darker treatment of the sub-genre. *Let the Right One In* eventually made $11 million in cinemas worldwide, a decent return given its modest budget and as a non-English language film.

As we have mentioned, during much of the 2000s Hollywood was in the midst of a remaking frenzy, and, given the critical reception to Alfredson's film, it was perhaps inevitable that it would be picked up for an American remake. Retitled *Let Me In*, this was the first theatrical production of the revived Hammer Films studio, who unsuccessfully approached Alfredson to direct. The job went instead to Matt Reeves, who had scored a critical and commercial hit with the found-footage monster movie *Cloverfield*. Like Alfredson's version, much of the darker material was omitted, and Reeves's film managed to be even more ambivalent about the vampire's gender than had the original. The remake was commercially unsuccessful, barely covering its $20 million budget, and reviews were noticeably less enthusiastic than for the Swedish film. Nevertheless, it found an outspoken fan in long-time genre icon Stephen King, whose appraisal of *Let Me In* as 'the best American horror film in the past 20 years' was used heavily in the publicity and packaging for the subsequent DVD release across all territories. Reinforcing his view, King subsequently rated the film as the best of any genre in his list of top films of 2010, as published in *Entertainment Weekly*. We will discuss the work of Stephen King, and his influence on the horror genre as a whole, in the next chapter.

Since the publication of his bestselling debut, Lindqvist (quickly and predictably labelled the 'Swedish Stephen King' [Turner 2010]) has built a reputation as a popular horror writer, with a number of novels and short story collections to his name. Though generally well received, none of his subsequent works have had the impact of his debut, which continues to have relevance in popular culture. 2011 saw the publication (much to Lindqvist's disgust) of a four-part comic book series *Let Me In: Crossroads*, which acted as a prequel to Matt Reeves' film. The same year saw the limited run of a Swedish stage version of the original book, adapted by Lindqvist himself, while English playwright Jack Thorne (co-writer of Shane Meadows' *This is England* television projects) wrote a 2013 stage adaptation which has enjoyed successful productions in the US, Australia, South Korea and elsewhere.

In 2016 a pilot for an American television series based on the book was filmed, but it never aired and the series was ultimately shelved. Nevertheless, television has continued to be a popular medium for the vampire in recent times, with such disparate series as *Van Helsing* (chronicling the adventures of a female descendant of Stoker's slayer in a dystopian world plagued by vampires), *The Strain* (based on Guillermo del Toro's series of novels) and *From Dusk 'Til Dawn* (a spinoff from the 1996 film) all attracting loyal audiences across multiple seasons. Of course, Hollywood's interest in the sub-genre has endured, with notable big-budget productions such as the continuing *Underworld* franchise, *Dark Shadows* (Tim Burton's 2012 update of the Barnabas Collins story), *Dracula Untold* (Gary Shore, 2014), and the conclusion of the *Twilight* saga, which managed to generate over $3 billion across five films.

Stephanie Meyer's 2015 reboot of the book series, *Life and Death: Twilight Reimagined*, suggests that there are yet more angles to be exploited from that particular brand of Romantic vampirism, but in the wake of Lindqvist and Alfredson's treatment film-makers have been keen to push the sub-genre in new directions. Derek Lee and Clif Prowse's low-budget *Afflicted* is particularly worthy of note in this respect. A self-funded feature that documents the aftermath of a vampire attack in the form of a travelogue, it uses the familiar aesthetics of documentary, reality television and 'found footage' to draw the viewer in. Combining the vampire myth with the modern-day trappings of GoPro, iPhone filming and online blogging, it is ultimately a comment on the self-destructive modern impulse to share all aspects of life online. While Lee and Prowse's film made little impact either critically or commercially, outside of the US the sub-genre has produced some important works, with the South Korean *Thirst* (Park Chan-wook, 2009) and the UK/German *Only Lovers Left Alive* (Jim Jarmusch, 2013) both nominated for the Cannes Palme d'Or. The critically acclaimed *A Girl Walks Home Alone at Night*, despite being filmed in the US, was publicised as 'the first Iranian vampire Western' and reaffirms the global appeal of vampire cinema.

More broadly, both *Afflicted* and *A Girl Walks Home* demonstrate a changing approach to independent film production that is becoming more prominent, particularly in the US. Since *The Blair Witch Project*, fans have been co-opted at an earlier and earlier stage into the evolution of a film, with new modes of production and consumption bringing the film-maker audience relationship ever closer. Whereas Prowse and Lee relied primarily on friends and family to raise backing for their film (with a top-up from Telefilm Canada), independent film-makers are increasingly turning to crowdfunding websites and apps. Crowdfunding allows the film-maker to bypass agents and studios, and pitch ideas directly to film fans, who donate as much or as little as they want in return for merchandise, a DVD or digital download, or even a part in the film itself. With *A Girl Walks Home*, director Ana Lily Amirpour launched an Indiegogo campaign to produce the film, based on a short work she had screened at an Iranian film festival.[9] Through innovations such as these, the 'active audience' we encountered in our previous chapter will be an increasingly powerful agent for contemporary horror.

When it comes to crowdfunding entire productions, it makes sense that such an approach would be restricted to low budget film-making. It's highly unlikely that a film-maker would be able to raise tens of millions of dollars in such a way; if their concept really was that popular then a Hollywood studio would surely snap it up. In the case of *A Girl Walks Home* the initial target funding of $55,000 was augmented by the involvement of The Woodshed, an independent production company established by actor Elijah Wood. Wood heard of Amirpour's project, saw the short 'proof of concept' film she had made, and agreed to be involved in the making of the feature version. With the availability of cheap digital video cameras and editing software, and sharing platforms such as YouTube, anyone can put together a short film and distribute it to millions of viewers around the world. All it takes is for the right person to see it at the right time, and a successful Hollywood career can be born – as we will see in our next chapter.

Bibliography

Badley, Linda (2010) 'Bringing it All Back Home: Horror Cinema and Video Culture' in Ian Conrich (ed.), *Horror Zone*. London: I.B. Taurus & Co. Ltd.

Badt, Karin (January 3, 2009) Let the Right One In: New Vampire Film with a "Beat". *Huffington Post*. Retrieved 17 February 2018 from https://www.huffingtonpost.com/karin-badt/emlet-the-right-one-inem_b_147966.html.

Billson, Anne (2011) *Let the Right One In (Devil's Advocates)*. Leighton Buzzard: Auteur.

Forrest, David (2013) *Social Realism: Art, Nationhood and Politics*. Cambridge Scholars Publishing.

Hutchings, Peter (2014) 'Northern Darkness: The Curious Case of the Swedish Vampire' in Hunt L., Lockyer, S. and Williamson, M. (eds.) *Screening the Undead: Vampires and Zombies in Film and Television*. London: I.B. Taurus & Co. Ltd.

Jones, Darryl (2002) *Horror: A Thematic History in Fiction and Film*. London: Hodder Arnold.

Newman, Kim (2003) 'Preface' in Schneider, Steven Jay (ed.) *Fear Without Frontiers*. Godalming: FAB Press.

Northlander (23 October, 2008). The Northlander Sits Down With The Writer Of LET THE RIGHT ONE IN! *Ain't it Cool News*. Retrieved 20 February 2018 from http://www.aintitcool.com/node/38839

Olney, Ian (2013) *Euro Horror: Classic European Horror Cinema in Contemporary American Culture*. Indianapolis: Indiana University Press.

Turner, Jenny (20 November, 2010) Harbour by John Ajvide Lindqvist – review. *The Guardian*. Retrieved 21 November 2018 from https://www.theguardian.com/books/2010/nov/20/harbour-john-ajvide-lindqvist-review

Vaux, Rob (14 July, 2010) *Q&A: Tomas Alfredson, Director of Let the Right One In*. Retrieved 11 February 2018 from http://let-the-right-one-in.com/woofy/36/qa-tomas-alfredson-director-of-let-the-right-one-in/

Weinstock, Jeffrey (2012) *The Vampire Film: Undead Cinema*. London: Wallflower.

Wolf, Leonard (ed.) (1993) *The Essential Dracula*. London: Plume.

Endnotes

1   To be fair, Hollywood's reliance on reboots, remakes and sequels was not restricted to the horror genre, with the percentage of productions based on pre-existing works skyrocketing across all genres since the mid-2000s.

2   Although Alfredson does not comment directly on her character's gender through the narrative, an older actress was brought in to dub Lina Leandersson's lines and give Eli a deeper voice.

3   Of course romance is not a new feature of the sub-genre. We have already mentioned that Universal's 1931 *Dracula* was released on Valentine's Day as 'the strangest love story ever told', and the last major (successful) adaptation of Stoker's novel, Coppola's big-budget 1992 version, was advertised with the slogan 'love never dies'.

4   There are exceptions of course, such as *Daybreakers* (The Spierig Brothers, 2009) and *Stake Land* (Jim Mickle, 2010).

5   The Hollywood remake is more to the point, showing a photograph of the Eli and Hakan characters together when Hakan was Oskar's age.

6   Again, Hollywood being Hollywood, the American remake conventionalises the Lacke character by making him a detective investigating the murders.

7   The train journey features in Lindqvist's short sequel-of-sorts, *Let the Old Dreams Die* (the next line from Morrissey's song) set some 25 years later. In it, Eli and Oskar are discovered to be in Barcelona, both still having the appearance of 12-year-olds.

8   Of course, *Twilight* was released in the US with a PG-13 rating, rather than the more restrictive R assigned to *Let the Right One In*.

9   https://www.indiegogo.com/projects/a-girl-walks-home-alone-at-night-feature-film#/

Chapter 13

'Mainstream' Horror

It

Andy Muschietti, US, 2017

Recommended viewing

The Conjuring (James Wan, 2013)
The Babadook (Jennifer Kent, 2014)
Split (M. Night Shayamalan, 2016)
Get Out (Jordan Peele, 2017)
The Shape of Water (Guillermo del Toro, 2017)
Hereditary (Ari Aster, 2018)

Introduction

When the *New York Times* magazine dubbed 2017 'The Year of Horror',[1] it was a high-profile recognition of the unprecedented levels of popularity being enjoyed by the genre. Almost overnight, it seemed that audiences' and critics' attitudes had changed, with box office records being smashed and horror-inflected films nominated for major awards. As cinemagoers flocked to see the latest releases, there was talk of a renaissance in horror cinema, of the genre as a whole becoming 'mainstream'. While high-profile cinema releases led to horror's first ever billion-dollar year at the US box office, in reality the genre's popularity had been growing steadily for a decade or more, fuelled by commercial and technological changes across the entire industry.

In this chapter we look at the parameters of the term 'mainstream horror', and how it relates to the genre as we have seen it develop throughout this book. For our case study we examine a film that succeeded in capturing the imaginations, and box office dollars, of traditional and non-traditional horror audiences around the world. Capitalising on renewed interest in the work of Stephen King, the 2017 adaptation of his epic novel *IT* quickly became the highest grossing R-rated horror film of all time. Encompassing many of the themes and ideas covered in our previous case studies, *It* provides a fascinating barometer for the state of horror cinema as we approach the third decade of the twenty-first century.

Background

The term 'mainstream' when applied to cinema is particularly vague, defined variously in terms of modes of production, commercial or critical popularity, genre, aesthetics, or a combination of these. At its broadest level, we can say that a mainstream film is one that succeeds in attracting a wide audience, unrestricted by age, sex, ethnicity or any other demographic. The film will be accessible and understandable to the average viewer, so will generally conform to the classical Hollywood style; self-consciously avant-garde and experimental films would not be considered mainstream. Finally, mainstream films, particularly those from major studios, will be produced with an emphasis on commercial success, and generally be accompanied by widespread marketing to reach as many potential viewers as possible. Nowadays, the term 'mainstream film' is largely synonymous with Hollywood blockbusters, such as the Marvel and DC Comics franchises. With release dates advertised months or even years in advance, the arrival of each entry is treated as a major cinematic event and accompanied by carpet-bombing promotion costing tens or even hundreds of millions of dollars. When sufficient films of a particular genre are achieving mainstream success we can say that the genre itself is (at that point in time) mainstream, and this is certainly the case with the superhero movies that have dominated the box office since the late 2000s.

Mainstream genre films, in fulfilling the above criteria, are notable for attracting large audiences outside of those who would normally watch a film of that genre. Putting aside the original cycle instigated by Universal in the 1930s (when the films' popularity was arguably due to the novelty of the images presented as opposed to widespread interest in a largely undefined genre), the first examples of what we would term 'mainstream horror' films came in the late 1960s and through the 70s. As we saw in Chapter 8, it was during this time that Hollywood invested heavily in the genre with films such as *Rosemary's Baby* and *The Exorcist*. Major productions based on best-selling novels, they were marketed to attract non-traditional horror audiences and succeeded with enormous box-office returns. The cycle resulted in relatively few films, however, and quickly ended following the relative under-performance of Kubrick's *The Shining*. In any case, by the end of the 1970s Hollywood had discovered the family-friendly blockbuster, and the future of mainstream cinema lay in the cross-generational appeal of action, adventure and sci-fi. In the eyes of film-makers and mainstream audiences, the horror genre had returned to the status of niche product.

For the makers of 'mainstream horror', the quandary is how to broaden audience appeal without diluting the very elements that define the genre in the first place. Films such as *Rosemary's Baby*, *The Exorcist* and *Carrie* succeeded by using the genre as a vehicle to address universal concerns, either explicitly or at a subconscious level, through conventional horror tropes. During the 1990s the major studios took two distinct approaches to squaring the circle, neither of which satisfied the core genre audience. When Hollywood appropriated the slasher sub-genre through commercially and critically successful films such as *The Silence of the Lambs* and *Se7en*, they carefully avoided using the 'horror' label. Like *Psycho* thirty years earlier, the lack of supernatural elements made it easier to market them through the more mainstream genres of thriller or crime drama; in the case of the above examples, the sub-genre of the 'serial killer' film served as something of an elision between the crime procedural and out-and-out horror. At the same time, big budget re-imaginings of the genre classics, *Bram Stoker's Dracula*, *Mary Shelley's Frankenstein* and *Wolf* (Mike Nichols, 1994) played up the films' Gothic and Romantic themes. Conforming to what Philip Simpson describes as 'horror event movies', these relied on 'star actors, star directors, narrative simplicity...stylistic gloss and technical virtuosity' to create something that 'appeal[s] primarily not to genre fans but those people who wouldn't normally be caught dead going to horror movies' (Simpson 2004:85).

With the 'horror event movie' reaching its zenith in *The Mummy* (Stephen Sommers, 1999) and the marketplace awash with bland remakes and *Scream* knock-offs, by the end of the 1990s many traditional horror fans were despairing for the genre's future. Fast-forward twenty years, however, and we find the genre enjoying its most successful period ever in terms of popularity, box-office takings and critical standing. While major studios may not be producing large numbers of horror films themselves, the genre is arguably as mainstream as it has ever been. To try and explain exactly how this situation came about we need to look at the development of the genre, and the film and broadcast industries as a whole, in the previous two decades.

The turn of the millennium saw the emergence of a number of independent production companies geared to the making of horror films, amongst them Dark Castle Entertainment (formed in 1999 initially to produce remakes of William Castle's films from the 1950s), Platinum Dunes (formed in 2001 and responsible for a number of remakes as discussed in Chapter 11) and Ghost House Pictures (formed in 2002 by *Evil Dead* creators Sam Raimi and Robert Tapert and responsible for the American remake of *The Grudge* [Takashi Shimizu, 2004] and its sequels). Whilst all of these are independent companies working on tight budgets, their films have generally been distributed by major studios and include titles that were extremely lucrative at the box office. By far the most commercially successful of this new wave of independents are Blumhouse and Lionsgate. Founded in 2009, Blumhouse had immediate success, with its first release *Paranormal Activity* bringing in almost $200 million worldwide. Produced over several years at a cost of just $15,000, the film uses the 'found footage' trope to relate the experiences of a young couple whose new home is apparently haunted. Featuring no gore and very little physical violence, *Paranormal Activity* captured the imagination of audiences much as *The Blair Witch Project* had ten years previously. In addition to the expansion of the *Paranormal* franchise, Blumhouse has gone on to release other popular genre entries including the *Insidious* series (2010–), the John Carpenter-produced reboot *Halloween* (David Gordon Green, 2018), and two of our recommended titles for this chapter, *Split* and *Get Out*.

Lionsgate is a production and distribution outfit formed in 1997 from what was Cinepix. From humble beginnings, they are now what would be termed a 'mini-major', producing popular films and television series across a variety of genres. During the 2000s, Lionsgate was responsible for the *Saw* and *Hostel* franchises – titles synonymous with what became widely known as 'torture porn' (a phrase coined by New York Magazine critic David Edelstein in his 2006 article 'Now Playing at Your Local Multiplex: Torture Porn'), a cycle of films that revelled in the no-holds-barred depiction of entrapment, suffering and bodily abuse. As with the majority of entries in the slasher and body horror sub-genre, the apparent *raison d'être* of these films was to present a parade of graphic and gory set-pieces, with the barest of narratives to lead from one to the next. Nevertheless, they attracted a fervent army of fans who were catered for by the aforementioned franchises and other films such as *House of 1000 Corpses* (Rob Zombie, 2003, also a Lionsgate release), *Wolf Creek* (Greg McLean, 2005), *The Human Centipede* (Tom Six, 2009) and their respective sequels. A pejorative label used with similar venom to that of the 'slasher' twenty-five years earlier, torture porn represented for many critics the lowest level of an already deprecated genre.

The torture porn cycle is frequently discussed in terms of a reaction to 9/11 and elements of the subsequent 'war on terror' such as extraordinary rendition and prisoner abuse in Abu Ghraib and Guantanamo Bay. Commentators have been keen to draw comparisons with the popularity of violent films in the late 1960s and 70s when, as discussed in Chapter 7, events such as the Vietnam War and Watergate pushed political tensions to similar levels. Although claiming not to be a political film-maker, Eli Roth has increasingly singled out the actions of the Bush administration as a driving force behind both the making, and the popularity, of violent films during this period (see Bernard 2014:78-80). However, as Mark Bernard suggests, a more direct link between the two periods can be attributed to the fact that the creative forces behind these more recent films (often referred to as the 'Splat Pack') grew up as horror fans watching such 1970s milestones as *Last House on the Left*, *The Texas Chain Saw Massacre*, *The Hills Have Eyes* and the like. A quick Internet search will return dozens of quotes from Splat Pack directors such as Roth, Alexandre Aja and Rob Zombie citing George A. Romero, Tobe Hooper and Wes Craven as major influences, and the gritty 1970s aesthetic comes through loud and clear in much of their own work. As such, their films can be considered a backlash against the watered down remakes that had invaded multiplexes in the wake of *Scream* – a 'taking back' of the genre – as much as a political statement. When the DVD of *Hostel* was outselling the latest *Chronicles of Narnia* in Wal-Mart (see ibid:58), one can imagine that Lionsgate was more than happy to indulge the film-makers in their moments of violent 70s retro-nostalgia.[2]

The launch of the DVD format in the late 1990s brought with it important changes across the industry, in terms of financing, marketing and consumption. As already discussed, the introduction of multi-region players and the wide availability of foreign discs through the Internet gave film fans access to titles that would previously have remained unseen. In addition, the ready availability of vast numbers of back-catalogue titles instigated a collecting culture that brought immediate dollars to the studios. Whereas for much of its life videotape had been rental-based (with little if any revenue returned to the studios), from the outset DVD was a retail business, with the studios receiving funds from every disc sold. DVD quickly became the fastest adopted home technology ever (see Langford 2010: 201), with users demonstrating an insatiable appetite for content. The addition of extra features such as commentaries and making-of documentaries made DVD even more attractive for buyers, and the practice of releasing films in a variety of editions (so-called 'double-dipping') was prevalent. As such, even within the first decade of the technology, it was not uncommon for films to take more in DVD sales than at the theatrical box-office (see ibid:199-203). In the case of torture porn titles, their 'unrated' DVDs, reinstating elements of gore and violence that had been removed to secure a theatrical R rating, proved extremely popular. For Lionsgate this approach was especially lucrative, with titles such as *Saw III* (the best-selling horror film on DVD in 2007) bringing in over $45 million from DVD sales alone (Bernard 2014:71). So while the *Saw* and *Hostel* series may not have been seen as major successes in cinemas, their profitability on DVD ensured that the series would continue. Indeed, *Hostel: Part III* (Scott Spiegel, 2011) bypassed a theatrical release altogether and went straight to DVD, saving the costs associated with striking and distributing film prints.

But for all the sound and fury generated by the torture porn cycle, its effect on the genre's direction as a whole has been limited. Although such films were released throughout the 2000s and into the 2010s, there were nowhere near as many entries as in the original slasher cycle of the early 1980s. As with any such cycle, the films themselves suffered from the law of diminishing returns, with even the most ardent fans growing sated of blood and guts. By the beginning of the 2010s, the most popular horror films commercially were those that took a more subtle approach to the genre. With the success of the ongoing *Paranormal Activity* franchise, the supernatural/ghost sub-genre was in the ascendancy. James Wan (director of the first *Saw* instalment) was the creative force behind the *Conjuring* franchise, based on the case files of real-life ghost hunters Ed and Lorraine Warren. *The Conjuring* (2013) was enormously successful theatrically, bringing in almost $320 million worldwide. Unusual for a direct sequel, this total was actually surpassed by *The Conjuring 2* (James Wan, 2016), while the spin-off *Annabelle* (John R. Leonetti, 2014) generated over $250 million. One interesting aspect of these three films is that well over half of their takings came from foreign (i.e. non-US) markets. For much of its history, domestic box-office was the predominant source of revenue for American-made films. This is now changing, with foreign box-office making up a higher percentage of theatrical takings. As such, film-makers and studios are increasingly conscious of how their films will be received by non-US audiences. China in particular has emerged as a major market for American films, with some titles (notably those in the Marvel Cinematic Universe) shooting scenes specifically for the Chinese audience. As an extreme example, *The Fate of the Furious* (F. Gary Gray, 2017) made 'only' $225 million of its $1.237 billion takings in the US, with almost half of the rest coming from China alone.

While the US box-office remains an important source of revenue for the industry, we can see that ancillary outlets have been making inroads and affecting how films are made, marketed and consumed. Stephen Follows, in his exhaustive data-driven survey of the horror film from 1911 to 2016, observed that although the number of horror films being produced worldwide had been steadily increasing throughout the twentieth century (to around 200 films, or approximately 5% of all feature films released, in 2000), in the years since the millennium this number had increased at an extraordinary rate, to well over 1000 films and around 12% of all releases in 2016. However, during the same period the percentage of horror films that opened at US cinemas dropped, from over 10% in 2000 to around 3% in 2016 (see Follows 2017:8-9). Returning to the torture porn titles discussed earlier, what we can see from the performance of these films outside of a cinema environment (in this case Lionsgate's success with the unrated DVD releases) is that measuring the current popularity of the horror genre solely through domestic box office returns can be misleading. While there is no doubt that 2017 was the 'year of horror' in terms of recognition of the genre by critics and the wider industry, as well as theatrical box-office success, the idea that mainstream audiences had suddenly decided that horror was what they wanted to see is questionable. In fact, the audience for horror had always been there, they just preferred to be terrified in the comfort of their armchairs.

In our previous chapter we mentioned the importance of television series such as *True Blood*, *Vampire Diaries* and *The Originals* in perpetuating the vampire's profile in popular culture. More generally, in terms of horror's popularity in the 2010s, one series above all others helped to stoke interest in the genre and to raise its profile on a worldwide scale. *The Walking Dead*, Frank Darabont's adaptation of a comic book inspired by *Night of the Living Dead*, debuted on American TV screens on Halloween night 2010 to instant critical and public acclaim. Within a week it had screened in well over a hundred different countries and was a confirmed worldwide success. Breaking records for television viewing figures in the US, it has consistently been the country's most-watched scripted television programme amongst adults (Otterson 2017). Alongside the action figures, board games, novels, calendars and all of the other merchandise that comes with popular culture success, the spin-off series *Fear the Walking Dead* launched in 2016 to further expand the TV universe. In the wake of *The Walking Dead*, series-based television has gone on to become an extremely important vehicle for screen horror, encompassing original ideas (*American Horror Story*), movie spin-offs (*Ash vs Evil Dead*, *Wolf Creek*, *Child's Play*), re-imaginings (*Scream*, *The*

Exorcist), prequels (*Bates Motel, Hannibal*) and remakes (*Rosemary's Baby*), with literally dozens of horror-themed series screening across various platforms and networks.

Discussing the differences between film and television with the *Los Angeles Times*, Mexican writer, producer and director Guillermo del Toro declared that when it comes to television series it was now necessary to 'plan it, structure it for binge watching', and that any series should be treated in its entirety as a 'three-act play' with the first third of the series being the first act, the middle third being the second act and the final third being the third act (Olsen 2017). In a logical progression of this, the first season of a continuing series can be seen as standalone, with subsequent seasons viewed as sequels rather than a direct continuation. (This was certainly the case with the makers of *Stranger Things*, discussed below, who made the conscious decision to name the second season *Stranger Things 2*.) Since the advent of 'binge watching' (through first DVD box sets and then streaming services), writers for television can now assume that their audiences are not necessarily watching over several weeks or months, perhaps forgetting key details as a result, and so can handle more complex storylines and characters. This allows content creators to take a more measured approach, with horror series such as those listed above offering scope for more involved conflicts, relationships and other sub-plots outside of the conventional genre tropes. As such, mainstream audiences who would have baulked at queuing to watch a horror film at the cinema have been happy to invite vampires, zombies, and serial killers into their living rooms on a regular basis.

Another factor influencing modes of production has been the global reach of the various broadcasting platforms. Streaming service Netflix provides content to over 200 countries around the world, with an increasing percentage of this content produced or funded by the company itself. Whereas with third-party films and television series it becomes necessary to navigate regional broadcasting rights, dictating which countries can access what content, programming produced by or for Netflix can be made available through its service across all countries simultaneously. Given the level of investment being made it is important that these films and series appeal to as many audiences as possible, cutting down on the need to create specific content for each region. Whilst the US will remain the largest market in terms of subscribers for the foreseeable future, an emphasis is placed on making films and series that will 'travel' and play well in overseas markets.

Of particular relevance to this chapter is the Netflix series *Stranger Things*, the first season of which was made available worldwide in the summer of 2016. Across eight episodes the search for Will Byers – abducted by a transdimensional creature dubbed the Demagorgon – attracted enthusiastic audiences in all territories. Set in 1983, the series foregrounded a 1980s aesthetic as well as familiar actors from the

period, and paid *homage* to the popular culture of the time. The series undoubtedly exists in the science-fiction/horror genres, and is aimed at evoking nostalgia
amongst those who had grown up with *ET*, *Gremlins*, *The Goonies* (Richard Donner,
1985) and the like. However, due to their control over the delivery system, Netflix
were able to market it to audiences across genre and age boundaries as a mainstream product. The Netflix 'dashboard' that each user sees is custom generated
based on that user's preferences and past viewing history. As such, the company is
able to promote content to each user in a format that makes them more likely to
want to view it; for a horror/science-fiction hybrid such as *Stranger Things*, if a user
commonly watches science-fiction content then it would appear as a new entry in
the science-fiction genre, if they're a horror fan than it would appear against horror. For more mainstream viewers, the series will appear high in the new or trend-
ing section with an image designed to appeal to whatever tastes that user has. So,
those who regularly watch comedy series will see a different image to documentary
aficionados, who in turn will see a different image to thriller fans.[3] In this way, audiences who would not normally choose to watch a particular product can be drawn
into it, and potentially develop an interest in seeing more of the same. In the case
of *Stranger Things*, the creators hoped to tap into a shared nostalgia for their own
personal influences, including the films of Steven Spielberg and John Carpenter,
and particularly the early novels of Stephen King. As King himself tweeted after
viewing the first season:

> Watching STRANGER THINGS is looking [sic] watching Steve King's Greatest
> Hits. I mean that in a good way.[4]

That we end this book with the work of Stephen King - a horror fan, writer and
critic who has been active in the genre for well over forty years – is perhaps fitting. While his own works date from the 1970s onwards, King's personal fascination with and love of the horror genre began as a child of the 50s. He has lived
through, and been influenced by, much of the film history we have documented in
the preceding chapters. This influence is evident throughout all of his genre works,
but none more so than in his 1986 novel *IT*. Through the previous twelve years,
Stephen King had built up a reputation as not only a successful horror writer, but
also an author whose work was avidly consumed by readers of all ages, interests
and backgrounds. Whilst critics invariably dismissed his books as popular junk unworthy of serious literary appraisal, the audience for his work grew at an incredible
pace. *Carrie*, his first novel, had an initial hardcover print run of 30,000 copies, with
his second *Salem's Lot*, dropping to 20,000. However, with the success of Brian de
Palma's film version helping to push *Carrie*'s paperback sales to almost 4 million,
from *The Shining* (1977) onwards the first edition print runs increased rapidly. In

1983 his eighth novel, *Christine*, was given a first run of 250,000, and three years later *IT* became the first of his novels to print one million first edition hardcover copies (see Skal, 1994:354-361).

King acknowledges the success of the 1976 adaptation of *Carrie* as having a major impact on his early career, telling the *New York Times* in 1979 that 'the movie made the book, and the book made me' (Lawson 1979). Certainly, the film was extremely successful both critically and commercially, and undoubtedly generated interest in the author's work. Following the success of *Rosemary's Baby* and *The Exorcist*, mainstream audiences had an appetite both for well-made horror films and well-written horror fiction. While the 'New Hollywood' horror cycle would quickly come to an end, fans who had been drawn to King through *Carrie* remained faithful, the 'Constant Readers' addressed by the author in his novels' introductions and afterwords. In terms of successful film adaptations of King's work, and certainly within the horror genre, *Carrie* has arguably remained a high watermark. Although many now consider *The Shining* something of a masterpiece (and the extended *homage* in *Ready Player One* [Steven Spielberg, 2018] confirms its status in 80s popular culture), at the time of its release it was very poorly received, particularly by the author himself, who remains resentful of the changes Stanley Kubrick made to his vision.

The perceived failure of Kubrick's adaptation did not deter film-makers from taking on King's other works, with no less than 15 feature films based on his novels and short stories released throughout the 1980s. Although some of these were critically well received (for example, David Cronenberg's *The Dead Zone*) or commercially successful (*Pet Sematary* [Mary Lambert, 1989]), the only one to achieve both was the non-horror *Stand By Me* (Rob Reiner, 1986). Based on his short story 'The Body', the coming-of-age movie was hailed as the most successful adaptation of his own work by King, who admitted to crying after watching the first screening. The story is set in the 1950s, and follows a group of preteen boys as they embark on a physical and spiritual journey into adolescence, while searching for the body of a boy who has been hit by a train. Devoid of any supernatural occurrences, the film concentrates on the characters of the boys, and plays on the nostalgia for childhood and the 1950s as detailed in King's story. These strengths – of characterisation and basically telling a good story, regardless of genre – are what continue to draw such a disparate collection of readers to King's work today.

In the same year as the release of *Stand By Me*, the publication of *IT* marked a turning point for Stephen King and the end of a particular phase in his writing career. Four years in the making, the author has described the 1,100-page novel as variously a 'final exam on horror', a 'final exam in writing on childhood', and 'the summation of everything I have learned and done in my whole life to this point' (see Cruz 2009, Strengell 2005:175, Magistrale 2003:184). With the vast majority of his writing by that time being in the horror genre, King found that he was frequently being asked where his ideas came from, what influenced him, and what his childhood must have been like. With *IT*, he decided to write a novel that would answer all of these questions, and would be his final word on the subject. The book's central theme of childhood had been a major element in practically all of King's work up to this point, with many of his stories concentrating on events as seen through the eyes of children, and detailing the trials and tribulations of the preteen and adolescent years. For King this is a time of rich imagination, a commodity he values highly on a personal as well as professional level:

> the purpose of the imagination, I believe, is to offer us solace and shelter from situations … which would otherwise prove unendurable. … the imagination which so often kept me awake and in terror as a child has seen me through some terrible bouts of stark raving reality as an adult. (King 1993:7)

With *IT*, King wanted to introduce the ultimate monster, a shapeshifter that could physically embody the greatest fears of its victims, terrorising them first as children and then as adults twenty-five years later. Growing up in the 1950s, King had been an avid reader of *Famous Monsters* magazine, and a devotee of Saturday matinees showing the latest creature features. The new novel would give him an opportunity to revisit the scares he had experienced from these cinematic monsters while at the same time exploring the more mundane adult fears that had replaced them. How would adults cope, he wanted to know, if the monsters of their childhood came back, *and they were real*? Would they be able to rediscover the power of imagination and defeat the evil that haunted them once and for all?

IT continued King's run of successful publications, topping the *New York Times* bestseller list for 14 weeks across 1986 and 1987. Rights to adapt the novel were quickly bought by the American ABC television network, with ambitious plans to turn it into an eight-hour miniseries directed by George A. Romero, who had worked with King previously on the 1982 portmanteau *Creepshow*. As it turned out, scheduling conflicts led to Romero leaving the project and in a cost-cutting exercise ABC pared it down to a three-hour TV movie in two parts. Still, when it aired in 1990 the adaptation was extremely well received by audiences and critics alike, with Tim Curry's performance as Pennywise the clown drawing particular praise. Modelled on the appearance of Lon Chaney's *Phantom of the Opera*, Pennywise was a source of nightmares for a generation of children and quickly became an iconic figure in the genre. Watching the 1990 adaptation today, it comes across as slow and not particularly well made or acted, despite featuring what was quite a well-known cast. Nevertheless, for many children of the 1980s and 90s the series was their first exposure to the work of Stephen King, and screen horror in general, and remains a potent source of nostalgia.

When Warner Bros. began planning a feature film remake of *IT* in 2009, it was the beginning of a long and bumpy road. Between then and the (first) film's release in 2017, the production went through numerous changes as an array of potential writers and directors became involved.[5] Originally planned as a single standalone film, an early decision was made to update the children's side of the story to the 1980s, rather than the 1950s. It would also be R-rated, meaning that material excised from the TV movie due to restrictions on sex, violence and language could be included. Best known at the time for his adaptation of *Jane Eyre* (2011), Cary Fukunaga was brought on board in 2012 to write and direct, and his first decision was to split the story across two films. Rather than crosscut between the child and adult lives of the protagonists as the novel and TV version did, the first film would concern itself entirely with the characters as children, and the second film with them as adults. Following New Line Cinema's success with *The Conjuring*, Warner Bros. moved the stalled project to its subsidiary studio in 2014. However, in mid-2015, with production due to begin within weeks, issues arose between New Line and Fukunaga over budgeting and the more character-driven approach that he wanted to take. Fukunaga left the project, and, while his ideas for the structure of the two films were kept and he would retain a screenwriting credit, the search was on for a new creative driver.

In 2006, Argentine director Andrés Muschietti, who up until then had experience only in television commercials, shot material for a short film in which two small girls are terrorised by a supernatural entity. Although just three minutes in length, it was two years before Muschietti and his sister, producer Barbara, edited and completed the film, at which point it was submitted to various international film festivals under the title of *Mamá*. This caught the attention of Guillermo del Toro, who makes a point of seeking out talented new film-makers through watching short films. With an interest in fantasy and childhood evident across much of his own work, del Toro was attracted by both the subject matter and the execution. As a result, he took the director under his wing, and worked with the Muschiettis in securing funding to write a screenplay for a full-length film, using the short as inspiration. The feature version of *Mama* was filmed at Pinewood on a soundstage shared with del Toro's giant monster epic *Pacific Rim* (2013), allowing close collaboration between the film-makers as it developed. A Spanish-US co-production, *Mama* combines the atmosphere of the popular Spanish supernatural films with the aesthetics and jump scares of more mainstream American horror films such as *The Ring* and

The Conjuring. Released in 2013, the result was a box-office hit for distributor Universal, bringing in almost $150 million worldwide on a $15 million budget.

Following the success of *Mama*, Muschietti was signed up to direct Universal's *The Mummy*, but departed after nine months citing creative differences. When Cary Fukunaga left the production of *It* Muschietti, a longtime fan of King and *IT* in particular, wasted no time in setting up a meeting with Warners. No doubt impressed by his skill in generating scares on a tight budget, he was hired and began pre-production immediately. Filming completed in mid-2016, and even though the film's release was over a year away there was already a high level of public interest. Images of actor Bill Skarsgård as Pennywise began circulating online, and comparisons were made with Tim Curry's interpretation. Those with nostalgic memories of the 1990 TV version looked forward to reuniting with Pennywise 27 years later, just as the story's children do as adults. Stephen King fans old and new were hoping that Muschietti could replicate the success of *Mama* with one of the author's most personal works. More youthful audiences were attracted by the themes and narrative elements it shared with *Stranger Things*, underlined by the presence in the cast of that series' Finn Wolfhard. Such was the level of anticipation that the advance trailer for the film broke Internet records with almost 200 million online views in its first 24 hours. If ever a horror film had piqued the interest of 'mainstream' cinema audiences then *IT* was it; the question was whether it could deliver on their collective expectations.

Textual Analysis

Derry, Maine, 1988: Housebound with the flu, 11-year-old Bill makes a paper boat for his younger brother, Georgie. When attempting to retrieve it from a storm drain on its maiden voyage, Georgie meets a clown-like creature that engages in conversation before biting his arm off and dragging him into the sewer. The following summer, refusing to believe that the missing Georgie is dead, Bill encourages his friends – Eddie, Richie and Stan – to spend their school holidays searching for him. They are soon joined by fellow outcasts Beverly, Ben and Mike and form the 'Losers' Club'. While also engaged in more everyday battles with bullies (both child and adult), they quickly discover that there is a dark supernatural force in Derry. 'It' is a shapeshifting entity that emerges every 27 years to feed on the local children. Drawing its strength from fear, It takes on the form of whatever scares its victim most, favouring that of a clown named Pennywise. After narrowly escaping It during a terrifying experience in a supposed haunted house, everyone except Bill and Beverly becomes too afraid to continue and the group disbands. However, when It takes Beverly, the Losers' Club reunites to find her and follow It into the sewers, which eventually lead to a well under the haunted house. Henry Bowers, a local bully who has murdered his own father while under the subliminal influence of It, attempts to kill them but is despatched down the well. Confronting It as a team, the Losers' Club are able to overcome their individual fears and force it back into hibernation. Meeting on a riverbank at the end of summer, Beverly reveals that she had a vision of them all returning to the scene as adults. The children make a blood pact to come back if they ever hear of It's reappearance in Derry.

As we will discuss later in this chapter, while 2017 may have produced some well-received horror films, there was a certain amount of resistance on the part of critics (and some film-makers) to labelling them as such. Thankfully, our case study suffered none of this, and proudly displays its genre credentials from the outset. Warner Bros. have long had a tradition of adapting their opening logo to suit the particular film it is introducing, and in the case of *It* the filtered and distorted shield and backdrop are accompanied by an unsettling rendition of 'Oranges and Lemons'. Non-diegetic nursery rhymes sung by children have become a familiar feature of contemporary horror films. A short-hand alert to the audience that something is awry, it also acknowledges the darkness often lurking behind the banalities of such songs; in this case the final lines of the rhyme help to give a visceral jolt in the film's library scene. As the Warner Bros. logo breaks up and reassembles into that of New Line Cinema, a thunderstorm begins, we hear an evil cackle, and a red balloon floats across the screen. Through the use of familiar horror elements the film-makers leave us in no doubt as to what kind of film we are about to watch, and set a foreboding tone before it has even begun.

This tone, as well as the thunderstorm, continues in the opening credits scene that introduces Bill, Georgie and Pennywise. Sent to the cellar to retrieve wax, Georgie's trip initially hints at a domestic horror setting familiar to audiences from contemporary paranormal films such as *The Conjuring*. However, while cellars, bathrooms and family garages do become sites of horror later in the film, the killing of Georgie takes place in the open and in comparative daylight. Shifting the action to the street for It's first attack quickly takes us out of the nuclear family and purely domestic horror and into something much broader. In the American Gothic tradition, *It* centres on a small town seemingly typical of the American dream in action, but which harbours dark secrets and an age-old evil. The fictional Derry brings together the urban and the rural, highlighted in numerous aerial shots that take us high above the trees before swooping down over suburban houses, transporting us down wide streets or across rivers and the surrounding countryside. An apparently idyllic setting, the Gothic trope of horror lurking beneath the surface of normality is explicit through the use of cellars, sewers and wells as the realm of It. Yet, as in Stephen King's original vision of an entire haunted city, danger lurks around every corner in the shape of both supernatural and-all-too human evil.

The narrative decision to focus solely on the children's story for the first film was a shrewd one. Not only does this make for a more cohesive work (certainly in comparison to the first episode of the TV adaptation), but by being firmly rooted in the 1980s the film is able to tap more fully into a nostalgia for 80s movies such as *Stand By Me*, *The Goonies* and *The Monster Squad* (Fred Dekker, 1987). This version of *IT* appeals to the nostalgia of movie audiences now in their late 30s and 40s, just as the novel (and the TV adaptation) evoked Stephen King's own 1950s' youth. From the opening scenes, however, it is clear that Muschietti's adaptation is attempting something subtler than just an 80s movie pastiche. Part of the joy of *Stranger Things*, at least for its sizeable 40-something audience, is that watching it is just like watching a TV series or movie when they were growing up. The viewer is not simply nostalgic for what is depicted on screen, but for the very manner in which it is depicted: the clunky title sequence, the throbbing analogue synth score, or the presence of popular 80s actors such as Winona Ryder and Sean Astin. In the case of *It*, the setting is still the 1980s but the aesthetics are not similarly constrained; there's no attempt to make it look or sound like an actual 80s production. Ignoring the obvious 'October 1988' subtitle there are relatively few clues in the opening scenes to the time period, aside from the movie posters in Bill's bedroom and perhaps the cars on the driveway. The soundtrack features the lush orchestral sound of a modern Hollywood studio film. The fact that Bill makes the paper boat from writing paper, rather than newspaper as in the novel, also resists the dating of these opening moments too overtly. A close rendering of the novel's opening pages, the nostalgia of these scenes is for childhood more broadly, for both innocent pastimes and the timeless fears of monsters in the cellar. The horror, when it comes, lies in the destruction of this innocence.

This theme of innocence lost continues through the introduction of Mike, as he embarks on a steep learning curve in the realities of life. Unable to pull the trigger to kill a sheep, Mike is warned by his grandfather that unless he starts to take responsibility he'll one day find himself in the position of said sheep. It is a metaphor that becomes all too literal later in the film when he finds himself staring down the barrel of the gun in the hands of Henry Bowers. Mike's status as an outsider stems predominantly from the fact that he's home-schooled, and that he lives outside of the town itself. Unlike in King's novel, the race politics of Mike and his family's position in Derry are downplayed; the racism in Henry's telling him to 'get out of my town' is implied rather than overt. That he is not a resident of Derry allows Mike's grandfather a privileged position as one of the few adults capable of seeing what's going on in the town and its effect on the residents. While Ben provides the background history of the unfortunate incidents in Derry, it is Mike's grandfather who effectively takes on the role of knowledgeable expert, educating him about the evil that stalks the town and bringing the folk wisdom that helps to explain It.

The addition of the farm scene allows for a neat segue from the doomed sheep being released from their pen to schoolchildren rushing out of a classroom at the end of term. The not-so-subliminal message of course is lambs to the slaughter, and it's one that is picked up again towards the end of the film when Henry 'baas' at the children down the well. Nevertheless, the general tone of the introduction to our 'heroes' is one of humour and excitement as the school year ends. Across one continuous shot we follow the four main male characters – Bill, Stan, Richie and Eddie – through the school corridors as they engage in fast-paced banter. They are obviously close friends and come across as witty and irreverent as they contemplate the summer of freedom ahead, moving swiftly past Henry Bowers and his gang of bullies with a combination of fear and loathing. The mood changes, however, when the camera switches to follow Gretta into the girls' toilets and the shot is broken as we meet our heroine Bev. The fact that she's smoking alone in the cubicle marks her as an outcast, and our sympathies are immediately with her over the bullying and aggressive Gretta and her gang. Bev's wit in responding to Gretta's taunts and her quick thinking in sheltering under her rucksack from the torrent of garbage are early indications of her self-confidence and resourcefulness. The key around her neck, meanwhile, hints at a less than ideal domestic situation.

The school corridor scene and that which follows, complete with police presence and 'Remember the Curfew' sign, are reminiscent of campus slasher films such as *Scream*, albeit with a much younger cast. As Gordie, the author-narrator of Stephen King's 'The Body' reflects, the friendships we have later in life are never the same as those we have when we are 12, and King seems particularly captivated by the late preteen/early teenage years. The child heroes of *It* are depicted at this crucial age, experiencing intense but frequently volatile and short-lived friendships, coping with the challenges of early puberty, and negotiating the boundary between childhood beliefs and adult versions of reality. King's original idea for *IT* came when walking over a footbridge and imagining a troll lurking below. For the members of the Losers' Club, adulthood can only be achieved by facing up to the troll (in the shape of their collective fears) and crossing the bridge. As with our previous case study, *Let the Right One In*, anything not relevant to the immediate experiences and relationships of the central characters has been omitted in the adaptation from novel to film. In this case, there is scope for adding explanatory background, and more details of It's transdimensional existence, in the sequel, but for this first entry the viewer is transported entirely into the world of its child characters. Every event is seen from their perspective; unusually for a modern horror film there are no obvious POV shots, and we are never invited to take the place of It or any of the adult characters.

When Bill, Richie, Eddie and Stan see the mother of the missing Betty Ripsom waiting outside school they are both sympathetic to the mother's plight and rational about the futility of her actions. Their conversation, and the subsequent intimidation of the boys by Henry's gang, targeting Stan for being Jewish and Bill for his stutter, further develops the dynamics of this children's world. Narrative moments such as these efficiently, and often humorously, establish the important characters and friendship groups but also insert a sense of threat through talk of curfews and tales of missing or murdered peers. The viewer is already aware of a distinctly supernatural evil lurking in the town through witnessing the attack on Georgie. However, Bill's emphatic belief that Betty Ripsom is missing and not dead tells us that he also believes his brother may still be alive. This is a clever departure from the novel, in which the characters are left in no doubt that Georgie is dead from the beginning. As such, the search for Georgie gives the main characters of the film purpose and acts as an important narrative thread. Bev's interaction with Ben introduces the final member of the Losers' Club, as he struggles with his bike and paper model of the Derry water tower. While Ben's infatuation with Bev is obvious, her good-natured teasing of his musical tastes sets up a bond between the two characters that is referenced throughout the film. The care she takes in signing his otherwise empty yearbook contrasts sharply with Gretta's malicious 'signing' of Eddie's plaster cast later. As in the novel Ben is the stereotypical 'fat kid' of the story, but the film gives the role more prominence in having him, rather than Mike, gathering the historical evidence of It's reign in Derry.

The reversal of the usual adult-child roles exemplified by the boys' observations on Betty Ripsom's mother is typical of the film as a whole, in which adults are peripheral figures and we are encouraged to adopt the (privileged) child perspective. As such, the film recalls what Robin Wood described as a 'curious and disturbing phenomenon' in the 1980s of 'films that construct the adult spectator as a child, or, more precisely, as a childish adult, an adult who would like to be a child'. Wood was referring specifically to films such as *ET* and the original *Star Wars* trilogy, which are identified as children's films but marketed to adults with the aim of satisfying 'a widespread desire for regression to infantilism' (Wood 2003:145-147). While Wood saw this as a negative and even dangerous development, Stephen King offers a contrasting view. In King's opinion, 'the job of the fantasy-horror writer is to make you, for a little while, a child again' (King 1982:456), to open up what he describes as the 'tunnel vision' of the third eye that comes with adulthood, and let the reader surrender to their imagination. Although hardly intended for a child audience, *It* also bears comparison with the 'children's horror genre', as described by Catherine Lester (2016). Discussing the popularity of films such as *ParaNorman* (Chris Butler and Sam Fell, 2012) and *Hotel Transylvania* (Genndy Tartakovsky, 2012), which feature conventional horror imagery and themes yet are produced for and marketed to children, Lester identifies some of the key elements of children's horror. These include the distancing of violence in the past, a happy or at least hopeful ending, the foregrounding of friendship and family rather than sexuality, and the absence of 'confirmation' of the monster by authorities due to the ineffectual nature of authority figures. All of these elements are present in this adaptation.

Described in the novel as 'the apotheosis of all monsters' (King 1986:18) It represents the summation of everything we have discussed over the previous twelve chapters. As stated throughout this book, the monster is a crucial part of the horror film's basic formula but its nature is dependent on the historical, cultural, political and geographical context in which a film is made and consumed. King's use of the term 'It' invites the reader to imagine the evil that stalks the town according to their own worst fears, and in terms of the film version the decision on what form It takes is an important one. One of the reasons given in the novel for It preying on children is that their fears are easier to embody in a physical form – the conventional monster – than are those of adults. While a reference remains in the advertising of *A Nightmare on Elm Street 5* (Stephen Hopkins, 1989) on the billboard of the Derry cinema, the possibility of It taking the form of Freddy Krueger was entertained but quickly rejected by the director as 'a bit too meta' (Gonzalez 2017). Certainly, Freddy's appearance would have been in keeping with the *modus operandi* of It as envisioned by King; in the novel It takes the form of familiar monsters from films such as *I Was a Teenage Werewolf* and Universal's *Frankenstein* and *The Creature From The Black Lagoon*. Muschietti's updated version replaces these with undoubtedly less-interesting generic zombies and ghost-like figures, though, of course, Pennywise the Dancing Clown remains as It's dominant form.

While Richie's admission to having a fear of clowns is not unusual, the term used to identify such a condition – coulrophobia – is relatively recent, with the Oxford English Dictionary dating its introduction to the 1980s. However, the ability of clowns to induce fear in cinema audiences was recognised far earlier. As Lon Chaney remarked, 'there is nothing laughable about a clown in the moonlight', and he credited the circus clowns he watched as a child with inspiring his interpretations of roles such as *The Phantom of the Opera* (see Clarens 1969:90). The figure of the menacing clown has been a popular one in the horror genre, particularly since the 1980s with films such as *Poltergeist* (Tobe Hooper, 1982), *Killer Klowns from Outer Space* (Stephen Chiodo, 1988) and *Clownhouse* (Victor Salva, 1989), through to the more recent *Clown* (Jon Watts, 2014) and *31* (Rob Zombie, 2016). Add to these the real-life case of 1970s serial killer John Wayne Gacy (who would attend children's parties and fundraisers under the guise of 'Pogo the Clown') and a general mistrust of clowns perhaps becomes understandable. Certainly, Tim Curry's interpretation of Pennywise in the 1990 miniseries has elements of the disturbed old man in clown costume that every parent fears turning up to their child's party. By contrast, Pennywise in the 2017 film is more of a 'real' clown inasmuch as he is a clown through a child's eyes; there is no sense of him being an ordinary human male in disguise. This works particularly well here, given that Pennywise interacts only with the children and not their adult counterparts.

Our first glimpse of Pennywise, as two points of light shining out from the darkness of the storm drain, recalls Georgie's earlier moment of fear in the cellar. However this is quickly forgotten when the clown moves out of the shadow, his brilliant blue eyes and buckteeth affecting an almost childlike innocence. Adopting the patterns of children's speech as he delivers their introductions and engages Georgie in conversation, Pennywise lures him closer with talk of the circus, of popcorn and cotton candy. This first appearance is in stark contrast to the images of Pennywise we see throughout much of the rest of the film, where his aim is to terrify rather than charm. Bill Skarsgård's own athleticism makes his interpretation of Pennywise a very physical one, whether leaping out of a coffin to frighten Richie or performing a terrifying parody of a dance routine when greeting Bev in his underground lair. The escapology act in emerging from the icebox in the haunted house, as he unwinds himself in front of Eddie's horrified eyes, is particularly grotesque. While such sequences provide some originality in the depiction of the monster, there are also numerous instances where the film reverts to tried and tested jump and scare tactics. Pennywise's uncanny speeded-up movements when rushing forward to attack his victims are familiar from contemporary supernatural films such as *Lights Out* and Muschietti's own *Mama* (and has long been a popular effect in J-Horror), while his emergence from the projector screen in Bill's garage recalls Sadako crawling out of the television

screen in *Ringu*. The scene where Bev is attacked by lengths of hair again echoes various J-Horror entries as discussed in Chapter 6, as well as the infamous 'tree rape' scene in the original *Evil Dead*, while the subsequent geyser of blood is reminiscent of Glen's death scene in Craven's *A Nightmare on Elm Street* (Fig 13.1).

Figure 13.1

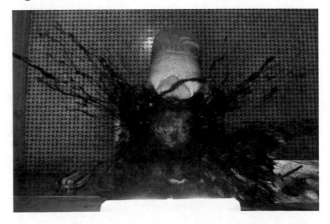

In the opening of *Danse Macabre*, his wide-ranging study of horror in the media, Stephen King describes the genre as existing on three distinct levels of emotion. The first level is terror, where nothing is shown and fear is generated through the imagination of the viewer (or reader). The second level is horror, where the viewer is explicitly shown the form of the monster and fear is generated through this. The third level is revulsion, where the viewer's gag reflex is stimulated through graphic depictions of blood and gore. While acknowledging a hierarchy within these definitions, King himself admits to the necessity of resorting to the basest level to generate fear:

> I recognize terror as the finest emotion... so I will try to terrorize the reader. But if I find I cannot terrify him/her, I will try to horrify; and if I cannot horrify, I'll go for the gross-out. I'm not proud. (King 1982:40)

Successful films that rely on the purely psychological emotion of terror are few and far between, with King giving the classic example of Robert Wise's *The Haunting*. To this we could arguably add more recent films such as *The Blair Witch Project* and *The Babadook*, but the paucity of other contenders demonstrates how difficult and restrictive it is for a film-maker to rely purely on the unseen or implied. In terms of the most popular genre films of the 2010s, contemporary film-makers tend to focus primarily on the dual emotions of terror and horror, with occasional bursts of revulsion.

At the beginning of our analysis we mentioned *It*'s opening sequence, with Georgie's fearful excursion to the cellar to retrieve wax for the paper boat. Although there is no actual threat to him there, this is probably the closest that the film comes to generating fear through terror, in terms of King's definitions above. Certainly, there are some suspenseful moments during the exploration of the sewers, or in the haunted house on Neibolt Street, but by this time the audience has seen the monster in the form of Pennywise and is aware of It's presence. As such, the tension here comes from wondering how and from where It will attack, rather than from our imagining what could be lurking in the shadows. However, there is an added layer of complexity working here, in that It is attempting to instill fear in the characters (and by extension the audience, given that they are our identification figures), and the scares are designed to work on two levels. The supernatural images that we see as an audience are in fact the creations of the child characters' imaginations, so that whereas the characters are made fearful through the emotion of terror, by contrast we as an audience are subjected to fear through both horror and revulsion. Our privileged position allows us to witness the products of the children's imagination while adult observers within the film remain oblivious. Existing at the border of childhood and young adulthood, the members of the Losers' Club are able both to see It and to recognise that the tricks used to frighten them are not entirely real. Unlike the *Nightmare on Elm Street* films, these visions are not merely dreams, as Mike attests: 'I know the difference between bad dreams and real life.' It is this self-awareness that Bill urges his friends to use as they confront their fears during the first visit to the Neibolt Street house.

While there are numerous instances of *It* using horror to instill fear, the Losers' Club's typical preteen preoccupation with 'loogies', vomit and the like ensures that there is also plenty of scope for generating revulsion. Julia Kristeva's theory of 'the abject' suggests that revulsion is generated by the loss of distinction between self and Other (see Kristeva 1982). In particular, the body's expelling of waste, vomit, blood and pus is both a signifier of bodily decay and a transgression of the borders between inside and outside, clean and unclean, alive and dead, with a corpse representing the ultimate abjection. The maintenance of the boundary between clean and unclean, or healthy and unhealthy, is central to Eddie and Stan's characters and provides moments of humour as well as horror. 'It' lives in filthy sewers, forcing them to wade through grey water full of 'piss and shit', and Eddie finds himself pursued by a zombie oozing pus and saliva. While the blood that gushes out of Bev's bathroom sink is in itself abject, the obvious association with menstruation plays on her anxieties of puberty and the transition to womanhood. This, in turn, references the very real horror of physical threat posed by her father when she is no longer his 'little girl'. Although the sexual abuse Bev suffers at the hands of her father is not made explicit in the film, it is strongly implied. For the male members of the Losers' Club sex is still something amusing and vaguely disgusting, with Richie in particular regularly engaging in innuendo. His description of Bev's sink going 'all Eddie's mom's vagina on Halloween' manages to evoke a suitably abject image.

Identified as It's entry point into the human world, and a realm over which it has complete control, the house on Neibolt Street is the site of many of the film's horrific scenes. The archetypal 'old dark house' and conventional 'Terrible Place' we have discussed previously, it has the outward appearance of the Bates' house from *Psycho*, albeit in very poor repair. Separated from the rest of the street, it is a dilapidated Victorian Gothic mansion with overgrown garden, gnarled trees and rusting fence unlike any of the other houses around it (see Fig 13.2). Although a deleted scene on the DVD shows the group mounting their bikes and fleeing in terror from the Neibolt house following their first encounter with It, the finished cut of the film (in which they seem to run out of the house and straight into Eddie's mother, in completely different surroundings) offers the possibility that the outward appearance of the house may in fact be influenced by the children's active imagina-

Figure 13.2

tions. Certainly, the Neibolt interior is the haunted house of a child's imagination, a theme park funhouse in which clowns jump out of coffins, heads emerge from mattresses and green acid slime advances across the floor. Canted camera angles are used frequently around the house, both inside and out, signifying its unstable position on the borders of reality and serving to unsettle the viewer. We're told that it's occupied by 'junkies and hobos', but see no-one but the leprous fiend of Eddie's worst nightmares, a dismembered Betty Ripsom and, of course, Pennywise. While the aesthetics of Betty Ripsom's torso hanging behind the 'not scary at all' door wouldn't be out of place in a *Saw* or *Hostel*, it is clearly a funhouse trick played by It, and results in a comic line reminiscent of *Shaun of the Dead*: 'Where the fuck were her legs?!'

If the exterior appearance of the Neibolt house is indeed affected by the presence of Eddie's mother then it is another subtle indication of the separate worlds that the adults and children inhabit. For the members of the Losers' Club the freedom of spending a summer outside is a recurring concern, often to Bill's annoyance: 'If you say "it's summer" one more fucking time...' Many viewers will look back on the 1980s (much as King's generation looked back on the 1950s) as a more innocent time, before the dubious attractions of social media, games consoles and mobile devices, and when it was apparently safe for children to venture out unsupervised. Aesthetically, the film's palette contrasts the bright summer light of the outdoors with dreary and claustrophobic interiors; dismal corridors in Bev's apartment and Eddie's house, for example, mirror the gloomy tunnels of the sewer system. It is in these darkened indoor spaces that the adults are generally found, often in a sedentary position in front of the It-infiltrated television show. That Eddie's mother tries to keep him 'locked inside this hell-hole' hints that she is aware of the threats inherent in the town but is unable or unwilling to explain them. The only mother with any real presence in the film, Mrs Kaspbrak recalls another of King's characters in the overbearing Annie Wilkes of *Misery*, as portrayed by Kathy Bates in the 1990 Rob Reiner film. Like Annie, her aim is to keep her charge inside the house through the invention of numerous ailments. Whilst she claims that this is for his own protection, Eddie recognises that it's his friends who have his best interests at heart, leading to one of the great comic moments in the film when he rebels over his fake medication: 'They're gazebos! They're bullshit!'

From the old woman who leaves Georgie to his fate in the opening sequence, to the threatening forces of Bev and Henry's fathers, the adult residents of the town are passive at best and downright hostile at worst. The overriding message of the film is that adults are not to be relied on; the kids are on their own. As in the rock war with the Bowers gang that foreshadows it, the final battle against Pennywise demands their combined strength, and unwavering loyalty to each other, to face off and (at least temporarily) defeat the danger. Whilst our central characters engage with the monster, each overcoming It in the physical guise of their greatest fears, they all survive relatively unscathed – very different to many of the films we have discussed previously. This is not the bleak horror of *Night of the Living Dead*, or the kill-fest of a slasher or torture porn entry, but a version of the genre in which evil does not necessarily triumph. The first kiss between Bill and Bev in the closing scene adds to the nostalgic appeal but also creates a hopeful ending. Pennywise's last word as he disappears down the well is 'fear', and it is fear, and the ability to overcome fear, that dominates *It*. Although Beverly was saved from death by not being sufficiently afraid, this is the only feeling she can recall when relating her vision of the group's older selves: 'I just remember how we felt. How scared we were.' Her premonition alerts us to the fact that the fight with It is not over, but we can have faith in the characters we have come to know, and in the pact they have made. As in the final scene of our opening case study, the joining of hands recalls the never-ending circle of fate (Fig 13.3). Just as It will return to feed again in 27 years, so the members of the Losers' Club are fated to reassemble for the next battle.

Figure 13.3

Reception and Aftermath

It would be safe to assume that for much of the project's development Warner Bros. did not see *It* as a major cinematic event. The film was released to US cinemas (and most of the rest of the world) in September, traditionally a quiet time for cinemagoers and known in the industry as a 'dump month'. Nevertheless, having adopted a saturation marketing strategy in the immediate run-up to its release, Warners and New Line publicly anticipated a domestic opening weekend of over $60 million. This would already make it the most successful opening for an R-rated horror film, and indeed for any film released in September. However, such was the anticipation around the film that it took over $120 million in the US alone that weekend, dwarfing its $35 million production budget. After spending two weeks at number one in the US charts it remained in the top 10 for a further five weeks, showing remarkable staying power for a horror film and demonstrating strong word-of-mouth support. By the end of the film's theatrical run, the US box office was over $325 million, with international takings pushing it over $700 million, making it by far the most commercially successful R-rated horror film ever. In terms of its critical reception the film received generally favourable reviews, with a number of critics drawing comparisons with *Stand By Me* and *Stranger Things* and lauding the performances of the young cast, although there was criticism of a reliance on jump scares and CGI effects (see Nyren 2017).

Warners' second highest grossing title of the year after *Wonder Woman* (Patty Jenkins, 2017), *It* demonstrated that the horror genre was as capable as any other of producing 'must-see' blockbuster films. That it did so without sacrificing its horror credentials made its success even more impressive, particularly when compared to the dismal performance only three months earlier of Universal's *The Mummy* (Alex Kurtzman, 2017). The first instalment in the studio's proposed 'Dark Universe' of classic monster re-imaginings, *The Mummy* was conceived and marketed as a mainstream summer blockbuster, and marked a return to Simpson's 'horror event movies' of the 1990s. In trying to appeal to non-genre audiences, Kurtzman's reboot played down the subject's horrific elements and instead presented a PG-13 Tom Cruise action adventure. At a time when the genre's popularity was riding high, Universal's attempt to bring their iconic characters into the mainstream would appear, on the basis of *The Mummy*'s reception at least, to be a misstep. While undoubtedly benefitting from a resurgent Stephen King brand[6] and the pop culture success of *Stranger Things*, *It* demonstrated that horror films were able to draw mainstream audiences without losing their essential genre characteristics.

It's commercial performance was the highlight of a year in which horror films regularly featured high in the box-office charts. Other genre entries to take top spot in 2017 included *Split*; *Alien: Covenant* (Ridley Scott, 2017); *Annabelle: Creation* (David F. Sandberg, 2017); and the *Saw* reboot *Jigsaw* (Michael and Peter Spierig, 2017). However, in terms of raising the genre's profile amongst mainstream audiences and critics, one film stood out more than most. *Get Out*, the debut feature by writer-director (and comedian) Jordan Peele, took over $250 million worldwide on a $4.5 million budget and received universally excellent reviews. Amongst literally hundreds of other award nominations, the film was nominated for Academy Awards in four categories, including Best Picture and Best Director, winning for Best Original Screenplay. Its inclusion in the Golden Globes shortlist for 'Best Motion Picture – Musical or Comedy', however, raised some familiar questions around genre categorisation. While Peele himself distanced his film from the horror label by assigning it to a genre he called 'social thriller' (see Zinoman 2018), its roots are undeniable. Coinciding with the release of *Get Out*, the director curated a film series at the Brooklyn Academy of Music featuring works that had inspired his debut, amongst them *Night of the Living Dead*, *Rosemary's Baby*, *The Shining*, *Scream* and *The Silence of the Lambs*.

Of course, as we have seen, the horror genre is no stranger to being manipulated by studios and film-makers in an attempt to appear more acceptable or attractive to audiences. From the list above, both *Scream* and *Silence of the Lambs* were marketed as thrillers at a time when the horror film was deemed to be out of favour with cinemagoers. With this in mind, it's worth returning to the question of genre, and in particular the idea of 'mainstream horror' as described in the opening of this chapter. We have mentioned already the influence of Guillermo del Toro in the career of Andy Muschietti, the director of our case study. Although his films generally highlight distinct fantasy elements, del Toro has never been afraid of being labeled a 'horror director', and is a vocal champion of the genre as a lifelong aficionado of monster movies, horror comics and literature. When *The Shape of Water* took Best Picture and Best Director awards at the 2018 Academy Awards it represented the culmination of a dream project that began over forty years earlier when, after watching *The Creature from the Black Lagoon* as a young boy, he didn't understand why the monster and the girl didn't get together at the end. A love story between a mute cleaner and a human-amphibian creature held in a secret military laboratory, *The Shape of Water* is an undoubted *homage* to classic Universal monster movies, and to Gothic horror more generally.

As mentioned throughout this book, horror film narratives frequently act as allegories for real-world issues, while at the same time functioning as a temporary escape from those same issues. With political and social tensions in the US and elsewhere running high following the election of Donald Trump to the White House, commentators were quick to assign the success of films such as *Get Out* and *The Shape of Water* to their explicit examination of contemporary issues such as racism, oppression and intolerance. To many critics, the fact that they do this through narratives of body snatching, brain transplants and fantasies in which the creature finally gets the girl is incidental. In choosing to look beyond genre labeling and concentrate on their underlying (non-generic) themes, critics' description of horror films such as these as 'mainstream' is perhaps understandable. Yet this is obviously not the whole story; not every horror film released into cinemas is rife with (not so) hidden meanings. While Andy Muschietti may describe *It* as 'a direct reflection of the "culture of fear" and "division" America has faced' in the year since Donald Trump took office (Chasmar 2017), it would be safe to say that this is not what drew record numbers into cinemas to watch the film.

Although horror has experienced ups and downs throughout the past hundred-odd years, it has consistently been amongst the most popular, and certainly most profitable, film genres, regardless of cyclical waxing and waning of fortunes. The simple fact is that audiences apparently enjoy being scared, and if a film can play effectively on universal fears then it will attract a wide audience. Yes, 'It' may appear as a clown, or a zombie, or whatever it is that personally scares the individual characters in the film, but behind this are the collective fears of growing up, of taking responsibility and of the unknown. That *It* succeeded so spectacularly in cinemas when marketed as an out-and-out horror film, not a 'social thriller' or 'Gothic fantasy', is undoubtedly a triumph for the genre, but, as noted in the opening section of this chapter, the audience for horror had been growing for some time outside of the multiplex anyway. If the genre has indeed crossed over into the 'mainstream' in terms of popularity then it is not an overnight phenomenon that can be attributed to any particular film, cycle or societal event.

To round off our discussion of 'mainstream' horror and hidden metaphors, it's worth mentioning the case of *The Babadook*, the debut feature of Australian director Jennifer Kent. A domestic psychological horror film, it tells of a widow raising a young son, whose grief over the death of her husband manifests itself into a physical presence based on a dark storybook character. Although the film received excellent reviews (including a recommendation via Twitter from *Exorcist* director William Friedkin, who ranked it alongside *Psycho* and *Les Diaboliques*) and international awards, it remained relatively unknown outside of its home country. That changed in 2016 when the title character became the subject of an Internet meme that bizarrely elevated it to the status of gay icon. While the initial cause of this is unclear (claims that Netflix had mistakenly added the film to its LGBTQ category were false), the film has gone on to become a cult classic in the eyes of the LGBTQ+ community, with representations of the monster appearing at pride marches around the world along with rainbow Babadook T-shirts, badges and other merchandise. The director herself has been reluctant to comment on any hidden meanings, but it seems that many in the LGBTQ+ community have identified with the film's depiction of the Babadook's Otherness within the family environment (it ends the film ostracised and living in a corner of the family's basement). If nothing else, *The Babadook* demonstrates the genre's ability to cross cultural boundaries and capture the imagination of non-traditional audiences, while at the same time delivering a well-made scary movie.

At the time of writing, horror is the genre *du jour*, experiencing a popularity that could scarcely have been imagined only ten years previously. Yet as we have witnessed throughout this book, cycles and fads come and go, and the genre's current state of heightened popularity will undoubtedly fall away sooner or later, only to rise again. Looking to the future of any film genre, but particularly one as dynamic as horror, is always something of a fool's game. However, the ongoing changes in modes of production, distribution and consumption we have detailed above provide plenty of scope for optimism. Horror has never been dependent on big-budget productions or commercial blockbusters, and will continue to find an audience even if this is outside of the multiplex. Online services such as YouTube allow film-makers to pitch ideas and find audiences with practically zero cost. While such avenues can lead to a successful Hollywood career, as in the case of Andy Muschietti or David F. Sandberg, whose short film *Lights Out* brought him to the attention of James Wan and into the *Conjuring* and DC Comics franchises, independent film-makers are increasingly able to fund, produce and distribute product without the need for studios or cinemas. In the case of Ti West's low-budget horror *The House of the Devil* (2009), its limited cinema run occurred only after it had been available for some time and proven popular on VOD (video on demand). Indeed, outside of major studio productions, a theatrical release is nowadays often seen as little more than an advertisement for the upcoming DVD and VOD release, through which much larger revenues can be generated. Alongside traditional television networks, streaming services are increasingly funding content themselves (with Netflix alone earmarking $8 billion for the production of original films and series throughout 2018 [Spangler 2018]), further disrupting traditional production and distribution methods. Driven by the need to attract and retain subscribers, the current popularity of the genre ensures that horror content will continue to be developed by service providers for the foreseeable future.

Through film, television and digital platforms, horror is today reaching a larger and more diverse audience than ever before. The genre exists on an ever-broadening canvas, where traditional vampires and werewolves sit alongside serial killers, poltergeists, zombies, possessed dolls, transdimensional clowns and even white Obama supporters. One of the key strengths of the horror film is its unpredictability. While drawing on the traditions and conventions laid down over the past hundred years, film-makers will continue to shock, surprise and terrify audiences with visions of horror limited only by the imagination. It is hoped that the case studies in this book, along with the associated viewing and reading lists, will stand the reader in good stead to tackle these monsters, whatever form they may take.

Bibliography

Bernard, Mark (2014) *Selling the Splat Pack: The DVD Revolution and the American Horror Film*. Edinburgh University Press.

Briefel, Aviva and Miller, Sam J. (eds) (2011) *Horror After 9/11: World of Fear, Cinema of Terror*. University of Texas Press.

Brown, Simon (2018) *Screening Stephen King: Adaptation and the Horror Genre in Film and Television*. University of Austin Press.

Chasmar, Jessica (12 September 2017) 'It' creators say film reflects 'culture of fear', 'division' in America. *The Washington Times*. Retrieved 27 March 2018 from https://www.washingtontimes.com/news/2017/sep/12/it-creators-say-film-reflects-culture-fear-divisio/

Clarens, Carlos (1969) *Horror Movies: An Illustrated Survey*. London: Secker & Warburg.

Collings, Michael R. (1986) *The Films of Stephen King*. Mercer Island, WA: Starmont Press.

Cruz, Gilbert (3 November, 2009) Stephen King on His 10 Longest Novels. *Time*. Retrieved 27 March 2018 from http://entertainment.time.com/2009/11/09/stephen-king-on-his-10-longest-novels/slide/it-1986/

Follows, Stephen (2017) *The Horror Report*. np: Stephen Follows. Available online from https://stephenfollows.com/horrorreport/

Gonzalez, Umberto (13 September 2017) 'It' Almost Included '80s Horror Villain Freddy Krueger, Director Says. *The Wrap*. Retrieved 27 March 2018 from https://www.thewrap.com/freddy-krueger-it-movie-80s-horror/

Jones, Steve (2013) *Torture Porn: Popular Horror After Saw*. New York: Palgrave Macmillan.

King, Stephen (1982) *Danse Macabre*. Futura: London.

King, Stephen (1986) *IT*. Hodder & Stoughton: New York.

King, Stephen (1993) *Nightmares & Dreamscapes*. BCA: London.

King, Stephen (2000) *On Writing*. Hodder & Stoughton: London.

Langford, B. (2010) *Post-Classical Hollywood: Film Industry, Style and Ideology Since 1945*. Edinburgh University Press.

Lawson, Carol (23 September 1979) Behind the Best Sellers: Stephen King. *The New York Times*. Retrieved 27 March 2018 from http://www.nytimes.com/books/97/03/09/lifetimes/kin-v-behind.html

Nyren, Erin (6 September 2017) Stephen Kings 'It' Reviews: What the Critics Are Saying. *Variety*. Retrieved 27 March 2018 from http://variety.com/ 2017/film/news/it-stephen-king-movie-review-roundup-12025491

Olsen, Mark (12 October 2017) TV horror vs. movie horror: Guillermo del Toro on telling scary stories across different mediums. *Los Angeles Times*. Retrieved 27 March 2018 from http://www.latimes.com/entertainment/movies/la-ca-mn-horror-guillermo-del-toro-storytelling-20171012-story.html

Otterson, Joe (24 October 2017) 'Walking Dead' Season 8 Premiere Draws Lowest Opening Ratings Since Season 3. *Variety*. Retrieved 27 March 2018 from http://variety.com/2017/tv/news/walking-dead-season-8-premiere-ratings-1202596402/

Rolls, Albert (2008) *Stephen King: a biography*. Greenwood Press: Westport.

Simpson, Philip L. (2004) *The Horror "Event" Movie*. In Hantke, Steffen (ed.) *Horror Film: Creating and Marketing Fear*. University Press of Mississippi.

Skal, David J. (1994) *The Monster Show: A Cultural History of Horror*. Plexus: London.

Spangler, T (27 February 2018) Netflix Eyeing Total of About 700 Original Series in 2018. *Variety*. Retrieved 31 May 2018 from https://variety.com/2018/digital/news/ netflix-700-original-series-2018-1202711940

Strengell, Heidi (2005) *Dissecting Stephen King: From the Gothic to Literary Naturalism*. University of Wisconsin Press.

Tizard, Will (14 November 2017) David Lynch on 'Twin Peaks', 'Arthouse' television 'Lynchian Fear'. *Variety*. Retrieved 27 March 2018 from http://variety.com/2017/film/global/david-lynch-twin-peaks-camerimage-1202615377

Wood, Robin (2003) *Hollywood from Vietnam to Reagan...and Beyond: Expanded and Revised Edition*. Columbia University Press.

Zinoman, Jason (18 January 2018) Why Are We Ashamed to Call 'Get Out' and 'The Shape of Water' Horror Films? *The New York Times*. Retrieved 27 March 2018 from https://www.nytimes.com/2018/01/18/movies/get-out-the-shape-of-water-horror-oscars.html

Endnotes

1   https://www.nytimes.com/interactive/2017/12/07/magazine/great-performers-horror-show-photos.html

2   This self-indulgent nostalgia reached its zenith with Robert Rodriguez and Quentin Tarantino's *Grindhouse*, a big-budget box-office flop notable mainly for its inclusion of 'coming soon' trailers for non-existent exploitation films by Eli Roth, Rob Zombie and others.

3   https://medium.com/netflix-techblog/artwork-personalization-c589f074ad76

4   https://twitter.com/stephenking/status/754699429047836672

5   It's well known that early in the life of the project, Ross and Matt Duffer unsuccessfully lobbied Warners in an effort to secure the directing job on *It*, and many of the elements they had in mind for their version would find their way into *Stranger Things*.

6   Following series such as *Haven* (2010-2015), *Under the Dome* (2013-2015) and *11.22.63* (2016), 2017 alone saw Netflix release well-received feature adaptations of *Gerald's Game* (Mike Flanagan) and *1922* (Zak Hilditch) as well as series based on his books *The Mist* and *Mr. Mercedes*. While *The Dark Tower* (Nikolaj Arcel, 2017) received poor reviews and a lackluster box-office return, plans were quickly put in motion for both a television series (from Amazon) and a theatrical sequel.

Index

Also in horror film studies from

Devil's Advocates

"The admirable Devil's Advocates series is not only essential — and fun — reading for the serious horror fan but should be set texts on any genre course." I.Q. Hunter, Professor of Film Studies, De Montfort University

"…a series which is finding itself at the forefront of academic studies of horror." Frightfest.co.uk

New Devil's Advocates are being published all the time.
Like the series on **facebook** Devil'sAdvocatesbooks — and follow it on DevilsAdBooks — for regular updates.

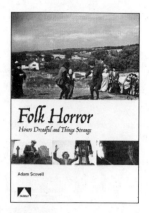

Folk Horror
Hours Dreadful and Things Strange
Adam Scovell

"...an invaluable resource for those who seek an introduction to both the central and more marginal entries in the folk-horror canon. ...There has been very little scholarly work on folk horror, [and] Scovell does an admirable job of collecting this work. ...you won't find a more comprehensive introduction to folk-horror texts." *Irish Journal of Gothic and Horror Studies*

"...this book is indispensable. Scovell proves himself an excellent writer as the level of research and consideration in this book is impeccable, yet it is not at all dry and is a captivating, flowing read for everybody interested in the subject matter..." *Folk Horror Revival*

The Films of Terence Fisher
Hammer Horror and Beyond
Wheeler Winston Dixon

"This book is a cinephile's dream, as well as an exemplary work of scholarship. Wheeler Winston Dixon illuminates the movies and the career of Terence Fisher in loving detail, bringing us close to an important director whose work now gets its proper due for the first time." Steven Shaviro, author of *The Universe of Things*

"Dixon's book is the definitive study of Terence Fisher, the director who spearheaded Britain's 1950s Gothic revival and put Hammer Films on the map of international horror cinema. An invaluable resource that belongs on the shelf of any serious horror fan or scholar." Ian Olney, author of *Zombie Cinema*

Frightmares
A History of British Horror Cinema
Ian Cooper

"...Cooper vividly captures the evolution of the British horror film via often underrated features from different decades, arguing that the UK genre scene has long revealed more about the national psyche than more respected art films, and highlighting the repeated convergence of high and low culture within the form. ...Cooper's admirably non-snobbish approach allows for thoughtful, appreciative study... Eminently readable and flab-free, FRIGHTMARES is among the most enjoyable studies of Brit horror to date... spotlighting strong unsung films and finding fresh takes on the old familiars." Frightfest.co.uk